ADVANCE PRAISE FOR
Ancient Christian Wisdom and Aaron Beck's Cognitive Therapy

"It is with great pleasure that I read this very erudite and yet beautifully written book. This journey into the modern world of cognitive psychology, accompanied all along by the writings of the church fathers, introduces us to two universes that crisscross and yet do not dissolve into each other. Father Alexis did not embark on this journey for purely theoretical reasons, although he distills theories very nimbly. He is a Christian theologian who wants to use both the resources of his tradition and those of cognitive psychology to make more effective the task of caring for those who suffer. His considerable learning, not least in his detailed exposition of Aaron Beck's thought, remains in the service of his calling."

Annette Aronowicz, Department Chair,
The Robert F. and Patricia G. Ross Weis Professor of Judaic Studies,
and Professor of Religious Studies, Franklin and Marshall College

"Father Alexis has innovatively woven together an account of cognitive psychotherapy and of the Christian struggle to realize an authentic spiritual life. This extraordinary volume, which draws on contemporary cognitive psychology and the Christian patristic tradition, is destined to become a popular manual for mental health and the spiritual life. It is easily accessible while maintaining depth of insight. One does not need to be a Christian, much less a believer, to appreciate the power of this book."

David Solomon, W. P. and H. B. White Director of the Center
for Ethics and Culture, Notre Dame University

Ancient Christian Wisdom and Aaron Beck's Cognitive Therapy

AMERICAN UNIVERSITY STUDIES

SERIES VII
THEOLOGY AND RELIGION

VOL. 313

PETER LANG
New York • Washington, D.C./Baltimore • Bern
Frankfurt • Berlin • Brussels • Vienna • Oxford

Father Alexis Trader

Ancient Christian Wisdom and Aaron Beck's Cognitive Therapy

A Meeting of Minds

FOREWORD BY
H. Tristram Engelhardt

PETER LANG
New York • Washington, D.C./Baltimore • Bern
Frankfurt • Berlin • Brussels • Vienna • Oxford

Library of Congress Cataloging-in-Publication Data

Trader, Alexis.
Ancient Christian wisdom and Aaron Beck's cognitive therapy:
a meeting of minds / Alexis Trader.
p. cm. — (American University studies. VII, Theology and religion; v. 313)
Includes bibliographical references (p.   ) and index.
1. Psychotherapy—Religious aspects—Orthodox Eastern Church.
2. Cognitive psychotherapy. 3. Beck, Aaron T. 4. Psychology, Patristic.
5. Orthodox Eastern Church—Doctrines. I. Title. II. Series.
BX342.9.P79T73   253.5—dc22   2010050257
ISBN 978-1-4331-1362-8 (hardcover)
ISBN 978-1-4331-2156-2 (paperback)
ISSN 0740-0446

Bibliographic information published by **Die Deutsche Nationalbibliothek.**
Die Deutsche Nationalbibliothek lists this publication in the "Deutsche
Nationalbibliografie"; detailed bibliographic data is available
on the Internet at http://dnb.d-nb.de/.

Cover Artwork: "Saint Paul Holding Scrolls"
courtesy of Saint Gregory of Sinai Monastery,
Kelseyville, California
and "Books of the Past" courtesy of Lin Pernille Kristensen.

The paper in this book meets the guidelines for permanence and durability
of the Committee on Production Guidelines for Book Longevity
of the Council of Library Resources.

© 2011, 2012 Peter Lang Publishing, Inc., New York
29 Broadway, 18th floor, New York, NY 10006
www.peterlang.com

Printed in Germany

To my parents

✠ Contents ✠

Part III. Human Practitioners and People in Need

Part IV. Strategies for Therapeutic Change

✠ Foreword ✠

This volume is a rare and important bridge between two worlds: that world within which cognitive psychotherapy developed and that world which sustains the spiritual therapy of the Christian fathers. What Father Alexis has accomplished is unique. Recently, there has been a trend to explore Indian and traditional Chinese approaches to medicine, although these have proven difficult to integrate into modern health care. This volume, in contrast, offers a serious Christian examination of psychotherapy in a fashion that can be integrated into contemporary mental health care. Remarkably, Father Alexis has produced a Christian study of psychotherapy that is no mere superficial or wooden reading of the Bible, but a study of mental health grounded in a Christianity that possesses two millennia of serious and nuanced reflection in the area.

In a readable and engaging fashion, Father Alexis [Trader] brings reflections on secular spirituality in the sense of psychological understandings of mental health into contact with traditional Christian understandings of spiritual health. As the therapeutic attempt to reduce excessive emotional reactions and self-defeating behavior by modifying the erroneous thinking and the maladaptive beliefs that underlie such behaviors, cognitive psychotherapy has a deep consanguinity with the disciplines engaged by the Christian fathers. Father Alexis has woven together an account of cognitive psychotherapy with an account of the Christian struggle to be granted union with God. This volume is a bridge between the concerns of psychotherapy and the concerns of ascetic discipline; it is destined to become a popular manual for mental health care workers and for those committed to the authentic Christian life. One does not need to be a Christian, or even a believer, to appreciate the power of the book's insights or the importance of the bridge Father Alexis has built.

Although this book is an easily accessible text, at the same time it maintains sophistication and depth of insight. The somewhat rare reliance on a wealth of original Greek and Latin patristic sources, many of which have never been translated into English, offers concrete empirical data about behavioral and cognitive issues for the layman and the specialist to ponder and even apply in daily life without creating a book that is difficult for the non-expert to read. This book has substantive scholarly foundations while being open to the average reader.

Yet one might ask: how could this bridge even be possible? How can Father Alexis have succeeded in connecting cognitive psychotherapy with the reflections of Christian ascetics on spiritual health? Father Alexis' metaphors such as "timeless truth and secular echoes" indicate the circumstance that with incarnate beings the spiritual will always be reflected in the psychological and the bodily. Our bodies are, after all, integral to our being. Christianity offers health and sanctification not only of soul but also of body. Although Christianity and the secular world appreciate mental and psychological health differently, it should come as no surprise that effective secular psychotherapy has a reflection within the psychological accounts and descriptions of the fathers, as well as the reverse.

For those who are Christian, Father Alexis discloses connections between traditional Christian insights into how to orient ourselves from ourselves to God, and insights into what is entailed in achieving in secular terms psychological health. This is not to suggest that Father Alexis embraces the commonplace, contemporary, misguided reduction of Christian experiences of God to immanent psycho-physiological findings. Throughout, Father Alexis recognizes that the meaning of psychological health in the two contexts is different, that the extension and intension of psychological health are not the same, but that the two notions are nevertheless importantly connected. He takes both senses of mental health seriously.

For those who are not Christian, Father Alexis offers an opportunity to rethink how one ought to conceive of mental health. Since the early 19th century, the dominant culture of the West has attempted ever more resolutely to understand everything, even health and flourishing, while embracing an atheist methodological postulate, that is, while acting as if God did not exist. This culture has increasingly sought to regard even mental health in a context within which life is approached as if it were ultimately meaningless. Secular accounts of mental health and psychotherapy are under such circumstances at best radically one-sided and incomplete. This is the case, given the context-dependent character of health. All accounts of successful adaptation require specifying the environment within which one will be well adapted, that is, be healthy. All accounts of health also require specifying the goal that the adaptation, the healthy behavior, is to achieve. Thus, the adaptations that are healthy at sea level are different from those for humans who have for generations lived in the oxygen-impoverished environment of high altitudes. Things also look different, depending on the goals of adaptation, depending on whether one is concerned about individual versus inclusive fitness (e.g., the sickle-cell gene supports inclusive fitness, the reproductive success of related, that is, heterozygous persons, in an environment with malaria and in the absence of effective anti-malarial drugs, although in homozygous individuals the trait does not contribute to their individual fitness, the life expectancy or reproductive success of the individual). So, too, mental health will look different in a world thought to be meaningless versus one in which the ultimate destiny of man is meant to be union with God. In this broader perspective, mental health, successful adaptation, will be defined in terms of the attitudes and behaviors that lead to salvation.

The point is that, rightly understood, that is, placed in the right context, cognitive therapy can be a support for the spiritual life. The understanding of the fathers also offers secular therapists insight into a broader perspective within which to appreciate cognitive psychotherapy. In this regard, Father Alexis' work demonstrates the practical value of patristic studies for contemporary life. It will likely inspire other similar endeavors. Father Alexis shows that much can be gained by letting patristic ideas critique us, rather than engaging in the more commonplace practice of critiquing the fathers from the perspective of our usually shallow wisdom and sophistication (a temptation for some scholars who make a living from such critiques).

The result is a creative reappraisal of the importance of cognitive therapy for Christians. As Father Alexis puts it, "Cognitive therapists echo patristic findings in a noticeably altered key and in an ontologically thin, but theoretically elegant form." The volume's cardinal insights into the parallel perspectives of cognitive psychotherapy and the ascetic teachings of the Christian fathers allow one to identify an unexpected resource for the spiritual life. At the threshold of the 21st century, there turns out to be Egyptian gold in cognitive therapy, to use Father Alexis' biblical metaphor, on which Christians can properly draw in the pursuit of mental health in the broadest sense of the term. This recognition is of profound scope and importance for a world in which challenges to spiritual and mental health are substantial, and where the pursuit of salvation is often encumbered by problems requiring psychotherapy. It is possible to integrate the Orthodox Christian pursuit of salvation with a major psychotherapeutic modality. Where one might have thought there would be tension, there is the promise of important areas of synergy.

This volume's appreciation of the resources of cognitive psychotherapy for enriching the spiritual life, as well as its grasp of the fruitfulness of examining the Christian fathers in order more deeply to appreciate psychotherapy, involves no novel doctrine. It involves only the perennial Christian recognition of how Christians can draw on the resources of the world in the pursuit of the kingdom of heaven. After all, Orthodox Christians drew on secular science and engineering in building the Hagia Sophia, the Great Church of Constantinople. Father Alexis has given a patristic introduction to and at the same time a patristic relocation of cognitive psychotherapy so that it can be engaged in recovering and sustaining the health of the soul.

H. Tristram Engelhardt, Jr.
Rice University/Baylor College of Medicine

✠ Preface ✠

This pastoral study in patristic theology and cognitive therapy represents an attempt to seek answers to questions that the particularities of life, training, and circumstances have set before me. From an early age, the predictive power of science captivated my mind, whereas the transfigurational love of Christ captured my soul. In the monastic republic of Athos, where venerable ascetics have discerningly cultivated a way of life that can and does produce the fruits of sanctity, I also encountered the products of a very different vine. In addition to the perennial givens of human passions and sin, a quite contemporary nexus of psychological issues seemed to be hindering some very good souls from receiving and living monastic counsels in such a way as to bring forth fruit one hundred fold. Starting out with the intuition that contemporary scientific approaches might have something significant to offer to resolve those issues, I began a venturesome exploration whose final destination seemed at times obscure. Notwithstanding at journey's end, the fathers' teachings comforted my soul, renewed my zeal, and gave me hope. They also provided me with familiar surroundings in which to lay the valuable tools from cognitive therapy, so that they too could be marshaled for the task of helping others lead a healthy life in mind and spirit. I believe that what I have written can be beneficial for many people. It has certainly been so for me.

Rigging a vessel and loading the ballast are hardly as invigorating as sailing on a bright blustery day, yet they are undisputedly crucial tasks for a long voyage at sea. In chapter one on method, we rig the sails for this study by selecting an appropriate model for relating two admittedly different approaches to human existence. In chapter two on worldviews, we stabilize our vessel with the presuppositional ballast of philosophical differences, lest we be carried away by gusts of unforeseen similarities. But in chapters three to five on theory and in chapters seven to nine on practical applications, we sail across an uncharted sea. Still, the impatient should feel free to weigh anchor with chapter three since they can always steer a course back to those earlier chapters if methodological and philosophical issues emerge as a troublesome reef. Chapter six in between the sections on theory and practice is also a pivotal exploration, for a focus on the human agent again allows worldview undercurrents to resurface and form a frothing, but not daunting, crest.

Embarking on the usually tranquil and predictably calming seas of cognitive therapy and patristic theology in a single expedition requires a great deal of skill to avoid tethered mines set by well-meaning, but explosive individuals in both camps. If my own skills have been lacking for the requisite maneuvers, I ask the reader's indulgence. Perceived bias in language is another minefield with which any writer in English must now contend. Whereas I confess that in Christ Jesus there is neither male nor female, I must admit that the demands of smoothly describing the dialogical relationships of therapy and of confession with consistently invisible gender neutrality has been more than this writer's talents could muster. Again, I request forbearance from those who read this work. Finally, a word concerning methodology may be helpful. Although critical approaches to patristic texts often maintain a suspension of judgment regarding belief claims, this book deals with practical knowledge and as such requires certain epistemic commitments, notably that the teachings on which the church fathers base their highly effective therapeutic approach are sound. The hermeneutics of suspicion, ever on the lookout for contradictory voices, cultural discontinuities, and conceptual inadequacies, is therefore unsuitable for the aims of the present study, while the hermeneutics of trust, and indeed love, is both premise and conclusion, alpha and omega.

At this point, I would like to express my deep appreciation to dear friends who have kindly read and wisely commented on this work as it was in progress, including: my adviser overseeing the Greek version of my doctoral dissertation, Dr. Anestis Keselopoulos; my former colleague from Saint Tikhon's Seminary, Dr. Harry Boosalis; Dr. Annette Aronowicz of Franklin and Marshall College; Dr. Bruce Foltz of Eckerd College; the clinical psychiatrist Manal Durgin, M.D.; and his grace, Bishop Sergios [Black] of Loch Lomond. Special thanks are also in order to Dr. H. Tristram Engelhardt who graciously agreed to write a foreword to this volume, to his wife Susan who kindly proofread the final version of the manuscript, and to Saint Gregory of Sinai Monastery, Kelseyville, California, for their help in cover design.

I also offer my gratitude to my spiritual father and elder, the Abbot of the Holy Monastery of Karakallou on Mount Athos, Archimandrite Philotheos, who gave me the blessing for undertaking this study, as well as to Eldress Nektaria and Nun Philothei of the Monastery of Saint Demetrios, who were quite supportive when I, their serving priest, would disappear for hours on end immersed in this project. Finally, I am grateful for my parents, Merrill and Mary Trader, whose strengths and yearnings underlie much of what I have striven to accomplish in the pages that follow.

✛ Abbreviations ✛

CCSG   *Corpus christianorum: Series graeca.* Vol. 1–69. Turholt, Belgium: Brepols, 1977–2010.

HPE   *Hellēnes pateres tēs ekklēsias.* Vol. 1–. Thessaoniki, Greece: Grēgorios ho Palamas, 1979–.

LCL   *Loeb Classical Library.* Vol. 1–403. Cambridge, MA: Harvard University Press, 1912–1989.

LSJ   Henry G. Liddell and Robert Scott. *Greek-English Lexicon.* Oxford: Clarendon Press, 1996.

MEN   *Mēnaion.* Vol. 1–12. Athens, Greece: Apostolikēs Diakonias tēs Ekklēsias tēs Hellados, 1980.

PG   *Patrologia cursus completus: Series graeca.* Ed. J. P. Migne. Vol. 1–161. Paris: J. P. Migne, 1857–66.

PGL   G. H. W. Lampe. *A Patristic Greek Lexicon.* Oxford: Clarendon Press, 1961.

PHIL   *Philokalia tōn hierōn nēptikōn paterōn.* Vol. 1–5. Athens, Greece: Astēr, 1982.

PL   *Patrologia cursus completus: Series latina.* Ed. J. P. Migne. Vol. 1–221. Paris: J. P. Migne, 1844–64.

SC   *Sources chrétiennes.* Vol. 1–. Paris: Les Éditions du Cerf, 1942–.

SYN   *Megas synaxaristēs tēs orthodoxou ekklēsias.* Vol. 1–12. Athens, Greece: Ēlias Bakopoulos Monachos, 2001.

Reason and Speech:
Timeless Truth and Secular Echoes

C ould an ancient mystical path of inner transformation, most rigorously pursued and explored by monks and hermits, possibly bear much resemblance to what now seems to be establishing itself as the standard psychotherapeutic approach to living an effective and rational life? Would they not of necessity lie worlds apart, reflecting two different mindsets, one pre-modern and the other modern and indeed post-modern—one rational and secular, and the other mystical and sacred? As the first century Christian theologian Tertullian asked: "What does Athens have to do with Jerusalem?"[1]

"And the *Word* was made flesh, and dwelt among us, and we *beheld* his glory, the glory as of the only begotten of the Father, full of *grace* and *truth*."[2] In this short verse, from the prologue to the Gospel of Saint John, the Beloved Disciple and Evangelist of the Word proclaims the apostolic experience of revelation to be the fount of the highest form of knowledge. But this needs to be properly understood not as the statement of a dogmatic claim, accessible only to faith, but rather as an invitation to a dimension of noetic or mystical experience that can lead to a radical transformation of the soul. Through the transfiguring *experience* of beholding Christ in glory, the apostles and saints experienced their senses being refined, their thoughts being made luminous, and they believed that they came to *know* the truth about humanity and the rest of creation. This knowledge attained through *theosis*, glorification or deification in Christ, together with the knowledge gained through their earlier experiences of purification [*katharsis*] from the passions and illumination [*phōtismo*] by the Holy Spirit[3] form the empirical foundation for the saints' counsels about the healing of the human person and the cleansing of the divine image within, counsels which reflect various aspects of that conceptually rich Greek term *logos* rendered according to context as reason, speech, and wisdom of God.

Since antiquity, philosophers and ascetics alike have known that reason and speech are the keys to the world of thought at both a personal and collective level. In the course of two thousand years, the saints (those who have pursued most successfully the threefold path of purification, illumination, and theosis) of ancient, traditional Christianity (which this study will maintain persists as a living tradition today in the Eastern Orthodox Church) have explored and recorded the mechanics and dynamics of spiritual transformation, known generally as *metanoia* or repentance, which begins with a change in a person's thought-life through the therapeutic use of reason and speech, and ends with the cure of the illness of the soul that since the time of the ancient church has been called *hamartia*, literally missing the mark, the disease of alienation of the soul from its truest end of joyful vision of God and things divine, that is, in short, sin. The saints have also found that selfish thoughts, left unchecked, lead a person to sinful acts, passions, habits, and eventually alienation from God and neighbor; whereas godly thoughts, when cultivated, guide a person by the grace of God to virtuous actions, habits, and ultimately purification from the passions, illumination by the Holy Spirit, and deification in Christ. Beneath the surface of this outwardly simplistic scheme lies an ocean of patristic texts providing a wealth of counsel and direction for making this good change a reality.

Remarkably, in our own very secular society, cognitive therapists are echoing these patristic findings, albeit in a noticeably altered key and in ontologically thin, but theoretically elegant form. These enticingly comparable, yet elusively dissimilar, resonances call for a nuanced Orthodox Christian response. Cognitive therapy's taboo-breaking discourse about the reality of mental states is surely a step forward from its immediate historical predecessor, behaviorism. Behaviorism was a scientifically framed psychological theory quite apt at predicting the reward-driven behavior of rats threading mazes, pigeons pecking feeders, and gamblers pulling slot machines, but highly unsatisfactory in dealing with the freedom and complexity of the human soul.[4] In responding to behaviorism, the Orthodox Christian could readily acknowledge the reinforcing influence of anticipated reward (e.g., the joy of mystical union with God, which since ancient times has been called *theosis*) or punishment (for instance, the anguish of separation from God) on human behavior. Notwithstanding, the Church's vision of humanity based on her experiential knowledge of the saint and sinner in the image of God could never be encompassed, much less elucidated, by the facile reductionism and crude, mechanistic determinism of American behavioralism.

By the 1970s, however, the vast landscape of American psychology had been radically altered by the accumulated weight of a series of studies indicating that statements about the effects of cognitive processes could be reliably predicted and scientifically tested. In this milieu, which would come to be known as the cognitive revolution, the clinical psychiatrist Aaron Temkin

Beck (1921–) completed research studies on depression, yielding results that were at marked variance from the expectations of the Freudian hypotheses being tested. These findings, together with Beck's clinical observations about the relationship between transient thoughts and emotions, led him to develop an evidence-driven procedure and a well developed theory of psychotherapy that would come to be known as cognitive-behavioral therapy.[5]

Alongside of Aaron Beck, other cognitive theorists, such as Albert Ellis, Donald Meichenbaum, George Kelly, Maxie Maultsby, William Glasser, Arnold Lazarus, Michael Mahoney, Vittorio Guidano, and Giovanni Liotti, developed similar therapies.[6] Among these figures, two thinkers are preeminent: Albert Ellis, the founder of rational-emotive therapy, often referred to as "the grandfather of cognitive therapy" and Aaron Beck, widely known as "the father of cognitive therapy." Our study will focus primarily on the writings of Aaron Beck and his coworkers[7] for several reasons. First, Beck's writings are "more scientific in their formulation, less dogmatic, and more well researched"[8] than those of Ellis. Second, Beck's approach not only subsumes Ellis's system based on the "action-belief-consequence" paradigm,[9] but also adds a vertical dimension, including deeper underlying layers of beliefs that are the ultimate source of problematic thinking.[10] Third, Ellis's system has been marginalized in clinical practice by Beck's approach.[11] Finally, Ellis's commitment to atheism and a sometimes-coarse hedonism lead him to judgments about rationality at such variance with Christian teaching that any fruitful dialogue is obstructed from the very outset.[12]

Succinctly defined, Beck's "cognitive therapy is a system of therapy that attempts to reduce excessive emotional reactions and self-defeating behavior by modifying the faulty or erroneous thinking and maladaptive beliefs that underlie these reactions."[13] On account of the empirical support demonstrating the effectiveness of cognitive therapeutic treatments, it has become for many syndromes the assumed and preeminent form of short-term therapy implemented in the United States and the United Kingdom.[14] In practical terms, this means that most psychiatric hospitals have programs in cognitive therapy; most university psychology curricula are required to teach courses about cognitive therapy; and insurance companies will only co-pay cognitive therapeutic treatments for certain disorders.[15] Given the expanding influence of therapy in Western culture and the shrinking authority of Christianity,[16] given the ubiquity of psychological modes of thought and the paucity of theologically informed ways of thinking in modern society,[17] Christian pastors would be well served by a balanced patristic evaluation of the tenets and techniques of cognitive therapy. Secular therapists, too, may be pleasantly surprised to discover that the territory they are just beginning to explore has been exhaustively mapped over two thousand years by intrepid voyagers of the spirit in the Eastern Church, men and women of whom the West has rarely been cognizant, let alone conversant. And it is hoped, too, that the lay reader may also take a certain interest in the exploration of the meeting of the mindset of ancient Christian asceticism and modern scientific rationality.

At first glance, the similarities between patristic pastoral tradition and cognitive therapy are indeed striking. Byzantine epistemology with its unity between *theoria* and *praxis* has been functionally described as "rationalism and empiricism,"[18] the very terms that could be used to characterize the epistemology utilized in cognitive therapy. In fact, the church fathers, as empiricists,[19] follow the pathway that underlies cognitive research—clinical observation followed by theoretical composition,[20] or put differently, empiricism and then rational discourse.[21] Both the fathers and cognitive therapists are committed to honesty and avoiding deception.[22] Both "assume limited freedom and a partial determinism."[23] Both are motivated by compassion for suffering people and a desire for their restoration to health.[24] Both recognize that talking can be a means for behavioral change.[25] Both affirm the centrality of the thought-life or meaning-making structures of cognition in psychological functioning.[26] Both view unhealthy thoughts about the self, the environment, and the future as a source for psychological problems.[27] Both recognize that the correction of the thoughts[28] or the purification of the thoughts is the foundational dimension of the return to health and wholeness. Both see the use of reason as instrumental in better human functioning.[29] Both assert that a human being is able to exert "personal control over thoughts and behaviors that promote change in a healthy direction."[30]

Given such similarities, it is not surprising that psychiatrists with training in Orthodox theology such as Fr. Vasilios Thermos and Fr. Adamantios Augoustidis identify patristic examples of what are currently known as cognitive therapy techniques.[31] Fr. George Morelli, an Orthodox Christian cognitive psychologist, is even more emphatic, stressing that "cognitive psychologists, using their own technical vocabulary, have demonstrated empirical evidence" for processes described in ascetic literature.[32] He even goes so far as to conclude that "the Christian spiritual tradition, including the prayers and practice of the Church, scripture and the writings of the spiritual fathers lends itself to an elegant integration with the cognitive therapy methods noted above."[33]

Although "an elegant integration" may be possible, care is required lest that integration either distort patristic teaching by putting it to foreign use or dull cognitive therapy's cutting edge by mixing it with material extraneous to strictly scientific method. Two simple yet related facts should always be kept in mind. First, the fathers were not cognitive therapists treating people suffering from anxiety or depression, but human beings striving to follow the commandments of Christ, to acquire the love that "seeks not its own,"[34] and to reach union with God. Second, cognitive therapists are not church fathers seeking to describe humanity in its ideal state or to answer ultimate questions, but mental health professionals attempting to reduce the symptoms of those suffering from various disorders so that these patients can function better in society. While certain domains of concern between cognitive therapists and the fathers coincide, the material that does not overlap will inevitably be considered more significant by purist cognitive therapists as well as by ardent followers of the patristic tradition.

Establishing and then evaluating a relationship between patristic pastoral tradition and cognitive therapy is an enterprise requiring both a brief comparison of worldviews underlying each orientation and an extensive juxtaposition of the discrete components that constitute each approach. On the one hand, a terse comparison between Orthodox anthropology based on revelation and the philosophical anthropology assumed by cognitive therapy should highlight stark differences between the two. On the other hand, an in-depth contrast between the constituent elements of cognitive therapy with their counterparts in the patristic tradition should point to startling similarities. Together, both perspectives should lead to an informed and fair Orthodox Christian response to cognitive therapy as well as an appreciation of Orthodox ascetic theology by cognitive therapists.

Of course, preliminary convictions inevitably influence subsequent conclusions. It is necessary to be frank about training and commitments at a personal level, for two reasons outlined by Dr. David Entwistle: "A valid critique can only come from the position of a person who is sufficiently informed so as to be working with actual disciplinary concerns, rather than a mere caricature or limited sample of disciplinary content"[35] and "The theorist's personal commitments will invariably influence the model that he or she proposes."[36] In terms of training, the writer's graduate work and personal life as an Athonite monk have been centered on Orthodox spiritual life and theology. Notwithstanding, earlier training in chemistry has provided the writer with sufficient grounding in the scientific method to appreciate its application in works written for mental health professionals.[37] In terms of commitments, the writer's ultimate loyalty lies with the patristic teaching of the Orthodox Church, whose practical guidance for striving to embody the virtues of the Gospel and to participate in the Church's mysteries begins with daily life and stretches into eternity. This devotion, however, in no way precludes a healthy respect for empirical findings in psychological research

utilized as applications to reduce human suffering. Obviously, prior commitments and training orient the writer toward some sort of approach involving
dialogue, if such a dialogue is indeed consistent with patristic tradition.

To decide whether that hypothetical "if" can become a statement of fact,
we will next turn our attention to historical relationships between patristic
theology and secular knowledge in order to discern a proper model that will
guide those Orthodox Christians sojourning in the desert of contemporary
society, so that they might constructively make use of cognitive therapy, the
present-day equivalent to the Passover gold of the Egyptians. Without the
guidance of Moses, the children of Israel took that gold and made a molten
calf to their perdition. With his guidance, they made an altar of gold for the
tabernacle of the law to their sanctification.[38] Whosoever "readeth, let him
understand."[39]

✠ PART I ✠

Methodologies and Philosophies

Egyptian Gold in a Christian Hand: Models for Relating Cognitive Therapy and Orthodox Pastoral Theology

I n *De doctrina christiana*, Blessed Augustine examines various tools for interpreting obscure passages in the Bible. Among the resources at the exegete's disposal, the bishop of Hippo includes the results of naturalistic and philosophical inquiry. Clothing his reflections in the language of scripture, he writes the following:

> The Egyptians not only had idols and heavy burdens, which the people of Israel hated and fled from, but they also had vessels and ornaments of gold and silver, and garments, which the same people appropriated to themselves when departing from Egypt. They set these items apart for a better use, not on their own authority, but by the command of God. In the same way all branches of pagan learning not only have false and superstitious fancies and heavy burdens of unnecessary toil, which every one of us ought to abhor and avoid, when Christ leads us to depart from the fellowship of the heathen, but also they contain liberal instruction which is better adapted to the use of the truth. Now this instruction is their gold and silver, which they did not create themselves, but dug out of the mines of God's providence.[1]

This fertile biblical analogy, likening pagan learning to Egyptian gold, not only warns of dangers and highlights benefits in the use of secular knowledge, but also directs us to where we should look in discerning a relationship between the believer and such knowledge that would be potentially beneficial to the soul. It suggests that we look to the history of those who experience themselves as called to be the people of God.

How then are Orthodox Christian pastoral theology and cognitive therapy to be related to each other? Guidance for a response to questions of this sort is usually sought by exploring the relationship between early Christian theology and secular knowledge in the form of ancient Greek philosophy. In so far as therapy takes the form of a value-laden[2] philosophy orienting its adherents in their interpretation of human cognition and behavior, this examination is illuminating. But psychology in general, and cognitive therapy in particular, have made titanic efforts to demonstrate that they are *not* speculative philosophies arranging unsubstantiated syllogisms in a logical order, but quantifiable sciences dealing with highly probabilistic psychometric variables. Given that cognitive therapy explicitly understands itself as a science and professionally situates itself within the field of medicine, it seems only fair first to examine the historical connection between the fathers' thought and medical science before later turning to the relationship between patristic theology and the philosophy of antiquity.

Church Fathers and the Practice of Medicine

Saint Basil the Great taught that "God's grace is as evident in the healing power of medicine and its practitioners as it is in miraculous cures."[3] This recognition of God as the Source in the therapeutic process brought about by both the physician's art and the Christian's prayer reflects "an enduring alliance between Christianity and classic culture including secular medicine."[4] This alliance forged by the fathers can be clearly seen in their acceptance of the Hippocratic-Galenic system of medicine that was prevalent throughout Byzantium. The fathers of the ancient church endorsed both medical principles and techniques including medication prepared from animal, vegetable, and mineral substances.[5] Physician saints—such as Saints Cosmas, Damian, Panteleimon, Sampson, and others—were among the best and brightest doctors in this medical tradition.[6] Skeptics might denigrate the importance of this patristic-medical alliance vis-à-vis psychological disorders by suggesting that the alliance was binding only in the case of bodily illnesses, but a closer look at the utterly naturalistic Hippocratic-Galenic system of medicine reveals the presence of diagnoses and treatments for psychological conditions such as mania characterized by pathological excitement and depression [*melancholia*] characterized by sadness and suicidal tendencies.[7] In fact, Saint John Chrysostom implicitly makes the distinction between a psychologically pathological condition and a demonic attack when he notes that "a profound sadness is more harmful to us than all the attacks of an evil spirit."[8] Furthermore, the fathers of the Eastern Church never characterized *all* mental illness as resulting from demon possession. Instead, they recognized three possible causes—organic, spiritual, and demonic—and directed their treatment accordingly.[9] Hence, from a patristic perspective, in so far as cognitive therapy belongs to the medical sciences, its findings, techniques, methods, and even theories are a valuable source of knowledge in dealing with mental illnesses once they are determined to be of a primarily psychological nature. Employing an exclusively medical paradigm, the fathers would object to the use of cognitive therapy only if it claimed etiological comprehensiveness and maintained opinions about matters concerning the faith.

It is also instructive to note how frequently the fathers used analogies taken from the practice of medicine to describe the spiritual father as a physician of souls,[10] the canons as healing remedies,[11] and the Church as a spiritual hospital. There are even twentieth century Orthodox theologians who assert that Orthodox Christianity belongs to the therapeutic sciences,[12] and that patristic tradition in its therapeutic orientation greatly resembles modern psychiatry.[13] The significance of this imagery becomes even more salient when contrasted with, for example, a philosophical metaphor that would view the Church as a philosophical society and the fathers as speculative philosophers. Such a metaphor is not simply unheard of within the Eastern Church; it is explicitly and vehemently rejected for fatally distorting the meaning of the Church and the process of salvation.[14] Thus, both as a historical relationship and at a rhetorical level, patristic thought and medicine have enjoyed a harmonious and peaceful co-existence.[15]

Turning from the Hippocratic naturalist-physician to the research-oriented cognitive psychotherapist, we observe what the patristic healers would see as the same human activity of eliciting the potential within God's creation through the use of reason. Today, it is the scientific method that guides the scientist in the accumulation of repeatable data that are arranged in such a way as to suggest reproducible causal and probable relationships between discrete events. When scientists make mistakes, the data or verified experience are not disqualified, but an inadequate interpretation or understanding of the data is.[16] In the process of interpretation, understanding, and theorizing, philosophical assumptions inherent in the scientific worldview are operative. For example, the idea that "a field of potential systematic progress exists" is a philosophical assumption without which a program of research would be inconceivable.[17] Sometimes elaborate new interpretive structures, not unlike philosophical systems of old, are built up around the data. Notwithstanding, even the ultimate rejection of a given theory does not necessarily imply the rejection of the verifiable data on which it is built. The facts simply call for an alternate explanation. There is patristic precedent for this distinction between rejecting a theory and accepting the facts. "Saint Basil acknowledges all scientific facts of natural science. But he does not accept the philosophical conceptions or interpretations of the facts that were contemporary to him: the mechanistic theory of the origin of the world, the teaching of the eternity and unbeginningness of the natural world."[18] Of course, facts and theory cannot always be so neatly disentangled, for the former inheres in the latter. Notwithstanding, a new framing of both fact and theory is always possible.

In so far as cognitive therapy is an applied medical science that reduces suffering from mental health disorders, there is patristic precedent for friendly collaboration between the two approaches. In so far as the findings of psychotherapeutic research are scientifically verifiable and repeatable facts, there is patristic precedent for both acknowledging and utilizing those facts. For the fathers, medicine, science, and technology evoke not fear, but gratitude to God when valued and employed in a way consistent with his providential plan for creation. Beckian cognitive therapy in both its scientific and medical aspects could evoke such a response. Notwithstanding, Beck's cognitive therapy is also built on certain philosophical principles and is imbued with a particular philosophical worldview, the scientific worldview. This aspect of cognitive therapy, explicit in Ellis and implicit in Beck, requires us to examine how the fathers viewed and utilized philosophical knowledge. This in turn will help us answer the pressing question: how are patristic theology and cognitive therapy as a philosophical value system to be related?

The American Protestant theologian Richard Niebuhr chronicles five historical answers in terms of the relationship between Christ and culture generally: opposition, merger, synthesis, tension, and transformation.[19] David Entwistle offers another set of descriptions for the interactions between psychologists and theologians: enemies, spies, colonialists, neutral parties, and allies.[20] Others speak of manipulative versus co-relational models in terms of credibility, convertibility, conformability, compatibility, and complementarity.[21] For the sake of simplicity, we can reduce these diverse models to three basic approaches: *rejection*, *identification*, and various intermediate modes of *inter-relation*. By briefly examining historical examples of each model, we can discern the preferred patristic approach. Of course, conceptual models are merely scholar's tools that can never fully describe how people behave and think in real life. The same person may utilize opposing paradigms in different situations. Nevertheless, these aids to thought can provide guidance in terms of overriding orientations.

The Tertullian Model: Resistance, Rejection, and Enmity

Early in church history, at a time in which persecution was rampant and merger with culture posed the threat of apostasy, it was not uncommon for Christians to reject Roman culture and Greek philosophy. This position can be observed in *The Shepherd of Hermas*, *The Epistle of Barnabas*,[22] and most markedly in the writings of Tertullian (145–220). It was a stance of such logical consistency, single-heartedness, and manifest fervor that it was then and even now remains an attractive approach.[23] After all, for the Christian, the perennial philosophical questions about knowledge, conduct, and governance found their most perfect answer in the revelation of Jesus Christ; the answers of the savants of old would be forever relegated to second place in terms of relevance and significance after Christ's victory over death, sin, and the devil. Without Christ, philosophy, science, and culture are, in Saint Paul's words, rubbish [*skybala*], because they are all mortal and subject to corruption.[24] Planted on this firm bedrock of faith, Tertullian exclaimed "Away with all attempts to produce a mottled Christianity of Stoic, Platonic, and dialectic composition. We want Jesus Christ....With our faith we desire no further belief."[25] For Tertullian, if a person becomes a Christian, *ipso facto* he must reject Athens and the Academy for the sake of Jerusalem and the Church. There was no other way.

This Tertullian response is echoed today by Protestant biblical counselors who are quick to detect the same lurking perils of apostasy when Christians mix their beliefs with psychology, the *modus vivendi* of modern culture. For instance, David Powlison notes the threat of beginning "to reason godlessly about behavior, mood, relationships, motives, and cognitions" and even twisting biblical quotations "to rationalize ideas that are intrinsically alien to the mind of God."[26] In other words, for these Protestant thinkers this mixing jeopardizes the possibility of salvation. For modern-day Tertullians, psychology is "a destructive infection in the life of the Church that prevents our understanding of ourselves, weakens our devotion to Christ, and replaces the Kingdom of God in the hearts of his people with such aims as individuation, self-esteem, feeling good, congruence, and satisfaction with life."[27] With such an evaluation of psychology, the most reasonable response would be the Tertullianesque exclamation—"Away with all attempts to produce a mottled Christianity of psychological composition!"

While the dangers feared by ancient and modern Tertullians are real and call for vigilance, a Tertullian position is problematic in terms of inner consistency. While ostensibly rejecting Stoicism with rigor, Tertullian's recommendations about modesty and patience always had Stoic overtones.[28] In other words, his culture was not an outer garment that he could cast off at will, but an inextricable part of his inner world. It enabled him to communicate with others, even as knowledge of Hellenic literature enabled the Apostle Paul to communicate with the Athenians when he said, "For in him we live, and move, and have our being; as certain also of your own poets have said, for we are also his offspring."[29] In like manner, Orthodox clergy make use of psychological principles, even if, unlike the Apostle Paul, they are afraid to acknowledge their source.[30] The scientific worldview is as ubiquitous as the products of technology that furnish our surroundings. *Bon gré mal gré*, our thoughts are clothed in scientific and psychological thought. An absolute categorical rejection of culture and philosophy was not possible then, and is not really possible now.

A combative mode also prevents any real dialogue from taking place. The only agreement that can be reached is that the other side is wrong and dangerous.[31] When modern-day Protestant Tertullians, such as Bobgan and Bobgan, try to discredit therapy and show how it fails to complement, conform to, and be compatible with Christianity, they often must rely on "contorted and contrived arguments to make their points."[32] For a Christian, this trust in one's own appraisal, this refusal to try to understand the other, and this failure to admit the possibility of one's own oversights, misinterpretations, and limitations are at odds with what Saint John Chrysostom calls the foundation of our own Christian philosophy, viz., humble-mindedness.[33]

It should also be noted that Tertullian is an important ecclesiastical writer, but not a recognized saint of the Orthodox Church. Others who have followed his radical anti-culture position, such as Count Leo Tolstoy (1828–1910), have extended their rejection of culture to a repudiation of holy tradition and been rightly excommunicated by the Russian Orthodox Church (1901). It has been perceptively observed that "at the edges of the radical movement the Manichean heresy is always developing."[34] As understandable as a model of resistance, rejection, and enmity may be, it is a position rife with inner weaknesses uncharacteristic of a discerning patristic approach.

The Model of Valentinus the Gnostic: Absorption, Manipulation, and Merger

Uncritically embracing the prevailing culture was the diametrically opposite approach championed by a figure who was a frequent target of Tertullian's energetic attacks: Valentinus (c. 140), the highly speculative and eminent propounder of the Egyptian-grown Gnostic heresy.[35] At that time, Persian dualism and Middle Platonism were the cutting edges of eclectic secular thought at both a popular and an intellectual level, playing a cultural role not unlike contemporary psychology. For the Gnostics, their neo-Platonic dualistic approach provided a "'scientific' and 'philosophical' interpretation of the person and work of Christ."[36] In place of the ineffable mystery of the God-man, utterly inaccessible to the limits of human reason, they presented an emanation of God called Christ descending on the man Jesus at his baptism and departing from him at the crucifixion.[37] Despite its phantasmagorical form, the Gnostics felt that their reasonable and logical Christology would only augment Christianity's attractiveness and power. The fathers, however, most emphatically disagreed.

Reading Valentinus's works, the ancient fathers would reach the conclusion of Saint Hippolytus (170–236): Valentinus "may justly be reckoned a Pythagorean and Platonist, not a Christian."[38] As a general rule, whenever science or philosophy is used "by means of heresies or other similar manifestations to replace or explain the functioning of charismatic theology, the fathers were categorical: they rejected such secular knowledge as demonic."[39] Thus with respect to Valentinus, Saint Irenaeus of Lyons exclaimed, "Let those persons, therefore, who blaspheme the Creator...by a perversion of the sense [of Scripture], as those of Valentinus and all the Gnostics falsely so called, be recognized as agents of Satan."[40] With one voice, fathers in the West, such as Saints Cyprian, Jerome, Hilary of Poitiers, and Ambrose of Milan as well as luminaries in the East such as Saints Athanasius the Great, Basil the Great, Gregory the Theologian, and John Chrysostom, all denounced Valentinus's misguided attempt to merge Christianity with secular philosophy and thereby transform Christianity into but another philosophy with a religious hue.[41] In like manner, the church fathers denounced similar mergers attempted in some of the works by Evagrius and Origen.

Obviously, a strong loyalty to certain aspects of contemporary culture can mitigate one's allegiance to Christ, so that "he is abandoned in favor of an idol called by his name."[42] Contemporary mergers between Christianity and psychology in which quietly and perhaps unwittingly "the gospel is replaced by a gospel of self-help and self-actualization"[43] are as perilous as the Gnostic-Christian mergers of old. In such cases, Saint Paul's warning to the Galatians comes to mind: "But though we, or an angel from heaven, preach any other gospel unto you than that which we have preached unto you, let him be accursed."[44] Richard Niebuhr aptly describes the merger process and its results as follows: "The terms differ, but the logic is always the same: Christ is identified with what men conceive to be their finest ideals, their noblest institutions, and their best philosophy....The Christ of culture becomes a chameleon; that the word *Christ* in this connection is nothing but an honorific and emotional term by means of which each person attaches numinous quality to its personified ideals."[45]

The dangers of the merger model are so dire that some could be tempted to follow Tertullian's example and abandon the entire endeavor to relate theology and psychology. For this reason, Christian psychologists rarely speak of merger, but of integration,[46] that is, the process of starting with a basic theoretical orientation such as Christianity and extending it by relating it to a different orientation such as psychology on the basis of shared presuppositions.[47] We should also not overlook the vast difference between Gnostic philosophies speculating about theogonies in the heavens and modern psychology describing the behavior of people on earth. We have already noted that neither psychology as a science girded by repeatable verifiable data nor therapy as a medical intervention is rejected by the fathers. Rather, they managed to maintain unadulterated devotion to Christ and at the same time to take seriously constructive offerings of culture as expressions of the Creator's wisdom inherent in his creation.[48] This suggests a third way of relating psychology and theology, "a middle course between the perils that would destroy a uniquely Christian understanding of humanity and those that would destroy psychology as a discipline."[49]

The Patristic Model of Clement of Alexandria:
Selection, Integration, and Transfiguration

Clement of Alexandria (150–211) and Saint Justin Martyr (114–165) were two contemporaries of Tertullian and Valentinus and paved the way for a third approach, "allowing for willing and intelligent cooperation of Christians with non-believers, while yet maintaining the distinctiveness of Christian faith and life."[50] Rather than setting Christianity against Stoicism, Clement would make use of both in directing the believer to the ultimate goal of leading a virtuous life. Thus, in his *Who is the Rich Man that Shall be Saved*, he begins with the Christian exhortation to gratitude for Christ's work, "For each of us he gave his life—the equivalent for all. This he demands of us in return: to give our lives for one another." Then, Clement selects from Stoic philosophy the tenet of detachment [*apatheia*] and incorporates it into his exhortation, "And if we owe our lives to the brethren and have made such a mutual compact with the Savior, why should we continue to hoard and shut up worldly goods, which are beggarly, foreign to us, and transitory?"[51] In this process, Stoic detachment is not only placed within the context of Christian love, but is also transfigured from a negative resignation concerning life in the world to a positive affirmation of the ultimate value of Christ's commandments.

Saint Basil the Great, in his *Address to Young Men on the Right Use of Greek Literature*, explicitly outlines the process at work in Clement's Christian use of Stoic material. He writes, "If, then, there is any affinity between the two literatures, a knowledge of them should be useful to us in our search for truth; if not, by emphasizing the contrast, the comparison will be of no small service in strengthening our appreciation for the better one."[52] Saint Basil's encouragement to search for affinity, make comparisons, and note contrasts suggests an approach of discerning openness, allowing for selection, integration, and transfiguration of secular insight. Such a discerning openness enabled the fathers to adopt elements from the Platonic tri-partite division of the soul—that is, to make use of the prevailing psychological theory of their day—without in any way committing themselves to Platonism at large.[53] This same openness can be seen in Saint Maximus the Confessor's *Theological Chapters*[54] in which selections from Aristotle, Plato, and the Stoics alongside church fathers are arranged in an anthology aimed at producing thought and behavior in line with the teachings of Christ.

Theologically, discerning openness is grounded in the Orthodox teaching that there is only one unified created reality in time and space from which the uncreated energies of the Triune God are never absent.[55] This presence of God historically in his Church and naturally in his creation enable the fathers to make use of material gained from empirical knowledge about the workings of God's world ("natural" or general revelation through created being) and God's working in the world ("supernatural" or special revelation in history). In addition to the unity between the natural and supernatural as well as between special revelation and general revelation,[56] the fathers also teach that the Church and the world form an organic unity, which means that "everything is potentially the Church and called to sanctification."[57] Thus, when frail and mortal thought opens up into the immensity of Christ the God-man, the whole panorama of creation and history are beheld from the elevated vantage point of the mind of Christ.[58]

The discerning openness encountered in Clement of Alexandria, Basil the Great, Saint Maximus the Confessor, and other fathers ultimately springs from their conviction about the comprehensiveness and transfiguring power of the Christian faith. This conviction gave the fathers the boldness necessary to go beyond an isolationist Tertullian ghetto. This faith illumined them with the perspicacity necessary to detect and reject Valentinus's tantalizing merger with deceptive teachings. Hence, Saint Basil instructed youth studying secular texts to selectively extract those elements that provide nourishment and could be harmonized with life's ultimate purpose—sanctification.[59]

Selective extraction and harmonization presuppose clarity about the teachings of Christ and a Christian worldview. This approach also assumes a relationship between theology and secular knowledge that is both asymmetrical and hierarchial. In terms of asymmetry, theology with its norms and values is given a place of logical priority over secular knowledge. In terms of hierarchy, concepts from secular learning "are placed properly within a larger overarching context of Christian theology."[60] Christian teaching thus provides a structure or framework into which useful aspects of secular learning can be oriented toward Christ and find their deeper meaning and ultimate significance. This hierarchal relationship between Christian theology and secular knowledge is not the relationship between a close-up and a panoramic photograph,[61] but rather it is akin to the relationship between a sentence governed by the rules for grammar and a group of words defined by the rules of lexicography.[62] Theology selects the appropriate words and puts them in order, without specifying the production of the words *per se*. This clarifies psychology's role in Christian thought. "Theology wants psychology neither as a servant nor as a master, but as a source of knowledge about that aspect of the created world which has bearing on theology."[63]

Such a relationship allows for psychological concepts to be situated and structured within the context of the Truth, to be transfigured by the vivifying experience of God, and to become vessels of glory.[64] This is what the fathers did when they borrowed technical terms such as *hypostasis* and *ousia* from Hellenic philosophical thought and invigorated them with a new content,[65] later employing them liturgically in the hymnography of the trinitarian canons of Sunday nocturns and elsewhere in the divine services of the Church.

In a contemporary setting, committed Protestant psychologists who endeavor to relate theology and psychology in a discerning way employ a variety of paradigms: neutral parties, allies, or parallel seekers. Those utilizing a neutral-parties model segregate distinct findings and correlate similar concepts. Those adhering to an allies model critique psychology using theology and critique theology using psychology, re-examining theological and psychological presuppositions when a discrepancy appears.[66] Those applying a parallel-seekers model seek psychological parallels, support, reinforcement, and modern examples of biblical teachings.[67] Although each of these models has its value and proper use, none of them really corresponds to the patristic model of discerning openness we have outlined above.

Some might malign this patristic approach as the theological imperialism of religious colonists or spies pilfering what they can from selective findings from psychology;[68] or even worse, some might liken followers of this approach to the "inquisitors who saw Galileo's science as legitimate as long as his theories did not transgress their theological proclamations."[69] Inquisitors, spies, and colonists, however, do not offer meaning to the otherwise meaningless and life to the otherwise dead. Orthodox theology does not stifle, steal, or exploit, but encourages, enriches, and uplifts knowledge about creation by embracing what is good, reorienting it toward what is best, and by the grace of God transfiguring it into something far better than it was before. This is not empty rhetoric, for "every tree is indeed known by his own fruit."[70] If the tree of Hellenic fine arts when nurtured in the garden of the Church could bear the extraordinary fruits of Byzantine iconography, architecture, music, and hymnography, there is no reason to doubt the possibility of a similar outcome with the discerning use of psychological knowledge.

Potential Benefits from an Approach of Discerning Openness

Employing the patristic approach of discerning openness with psychological concepts would allow them to be anchored within a narrative that stretches from creation to the consummation of all things and that can provide them with an ontological depth that is able to respond to existential problems for which psychology has no satisfactory answer. In the face of guilt and condemnation, emptiness and meaninglessness, the twists of "fate" and death,[71] psychology is fundamentally limited.[72] Within a theological framework, however, the deeper meaning of life as revealed by faith in God and in Christ's victory over death brings divine consolation and healing to those troubled by such issues.[73] For a person who has never received a parent's love, but only abuse, or for someone suffering from real guilt, psychology is ill equipped to supply an answer; only Christ's love, the possibility of real repentance, and divine forgiveness as encountered in the Church can offer what no psychologist can.[74]

Apart from a theological framework offering healing to spiritually wounded human nature, the incarnation of God the Word, his death on the Cross, his Resurrection, his Ascension into heaven, and his Second Coming transfigure both anthropology and our understanding of the potential Christ has provided for us.[75] The closed world of the psychology of fallen man can open up into a psychology of the new Adam that operates according to a different set of "psychological laws" as seen in the lives of the saints (see chapter 8). Thus, even as psychology offers a descriptive account of how fallen man functions, thinks, and behaves, so theology can provide prescriptive and normative advice for the life, thought, and behavior of the new man in Christ.[76] "Psychology cannot tell people how they ought to live their lives," as the renowned psychologist Albert Bandura observed. Something hierarchically superior and existentially deeper is required for that. Psychology "can, however, provide them with the means for effecting personal and social change."[77]

Given that the Church finds man in his fallen condition, the condition in which psychologists study human nature, psychological data can help clarify the pastor's thought with important knowledge about human emotions.[78] In this case, psychology serves an assisting, preparatory, and pedagogical role by its guidance toward healthy mental processes.[79] In particular, cognitive therapists have developed, researched, and tested additional tools for dealing with cognitive distortions, not unlike some patristic advice.[80] In the proper framework, these tools can be employed today, even as Clement of Alexandria's Stoic exhortations were utilized in his time, and thereby aid Christians in their striving toward Christ. As Elder Païsios put it, "Those who have clouded their minds with science will naturally have more tools for their work, if by the grace of God their minds become clear."[81]

The Approach of Choice: Some Conclusions about Method

Our brief survey of how church fathers, ecclesiastical writers, and proponents of heresy have used the proverbial gold of the Egyptians can now furnish us with guidance for a patristic approach to and evaluation of cognitive therapy. The historical friendship between the fathers and Hippocratic-Galenic medicine disqualifies a dismissive Tertullian response. In so far as cognitive therapy is a medical treatment that does not claim exclusive etiological comprehensiveness or seek to encompass regions outside its expertise, such as the spiritual realm, the facile rejection of the Christian zealot is no longer an option. Obviously, an unreflecting merger à la Valentinus would be not only wrong and irresponsible, but also, according to the fathers, demonic.

The remaining option is the approach seen in figures such as Saint Basil the Great and Clement of Alexandria, an approach of discerning openness that selects, incorporates, and transfigures. This strategy is implicitly asymmetric and hierarchal by virtue of the eternal value of salvation in Christ in contrast with the fleeting significance of temporary psychological well-being. With this approach, Christian teachings act as a filter admitting some concepts, rejecting others, and in other instances suggesting alternatives. To be successful, this patristic approach requires clarity in terms of a theological mindset capable of placing valuable insights from cognitive therapy into their appropriate niches within a Christian conception of the world and system of values. This is no simple task. Immersed as we are in a scientific worldview, our thought patterns are often unwittingly guided in a direction quite different from that of the fathers. What was for them a natural perception must often be for us a matter of deliberate and continuous choice.[82]

We do, however, have the privilege of being able to choose to be methodologically guided by the fathers on the sojourn before us. An Orthodox Christian theological worldview can be outlined and serve as a standard for evaluating the implicit *Weltanschauung* of cognitive therapy. Relevant pastoral advice and ascetic teachings by the fathers can be selected and arranged in order to form a patristic context for examining discrete components of cognitive therapy. In this way, we can strive to follow along the bold path of those conquerors of death into the promised land of the Church where "the mystical trumpeters of the Spirit"[83] proclaim the truth of the faith: "all things are possible to him that believeth"[84]—Egyptian gold can be forged into a censer by a Christian hand.

CHAPTER TWO

Worlds Apart:
Myth, Method, and Metaphysics

When Saint Gregory Palamas likened the identification of useful secular knowledge within Greek literature to the extraction of organic material from a serpent for pharmaceutical use,[1] he was describing the painstaking process of filtering a non-Christian system of thought through a lattice of Christian doctrine, so that harmful elements could be removed and beneficial elements could be retained in order to provide healing in the context of the believer's lives. He was also implicitly affirming a basic principle of faith: "Christian teaching illumines created reality and the events of history."[2] In the case of Hellenic wisdom, Saint Gregory Palamas discerningly wielded the two-edged sword of Christian revelation to cut off both the allegorical head of the serpent, secular opinions about divinity, and its tail, pagan myths about creation. In like manner, an Orthodox Christian theological worldview can be employed as a frame of reference for evaluating the philosophical worldview underlying cognitive therapy, thereby removing what is false and misleading so that what is true and informative can be put to a proper use.

Worldviews, as they relate to psychology, provide background theories about human nature and the universe, a diagnosis of the human condition, and a prescription for its healing. In other words, they respond to four basic questions: Who am I? Where am I? What is the problem? and What is the cure?[3] An Orthodox Christian conception of the world provides answers to these questions through the testimony of scripture and tradition about the Triune God and his relationship to the human race. In cognitive therapy, the answers to these questions arise from Renaissance, early modern, and modern philosophies that served as sources for, or were derivatives of, scientific thought. On the one hand, we can choose to listen prayerfully to a narrative about creation, the image of God in man, the fall, and salvation in Christ that makes up the worldview that informs the Christian's choices, thoughts, and action. On the other hand, we can elect to accept intellectually alternative descriptions about human origin and nature drawn from empiricism, rationalism, atomism, materialism, evolutionary theory, naturalism, and pragmatism. Individually, these philosophies serve as inspiration for the method and theory of cognitive therapy; collectively, they crystallize into a worldview that therapists use as their guiding star for suggesting adaptive thought and behavior.

Even before we examine the two sets of answers to the worldview questions noted above, the divergent sources of authoritative knowledge from the two approaches seem to suggest irreconcilable epistemological differences. The Christian makes use of faith—"I believed, and therefore have I spoken"[4]—as a basis for understanding,[5] while the scientist appears to accept nothing by faith—*nullius in verba*[6]—but only that which is arrived at from tangible data, through formal inference, and by the right method.[7] Notwithstanding, a Christian is not someone who believes just anything, but a person who believes in God and makes use of this faith to illumine all things,[8] because he has discovered through faith an ever-flowing fount of knowledge far deeper than any cistern of mortal wisdom.[9] A scientist, *pace* logical positivists, is not someone who dogmatically rejects all belief or traditional ways of knowing as meaningless or superstitious, but an individual who seeks to understand the natural order through the formulation of causal laws and probabilistic correlations, because such formulations have explanatory power. Nothing in principle hinders the scientist from embracing faith or the believer from engaging in science.

The ostensible epistemological differences between the use of faith and the application of the scientific method in fact are differences in subject matter and aim. The subject of the Christian faith—the unlimited, infinite, and eternal God who became man—cannot be understood by limited, finite, and temporal measurements and approaches that characterize the scientific method.[10] The subjects explored by science are amenable to scientific investigation because they are limited in time and space. It is not a matter of science versus faith, but of selecting the suitable method and instruments for each field of inquiry. In the case of the Orthodox Christian faith, the spiritual heart refined by the hesychastic method and illumined by the Holy Spirit provides a fitting instrument for the aim of supra-rationally [*agnōstōs*] "knowing" the infinite Triune God through the revelation of Christ. Notwithstanding these methodological differences, faith requires neither the sacrifice of reason[11] nor the rejection of the scientific method in its appropriate realm.

While faith and science need not be at odds, scientists and theologians with insular agendas can be at loggerheads. Such estrangement can be irreconcilable when the subject matter is the human being. After all, humanity as part of the natural order is a valid subject for scientific inquiry, while man viewed as a being in the image of God is an apt subject for the light of faith. As we suggested in the previous chapter, an open approach of selective integration incorporating information from both sources seems to be the preferred strategy of the fathers. Secular scientists may well scoff at what they view as the mixing of reason and mythic thought, but it is precisely mythic thought that can "unify and gather together the shards of reality,"[12] so that they might discern the value of the forest, and not just the species of the trees. Reason stripped of myth has unquestionably produced impressive technological advances, with cognitive therapy numbered among them, but as the German Romantics rightly pointed out, man stripped of myth is stripped of his humanity and deprived of his ability to see.[13] In Christianity, however, believers experience their eyes being opened to the heights of a God-revealed faith capable of replacing the soaring mythology of ancient Greece, because the Christian narrative is understood to be not only illumining and unifying, but also historical and true.

The three-layered narrative of creation, the fall, and redemption offers a background theory about the universe, human nature, the human predicament, and its resolution. Notwithstanding, the ultimate meaning of each of these worldview elements is fully unveiled only at the end of the sketch. For this reason, we will first walk through the whole Christian narrative as it relates to the structural, ontological, and phenomenological character of human nature, and then when the worldview elements have been gathered in, we will lay out the corresponding Christian conception of the world. In like manner, we will also wade through the philosophies instrumental in the development of modern science in order to extract the *Weltanschauung* that seeps into cognitive therapy as well.

Beholding the World in the
Light of the Christian Narrative

The World in the Beginning:
Creation *ex nihilo* and *ad imaginem Dei*

The core of an Orthodox Christian worldview consists of the revelation that the Holy Trinity, "the Father through the Son and in the Holy Spirit created all things"[14] *ex nihilo* out of a superabundance of love and goodness. This revealed truth, verified by the experience of the saints throughout history, has a number of consequences. First of all, the cause and purpose of all things, including man, are found in the Triune God, that is to say, his love and his goodness.[15] Second, the chief principle that shapes Christian theological and philosophical thought is the contradistinction between the uncreated God and the created cosmos. Only the Holy Trinity is absolute and unchanging; all creation, spiritual and material, is relative and subject to change.[16]

Related to the radical difference between the uncreated and the created is the distinction between God's essence and energies.[17] The unapproachable and by essence transcendent God not only draws nigh to creation through his uncreated energies, but he also touches each created being with these energies that vary according to the receptivity of the created being participating in them.[18] There is thus no aspect of created reality that can be conceived of apart from the uncreated divine energies. Physical objects, for instance, owe their physical being to the uncreated energy bestowing physicality on them; living things are alive by virtue of the uncreated energy providing them with life; reasoning beings are rational on account of the uncreated energy granting reason; and beings receptive of *theosis* are deified by the deifying uncreated energy of God.[19] The doctrines of creation *ex nihilo* and of the divine energies jointly suggest that through the uncreated energies, reason is weaved into the very fabric of reality, while irrationality suggests a fraying of the carpet by turning away from God and returning back to the non-being from which creation was formed.[20]

According to Genesis 1:26, humanity is theologically fashioned in the image and likeness of the Creator and charged with lordship over creation. What distinguishes man from beast is not the presence of reason, but his creation in the image of God and the stewardship with which his Maker entrusted him.[21] These theological aspects of human nature are intimately related. The image of God was meant to illumine human activity in the world, so that by governing creation with divine goodness, Adam and Eve would grow in virtue and reach the likeness of God by divine grace.[22] Hence, the image of God can be seen as an inner wellspring watering human activity and human life with motivation, purpose, and meaning beyond this transitory world. It implies that our relationship with our Archetype is at the center of our humanity.[23] The image of God in man also suggests an innate human receptivity to the divine that enables people to live with their Benefactor, to see their Redeemer, to imitate their Savior, and to be transfigured into the very likeness of God.[24] It also entails an inherent dynamism toward perfection,[25] for that which is in the image strives toward God's likeness. Human wisdom, for example, naturally stretches upward to divine wisdom; human knowledge spontaneously reaches out to divine omniscience;[26] and so all human faculties, thoughts, and desires find their aim and destination in the infinite perfections of God in whom the human being is called to be deified by grace.[27] For the fathers, if man's greatness is found in the image of God rather than in the rational faculty *per se*, it is because the image is the source of his capacity to be deified.[28]

Of course, reason and freedom are important aspects of our being in the image of God, for we were meant to use those gifts in order to live in virtue, imitate our Heavenly Father, attain the likeness, and be deified by grace.[29] The fathers locate this capacity for self-determination by the free will and reason in the *nous* or spiritual heart, the faculty of the soul by which a person transcends himself and enters into communion with God.[30]

According to the church fathers, what it means to be made in God's image can be understood only by looking to Christ, the image of the invisible God. Man is in fact "an image of the Image" who is Christ.[31] Christology thus becomes the key to Orthodox Christian anthropology, which is literally theanthropology.[32] Panagiotis Nellas notes "man is logical, because he is created in the image of Christ who is the hypostatic *Logos* of the Father...man is creative, because he is in the image of the *Logos*, the Creator *par excellence*."[33] One could also say that a human being is logical to the extent that he participates in the *Logos*.[34] But even further, every human soul can recognize and experience Christ's work, resurrection, and kingdom as his own, because he is in the image of Christ.[35] All this being said, the image of God in man remains, in the final analysis, a mystery of unfathomable depth, apprehended in part only to the extent that a person sees God. Saint Gregory of Nyssa asks, "How then is man, this mortal, passable, short-lived being, the image of that nature which is immortal, pure, and everlasting? The true answer to this question, indeed, perhaps only the very Truth knows."[36]

A Fallen Humanity and a Fallen World: the Ancestral Sin

Obviously, this majestic description of God, the world, and human nature is at variance with the violence, sickness, and human dysfunction of every sort that plague human lives and necessitate such institutions as prisons, hospitals, and mental health facilities. The opening Genesis account, however, does not seek to describe the vagaries of current existence, but to unearth a core of divine goodness and relatedness to God, discovered by the prophets, apostles, and saints, but revealed most perfectly in Christ Jesus. The tragedy of the present world can only be understood theologically by considering the second half of the Genesis story that describes how the misuse of human reason and freedom radically altered creation. The sacred history of the fall forms a second phenomenological layer over the Christian understanding of humanity and the universe in its pristine state.

At its root, the fall is a sundering of a connection inherent in man's creation in the image of God: namely, the relationship between the created and
the uncreated realm. Given that humanity was created *ex nihilo*, the very core
of human life necessarily changes with an alteration in man's relationship to
the fount of all being, the uncreated God.[37] Instead of following the natural,
positive, and dynamic path of the remembrance of their Maker, obedience to
their Lord, friendship with their Provider, and development into the likeness
of God with the support of the healing and life-giving divine energies, Adam
and Eve chose the unnatural, negative, and destructive path of forgetfulness,
disobedience, enmity, alienation, emptiness, and death by separating themselves from the Giver of life.[38]

The wrong choice of the ancestral sin was not just a detour from the
journey toward perfection. It was a dead-end characterized by a deluded state
of irrationality[39] and pride[40] in which man disregarded the very boundaries
separating the created from the uncreated realm.[41] Although the divine image
was not erased by the fall, it was darkened, thereby permitting human reason
to grow indolent and lose its ability to clearly see the things of God. Instead of
being directed toward the Giver of Light, human reason turned with blind
selfishness toward creation and fell under the shadowy influence of the
imagination that encouraged all manner of illusion, prejudice, superstition,
and idolatry to grow freely.[42] As a result of separation from God, human
beings became more vulnerable to the devil's influence as they became
intimately acquainted with corruption, sickness, and death, foes that human
freedom and reason could not overcome.[43] When Adam and Eve were girt
with garments of skin, human nature was clothed with dead matter, altering
life into a struggle for survival in which instincts and passions would displace
God-implanted reason.[44]

Notwithstanding, God in his providence continued to lovingly preserve
the world as a whole and the human race in particular, wisely guiding all
things to the goal he had assigned to them.[45] He sent his prophets, revealed the
law, and in the fullness of time became man in the cosmically immense person
of Jesus Christ.[46]

The World's Salvation: Christ's Wondrous Work

From an Orthodox Christian perspective, human salvation in Christ is a
divine mystery of infinite complexity wrought by everything Christ did and
does, said and says, was and is, and ever shall be. Through his incarnation,
nativity, baptism, transfiguration, passion, death on the Cross, resurrection,
and ascension, Christ did what no human being could do—he saved humanity

from sin, death, and the devil so that man might be renewed, illumined, perfected, and deified.[47] The person of Christ, his teachings, and the events in his earthly life are inexhaustible sources of meaning, healing, and salvation. They are the salve that bestows vision to eyes that otherwise would never see, enabling Christians to interpret themselves, their neighbors, and their world in the light of Christ. These world-changing events are the *sine qua non* of any Christian worldview and form the decisive third layer that defines the Christian narrative as well as Christians themselves.

Since human nature was altered by the fall, God the Word became man in order to heal mortal and corruptible human nature in himself[48] by uniting it with immortality and incorruptibility.[49] Through the incarnation, the infinite God has shown that an inseparable union between God and man is perfectly normal, natural, and fitting for a human being.[50] In the God-man, God becomes man and man becomes God. Hence, the incarnation itself reveals that salvation is nothing less than deification in Christ or union with God.[51] As the incarnation naturally points toward deification, it also gives meaning and purpose to every aspect of human existence.[52]

In Christ's wondrous life and life-giving work, "God in his entirety gives himself unsparingly to man in his entirety."[53] By virtue of who Christ is as the Logos who created all things, the various moments in the work of salvation have a cosmic significance whose wisdom far exceeds the reaches of the human mind, but is deeply felt by the believing heart. Ever moved by love for fallen man, Christ's every word and deed were as the creed puts it, "for us men and for our salvation." Saint Gregory the Theologian refers to Christ's nativity, baptism, miracles, and crucifixion as a "sort of divine education for us."[54] Blessed Augustine comments on these events being "so ordered that the Christian might model his life on them, not merely in a mystical sense, but in reality."[55] When Christ was baptized in the Jordan, human nature was ineffably made worthy of the bath of incorruption and the forgiveness of sins.[56] When he arose from the waters, the Holy Spirit descended on our common nature by descending on him. And when the voice of the Father bore witness to the Son, the Holy Trinity was revealed to the world as the source of our salvation.[57] A similar epiphany occurred when Christ was transfigured on Tabor, transfiguring our human nature by his divine nature, so that the image of God in man might shine forth more gloriously than the sun. When Christ suffered and died on the Cross, he healed our human nature wracked by sin, transforming death into an entrance to life eternal, and redirecting our human will toward the good through the power of his love.[58]

When Christ arose from the dead, he killed sin, trampled down death, and crushed the devil, thereby utterly vanquishing the three enemies that tyrannized the nature of human beings since the fall. In so doing, he also granted humanity forgiveness of sins, eternal life, unfading joy, and his great mercy.[59] The resurrection of Christ is what fills the Christian heart and mind with ever-burgeoning optimism and unfaltering courage. In fact, Christians are Christians only in so far as they live the resurrection of Christ and make it their guiding light in life as well as in death.[60] In the luminescence of Christ's resurrection, believers see death as a sleep from which Christ will awaken them.[61] Christ's victorious resurrection shines radiantly through "the apostleship of the apostles, the martyrdom of the martyrs, the miracles of the wonderworkers, the faith of the believers, the love of those who love, the hope of those who hope, the fasting of those who fast, the prayer of those who pray," for apart from the resurrection of Christ all these things remain inexplicable.[62] Finally, when Christ ascended in glory, he lifted up human nature beyond the highest heaven to the right hand of God the Father, thereby placing man inaccessibly beyond mortality's reach. By his ascension, Christ showed fallen humanity the immensity of his love and the ultimate purpose of his incarnation: to see his children deified, glorified, and dwelling with God forever.[63]

If the remedy for human suffering is found in the person and life of Christ, the believer can partake of that remedy by entering his Body, the Church, the new space Christ created in an old world.[64] As God the Word became man at the Annunciation to save human nature, so Christ the God-man became the Church at Pentecost to enable each and every human being to become a living member of his Body, to be transfigured into his likeness, and thereby to make Christ's salvific victory over sin, death, and the devil his own.[65] This transfiguration takes place through the Church's Holy Mysteries and the holy virtues that make it possible for the believer to live the events in Christ's life as his own life and to receive his teachings in all their salvific fullness.[66] In other words, human restoration, transfiguration, purification, illumination, and deification are wrought through the grace of the Holy Spirit received on the one hand through baptism, chrismation, the Holy Eucharist, and all the other mysteries and liturgical services that make up the sacramental life; and on the other hand, through faith, repentance, noetic prayer, fasting, vigil, humility, love, and all the other virtues that constitute the life of ascetic struggle. Thus, through the indivisible union of the virtues and the mysteries, the believer's prayer "Thy will be done on earth as it is in heaven" becomes a reality: his will is aligned with the will of God, even as Christ's human will was in harmony with his divine will.[67] In practical terms, this means that in the Church, a person's love of self [philautia] is transfigured into love of neighbor [philadelphia],[68] which is the very source of the divine economy.

Divine Revelation to the World and
an Orthodox Christian Worldview

Making use of the above three-layered sketch of creation, the fall, and the work of Christ as a map, we can point out the characteristics of an Orthodox Christian theological conception of the world as it relates to psychology. When the Christian asks the question, "What is a human being?" divine revelation about creation tells him that man is a dynamic being subject to change, either growing toward or falling away from God. His inner structure should guide him in goodness. Patristic teachings about the image of God reveal that man is a theological being with receptivity to and a dynamic élan toward God and divine perfection that can be seen incarnate in the person of Jesus Christ. Human rationality and freedom are integral parts of human nature, but their value is dependent on their responsible use as tools for growing into the likeness of God and for wisely governing self and creation. The account of the fall indicates that in terms of phenomenology, man is easily deceived and often forgetful of God. This forgetfulness can lead to a state of pride in which man no longer properly judges the boundaries separating the created and uncreated and in which his rationality becomes irrational under the joint influence of the imagination and the devil. Human reason and freedom are further weakened by the presence of corruption and death, which turn life into a struggle for survival. Finally, the work of Christ reveals that man is a being of great complexity and immense value. Above all, he is loved. For human beings, it is normal and natural to be united to God. Union with God implies that the image can be restored and the likeness can be attained. In the Church through the mysteries and the virtues, people can be purified, transfigured, shown to be victorious over sin, death and the devil, be resurrected and ascend to the Father. The lives of the saints demonstrate that these are not empty words, but by the grace of God, achievable goals.

When a Christian asks, "What is the world?" Orthodox teaching on creation answers that the world was created by God out of love and goodness and saturated with a purpose infinitely greater than itself. Being absolutely distinct from the Creator by essence, nothing in this world is worthy of worship, yet everything in it acquires value by its contact with him through his uncreated energies. The heart of reality is thus both good and meaningful. Notwithstanding, creation is utterly dependent on God and subject to change. To unpurified eyes, however, nature's goodness and meaningfulness are no longer transparent, because fallen man's reason has grown dark through pride, selfishness, fear, and a swollen imagination. Moreover, corruption, sickness, vice, sin, and death are ever-present realities in the world. Notwithstanding, for the Christian, all of creation has been purified by the coming of Christ.

Sickness, corruption, sin, and death after Christ's victory are no longer the invincible fear-inspiring enemies that they once were. In the Church, the eyes of believers are purified through the mysteries and virtues of Christ, so that they can see through the phenomenology of the suffering fallen world to the ultimate nature of creation and the consummation of all things in the kingdom of God, where Christ is "all in all."[69]

We have already touched on the answers to the two remaining questions. What is amiss in human affairs and life? According to the account of the fall and subsequent sacred history, human misery stems from forgetfulness, disobedience, and a broken relationship with God, accompanied by selfishness, pride, irrationality, delusion, a lack of self-control, movement toward non-being, and a fearful subjugation to corruption, sickness, death, and the devil. What is the remedy for this situation? According to patristic interpretations of Genesis and the work of Christ, man's salvation is possible through remembrance of God, through unceasing prayer and thanksgiving, a restored relationship with the Holy Trinity through the mysteries of the Church and a life of virtue, and filial obedience to God that are accompanied by love for one's brother, humility, clear-sighted reason, self-control, continuous movement toward Christ, and freedom from the fear of corruption, sickness, death, and the devil.

Explicit Method and Implicit Metaphysics: Underpinnings of the Worldview of Modern Science

Novum Organum: Empiricism, Rationalism, and Atomism

Unlike the Christian conception of the world that can be discerned by recourse to a narrative revealing the ultimate meaning and purpose of man and creation, the *Weltanschauung* underpinning cognitive therapy can be gleaned from purportedly non-metaphysical theories about nature and the human organism that are derived from scientific observations and methods. We can ferret out this worldview with a brief historical survey of the major philosophical movements embedded in modern scientific thought as it grows increasingly secular and ever more mythically sterile from the period of the Renaissance to the Second World War. Our aim, then, is to discern value systems and worldview elements contained in these philosophical systems and passed on to cognitive therapy. Historically, the theories espoused by various philosophical movements gradually eclipsed the earlier narrative of scholasticism and inspired the construction of progressively more expansive theories to replace it. Although Orthodox Christianity views scholastic theology as heretical on various counts, it is still a Christian heresy and not another religion. When the soaring gothic spires of scholastic thought began to crumble during the Renaissance, the initially Christian worldview that inspired them began to be replaced with alternatives to religion that could no longer be qualified as Christian at all.

If anything was "reborn" during the Renaissance, it was the pre-Christian philosophical position of humanism, namely, that "man is the measure of all things."[70] It would be expressed in the opposing and often competing forms of Sir Francis Bacon's (1561–1626) optimistic experimental empiricism and René Descartes' (1596–1650) confident skeptical rationalism.[71] Empiricism with its focus on experimental observations and rationalism with its concentration on speculative principles are the two foundational approaches that undergird scientific research and the worldview of modern science.[72] As empiricists, scientists gather knowledge from sense experience. As rationalists, they use reason to analyze their observations.

When cognitive therapists stress the importance of experimentation and careful observation as sources of personal psychological knowledge, they are being true to their Baconian heritage. When they rigorously apply logical analysis to evaluate beliefs or assumptions and when they break problems and goals into smaller steps, they are adhering to a classically Cartesian paradigm and method.[73] From both approaches, cognitive therapy inherited the Renaissance notion that knowledge is power and should be put to practical ends.[74]

The Baconian use of observation, experimentation, and logical analysis can be viewed as an expression of human striving for perfection inherent in the image of God. They can also be considered fitting tools for fulfilling the divine mandate to govern creation. The patristic acceptance of Hippocratic-Galenic medicine suggests an implicit approval of Hippocratic systematic observation as well as a tacit assent to Galen's sophisticated experimental procedures. Bacon's arguments for limits to the scope of science[75] are also consistent with the broad patristic etiology for mental illnesses referred to in the previous chapter. Although the fathers do not denigrate the use of reason when aligned with the faith (see chapter 5), Descartes' rationalism, not unrelated to rationalistic scholasticism in which he was Jesuit-trained, is more problematic, because it involves a skepticism about supra-rational ways of knowing, a belief in the unlimited scope of scientific inquiry, and a tacit approval of questionable and even fictional assumptions if they prove to be serviceable.[76] When reason is idolized, when observation is arbitrarily restricted, and when traditional sources of knowledge from revelation are devalued, narrow empiricism can result in a simplification and flattening of reality that makes life shallow, while unbridled rationalism can culminate in a disembodied estrangement from reality that replaces life itself with a hollow abstraction thereof.[77]

Notwithstanding, empiricism and rationalism would leave the next generation awestruck by the spectacular achievements of the founding fathers of the Enlightenment, Sir Isaac Newton (1643–1727) and John Locke (1632–1704), who rationally examined the results of empirical investigation with an atomistic approach. In its Enlightenment form, atomism seeks to establish relationships between simple ideal factors in order to explain complex composite reality. This approach enabled Newton to frame the laws of motion and Locke to develop a scientific theory of knowledge. When cognitive therapists encourage their patients to solve their problems via method, measurement, and technique, when they help them to make a better fit between a personal interpretation of a situation (hypothesis) and the situation itself (empirical data) by altering a single variable, when they conceptualize a client as "a collection of behavioral and cognitive habits and predispositions," they are operating within classically Newtonian and Lockian tradition.[78]

Even as empirical methods within certain limits do not pose a problem for Orthodox Christians, so atomism that interprets reality by breaking it down into distinct separable elements is not problematic as long as an atomistic approach does not exclude holistic alternatives. As in the case of empiricism, atomism as a method is not particularly ambiguous. When the fathers would analyze an impassioned thought by breaking it down into a neutral concept and emotional charge or passion, they too were adhering to an atomistic approach.[79] However, if the therapist uses an atomistic approach to replace an understanding of the human person as a responsible moral agent in the image of God with a conglomeration of cognitions and behaviors, the therapist is in danger of reducing the human being to a biological organism with no theological, spiritual, or moral significance.

Metaphysics Concealed: Naturalism, Positivism, and Materialism

The triumphs of Newton's method together with Locke's effective application of that methodology to the process of human understanding influenced not only the next wave of scientists and philosophers, but also the succeeding generation of Western religious thinkers and figures who accepted the proposition that reason is the only instrument apt for solving human problems.[80] When these "enlightened divines," who were truly in the dark about things divine, espoused Locke's opinion that reason should also judge revelation, they found themselves later embracing his rejection of God's direct intervention in history and in the world.[81] These positions, however, are not intrinsic to empiricism, rationalism, or atomism. In other words, relying on sense experience, using reason, and isolating distinct aspects of a phenomenon do not necessitate deism. The rejection of an active God is not a scientific finding, but a metaphysical assumption that Orthodox Christian theology is obliged to reject. Frederick Copleston remarks, "The idea that scientific advance pushes metaphysics out of the picture is mistaken. Metaphysics simply reappears in the form of concealed assumptions."[82] The historically contingent theological assumption of an inactive deity proposed by the deists would become a basic principle in scientific explanations, a ground rule in physics, chemistry, biology, psychology, and by extension cognitive therapy.[83] Since God never intervenes according to the philosophy of naturalism, whatever exists must be explained exclusively in the natural terms of scientific theories. While naturalism, the theory that everything arises from natural causes, may be a useful assumption in research, its consequences in terms of an overall worldview blind even when its premises illumine.[84] The blinding effect of this useful assumption would only increase as naturalism would take on new forms as positivism, materialism, and in evolutionary theory.

While naturalism was not atheistic *per se*, its inherent agnosticism had the effect of turning people away from Western Christianity. This can be seen in Auguste Comte's (1798–1857) empirical positivism, an expression of naturalism that explicitly denied the validity of any knowledge apart from the observed facts and descriptive laws that make up scientific theory. For Comte, only those of immature mind take recourse to God as an hypothesis to explain that which they do not understand.[85] In fact, Comte envisioned scientists and positivist philosophers replacing the church hierarchy, and Humanity (with a capital *H*) taking the place of God as an object of worship.[86] In the twentieth century, logical positivism prepared a similar manifesto with a linguistic twist maintaining that any metaphysical theory about the world, including all religious statements, was meaningless, because metaphysics cannot be verified by observation and experimentation.[87] Although modern positivists may not explicitly set out to form a religion of science, their rejection of established religion is quite similar to their Comtian predecessors. Unfortunately, a positivist approach à la Comte is widespread in contemporary psychology.[88] The naturalist model with its positivist tendencies is clearly the paradigm within which cognitive therapy seeks the sources of dysfunctional behavior and thinking.

Another close cousin of naturalism was materialism, a philosophical position that views all observable facts as dependent on physical processes or reducible to them. In its sensationalist form represented by the works of Julien de La Mettrie (1709–1751), man could be purportedly understood by viewing the human being as a mere machine or even a plant.[89] Everything functions according to deterministic mechanical laws; differences between humanity and the rest of nature are just a matter of degree or in Diderot's (1713–1784) terms "physical organization."[90] Pierre Cabanis (1757–1808) even went so far as to assert that "the brain secretes thought just as the liver secretes bile."[91] Within such a paradigm, there is little room for the mental or the spiritual, much less the uncreated. Psychologists who look to rats solving mazes or computers yielding output in order to understand human behavior and thought are working in a thoroughly materialistic model. The information-processing model used in cognitive therapy is also an example of a materialistic approach.[92]

Method or Metaphysics? Evolutionary Theory and Related Philosophies

Within the milieu of deist-inspired naturalism, omni-competent positivism, deterministic materialism, and highly competitive progress-oriented industrial society, Charles Darwin used his acute observational skills and speculative faculties to frame a theory reflecting his age, to wit, the initially retrodictive theory of evolution. Evolutionary theory completed the naturalistic account of the human organism and its place in the universe. Based on evolution, psychologists would adopt an anthropology maintaining that "the characteristics and abilities that make us *Homo sapiens* have been shaped by natural selection. We are what we are because we have survival value—not just as individuals, but also as a species. We are the largely accidental result of particular environmental pressures acting on the available genetic material."[93] Moreover, materialistic evolution ultimately assumes that human beings and human thought "were once latent in a fiery cloud," and would one day be as though they had never been.[94] In a world defined by evolutionary theory, reality is seen as being determined by chance, natural laws, and inertia. In such a framework, the only remaining values are growth and survival.[95]

Evolutionary theory is whole-heartedly embraced by cognitive therapists as a background theory that shapes their vocabulary (for instance, thoughts are adaptive or maladaptive) and provides hypothetical explanations for mental states associated with hostility, anxiety, and sexual attraction.[96] According to cognitive theorists, present-day *maladaptive* egocentric biases, self-defeating beliefs, and negative meaning assignment had survival value at an earlier stage and particular environment in the evolution of our species when such reactions and cognitive shortcuts were *adaptive*.[97] Applying evolutionary theory as an explanatory model for psychopathology, Beck opines,

> Our environment has changed more rapidly than our automatic adaptive strategies— largely as a result of our own modifications of our social milieu. Thus, strategies of predation, competition, and sociability that were useful in the more primitive surroundings do not always fit into the present niche of a highly individualized and technological society....Egocentricity, competitiveness, exhibitionism, and avoidance of unpleasantness may all be adaptive in certain situations but grossly maladaptive in others.[98]

Thus, psychopathology is understood as a mismatch between human beings and their suddenly (in evolutionary terms) altered environment. What is now abnormal and pathological was once a quite normal survival mechanism in terms of "defense from predators, the attack and defeat of enemies, procreation, and energy conservation."[99] This explanation makes sense, especially if one has already accepted the philosophical assumptions of naturalism, materialism, and positivism.

Although some Orthodox Christian theologians have attempted to reconcile evolutionary theory as a scientific description of a natural process to creation in Genesis as a theological account of causation,[100] no reconciliation has been greeted by unanimous approval, simply because evolutionary theory is *more* than a description of a process and Orthodox theology of creation is *more* than a statement about causation. And that something more on either side should not be allegorized away. It is beyond the scope of this study to discuss or pass judgment on evolutionary theory. Notwithstanding, metaphysical positions that are conveyed during cognitive therapy and that have their roots in evolutionary theory and its forebears should be evaluated.

Naturalism, materialism, positivism, and evolutionary theory are in their purist forms all closed paradigms limiting reality to natural causes, matter, scientific explanations, or all of the above. They also contain metaphysical assumptions about reality that are incompatible with Orthodox Christianity. The American philosopher and psychologist William James would even find such paradigms insufficiently empirical in so far as they refuse to take seriously religious experiences, since they label those experiences as supernatural, spiritual, and not subject to scientific investigation.[101] These philosophies share a number of serious metaphysical, theological, and anthropological defects. Metaphysically, they tend to turn scientific observations about physical and biological entities into "the highest court of meaning that determines what is the truth."[102] Theologically, they deny the existence and thus the possibility of knowing the uncreated God, despite a host of quite sane witnesses to the contrary. By their rejection of miracles, they also dismiss the notion of Divine

Providence and God's interventions in history.[103] In terms of anthropology, they preclude the possibility of an "immaterial" part of man, namely the soul, surviving death.[104] They also enclose human freedom within a prison of causality in which man is determined inwardly by his genetic code and outwardly by his environment. When they liken the human being to a complex animal or a slow computer, they not only debase man, but deprive him of responsibility, for "who among us would hold either an animal or machine morally accountable for its performance?"[105] In an evolutionary framework of the adaptive versus the maladaptive, virtue and sin become meaningless concepts. It should hardly surprise us that one of Ellis's articles is entitled, "There is no place for the concept of sin in therapy."[106]

Metaphysically and theologically, an exclusively evolutionary rationale for thought and behavior undermines fundamental theological beliefs about Providence and morality. Notwithstanding, the idea of adaptation to a given situation can provide supplemental information on a practical level that is hardly irrelevant to the believer who primarily examines a situation employing the existential, theological categories of sin and virtue. Natural selection, adaptation, species modification, and predictions about maladaptation as scientific data can also be accepted without unreservedly endorsing retrodictive evolutionary theory concerning the origins of life and the descent of man. Since cognitive therapists employ evolutionary psychology as a useful explanatory model for observed dysfunction without requiring the patient to metaphysically acquiesce to that model, they can easily practice cognitive therapy without relying on it.

Some charge Beckian cognitive therapy with "imposing an Enlightenment ethos on its clients by its ahistorical and acontextual scientific script."[107] The historical-philosophical underpinnings of cognitive therapy outlined above would lend credence to such a charge. Although explicit advocacy of metaphysical naturalism and logical positivism are not characteristic of Beck's works, such philosophies fit all too comfortably in a cognitive psychotherapeutic context, and they are certainly more compatible than an explicit Christian outlook is. If a particular therapist does advocate logical positivism, the spiritual and moral dangers in therapy from a Christian perspective can be immense.

Albert Ellis's philosophically oriented version of cognitive therapy offers an instructive example of the direction of therapy that wholeheartedly embraces both metaphysical naturalism and logical positivism. Ellis's "elegant solution" in rational-emotive behavioral therapy is the acquisition of an all-embracing rational philosophy of life.[108] Although someone subscribing to metaphysical naturalism or logical positivism might find his advice rational, a practicing Christian of any ilk would be hard-pressed to agree. For instance, Ellis claims that there is no such thing as right and wrong,[109] or even good and bad, but only thoughts, feeling, and actions that further or that sabotage one's goals and purposes, which ultimately translate into maximizing the amount of pleasure a person receives in life.[110] In such a framework, promiscuity is advisable,[111] and suicide is permissible.[112] Ellis even opines that religiosity is "in many respects equivalent to irrational thinking and emotional disturbance," and should ideally be eliminated in the therapeutic process.[113] Obviously from a Christian perspective, his final psychological cure leads to a spiritual sickness unto death far worse than any presenting illness.

Notwithstanding, naturalism, materialism, and positivism have their moment of truth or they would hardly be so influential. There are natural causes. Matter and motion are fundamental constituents of reality. Scientific explanations produce results and generate further scholarship. Christian anthropology also sees man as part of the created realm and thus amenable, though never reducible, to theories and methods applied to other aspects of that realm.[114] This suggests the possibility of separating *methodological* naturalism, materialism, positivism, and evolutionary theory from their *metaphysical* counterparts. There is a compelling precedent for such a separation. Medicine, including Hippocratic-Galenic medicine, has always operated within a paradigm of *methodological* materialism. Surgical procedures and pharmaceutical interventions hardly make sense under any other model. Many fathers had no objection to methodological materialism employed by Hippocratic-Galenic medicine, which simply maintained that "empirical methodologies are the best way of obtaining knowledge about some subjects." However, an all-embracing metaphysical materialism that views supernatural claims as *a priori* impossibilities[115] and that dismisses all theological interpretations as unnecessary or meaningless[116] is folly, for the psalmist, who has explored the heights and depths of human existence, has also verified that only "the fool hath said in his heart, there is no God."[117]

That "theoretical formulations that are built on non-Christian or even anti-Christian presuppositions still have the capacity to generate verified and verifiable observations of human nature that had never before been suggested by Scripture"[118] need not be a vexed question. A theory can be a methodologically useful tool with predictive power without being metaphysically or even empirically true. Ptolemy's successful predictions of eclipses and the flat-earth model used by engineers are good examples of models that may be methodologically useful, but are factually quite mistaken.[119] Technically speaking, "scientific theories are neither true nor false, but rather more or less useful for explanatory and predictive purposes."[120] In other words, the use of methodological naturalism and materialism for practical reasons does not require a commitment to the truth-value of their metaphysical counterparts.

Practically speaking, however, it seems unlikely that someone could adhere to *methodological* naturalism, materialism, positivism, and evolutionary theory and remain immune to the *metaphysical* pull of these philosophies. It is psychologically naïve to suppose that one could use such working hypotheses on a daily basis and not be seduced into applying such thought forms in other areas of life and faith.[121] A safer approach would involve explaining some of the verifiable results of cognitive therapy by another background model. For example, the fact that logical thinking and exerting mastery over oneself and the environment result in psychological health can also be explained theologically by the account of creation in the likeness of the Logos and the God-given task of lordship. In the believer's mind, a Christian view of personhood may well provide a better and motivationally more compelling explanation for the success of cognitive therapy.[122]

A Pragmatic Postscript: As long as it works

A final major philosophical trend that can be discerned in cognitive therapy is the American pragmatism of C. S. Pierce (1839–1914), William James (1847–1910), and John Dewey (1859–1952). Pragmatism is a method for attaining clear thinking about a position by considering the practical consequences of holding that position.[123] When cognitive therapists ask their patients what are the practical results of maintaining a belief or when they devise experiments for them to test a conviction, they are operating within the paradigm of pragmatism. Beck's practical-scientist model fits perfectly within Dewey's pragmatic views that "the total process of hypothesis, deduction, controlled experiment simply reproduces in a much more sophisticated and complex form the process of inquiry which is stimulated by some practical problems in every day life."[124] In fact, some writers refer to the broader philosophy underlying this cognitive approach as pragmatic rationalism. From rationalism, it takes the use of careful reason and analysis; from pragmatism, it makes the experiential and empirical usefulness or workability of thoughts and beliefs the criterion for their rationality.[125] Although pragmatic rationalism seems very reasonable, it is not without its dangers. Using what logically makes a person feel good as the basis for constructing that person's views about reality can lead to functional relativism in which no truth-claims exist except for maximizing rewards and minimizing punishments.[126]

Our survey of the major philosophical movements whose orientations are weaved into cognitive therapy might justifiably prompt a psychologist to object to the omission of major figures in the history of psychology whose direct influence and contribution to cognitive therapy can be easily discerned.[127] Our aim, however, has not been to establish sources for specific cognitive psychological concepts, but wider value-systems and approaches whose presence in cognitive therapy evokes an overall worldview. In passing, we have noted potential problems in these philosophical approaches for the Orthodox Christian. Although the presence of these philosophies in cognitive therapy may be rightfully disturbing to a committed Christian, it may be possible for the cognitive therapist to rely on the methods of Baconian empiricism, Newtonian atomism, limited Cartesian rationalism, and limited American pragmatism on a scientific practical basis without committing himself to the philosophical positions of naturalism, materialism, and positivism. If so, Saint Gregory Palamas's "what is useful and perhaps very much so" in cognitive therapy may still be made available for Christian use. With this aim in mind, we will at last critique the *Weltanschauung* inherent in cognitive therapy in the light of the Orthodox Christian conception of the world that we sketched at the beginning of this chapter.

Seeking a Common World Between Divergent Worldviews

Standard scientific cosmogony holds that the cosmos, life on earth, and human beings all emerged or evolved as a matter of chance interactions within the limits imposed by fortuitous fundamental constants and laws. The human organism and its world are understood in terms of mechanistic and deterministic models devoid of any reference to God. *Homo sapiens* is just a species among other species, an organized organic structure alongside of other such structures. The only values left standing in this utterly materialistic universe are survival and growth. The ultimate fate for all species and stars is extinction and death.

While cognitive therapists as members of the larger scientific community may assume this bleak picture of reality, it is neither intrinsic to therapy, nor to cognitive therapeutic interventions. In fact, an explanation of the eschatological implications of a scientific worldview in which the universe ultimately suffers *the heat death* would certainly be contraindicated in working with depressed patients. Given the Christian understanding of the fall, given the reality of death and corruption, given the dimness of fallen man's spiritual vision, scientific cosmology provides an intelligible account of reality. Christian revelation, however, uncovers a world alive with God's presence, love, and goodness. Neither the universe nor man is understandable without reference to God who is quite active in time and space. For the believer, the ultimate value in the universe is Christ; the highest aim is eternal union with him.

Obviously, these two background theories are too disparate to allow for any rapprochement. Both are to a certain extent a matter of faith and a matter of experience. Although cognitive therapy assumes the prevailing scientific cosmology, cognitive therapy can still be practiced without it if the therapist chooses to do so. Background theories may be used in explanations of certain conditions, but such explanations are not central to all therapeutic interventions. The central tools of cognitive therapy are derived from empiricism, rationalism, atomism, and pragmatism, methods that are employed daily by the Christian and non-Christian alike.

As for the nature of man, cognitive therapists understand the human organism in both self-deifying and reductionist terms. On the one hand, *Homo sapiens* are seen as autonomous active beings with powerful observational and rational skills that can alter both reality and their view of reality when guided by the proper method. On the other hand, they are regarded, irrespective of their outer garb, as naked apes conditioned by learning experiences and still reacting according to outmoded survival instincts evolutionarily honed in a more hostile physical environment.[128] Thoughtful human action can alter the hominids' corner of the universe in constructive ways even as instinctual reactions can do so with destructive consequences. Notwithstanding, such alteration lacks any meaning aside from survival value.

While Christianity also recognizes human rational and observational skills, their merit is dependent on their use. The human being is understood primarily as a theological being whose greatest worth lies in his being loved by God to whom he is receptive and in whom he can be deified. This implies that human life should be characterized by humility and gratitude. If rationality and observational skills are not humbly and gratefully used in accord with the higher aim in human life, if they draw man farther away from God rather than closer to him, this misuse overturns the very structure of human nature.

Cognitive therapy's exaltation of autonomous rationality is cause for concern. For the Christian, reason [*logikotēta*] and the *Logos* are etymologically and logically inseparable. If they are separated, we are dealing then not with reason, but with sin, "a rational force of Satan"[129] that so twists human reason that the unreasonable appears reasonable and the sensible appears senseless. In other words, autonomous rationality is not a characteristic of human nature, but of the fallen human will. It can be healed by humble submission to God through the virtues and mysteries of the Church. Significantly, Beck admits that humility "is not a concept that I think about."[130] Cognitive therapy's optimistic take on human nature in terms of acontextual rationality should be modified for Christian use by associating genuine rationality with humility and a desire to learn divine wisdom through living according to the teachings of Christ.

The reductionist aspect of cognitive therapy's understanding of man is also problematic. A human being is more than a vehicle for genetic material striving for immortality against the impersonal forces of the environment. Environment and genetic make-up are important factors in human development, but human behavior has at times managed to elude their predictions and to demonstrate the possibility of real freedom.[131] Moreover, one's surroundings and heredity are not happenstance, but part and parcel of Divine Providence for every living thing. Human thought and behavior should not be reduced to a good or bad fit with the environment as though man were a rat in a Skinner box. Since every human being is fashioned in the image of God, his or her thoughts and behaviors can be evaluated according to their consonance or dissonance with the divine energies. Man as a theological being is needed to compensate for the reductionistic view of *Homo sapiens* as a biological entity.

In terms of a diagnosis of the human condition, cognitive therapy locates the sources of human psychological dysfunction in "(1) egocentric biases leading to inappropriate anger, envy, cravings, etc., and false beliefs, (2) underlying self-defeating beliefs that reinforce biases, and (3) attaching negative meanings to events."[132] These dysfunctional cognitive habits and reactions are seen as stemming from unfortunate conditioning and learning experiences, symbolic misinterpretations during childhood, and the lack of fit between evolutionary-driven reactions that had survival value in prehistoric times and contemporary conditions for which they are inappropriate.

Despite the etiological differences we have already considered, the cognitive therapeutic observations about psychological dysfunction are not inconsistent with what Christians see in the results of the fall and a state of sin: namely, prideful selfishness, a swollen imagination, and a fear of death and corruption that warps human judgment. The language differs, but the concepts certainly converge. Interestingly enough, this aspect of cognitive therapy rests firmly on clinical observation, empiricism, rationalism, and atomism, philosophical scientific approaches that Christianity can accept with certain reservations about their scope.

The model behind cognitive therapy usually frames the prescription for the human predicament in terms of empirically measured symptom reduction, which means a decrease in discomfort and pain. Symptom reduction is to be achieved by correcting thinking errors, self-defeating biases, and beliefs through the use of observation, analysis, and experimentation that characterize modern science. Cognitive therapists seek to strengthen their patients' ability to observe and analyze their thoughts and reactions by training them as practical scientists and by providing them with cognitive tools and methods that produce more logical, veridical, and adaptive cognitive processes.

While reducing melancholic feelings in the depressed, anxiety in the agoraphobic, and cravings in the addict are all worthwhile aims, the Christian does not view all pain as pathological. There are instances in which pain of heart has a transfigurational potential that should not be avoided by analgesic means. In the Christian understanding, healing and symptom reduction are no more synonymous than cure of an ailment and a painkiller masking that condition.[133] Nevertheless, if other positive functions of pain especially in repentance are recognized, cognitive therapy's goal of symptom reduction could be adopted as a subgoal in the larger Christian aim of union with Christ.

The believer's struggle for purification, illumination, and deification through participation in the mysteries and an ascetic life of virtue is in stark contrast to the repertoire of cognitive techniques and methods that cognitive therapists offer their patients. While the techniques and tools of cognitive therapy have been clinically shown to be effective, "an over-reliance on techniques can lead to a secular, humanistic way of looking at the world in which a person's primary faith is in the power of scientifically validated technologies."[134] The sense of self-efficacy that these tools are intended to give the patient can also lead to a sense of self-sufficiency or autonomy apart from the Giver of Life, which for the Christian simply repeats the drama of the fall.[135] C. S. Lewis noted, "For the wise men of old the cardinal problem had been how to conform the soul to reality and the solution had been knowledge, self-discipline, and virtue. For magic and applied science alike the problem is how to subdue reality to the wishes of men: the solution is a technique; and both, in the practice of this technique, are ready to do things hitherto regarded as disgusting and impious."[136] If such words seem unduly harsh, one need only consider Ellis's example of how he cured a female patient of guilt over promiscuous sexual relationships by providing her with analytical cognitive tools that enabled her to continue to have non-marital sex and feel no guilt.[137] For a Christian, good reasoning apart from a hierarchy of values and virtues, outside a living relationship with God, is no panacea for human ills. The techniques of cognitive therapy need to be situated in a framework firmer than abstract rationality. Since the therapist's view of what is rational tends to become an ultimate authority in cognitive therapy, the therapist's own belief system and larger worldview play a disturbingly critical role.

Notwithstanding, logical thinking in itself is surely better than illogical thinking. As we saw earlier, Christianity teaches that reason is woven into the fabric of creation and that man is logical because he is in the image of the *Logos*. When logical thought processes are put within their proper context, one can also learn to act in accord with divine wisdom. Techniques to clear up faulty inferences, to reduce egocentric biases, and irrational pessimism can then be used alongside of the tools and methods that the fathers have adopted in their own ascetic struggle. If the techniques and tools of cognitive therapy are utilized by the patient under the direction of a Christian therapist in conjunction with the sacramental life and struggle for virtue, both psychological healing that can enlarge a person's sense of freedom and agency as well as spiritual healing that enables the person to choose the good can be achieved.[138]

Slaying the Serpent to Rescue the Remedy

Saint Gregory Palamas's advice on the use of secular wisdom has been quite apt for the worldview evaluation of cognitive therapy. First of all, Saint Gregory counseled that we slay the serpent of secular wisdom by eliminating the conceit that it attaches to the one using it. In the case of cognitive therapy, autonomous rationality via the scientific method needs to be humbled or put into perspective by the ultimate goals of human existence revealed in Christ. Reason [*logikotēta*] in harmony with the *Logos* is a useful tool for the Christian, but autonomous rationality not only fails to define human nature, it reflects a misuse of the faculties of the soul. In fact, disparate results that rationality yields according to the underlying worldview demonstrate that rationality on its own is an insufficient guide for a meaningful life. Who can remain conceited about such insufficiency? Second, Saint Gregory recommended that we cut off the serpent's head and cast it aside by discarding secular principles about divinity. In the case of cognitive therapy, the Orthodox Christian is obliged to reject the assumption that God is not active in history, that Divine Providence is not present in the life of the world and the individual, that man can be understood sufficiently without reference to God, and that religious beliefs are no more than "nuisance variables that affect what a client values."[139] The removal of such presuppositions and their replacement with the corresponding Christian beliefs can help put rationality on a firm foundation. Third, Saint Gregory advised that we sever the serpent's tail and cast it aside by discarding secular mythology about things created. In the case of cognitive therapy, it means casting aside the mythologies of metaphysical materialism and logical positivism and at least certain presuppositions assumed by evolutionary theory. It means rejecting the myths of man the computer and man the evolved animal as all-embracing anthropologies, and replacing them with the revelation that man is in the image of God, created "a little lower than the angels,"[140] but through sin becoming "like the beasts that perish."[141] If we adjust the overall worldview of cognitive therapy in these ways, the discrete components of Beck's cognitive theory of psychopathology and therapy can be explored in hope of finding what Saint Gregory refers to as "an excellent, effective, and most useful therapeutic antidote"[142] not only for psychological disorders, but also for difficulties in the thought-life that every Christian soul confronts in the struggle to follow Christ.

❦

✠ PART II ✠

Theories of Thoughts, Pathology, and Recovery

CHAPTER THREE

A Patristic Voyage
through the Cognitive Model

Some Maritime Knowledge: Charts, Shoals, and Winds

In chapter one, we decided that the best method for making use of the Egyptian gold of cognitive therapy would involve an approach of discerning openness in which patristic teachings would be given logical priority over psychological concepts and serve as a context in which those concepts would be situated. In the previous chapter, we concluded that the therapeutic practices of cognitive therapy should be separated from certain metaphysical assumptions that are no less dangerous than the proverbial serpent of old. Now in this chapter, we leave those metaphors behind and begin the actual task of mining the allegorical gold and extracting the healing elixir of cognitive therapy. We will do this by examining the basic mechanisms underlying psychopathology according to the cognitive model: viz., meaning assignment, automatic thoughts, and schemata or beliefs.

In line with our chosen method, we will first introduce each psychological concept and then more extensively present related patristic teachings that will be translated into modern idiom when necessary. In other words, at times we will attempt to formulate patristic teachings in cognitive terms, so that the two approaches can more easily enter into dialogue. Having thus established a patristic context, we will then lay out the psychological concept in further detail and finally compare the offerings of both approaches. Before embarking on this twofold exploratory voyage, we will give an overview of the cognitive model in order to provide a framework within which concepts from cognitive therapy make sense. This summary will serve as a navigational chart for the cognitive sea that we wish to cross. We will also point out the shoals to be avoided as we juxtapose patristic texts and psychological concepts.

We can easily charter the cognitive model by looking out for the three channel markers: (1) meaning assignment, (2) automatic thoughts, and (3) schemata or beliefs. In simplest terms, cognitive therapy is based on the common-sense notion that thoughts come in between events and feelings.[1] The cognitive model maintains that the way a person behaves in a situation and emotionally responds to it depends on how he interprets and *assigns meaning* to that situation. For example, when Elder Païsios notes that a person's countenance becomes radiant after a humble thought and dark after a thought of pride,[2] a cognitive psychologist would suggest that he is referring to a humble versus a proud *interpretation* of a situation in relation to self, an interpretation whose emotional and spiritual signatures are left written on that person's face. According to cognitive theory, this interpretive process takes place very quickly on the basis of assumptions (*intermediate schemata* or *beliefs*) learned during earlier experiences, and is accompanied by *automatic thoughts* passing through a person's mind.[3] If someone's interpretative framework happens to be dysfunctional, it will leave him or her vulnerable to mood disorders and maladaptive behavior. This etiological principle has therapeutic significance: it implies that mood disorders and maladaptive behavior can be treated by realistically re-evaluating and modifying dysfunctional ways of processing information.[4] In other words, treatment entails altering that person's beliefs or schemata. Therapy is thus an educational process in which the therapist trains the patient in the use of empirical and rational tools in order to provide him with a broader interpretative framework that can make sense of his experience[5] and enable him "to think and act more realistically and adaptively about his psychological problems."[6] This pragmatic state of adaptive realism is the final destination of any voyage into cognitive therapy.

On our particular odyssey, however, we will also use the ancient fathers as a compass. Along the way, we will strive to avoid certain shoals whenever we locate parallels between related ideas. The primary danger is to reconcile corresponding concepts by turning one notion into a linguistic equivalent of the other.[7] Of course, some translation is necessary if there is to be any communication whatsoever between the two approaches. Notwithstanding, when we endeavor to extend the communicative value of any text, we must avoid distancing that text so thoroughly from its original context that its primary meaning is lost. Moreover, a concept-for-concept translation can imprison us within a theoretical world of our own making in which differences between patristic wisdom and psychological findings disappear as otherwise distinct concepts merge.[8] For this reason, whenever we discover clear compatibilities, we will try to act as careful helmsmen who remain vigilant for potentially hidden incompatibilities or additional connotations beneath the waters' surface that may be more significant than the up-jutting area of semantic overlap.

Finally, like seafarers of yore, we will have to be sensitive to subtleties like inauspicious winds and cambered shadows whose navigational significance the fair-weather sailor can hardly fathom. Earlier, we mentioned that the fathers and cognitive therapists have different aims, methods, and vocations, even though they are both concerned with human thought and behavior. The concept of tacit knowing may account for patristic silence about, but not necessarily ignorance of, certain aspects of human psychological processes that cognitive therapists have uncovered. According to Michael Polanyi, "in an act of tacit knowing we attend *from* something for attending *to* something else."[9] He uses the example of recognizing a person's face. We attend to someone's face and away from the individual features such as the nose, lips, or eyes. In other words, we have an explicit knowledge of the face as a whole, but only a tacit knowledge of the isolated features. Since our knowledge of a particular feature is only tacit, we would not be able to identify a particular nose among a series of noses, although we clearly recognize it as part of a familiar person's face.[10] In like manner, the fathers may have tacit knowledge of certain psychological interconnections that they may not articulate, because their attention is focused on the cumulative effect of those interconnections on man's relationship with God. When this is the case, their silence need not be interpreted as ignorance, for it may well be an indication of tacit knowledge that the findings of cognitive psychology can help disclose.

Having laid out our two-fold voyage, consulted our navigational chart, noted the shoals, and become aware of certain subtle nautical signs, we are at last ready to heave anchor and set sail for the central concept of the cognitive model: the meaning we assign to what we experience.

Meaning Assignment: A Meeting Place for Stoics, Fathers, and Psychologists

The basic concept in the cognitive model affirms that the way people feel and behave stems not from a situation in itself, but from the way in which they interpret or construe that situation.[11] As Albert Bandura put it, "Humans do not simply respond to stimuli; they interpret them."[12] This principle can be traced back to Epictetus, who wrote in *The Encheiridion*, "It is not things themselves that disturb men, but their judgments about these things. For example, death is nothing dreadful, or else Socrates too would have thought so, but the judgment that death is dreadful. This is the dreadful thing. When, therefore, we are hindered or disturbed, or grieved, let us never blame anyone but ourselves, that means our own judgments."[13] Significantly, this quotation, repeatedly cited by both Beck and Ellis is also quoted in full and without alteration in the Christian paraphrase of Epictetus's *The Encheiridion* that is attributed, albeit erroneously, to Saint Neilus the Ascetic.[14] At this juncture, patristic theology and cognitive therapy set their course from guidance proffered by the self-same stoic star. This joint use of a single source can only generate mutual respect. Of immediate interest is where that star leads each respective vessel.

Saint Ambrose of Milan writes, "Anyone who examines more closely these matters will perceive what great assistance the wise man finds and what great obstacles the foolish encounter in the very same things...For we have both wars in peace and peace in war."[15] In other words, the interpretation of a situation determines the range of available strategies for responding to that situation. Wisdom involves adaptive and constructive interpretations that can lead a person to beneficial responses even in the worst and most destructive of conditions. For Saint Ambrose, this observation is, moreover, an empirically verifiable fact. In a similar vein, Saint John Cassian notes, "The roots and causes of our offenses lie not in others, but in ourselves."[16] For the saint, an etiology of maladaptive thought and behavior primarily requires introspection, rather than an investigation of situational factors.

Abba Dorotheos espouses the same Stoic teaching when he writes, "For everyone is benefited or harmed by his own state, for no one can harm another." He gives the example of three different people who saw the same gentleman standing at a street-corner, but who had quite dissimilar interpreta-tions of his behavior. One person assumed that he was waiting for a prostitute; another suspected that he was preparing for a robbery; and a third thought that he was going to a friend's house for prayer. One event with three radically divergent interpretations demonstrates that what one sees depends on how one interprets. In cognitive terms, one could say that meaning assignment determines perception. The fathers, however, stress that how one interprets an event also depends on one's spiritual state.[17]

Elder Païsios draws on this same teaching when he explains why the same incident is viewed by one person as a blessing, but by someone else as a tragedy. He characteristically remarks, "Everyone interprets events in a way that is consistent with his own thoughts. Everything can be viewed from its good or bad side." The elder then mentions the case of someone hearing thuds from the apartment above. A pious individual with good thoughts will think, "He's making prostrations," whereas a religious person lacking such thoughts might think, "He's dancing all night long." Like Abba Dorotheos, Elder Païsios also observes that a person's conclusions about an incident are dependant on "the spiritual content of his soul,"[18] or as he puts it elsewhere, on the "dictionary" that the individual tends to use.[19] Viewing the soul's contents in terms of having or not having good thoughts indicates that a good dictionary—meaning an interpretative framework with constructive beliefs or schemata—needs to be in place for good thoughts to arise spontaneously.

The monastic fathers make a noteworthy addition to the initial Stoic idea that reactions depend on interpretations. Whereas cognitive therapists strive to make their patients' interpretations veridical and objective, the fathers believe that it is more important to spontaneously fulfill Christ's commandments to "love one's neighbor"[20] and "to judge not"[21] than to accurately perceive a situation. Meaning assignment, like all else, should be "subjected unto Christ."[22] Given that cognitive psychologists admit that initial interpretations are often inaccurate and egocentrically biased, the patristic advice about non-condemnatory and loving initial reactions to events is not as naïve and unrealistic as it may first seem. In other words, the patristic stance can also correct initial innate biases and lead to more accurate assessments.

Saint John Chrysostom recounts for the faithful two graphic hypothetical examples to teach them about the importance of how they interpret their station in life and the situations that they encounter. First, he has them consider the case of a poor junk collector who is disturbed, because he does not have more possessions. If that person were to receive those desired goods, but continued to interpret his world through the lens of what he does not have, he would still be upset. Saint Chrysostom has this person progressively ascend the political, social, and economic ladder to an objectively and measurably improved status. The saint notes that even if this person were to be crowned king, he would still be distraught, because other kings are greater than he is. Saint John then has the faithful consider the diametrically opposite case of a king who is accustomed to finding solace in the positive aspects of his situation. If this ruler were to be removed from office, but still has his goods and chattels, remembering that fact will console him. If his possessions are taken away from him, but he still has food to eat, focusing on that blessing will comfort him. Inverting the former example, Saint Chrysostom has this figure descend the political, economic, and social ladder rung by rung until the former ruler finds himself in prison. Even there, this truly wise ruler of himself considers that he is alive and finds consolation therein. Thus, the saint concludes, "It is not then wealth that is the foundation of pleasure, nor poverty of sadness, but our own judgment and the fact that the eyes of our mind neither see clearly nor remain fixed in one place, but flutter abroad."[23] From these vivid examples, he not only comes to the conclusion of Epictetus, but also diagnoses the source of dysfunctional interpretations in distorted mental representations and a misdirected focus of attention. He advises the faithful to keep their minds turned toward the really good things to come whence the soul can drink from an ever-flowing fount of refreshment.

Among the texts of patristic literature, the Christian redaction of *The Encheiridion* of Epictetus spuriously attributed to Saint Neilus the Ascetic most closely approaches the thought of cognitive therapists. This paraphrase, which excises any unacceptable pagan elements and sparingly alters the phraseology and terminology of the original, is quite significant, for it makes the text legitimate for Christian use.[24] In this work of Epictetian origin, it is noted that even if something bodes ill for one's reputation, property, or family, it is possible to interpret that change in a good way.[25] In an insightful paragraph akin to certain passages in Beck's *Prisoners of Hate*, the Christian version of the *Encheiridion* reads: "Remember that it is not the person who insults you, speaks badly of you, or hits you, but it is your idea that he supposedly curses you. When someone makes you angry, know that your own idea made you angry. For this reason, try not to be dominated by the imagination, because if you gain a little time and delay, you will easily keep yourself in check."[26] This passage contains several instructive observations about cognitive processes. First, anger is provoked by our interpretation of someone else's behavior as unpleasant rather than by the behavior in itself. Second, the seemingly combative person and our mental *image* of that person are not the same. Third, when our imagination embellishes our interpretation, the offense seems far worse than it in fact is and this exaggerated interpretation incites us to react. Fourth, if we fight against the tendency to elaborate on the initial image and refrain from reacting to it, we can reacquire our self-composure.

In addition to the case of hostility, the fathers were well aware that meaning assignment directly influences mood. Saint John Chrysostom observes that irrational fears can spring from incorrect meaning assignment. For example, someone in the dark might be afraid of a dangling rope if he mistakes it for a live serpent.[27] Saint Theodore the Studite characteristically notes, "We feel radiant when we think about something good, and then we become dark and gloomy when we entertain somber thoughts...The change is volitional and within our own power."[28] The light imagery (being light or dark) may tacitly suggest that good thoughts also enable one to see farther and more clearly, whereas dark thoughts cloud one's mental vision. Saint Theodore does not limit mood-altering thoughts to evaluations and judgments, but also includes images that evoke good and bad sentiments. As an example, he draws attention to how we awaken from a nightmare feeling disturbed, whereas we are roused from a pleasant dream feeling joyful.[29] These passages point to a variety of interpretive processes that affect mood and over which the individual has a varying degree of control.

Finally, according to the fathers, the way in which a person assigns meaning coalesces into traits that shape character. Saint Symeon the New

Theologian asks why is one person easily moved to compunction, whereas someone else remains untouched. He replies that being sensitive or hard-hearted depends on an individual's disposition, thoughts, and actions. In psychological terms, disposition can be seen as an interpretative framework, thoughts can be understood as the automatic thoughts generated by that framework, and actions can be construed as behavior consistent with those thoughts. The saint also concludes that if a person's disposition and thoughts are modified, the very character of that individual will change as well.[30]

In summary, the fathers were quite mindful of the overall importance and etiological significance of meaning assignment for successful human functioning and the virtuous life. They recognized that our perceptions are channeled through our interpretations of our situation, interpretations that are often influenced more by our imagination than by objectively measurable external reality. Interpretations in the form of thoughts and images shape our views of others and ourselves. Good thoughts bring us joy, increased insight, and wisdom, whereas bad thoughts can throw us into a state of melancholy, confusion, or even folly. According to the fathers, thoughts not only give rise to emotional reactions, but also coalesce over time into character traits. If we alter our way of interpreting, we can bring about changes in mood and character. The patristic consensus also views our soul's orientation to God and things eternal as decisive in the way we interpret reality. Finally, the commandments to love our neighbor and not to judge our brother act as filters through which a Christian should first assign meaning to whatever he or she sees and hears.

Having set our sextant to the north star of patristic teaching on interpretive processes, we can now shift course and consider in more detail how cognitive therapists understand meaning assignment. According to Beck, "The function of meaning assignment (at both automatic and deliberate levels) is to control the various psychological systems (e.g., behavioral, emotional, attentional, and memory). Thus, meaning activates strategies for adaptation."[31] In other words, an individual interprets a given event and has an automatic thought that expresses his personal interpretation. That interpretation, in turn, becomes the first link in a chain reaction resulting in a change in how that individual feels, what he recalls, what he focuses on, and how he behaves.[32] For example, if a person interprets a situation as dangerous, he might have a fleeting thought such as "I'm in danger," and then feel anxious; if he interprets an action as deliberately causing him injury, he might think "I've been wronged" and feel angry; if he views a gesture as an expression of love, he might have the thought "I'm loved," and feel joy.[33] In like manner, if an individual interprets a change as a loss, he might think, "Now I'm alone," and feel sad.[34] These psychological processes are all perfectly normal. In psychopathology, however, a person's meaning assignment is skewed, excessive, or inappropriate, causing dysfunctional thoughts, uncomfortable emotional states, and maladaptive strategies for behavior.[35] For instance, people suffering from anxiety interpret situations that are perhaps mildly threatening as extremely dangerous; people suffering from depression interpret every setback as proof that they are dismal failures, and so on.

Problems arising from meaning assignment, however, are not limited to psychopathology. Beck notes that in marital relationships, over-reactions and quarrels occur when one spouse interprets the other spouse's behavior as uncaring or disrespectful. For example, a wife who sees her husband's clothes thrown on the floor interprets that bundle of fabric as proof that her husband does not care about her and views her as a maid. For the wife, the clothes on the floor symbolize how her husband deliberately tramples on one of her deeply held values: a husband should care for and respect his wife. Her husband who may have been handling his clothing in this way since he was an adolescent is likely quite unaware of the symbolic value that the clothes on the floor have for his wife, so that he will view her angry accusation as unreasonable. Thus, mutual mistakes in meaning assignment inevitably lead to a serious marital clash in which both sides misinterpret each other.[36]

Likewise in the more general case of hostility, Beck notes, "Delays and frustrations do not in themselves necessarily produce anger. The crucial element is the *explanation* of the other person's action and whether that explanation makes the other person's behavior acceptable to us."[37] For example, if Cain interprets Abel's frustrating behavior as intentional, Cain will see himself as a wronged victim and feel distress. To compensate for the uncomfortable feelings of weakness, Cain will also empower himself with feelings of anger that may swell into violent behavior. The problem in this sequence is that for Cain to accurately know why Abel did something that irritated him, Cain would have to be able to read Abel's mind, a task usually requiring a stretch of the imagination for seers and soothsayers alike.[38] Unfortunately, mind-reading and the imagination join forces in destructive ways. In a remark reminiscent of the earlier passage from *The Encheiridion*, Beck writes, "People in conflict perceive and react to the threat emanating from the image rather than to a realistic appraisal of the adversary. They mistake the image for the person....The fixed negative representation is backed up by selective memories of past wrongs, real or imaginary, and malevolent attributions."[39] Since a person is usually more provoked by what he supposes others think and feel about him (e.g., "They think I'm stupid," or "they don't like me") than by what they actually say or do, Beck advises those of us who are prone to anger to decrease the importance we place on how other people evaluate us.[40]

Both the fathers and cognitive psychologists recognize that meaning assignment or the interpretation of events inevitably affect mood, behavior, and character. Both recognize that meaning assignment often makes use of the imagination or mind-reading. On the one hand according to cognitive therapists, when meaning assignment is extreme, an individual is vulnerable to transient emotional disorders or may exhibit symptoms of enduring personality disorders. On the other hand according to the fathers, when meaning assignment assumes the worst in others and in one's situation, a person is vulnerable to the sins of misjudging others and being ungrateful toward God. In other words, each approach defines the problem in meaning assignment differently and has differing standards for normality.

In the mind of the fathers, negative meaning assignment not only harms one's relationship with other people, but also one's relationship with God. Christ's life and teachings reveal that for man in the image of God, it is natural to love others and to refrain from condemning one's neighbor. For cognitive therapists, negative meaning assignment may be normal and non-problematic if it is not excessive. This contrast has a flip side. Whereas the fathers encourage positive meaning assignment by generating good thoughts as a footpath leading to wisdom and perspicacity, cognitive psychologists would emphatically disagree with that tactic, which they view as a pathway ending in cynicism and disillusionment. In fact, cognitive therapists vehemently defend themselves from the charge that cognitive therapy is merely a new manifestation of Dr. Norman Vincent Peale's *The Power of Positive Thinking*.[41] Notwithstanding, they would admit that negative meaning assignment often leads to emotional states in which a person's mental field of vision is narrowed and his conclusions are biased. If positive thinking is put in the context of God's love and providential plan, the falsification of a positive interpretation that would drive a non-believer to disillusionment could lead a Christian to compassion and prayer. At this point, patristic wisdom can open up secular cognitive therapy to other possible ways of interpreting, responding, and acting.

Cognitive theory does make connections between thoughts and emotions with considerable precision and well-defined clarity. In particular, cognitive theory notes how meaning assignment activates attentional and memory systems. It also locates the source of interpersonal conflict in the often-unwarranted attribution of intentionality to the behavior or words of others. Awareness of the fallibility of meaning assignment and the special meaning of actions to an individual could make for more peaceful interpersonal relationships. Replacing negative interpretations of other people's behavior with more positive explanations can make a person more virtuous as well. At this the first docking in our passage through the cognitive model, therapists and Christians have a good deal to gain from listening to one another.

Patristic Thought and Automatic Thoughts: Self-monitoring and Beyond

We can now set our course for the next channel marker in the cognitive model: the appearance of automatic thoughts. Meaning assignment is not a premeditated process, but a rapid evaluation of a situation. We know that meaning assignment has taken place by what Beck calls the automatic thoughts that we have about our present state of affairs. In addition to explicit thoughts and ideas that we may develop or express, we also have other brief bursts of thought that are used for internal communication consisting of "self-monitoring, self-appraisal, self-evaluation, self-warning, and self-instructions."[42] The first step in cognitive therapy is for patients to become aware of their automatic thoughts. In like manner, the first step in Christian spiritual warfare is for believers to become mindful of their sinful thoughts. According to Saint John Cassian, as long as wrong thoughts remain hidden, they hold sway over a person; but once they are discovered, they immediately are weakened even before one begins the task of discerning whether they are good or bad.[43] Cognitive therapists would wholeheartedly agree.[44] This parallel between the two essentially therapeutic approaches to the thoughts suggests that each approach may offer material of interest to the other.

The fathers comment on the characteristics, composition, causes, and effects of the thoughts, because man's contribution to salvation is to a large extent dependent on the thoughts that he entertains. In the Mosaic Law, it was understood that a covenantal relationship with God consisted in loving the Lord with all one's heart, soul, and might.[45] In the Gospel according to Saint Matthew, Christ summarizes this first and great commandment as loving the Lord with all one's heart, soul, and mind.[46] Although heart, soul, and mind are not interchangeable terms, they are all used in scripture to refer to inner "places" where thinking processes occur.[47] Elsewhere in the New Testament, Christ extended the Ten Commandments to include underlying sinful thought processes that are the source of sinful behavior, "for out of the heart proceed bad thoughts, murders, adulteries, fornications, thefts, false witness, blasphemies."[48] The fathers thus had good reason to study the thoughts and closely observe them.

Given the scriptural emphasis on the thoughts as intimate expressions of a person's relationship with God, it was natural for the ancient fathers to focus on the moral valence of the thoughts, with morality understood in terms of human receptivity or resistance to divine grace. Patristic texts distinguish among thoughts that are angelic, demonic, and human.[49] Although some fathers view this as a distinction among good, bad, and vain thoughts,[50] or among supernatural, unnatural, and natural thoughts,[51] the distinction is meant to describe existential orientations, rather than to generate moralistic pronouncements. There are thoughts that ascend to the uncreated Trinity serving God wisely, thoughts that descend to the abyss of non-being rebelling against the good Lord foolishly, and thoughts that remain on an earthly plane being concerned with daily human functioning. Angelic thoughts are in harmony with the image of God in man and imbue the soul with delight in God's law, whereas demonic thoughts provoke lawlessness, lust, and sensual impulses.[52] The notion of lawlessness leads Saint John of Karpathos to graphically personify demonic thoughts as "gamblers, poisoners, pirates, hunters, defilers, murderers, and so on."[53]

Elaborating on the threefold division among the thoughts, Saint John Cassian observes that the believer conceives of angelic thoughts when he is illumined by the Holy Spirit. This illumination sets the soul aflame with spiritual zeal, moves her to compunction, or reveals to her heavenly mysteries. These godly thoughts strengthen the will and lead the believer to God-pleasing behavior. Demonic thoughts are hatched from musings about sensual pleasures or about an illusory good that is in fact evil. These thoughts weaken the will and lead to sinful conduct.[54] Angelic thoughts are thus divine gifts guiding the soul to a safe harbor, whereas demonic thoughts are temptations casting her into an open and raging sea.[55] Human thoughts involve ideas automatically arising "from ourselves, when in the course of nature we recollect what we are in the process of doing or have done or have heard."[56] Recollections on what a person is in the process of doing certainly suggest the evaluative automatic thoughts of cognitive therapy.

Evagrius, Saint Maximus the Confessor, and Saint Peter of Damascus make a similar taxonomy of the thoughts focusing on how they are composed and the way they shape perception. These monastic fathers distinguish between the simple thought, the composite thought (a concept combined with a passion), and dispassionate *theoria*.[57] According to Saint Peter of Damascus, human thought is exemplified by "an abstract conception arising in the heart of some created thing...Demonic thought consists in a conceptual image compounded with passion....Angelic thought, finally, is comprised of the dispassionate *theoria* of things."[58] Evagrius illustrates how ascetics classify the thoughts by considering three approaches to the "concept of gold." Human thought frames a simple image of a lustrous yellow precious metal that it calls gold. Demonic thought identifies that image with wealth and power recasting gold into an object of greed. Angelic thought ponders on how gold is scattered providentially in the depths of the earth, cleansed with water, purified by fire, and crafted into vessels for the tabernacle of the Lord.[59]

From the above example, we can see that the special meaning attached to a simple concept can have theological implications that define the spiritual character of that thought. On the one hand, thoughts that are accompanied by a mindless affection or an unreasoning hatred for some object are demonic, because they lead to apostasy from God. To abhor something irrationally is to blaspheme the Creator, whereas to adore it mindlessly is to fall into idolatry. On the other hand, thoughts that dispassionately and theologically widen a person's field of vision are angelic; and consequently, they include veridical, humble, and hopeful notions that inspire both faith in and love for God.[60] Human thoughts as information formerly received through the senses in turn become opinions that may be right or wrong. Although Evagrius's example of the three kinds of thoughts is clear-cut, other fathers were aware that a tidy classification was not always possible, since, as Saint Gregory Palamas noted, thoughts can be framed "impassionately and dispassionately or in a state between the two" [empathōs, apathōs, mesōs].[61]

The threefold distinction among the thoughts implies that human thoughts as simple conceptions stemming from the senses are a given, but angelic and demonic thoughts as gifts or temptations from the outside involve some degree of free choice. While it is not in a person's power to decide whether a demonic or angelic thought will pass through one's mind, people can choose to act on it or to ignore it.[62] Upon determining the origin of a given thought, a person is quite free to reject the thought or admit it by lingering on it.[63] No matter how enticing a demonic thought may be, it can only urge, not coerce.[64] This can be seen both in the account of the fall and of Christ's temptation in the wilderness. Being made in the image of God, each human being receives as a royal birthright the sovereign power of the intelligence and the free will.[65] In fact, Saint Nicodemos of the Holy Mountain, well aware of the radiant examples of the martyrs and great ascetics, writes, "God bestowed on our will so much freedom and power, that even if every kind of sensual provocation, every kind of demon, and the entire world united to take arms against our will and vehemently to make war against it, despite all that, our will remains entirely free to despise that attack and will what it chooses to will or not will what it does not choose to will."[66]

Free choice and self-determination as they relate to the mental life also imply accountability. Acting on demonic thoughts is blameworthy, whereas acting on angelic thoughts is worthy of praise.[67] Saint Jerome notes, "God will not immediately punish us for our thoughts and resolutions, but he will send retribution on their offspring, that is, on the evil deeds and habits of sin which arise out of them."[68] Consequently, it behooves Christians to search their thoughts, to test their conclusions, and to make the necessary modifications in order to avoid committing deeds worthy of punishment. With a full awareness of the cognitive roots of behavior, Saint Gregory of Sinai writes, "There can be no action, either for good or evil, that is not initially provoked by the particular thought of that action."[69] Saint Mark the Ascetic observes that the mind naturally races ahead in thought, and the body follows behind in action.[70] These observations have logical consequences. Blessed Augustine notes, "It is impossible for a man's acts to be evil, whose thoughts are good, for acts issue from thought."[71] He also likens the mind to a throne on which an emperor is seated and issues his decrees. If Christ is seated on that throne, the directives will be for good; but if the devil is perched thereon, they will be for evil.[72]

Man, however, is not merely a slave who must account for his deeds, but also a free individual who is obliged to answer for his words and thoughts.[73] While the appearance of a demonic thought is as forgivable as a dream in the night,[74] the cultivation of that thought warrants punishment, for such cultivation relentlessly drives the ship of the soul into the rocks of perdition. In contrast, the rejection of demonic thoughts makes the soul worthy of a crown,[75] even as the reception of angelic thoughts clothes the soul with consolation.[76] Given the rapidity of the thoughts, a person can suffer defeat or secure a victory in an instant.[77] For this reason, Elder Païsios would remark that a person's salvation can be gained or lost quickly: it is not just a matter of minutes, but of seconds.[78]

What does it mean to cultivate a demonic thought? According to Saint Isaac the Syrian, the cultivation of a demonic thought does not refer to agreeing momentarily with a bad thought, but to looking shamelessly at it and accepting it as true, right, and desirable, instead of considering it repulsive.[79] In the case of pride or heresy, "it is possible for a single thought to separate someone from God if that person accepts it and agrees with it."[80] Refusing to cultivate demonic thoughts does not have an exclusively negative connotation. For the fathers, rejecting bad thoughts purifies the heart, increases humility,[81] and expresses the believer's friendship with God.[82]

In addition to rejecting bad thoughts, it is equally essential to cultivate good ones (see chapter 9). One of the reasons for assiduously reading the scriptures, compunctiously singing the psalms, and fervently offering prayers is that such practices improve the quality of the believers' thoughts.[83] According to Elder Païsios, "a good, pure thought is more powerful than any ascetic activity...and helps in a more positive way."[84] In fact, he maintains, "The entire spiritual life depends on the thoughts."[85] With good reason, the Church's liturgical texts contain frequent encomia of the martyrs, for these saints were able to endure a most painful death by remaining courageous in thought.[86] Even more importantly, thoughts are also a means of communication with God. As Clement of Alexandria puts it, "the thoughts of the saints cleave not only the air, but also the entire world."[87] Saint John of Karpathos mentions the example of the hemorrhaging woman in the Gospel who received healing because of her thought, "If I can but touch the hem of his garment, I shall be healed."[88] Given the soteriological importance of the thoughts, man's most deadly enemy is his own mind, for his thoughts are voluntary, but their outcome is involuntary.[89]

The reader may well wonder why we have allowed ourselves to drift so far from the coast of the cognitive model. We have done so because of the vantage point that such a distance offers. From the above excursion, we can see that, for the Christian, thoughts are etiologically complex and have an impact that extends beyond psychological functioning. While automatic thoughts include simple human thoughts, those thoughts may also be composite, that is, under the influence of the passions. Finally, the consequences of the thoughts are far-reaching in terms of a person's present and future relationship with God. These teachings, which are foreign to non-believers, should offer Christians additional motivation to watch over their thoughts and improve them.

Drawing nigh unto the shore of the cognitive model, we can now consider how various fathers commented on the nature of the thoughts in general. Blessed Augustine refers to the thoughts as "speeches of the heart" [*locutions cordis*] or "inward speeches" that are "acts of sight" recounted by "the mouth of the heart."[90] This inward speech [*endiathetos logos*] is, according to Saint Maximus the Confessor, "a movement of the rational part of the soul without speaking out loud [*aneu tinos ekphōnēseōs*]."[91] Elsewhere, Blessed Augustine likens speech to Hermes running back and forth between interlocutors or negotiating between merchants.[92] With inner speech, however, the dispatcher and receiver of the message are one and the same person. There seems, then, to be some tacit knowledge that a person speaks silently to himself in a way analogous to what cognitive theorists call self-talk or automatic thoughts. Furthermore, Saint Gregory of Sinai calls thoughts "mental images" that are motives for action.[93] This implies the existence of thoughts meant for shaping a person's behavioral response, but not necessarily intended for dialogue with others or any kind of vocalization. As an act of sight, speeches of the heart can quickly encompass an entire situation even as a painting can portray what a thousand words will never embrace. Comprehensiveness and rapidity, in turn, imply that these inward speeches cannot always be adequately translated into spoken words.[94] Even when they are appropriately rendered, "the tongue needs words and a long recital of intermediary speech" to reproduce the thoughts in full.[95]

The uncontrollability of quickly moving thoughts is another common theme in ascetic literature. According to monastic luminaries, the nature of the mind is such that it "never ceases to beget" thoughts,[96] for the mind is never idle, but continuously in motion and musing on many things.[97] Moreover, when the mind is disturbed (i.e., in a state of spiritual warfare), the thoughts become "capricious and hard to control."[98] Thoughts are, in fact, sometimes defined as "simple and ungovernable energies of the mind,"[99] which whirl about "like snow flakes in the winter or clouds of mosquitoes in the summer."[100] The speed of successively shifting thoughts sometimes makes their identification difficult. Saint John Climacus refers to a "flick of the mind" [pararripismon noos], a thought that seems to appear "without the passage of time, without word, or image...swifter or more indiscernible among spirits. It manifests itself in the soul by a simple remembrance, which is instantaneous, independent, inapprehensible, and sometimes even unknown to the person himself."[101] Significantly, all the adjectives that the good abbot of Sinai uses to describe a "flick of the mind" could be employed with equal precision to delineate an automatic thought.

By referring to flickering thoughts as simple remembrances, Saint John Climacus also points¹ to a relation between situational thoughts and deeper cognitive structures such as memory systems. Saint Ilias the Presbyter suggests this when he writes, "Thoughts gather about the soul according to its underlying quality."[102] Although flickering thoughts may be unknown, they nevertheless signal their existence. Saint Theophan the Recluse notes that there are subtle thoughts that "go unnoticed at the hour of their appearance in the heart, and are revealed only later by action,"[103] or as Tertullian observes, by the expression on a person's face.[104]

The fathers are well aware of the inaccuracy of many thoughts. Saint Gregory Palamas notes that many thoughts are no more than blind wanderings of the mind without any accurate understanding of what it imagines.[105] In fact, according to Saint Maximus, the thoughts are the product of reason [logikē] responding to sensation by means of the imagination [phantasia],[106] or to employ the English cognates, the thoughts can be viewed as fantasy wrestling with logic over the meaning of perception. Being filtered through the imagination, a person's thoughts can hardly be viewed as absolute truths. Notwithstanding, the presence of reason can convince the individual of their truth-value.

Finally, although the fathers speak at length about angelic, demonic, and passionate thoughts, as well as flights of the imagination, they also consider organic sources for the ideas that pass through the mind. Saints Isaac the Syrian and Nicodemos of the Holy Mountain both mention that physiology affects the thoughts. Physiology as "will of the flesh" or "passionate human nature" chiefly produces thoughts relating to pleasure or pain.[107] In addition to a person's physiological condition, Saint Maximus the Confessor notes the role of sense impressions and recollections in the generation of thoughts. Although physiology, sensation, and memory have a certain objectivity, that objectivity is altered by the relation that these sources of thought have to underlying passions.[108] Of these three natural causes of the thoughts, the most troublesome thoughts are those arising from the memories.[109]

In summary, the patristic understanding of thoughts is rich in observational sensitivity and theoretical sophistication. Long before modern cognitive psychology, the fathers of the ancient church expounded on quickly-moving thoughts that are hard to control and dependent on one's immediate environment. Sometimes these thoughts are unuttered speeches of the heart directed to the self and intended to motivate a person for action. At other times, they are not only unvoiced, but also unperceived. Notwithstanding, the fathers teach that their presence can be detected by a shift in mood or by a change in facial expression. Although these thoughts are often blind and inaccurate products of the imagination, they have a logic of their own that exerts considerable persuasive, though not coercive, influence on behavior. Finally, the fathers recognize that the thoughts, like man himself, belong to two worlds—biological and spiritual. A person's thoughts are on the one hand grounded in physiology, sensations, and memories, and on the other hand influenced by positive and negative spiritual forces. These two factors, the biological and the spiritual, can never be fully separated, for as a human being is a unity composed of body and soul, so the thoughts issue forth from that unity, rather than from the body or the soul in isolation.

Having surveyed patristic views on transient thoughts, we can turn the helm of our investigation back to the cognitive model and its parsimonious description of automatic thoughts. According to cognitive theory, automatic thoughts are distinct from what we normally associate with particular thoughts or ideas. Unlike conventional thoughts that are communicated to others, automatic thoughts are internal communications directed to the self. They comment on the self's behavior (e.g., "I don't understand this chapter"), the behavior of others (for instance, "She's angry with me"), and predict the consequences of behavior (e.g., "I'm going to fail").[110] This is why Ellis calls them *self-statements*, a reformulation of the Skinnerian term *self-observation*.[111]

Beck refers to these thoughts as *automatic thoughts*, because they seem to be produced automatically without any effort of the will or active concentration of the mind. In general, a person is unaware of these thoughts, because he does not pay attention to the way in which "he ceaselessly interprets (or misinterprets) events, monitors his own behavior, makes predictions, and draws generalizations about himself."[112] Nevertheless, these thoughts, in the form of words or images, have a direct effect on the tone of a person's voice, the expression on his face, and the mode of his behavior.[113] Because these thoughts are uncritically accepted as true, they often determine a person's corresponding emotional and behavioral responses.[114] Beck also likens these thoughts to subliminal advertising that is effective, because it goes unnoticed. If, however, automatic thoughts are recognized, the influence of their subliminal messages is greatly mitigated.[115]

To become aware of these thoughts, the patient learns to detect them by asking himself the question "What was just going through your mind?" whenever he notices a change in mood. If a particular thought is in shorthand form (for instance, "Uh oh!"), that thought can be spelled out if the therapist asks the patient what the thought means (e.g., "Uh oh!" might mean "I won't manage to finish this in time").[116] If the patient has trouble recalling an automatic thought that he had when he felt distressed, the therapist can have the patient describe the setting, imagine the situation visually and audially, or even role-play a dialogue in which his mood shift occurred, so that the thought can be caught afresh.[117] Once the dubious automatic thought is uncovered, it can be challenged, used to discover an underlying schema, or replaced with a more adaptive thought.[118]

Both saintly monks and cognitive theorists make similar observations on rapid thoughts that are often difficult to identify and hard to control. They both recognize the relationships between thought and mood as well as between thought and behavior. Cognitive psychologists explicitly note that these thoughts involve evaluations about self, others, and consequences. In patristic literature, the concepts of "inner speeches" and "motives for action" indicate a tacit awareness of the cognitive concept of evaluative self-monitoring. Cognitive theorists also note that we are unaware of automatic thoughts, not only because of their speed (as the ascetics likewise observe), but also because people have a life history of not paying any attention to them. Cognitive therapists furthermore suggest simple ways to uncover them by first asking "what was going through your mind," and second by imaginatively recreating the situation and asking the question again. These are valuable tools and additions.

As we have noted earlier, the fathers classify thoughts as angelic, demonic, and human. Some cognitive psychologists might be prone to reject this classification as a pernicious vestige of medieval superstition. For an Orthodox Christian, however, the presence of angelic and demonic forces is a non-negotiable component of Christian belief according to the testimony of Holy Scripture and Sacred Tradition. Even if a cognitive therapist metaphysically rejects this distinction, he might find it to be methodologically useful in terms of motivation when working with patients who are conscientious Orthodox Christians. The patristic etiological understanding of thought as the product of reason and imagination may also prove helpful in explaining both the logical persuasiveness and the fantastic inaccuracy of many automatic thoughts. At this midway dock on our voyage through the cognitive model, each side once again has much to offer.

Of Beasts and Babes: Alternate Perspectives Conveyed by Passions and Schemata

Having explored meaning assignment and automatic thoughts, we can once more put to sea and head for our final destination in the cognitive model, the underlying source of both meaning assignment and automatic thoughts: schemata or core beliefs. According to cognitive theory, we learn to respond to our surroundings by employing meaning-making structures called schemata or core beliefs, so that we can interpret how a particular situation relates to the self.[119] These schemata enable people to organize their mental representation of reality quickly and with a minimum amount of reflection. They are often characterized as primitive, because they are reminiscent of the global, absolutist, and invariant thinking processes of children[120] as well as the non-volitional reactions of animals.[121] Both the notions of reasoning like a small child and reacting like a wild beast suggest a relationship to the patristic concept of the passions that according to Saint John Chrysostom are the offspring of an imperfect mind and childish judgment,[122] and according to other fathers are like mental beasts [thēras noētous][123] in so far as they provoke people to behave like animals in the wild.[124] If according to the cognitive model, emotions are schema-driven affective reactions to the environment and if the emotions are, as one Orthodox Christian psychologist suggests, "the voices of the passions,"[125] we would expect to find considerable overlap between the cognitive concept of schema and the patristic understanding of the passions.

The ascetic term *passion* refers to "a bad disposition of our inner man" [*tōn kakōn diatheseōn tou entos anthrōpou hēmōn*][126] that is at the root of sinful thoughts and deeds. If the classical Greek concept of the inner man overlaps with the modern psychological concepts of personality and consciousness, the passions can also be understood in more modern terms as discrete mental states that orient or, rather, disorient a person in specific situations. Since Saint Gregory Palamas views the passions as "paths that are always crooked and perverse,"[127] they can likewise be construed as misleading cognitive maps that deceive a person into making decisions that take him off the strait and narrow path of virtue. Saint John Climacus describes a passion as "that which persistently nestles in the soul for a long time, forming therein a habit, as it were, by the soul's longstanding association with it, since the soul of its own free choice clings to it."[128] Several important notions are contained in this passage. First of all, passions are habitual modes of responding formed over time, which indicates that they are learned—or to be more precise, over-learned—ways of reacting. Second, since a person chooses to invest himself in the passions, they adhere to him in a profoundly individualized way. As habitual, persistent, and individualistic modes of reacting, the passions tend to grow rigid and difficult to change if they are left unchecked.[129] Thus in psychological terms, passions can be defined as disorienting, inflexible, and idiosyncratic cognitive maps marking out behavioral pathways that are reinforced over time and resistant to change. In moral terms, they are characterized as evil, crooked, and perverse, because they entice man away from God, the Source of life.

Saint Maximus the Confessor notes that a passion always consists of an interaction involving a perceptible object, the senses, and the faculties for reasoning, desire, or aggression.[130] In modern parlance, each passion entails a person's environment, his perception of that environment, and his mode of processing what he perceives. Given this conceptual model, a passion manifests itself when the object of that passion is present, but remains hidden or dormant when it is absent.[131] The patristic description of a person being mentally bound to the object of a passion[132] can be likened to what psychiatrists observe in the case of obsessions, for in both cases, passion-related thoughts engulf the mind[133] and exclude thoughts unrelated to the passion. Obsessional thoughts are in fact reliable portents that a passion is present.

Passions can be considered normal or positive when they are shaped by right reason and the remembrance of God, but they are regarded as abnormal or negative when they stem from the irrational reactions of a person who has forgotten his Maker.[134] In the negative sense in which the term *passion* is customarily used, it implies a sickness of the soul and a deviation from reason,[135] or what psychologists would call a pathological mental state. Examples of such passions include "anger, vainglory, love of pleasure, hatred, evil desires, and the like."[136] Although the list of passions is quite long,[137] it can be generated from the three core passions of the love of pleasure, the love of silver, and the love of glory,[138] or from the two most comprehensive passions of pleasure and pain.[139] Whereas some passions are inter-related and mutually supportive,[140] others are mutually exclusive, even as "pleasure does not allow for pain; nor sadness joy; nor gloom, gladness."[141]

When someone is under the influence of a passion and in a state of forgetfulness of God, the human mind, according to Saint Gregory Palamas, becomes "creaturely or demonic. Having strayed from the principles implanted in its nature, it begins to be overcome by a desire for the acquisition of foreign objects and an insatiable love for gain. It then betrays itself to every form of fleshly desire, knowing neither barrier nor limit to pleasure."[142] The passions are thus unnatural in the sense that they distort the image of God in man and motivate him in ways that can be obsessive, savage, and even demonic.

Saint Maximus the Confessor describes what it means to be in this creaturely mindset. Thought processes are restricted to a dualistic algorithm in which sensual pleasure is the sole good and bodily pain is the only existent evil. To emerge from this frame of mind, a person should replace the pleasure-pain criterion with the distinction between God's eternal glory that is truly good and the transitory processes of corruption and decay that are not.[143] The saint traces the source of a creaturely mindset to a person's irrational relationship to the senses for the sake of obtaining pleasure.[144]

The fallen human condition has a number of consequences. It makes the pleasurable passions appear attractive and the arduous virtues unappealing.[145] It prevents people from discerning their best interests, so that they fail to live virtuously, to acquire spiritual knowledge, to partake of true life, and to see the Uncreated Light.[146] Unable to function properly, the human mind becomes dense,[147] falls under the tyranny of the senses,[148] and embraces irrationality instead of knowledge.[149] In such a state, thinking becomes simplistic, superficial, and disinclined to carefully explore causal factors.[150] Becoming mentally dense, however, does not mean becoming slow-witted. The mind is far from inactive; it is full of thoughts, conceptions, and images.[151] These irrational passionate thoughts are especially bound to anger or primitive desires, "since those passions are common to us and the irrational animals." In addition, there are passions that are not characteristic of animals, but of demons. These passions include the more complex mental states of pride, vainglory, and envy.[152] Such passions are also rooted in ignorance. Pride, for instance, results from an ignorance of divine help and human fallibility.[153]

In summary, passions can be understood in modern psychological terms as obsessive pathological mental states in which human reasoning processes cease to function normally. These idiosyncratic and environmentally triggered modes act as dysfunctional cognitive maps that disorient the mind, overwhelming it with thoughts and shutting out contradictory cognitive sets. Following these cognitive dysfunctional maps, thought processes become superficial, simplistic, and dualistic: pleasure-good, pain-evil. Moreover, the mind can envision no further than what it immediately senses. In a state of ignorance about possible causes in a situation, people influenced by the passions are also lacking in spiritual knowledge and unable to discern their best interests. The passions are also situation-dependent structures that are activated when an object of passion is present, but latent when it is absent. Over time, they become increasingly inflexible and resistant to change, forming interlocking networks of similarly dysfunctional cognitive maps. There is something primitive and childish about passionate states, for their external manifestations bear a striking resemblance to the behavior of animals on the prowl (desire), predators ready to pounce (anger), or children in a tantrum.[154] For the fathers, this is not a natural state, but a departure from the qualities inherent in man as created in the image and likeness of God.

Childish thought and brutish behavior are also crucial issues for mental health professionals, even if they may partially justify such thought and behavior as natural even in adult human beings. Cognitive theorists explain such disruptive reactions with the concept of schema, the final channel marker in the cognitive model. Piagetian stage theory has demonstrated how children struggle to make sense out of their surroundings by paying attention to certain aspects of any given situation, discerning a pattern, assigning a meaning to that pattern, and making up rules and assumptions for dealing with that situation.[155] Those meanings, rules, and assumptions are called schemata, because they give structure to a person's mental representation of the world. As children mature, they learn to respond quickly to comparable situations in similar ways on the basis of these previously formed schemata or beliefs.[156] Judith Beck notes that people's beliefs about themselves, others, and their world are often never put into words, but are simply accepted, even in adult life, as absolute truths about reality that their thoughts and behavior *must* obey.[157] Being formed in childhood, schemata tend to be as exaggerated and absolute as the reactions of a two-year-old child fearful of a snarling dog. Being employed in the same fashion for a docile lap dog and a ferocious bulldog, these schemata also tend to be global and over-generalized. Although developmental schemata, such as the phobic rule "*always* avoid dogs," serve their function in early childhood, they are often quite inadequate in adult life.[158]

In addition to the idiosyncratic schemata/core beliefs formed during development, other more universal schemata seem to be a part of innate preprogrammed human behavior and related to the reactions of animals under threat. In other words, just as animals instinctively react to danger by making use of preprogrammed survival strategies, so human beings respond to sudden threats in similar primitive ways. Introductory biology textbooks refer to the classic case of threatened animals rapidly determining whether they should fight, flee, freeze, or faint.[159] A human being under threat behaves in like manner: he uses schemata in the form of rigid rules to compress "complex information into a simplified, unambiguous category as rapidly as possible" and to calculate whether or not a given situation is dangerous. The individual crudely evaluates the environment in dichotomous terms as being harmless or harmful,[160] and then involuntarily reacts emotionally, physiologically, and behaviorally. For example, in the case of anxiety, someone about to give a speech interprets his situation using vulnerability schemata that lead him to conclude that he is in danger of embarrassment. That person will then feel tense, experience an increased heart rate, and speak with difficulty.[161] Although this involuntary primitive reaction interferes with a person's immediate goals, in more dangerous times it offered protection from reckless behavior[162] and motivation to alter unfavorable situations by either escaping from them or removing the source of frustration.[163]

Although developmental and primitive schemata enable an individual to scan his surroundings for schema-relevant information and to reach a quick conclusion about that situation, they also block out incompatible information, so that a person tends to "see what he expects to see instead of what is actually present in the situation."[164] For example, the infatuated are under the influence of such positive schemata with respect to their beloved that they can see neither flaw nor defect.[165]

As tools for decoding particular situations, schemata are dormant if no information can be found in a situation to activate them. They vary in terms of the number of situations in which they can be used, their capacity to be modified, and their intensity when activated.[166] Close to the surface of a person's consciousness are intermediate schemata or beliefs that are made up of rules, attitudes, and assumptions about various situations. These schemata focus on safety versus danger and pleasure versus pain.[167] Further from a person's awareness are core schemata with rigid and global ideas about oneself and others.[168] These core beliefs tend to revolve around notions of perceived helplessness in terms of competence and control as well as notions of perceived unlovability in terms of acceptance.[169] Although people are no more aware of their schemata in the form of rules and core-beliefs than they are of the grammatical structures that they use when speaking, these schemata have a great influence on how they react.[170]

In psychopathology, a person consistently and inappropriately relies on certain sets of schemata even in situations that offer very little evidence to support them. By focusing solely on the minimal amount of information that confirms the schemata, the person maintains and strengthens them.[171] For example, in depression, a person's thoughts are dominated by self-constricting schemata and guided by unconditional rules, so that any shortcoming that the depressed person detects only confirms his belief that he will always be a failure.[172]

These dysfunctional schemata cause the patient, and sometimes those around him, a great deal of discomfort. The primitive rules that act as "coding systems to define the personal meaning of a particular behavior" fail to take into account the needs and wishes of other persons,[173] so they often lead to unnecessary conflict. Since these schemata exaggerate personally relevant details in a situation and minimize or exclude other objectively important factors, they lead a person to egocentric and excessively broad conclusions.[174] Furthermore, since misidentifying a single danger in a harsh environment could prove fatal, there is a built-in bias to primitive schemata that are set to detect every danger and foe at the cost of occasionally mistaking a friend for an enemy.[175] In other words, such schemata tend to make a person excessively suspicious and unduly fearful. Schemata thus ignore the array of factors responsible for any event and force a person "to focus 'on the one single cause' and exclude other possibilities."[176] A few examples should suffice to illustrate how a person's schemata and best interests can be at cross-purposes.

In an anxiety disorder, the sufferer not only scans the environment for menacing signs, but also reacts to imaginary dangers, because his schema functions as a "hypersensitive alarm system" that keeps sounding false alarms about perceived dangers outweighing his ability to cope. Like a deer caught in the headlights, the patient freezes up, tries to escape, or even faints. The schema literally keeps the patient's "attention bound to stimuli perceived as threatening,....Because the patient 'uses up' a large part of his cognitive capacity by scanning for threatening stimuli, the amount available for attending to other demands is severely restricted."[177] Although the patient does not want to be anxious, he can do little about his anxiety symptoms once his vulnerability schemata are activated.

An example that more closely approaches patristic notions of passion is observed in the schemata of those struggling with substance abuse. When an addicted individual sees a cocaine pipe, he starts to feel a craving to use cocaine. For the addict, a cocaine pipe is not a neutral stimulus, but a trigger that activates a schema that identifies the pipe with the pleasure experienced when using the pipe, thereby producing preliminary pleasurable sensations. Other schemata are also activated such as "using is necessary for my happiness." These schemata block out other interpretations such as "drug abuse will harm me" and set in motion emotional, physiological, and memory systems that prod the addict to engage in drug-related behavior.[178]

It requires much effort for people to modify dysfunctional schemata, both because they have difficulty adopting a new and unfamiliar interpretation of familiar situations, and because even dysfunctional schemata seem to provide short-term benefits.[179] Usually, the cognitive therapist will work with a patient's dysfunctional core schemata midway through therapy after the patient has seen how helpful cognitive methods have been in evaluating automatic thoughts and schema-based assumptions.[180] It is often not feasible to completely dismantle dysfunctional schemata, but it is frequently possible to modify or reshape them by making them more flexible, more veridical, and less egocentric, as well as by narrowing the range of situations in which a given schema is used. For example, if a patient suffers from paranoia, it would be unrealistic to try to have him view everyone and every situation without suspicion, but it may be possible to teach him to trust specific people under certain circumstances.[181]

Having circumnavigated both patristic notions of the passions and the cognitive concept of the schemata, we observe that they are like unto similar islands with quite distinct coastlines. In terms of similarity, both dysfunctional schemata and sinful passions can be viewed as pathological mental states that are habitual, inflexible, idiosyncratic, and biased. Under the influence of both passions and schemata involving danger or pleasure, thinking becomes simplistic, dualistic, and causally un-nuanced. Both passions and schemata are dependent on concrete situations in which some object or information serves as a trigger activating the schema or enflaming the passion. In the absence of that object or information, they both remain latent. Once the schema or passion is deployed, they both unleash a flood of related thoughts and block the flow of incompatible ones. Both sinful passions and dysfunctional schemata tend to sabotage a person's best interests and higher goals. Hence, some sort of therapeutic intervention is called for in both cases. Although the complete dismantling of a schema or the total mortification of a passion is neither feasible nor advisable, modifying a schema and transforming a passion are both possible and salutary, albeit laborious.[182]

Among the distinct features observed along each coast, the most prominent difference involves how dysfunctional schemata and sinful passions are characterized. For the monastic fathers, passions motivate man in unnatural ways, inconsistent with the divine image, and inconceivable for someone who actively keeps God in his thoughts. Dysfunctional schemata may impair human functioning, but sinful passions also damage man's relationship with God and encumber his salvation. For the fathers, excessive egocentricity not only produces broad and subjective conclusions, but also leads to a creaturely or even demonic state. Furthermore, there is a significant connotative difference between the passions being portrayed as brutish and childish and the schemata being characterized as a continuation of primitive and juvenile modes. The fathers are speaking allegorically, whereas psychologists are making a quite literal statement. A literal reading inclines psychologists to explore the characterization more analytically and extensively as well as to base their conclusions on studies of child development and animal behavior. It also leads them to do so in non-moral terms. The patristic allegorical approach, however, rings true with our deepest intuitions. There is something fundamentally wrong about an adult behaving like a child or reacting like a beast. The personality theorist Gordon Allport comments on this condition as follows:

> Picture, if you can, an adult who is extremely destructive of property, insistent and demanding that every desire be instantly gratified, helpless, and almost totally dependent on others, unable to share his possessions, impatient and prone to tantrums, violent and uninhibited in the display of all his feelings. Such behavior, normal to a two-year old, would be monstrous in a man. Unless these qualities are markedly altered in the process of becoming we have on our hands an infantile and potentially evil personality.[183]

The amoral language of biology may have its therapeutic uses, but the moral language of the fathers touches a basic truth that is intrinsically healing: the human being is not meant to remain a child or to behave like a beast, but to resemble God incarnate.

Other intriguing connections between the contours of both concepts emerge from a comparison of negative core schemata and core passions. Although both ascetics and cognitive theorists identify the centrality of the core passion or schema regarding pleasure and pain, the conceptualizations are radically different. Psychologists accept the human need for pleasure as natural and relate it to being loved and accepted, whereas the fathers not only refuse to make sensual pleasure a basic value, but also consider it to be a consequence of the fall, a potential danger in a fallen world, and a slippery path leading to the forgetfulness of God. Cognitive psychologists also note the importance of schemata concerning safety versus danger or competence and control versus helplessness. Perhaps, core schemata regarding helplessness can be correlated to core passions concerning the love of silver and the love of glory. In like manner, core schemata regarding unlovability may be related to the core passion concerning love of pleasure. If this is the case, passions associated with the love of silver and love of glory can be viewed as a misguided strategy (or in cognitive terms, as dysfunctional schemata) for dealing with a sense of helplessness. Similarly, love of pleasure can be conceptualized as an improper means (dysfunctional schema) for coping with unlovability. When framed in this way, one can appreciate the spiritual and psychological value of the patristic exhortation concerning the remembrance of God. If a person recalls that God is his helper, amassing wealth and attracting fame no longer offer additional security. If he recalls that God loves him, sensual pleasure in no way increases his sense of being loved. Moreover, the martyrs, who feared neither danger nor pain, demonstrated that by the remembrance of God and the love for God, the human being can acquire true freedom from passions and core schemata alike.

Noteworthy similarities, intriguing connections, and distinct characteristics vis-à-vis both concepts suggest that when we examine one concept, knowledge of the corresponding concept can provide supplementary information of use to the pastor and psychologist alike. Even if a pastoral counselor or cognitive psychologist ultimately rejects as inappropriate the perspective that the corresponding approach offers, the additional knowledge will expand the range of available hermeneutical choices and etiological explanations.

For example, the pastor might consider whether what he labels as a passion might be complicated by additional causal considerations such as the fact that during childhood, people often misinterpret themselves, significant others, and their world as well as the fact that those interpretations often linger on into adult life. For instance, the passions of foolish talk and jesting might be rooted in a child's belief "if I make people laugh, they will love me." Histrionic personality disorders thrive on beliefs about displays of this sort. It would prove helpful for the pastor to realize that people rarely verbalize such beliefs, although they implicitly accept them as absolute truths. Undermining such beliefs would be instrumental in weakening the passion. In like manner, the pastor might also consider the possibility of personal rules and assumptions that play an important role in supporting a given passion. In the previous example, dismantling the childhood assumption about lovability should be helpful in fighting the passion. It may also be profitable to consider what the passion seems to offer a person in terms of short-term benefits and rapid information processing.

The psychologist, in turn, might widen the notion of schemata by including a person's interpretation of his relationship to God. The absence of remembrance of God, fundamental in activated passions, could also play a role in supporting dysfunctional schemata. This means that the remembrance of God may have therapeutic value in modifying dysfunctional schemata by changing a person's focus and by attracting the transfiguring power of divine grace. There is some scientific warrant to this proposition. McMinn and Campell note, "In an unpublished doctoral dissertation, Stavros (1998) found that meditating on the Jesus prayer for thirty days reduced anxiety, along with depression, hostility, and interpersonal sensitivity."[184] The psychologist could also offer the Christian additional motivation for change by noting how a dysfunctional schema that coincides with a particular passion should be modified, so that the patient's way of responding will conform with the image of God.

The Cognitive Model: Some Retrospective Conclusions

Looking back over the log of our twofold voyage, our entries indicate that patristic thought and cognitive theory encounter each other in beneficial ways at every channel marker along the cognitive model. The church fathers would concur with cognitive theorists who assert that meaning assignment affects mood, behavior, and character, that rapid automatic thoughts meant for the self alter mood and motivate action, and that schemata in the form of primitive and juvenile modes of reacting sabotage one's best interests. The fathers would also likely commend cognitive therapists for the clarity of their model and their perceptive observations. At each channel marker, however, the ancient mariners of the Spirit would gently remind present-day psychologists that meaning assignment also reflects one's relationship with God, that thoughts also have a spiritual dimension with eternal repercussions, and that man is also called to rise above primitive and juvenile schemata to "the glorious liberty of the children of God."[185] These reminders bring glad tidings of salvation and the potential for transfiguration to the cognitive model, thereby including it as a passenger on a voyage beyond the shallows of adaptive psychological functioning unto the deep waters of eternity itself.

CHAPTER FOUR

A Comparative Anatomy of Psychopathology: Thoughts, Self, and Childhood

In the previous chapter, our patristic voyage across the cognitive model skirted along the coast of psychopathology, but did not give us the opportunity to stop and focus on the objective features of the coastline or to discern the unifying quality that subjectively captures that terrain. Notwithstanding, our coastal observations are sufficient to summarize the process of psychopathology. According to the cognitive model, psychopathology manifests itself when someone inappropriately and dysfunctionally uses primitive and juvenile schemata, thereby generating distorted automatic thoughts that express inaccurate and detrimental interpretations about himself, others, and his world. These cognitive events set in motion excessive emotional reactions and maladaptive behavioral responses that cause distress for the individual who may then manifest symptoms that define clinical syndromes and disorders.

In this chapter, we will turn from a description of the cognitive processes underlying psychopathology to an "anatomical" examination of that pathology as it is objectively observed in the form of specific cognitive distortions and subjectively defined in terms of excessive egocentricity and maladaptive schemata formed during childhood. We will strive to construct a comparative anatomy in which patristic teachings on bad thoughts, *philautia*, and the raising of children form the major structures to which the psychotherapeutic concepts of cognitive distortions, egocentricity, and childhood factors will be compared. As anatomists begin with easily observable surface structures and dissect their way into organs otherwise hidden from sight, so we shall begin with an examination of cognitive distortions that can be readily recognized, continue with an investigation of egocentricity, and conclude this chapter with a consideration of childhood factors.

Bad Thoughts and Cognitive Distortions

Our initial incisions open up notions of bad thoughts and cognitive distortions. Stemming from their personal experience in the spiritual life, the fathers composed lists of thoughts that are obstacles to loving God and neighbor, and are therefore characterized as bad or demonic. Originating in his empirical research on depression, Aaron Beck recorded specific cognitive distortions and thinking errors that prevent someone with depression from realistically evaluating himself, his world, and his future. Beck defines a maladaptive thought as an "ideation that interferes with the ability to cope with life experiences, unnecessarily disrupts internal harmony, and produces inappropriate or excessive emotional reactions that are painful."[1] These two contexts are admittedly as different as the commandment "Be ye perfect for the sake of the kingdom of heaven" and the prescription "Be ye functional for the sake of human society." Notwithstanding, the two concepts focus both on mistakes in judgment producing harmful results and on the beneficial correction of those errors.

For example, Saint John Chrysostom notes, "The Church not only saves irrational people, but also transforms them....When a greedy and rapacious person enters a church and hears the divine words of teaching, he changes his opinions and instead of a wolf, he becomes a lamb."[2] In psychological terms, the irrationality of greed is corrected by a new learning experience in the Church, thereby altering a person's beliefs and thoughts as well as producing behavioral change. In spiritual terms, divine grace present in a liturgical setting together with the transfiguring power of Christ's teachings bring about repentance: a change in a person's way of thinking and manner of life. The thought of greed *per se* is as irrational and destructive as a wolf, for it prevents the person entertaining it from dwelling peacefully with the other sheep of Christ's rational flock. In cognitive therapy, Beck notes that a patient's distortion of reality and illogical thinking can be corrected in the therapeutic session by objectively appraising reality and examining the logical consistency between a person's premises and conclusions.[3] Although no one-to-one correspondence between bad thoughts and thinking errors is immediately apparent, common themes of irrationality, corrective learning, and altered perspectives invite further examination, which may suggest other points of intersection where knowledge from one approach might elucidate our understanding of the other.

Patristic Approaches to the Concept of Bad Thoughts

Ascetic tradition singles out eight principal bad thoughts that encompass and engender all the other sins that the mind can commit.[4] The eight bad thoughts include gluttony, unchastity, avarice, anger, dejection, listlessness, vainglory, and pride.[5] They are the conceptual analogues to specific behaviors, for "what the body acts out in the world of things, the *nous* acts out in the world of conceptual images."[6] Hence, the thoughts can be formulated in behavioral terms as the gluttonous behavior of someone overeating, the unchaste conduct of someone having illicit sexual relations, the avaricious actions of someone gambling, and so forth. This patristic connection between thought and behavior links the subjective reality of the eight bad thoughts to the objective reality of concrete actions that can be observed and measured by an external observer.

Furthermore, if bad thoughts can be formulated in behavioral terms, their antidotes can also be framed in like manner. For example, in a text attributed to Saint John of Damascus, the author notes that "gluttony can be corrected by self-control, unchastity by desire for God and longing for future blessings; avarice by compassion for the poor; anger by goodwill and love for all men; worldly dejection by spiritual joy; listlessness by patience, perseverance, and offering thanks to God; vain-glory by doing good in secret and by praying constantly with a contrite heart; and pride by not judging or despising anyone in the manner of the boastful Pharisee, and by considering oneself the least of all men."[7] For each bad thought, the believer is provided with an incompatible set of thoughts to be cultivated, so that a given bad thought can be cut off by that incompatibility. A behavioralist might suggest that we apply the patristic concept-action connection to this list of antidotes. In other words, the more subjective mental states such as desire for God, compassion for the poor, and spiritual joy can be operationalized (i.e., made behaviorally observable) by asking what would someone be *doing* consistent with desire for God, compassion for the poor and spiritual joy, and then suggesting that the person act accordingly.[8]

The eight bad thoughts can also be framed in more cognitive terms as "mistaken judgments about concepts" [*hē esphalmenē krisis tōn noēmatōn*][9] or as misleading impressions about the pleasure some perceivable object will bring.[10] This formulation bears a significant resemblance to the idea of cognitive distortion. In a Protestant adaptation of Ellis's system of irrational beliefs, William Backus defines sin as putting a mistaken belief into action. For example, "Envy can be defined as the misbelief that it's best to prevail over others....Greed is the misbelief that the highest good lies in owning things purely for the sake of possessing them."[11] Applying Saint Maximus's definition of "mistaken judgment about concepts" to the eight bad thoughts, we can similarly express those thoughts in terms of particular errors. For example, gluttony, unchastity, avarice, anger, vainglory, and pride involve obvious mistakes in judgment that respectively transform excessive eating, sensuality, possessions, revenge, one's image, or oneself into the highest good. Sorrow for a being created by a loving God as well as listlessness for a being whose life is numbered in days can be seen as misevaluations at an existential level. The value of this cognitive approach lies in its emphasis on personal choice, which provides motivation to strive for virtue through the natural human desire to see clearly and not make mistakes.

Mistakes are made when an individual is either not adept at working with the appropriate standard or when interference prevents or distracts a person from using it. Since the standard of the gospel is a given for the ancient ascetics, they emphasized the problem of mixed signals: that is, the coexistence of ideas that conceal the eight bad thoughts, so that the latter slip by unnoticed. For example, the thought of gluttony is often camouflaged by the "reasonable" pretext of preventing bodily illness; the thought of avarice is disguised by "prudent" concerns about old age. In other instances, the thought is not camouflaged, but the attention shifts to another issue that eclipses the bad thought. For example with the thought of fornication, the conviction that the fleshly impulses will not subside makes room for the belief that only by satisfying those desires will a person feel relief.[12] In all these Evagrian examples, a person who has made the mistake of acting on one of the bad thoughts has previously accepted permission-giving beliefs that seem reasonable or feel compelling. Thus, the monastic fathers point out these beliefs that are really sly self-dispensations, so that the believer will recognize them, be able to judge them with increased objectivity, and by the grace of God avoid the mistake in judgment and ensuing sin.

The classical patristic list of eight bad thoughts is meant to provide the believer with an easily remembered set of mutually exclusive, but collectively exhaustive categories that he can use as an aid or standard for diagnosing his own thoughts.[13] This additional knowledge in turn should clarify the believer's choice about accepting, rejecting, or acting on a given thought. By utilizing this list in both cognitive and behavioral ways, the fathers greatly expand its value as a resource. The identification of permission-giving thoughts gives the believer a kind of cognitive litmus test for the presence of some of the eight bad thoughts, whereas the description of the thoughts in behavioral terms prevents the list from becoming an abstraction unrelated to the active life.

Saint Anastasius of Sinai provides a different scriptural list with eight sinful thoughts:

1. Ignorance as with Laban
2. Deception as with Eve
3. Enthusiasm as with Peter
4. Forgetfulness as with Moses who did not love God at the rock
5. Tyranny as with Darius who handed over Daniel
6. Disbelief as with Lot's wife
7. Contempt as with Gehazi who disdained Elisha
8. Evil disposition as with the Pharisees who hid the resurrection.[14]

Although this list is formulated in behavioral terms as the actions of particular biblical figures in concrete situations, each of these sins also involves the cognitive component of a mistaken judgment in which the immediate consequences of those actions are overvalued, whereas their long-range repercussions are overlooked. The fundamental error in these bad thoughts is a failure to give appropriate attention to the spiritual dimension of the situation. In retrospect, we note that the same oversight is common to the more conventional list of eight bad thoughts that we discussed earlier.

In addition to mistakes in judgment related to the eight bad thoughts, saintly monks also note other thinking errors that cause the believer to stray from "the narrow way that leads to life."[15] In particular, they note mistakes such as diverging from the mean of virtue, making conjectures about the thoughts of others, predicting the future, and thinking under the influence of anger or desire. These errors have surface similarities with the cognitive distortions of *magnification-minimization*, *mind-reading*, *catastrophizing*, and *emotional thinking* that we will examine shortly.

Saint Basil the Great remarks, "The upright in heart have thoughts that are inclined neither to excess nor to deficiency, but are directed toward the mean [*to meson*] of virtue."[16] This quintessentially Aristotelian understanding of virtue as the mean is widespread in patristic literature and noted elsewhere.[17] Of interest for the present discussion is how a thought can be classified as virtuous when aligned with the mean of two excessive qualities and as passionate when aimed at what can be considered an exaggerated or deficient form of what would otherwise be a virtue. For example, Abba Dorotheos of Gaza sets forth Aristotle's illustration of "courage as the mean between cowardliness and brazenness."[18] The value of this model lies not so much in supplying worthy goals for thought and action as in providing an objective and dispassionate way to evaluate cognition and behavior by placing them within a continuum of possible responses. For the fathers, distinctions are never abstractions, but direct outgrowths of life itself. In fact, according to Saint Maximus the Confessor, the conceptually accurate and useful tool of understanding virtue in terms of the mean that avoids deficiency and excess becomes obsolete once a person has learned to recognize in practice God as the true cause of the virtues. Living according to the mean, one becomes blessedly unaware of excesses.[19]

An interesting application of the concepts of excess, deficiency, and the mean is the patristic view that superstition and atheism are extremes characteristic of the unlearned.[20] Saint Gregory of Nyssa notes, "The devout person is neither an atheist, nor superstitious, for to deny the existence of God and to believe in many gods are equally impious."[21] Christian opposition to atheism is common knowledge.[22] It is less widely known that superstitious beliefs and practices are also condemned by the twenty-fourth canon of the Council of Ancyra and the eighty-sixth canon of the Council of Carthage.[23] Cognitive therapists who are concerned about the interference of superstitious beliefs on human psychological functioning would find such ecumenical decisions heartening. They would also benefit by examining the patristic alternative to atheism and superstition, namely, the royal way of piety. This mean, which avoids both ignorance and superstition, is characterized by a knowing prudence that is acquired by patience, abstinence, and obedience to the commandments of Christ.[24]

A third conceptual tool that some fathers employ as an aid to identifying mistakes in judgment is the originally Platonic tripartite division of the soul into the rational, aggressive, and desiring aspects [to *logistikon*, to *thymikon*, and to *epithymētikon*].[25] In this framework, sin is conceptualized as the use of these faculties in a way that is contrary to nature or that overturns the innate hierarchy according to which "our rational faculty should control our aggressive tendencies and our desires with wisdom and skill, regulating them, admonishing them, correcting them, and ruling them as a king rules over his subjects."[26] When thoughts passionately or vehemently give orders, they usually stem from the faculties of desire or anger instead of the reasoning faculty and are consequently fallacious.[27] In psychological terms, someone with such thoughts exhibits a cognitive distortion known as *emotional reasoning*.

The commandment "judge not," mentioned in our discussion of meaning-assignment, led other fathers to identify another common thinking error in our tendency to assume that we know what someone else is thinking. Saint Jerome reminds us that "speech does not express the thoughts of our own minds. How much more dangerous is it to judge another man's heart!"[28] The danger, of course, is that we misjudge someone's intentions and thus come to a mistaken conclusion about him or her. According to Blessed Augustine, such mistakes are the inevitable outcome of unreliable premises. After all, "we do not see the thoughts of one another's hearts; and our opinions about each other are sometimes better and sometimes worse than what is warranted by reality."[29] With discriminative acuity, the saintly bishop of Hippo observes that if we judge someone regarding a vice, our assessment of that person may be wrong, whereas our judgment concerning the distinction between virtue and vice might be quite sound. The soundness of that distinction is the culprit that deceives us into accepting our conclusions about what is in fact cloaked by the "thick darkness of the human heart."[30]

Although the fathers consider it presumptuous to speculate about the contents of another's heart in view of the fact that we are not even fully aware of our own thoughts, they, nevertheless, do allow for an exception for the saint who recognizes the thoughts of another by the Spirit of truth,[31] even as the Gospels portray Christ perceiving the thoughts of others.[32] If we cannot discern what is hidden in that way, we should not come to a conclusion about someone on the basis of appearance.[33] To do so, according to Kallistos Aggelikoudis, is as foolish as it is for a blind man to attempt to read a book.[34]

Related to the fallacy of presuming what someone else is thinking is the error of predicting the future apart from divine inspiration. According to Saint John of Damascus, the ability to see into the future is not a trait of human nature; even the human nature of Christ would not have that attribute if it were not for the hypostatic union that deified human nature with the knowledge of the future.[35] As Saint Gregory the Wonderworker notes, "It is impossible for a human being to know anything, or to learn from another human being either what has been from the beginning, or what shall be in the future."[36]

In summary, the church fathers made use of a variety of conceptual diagnostic models to identify thoughts that are both mistakes in judgment and hindrances to the believer in his struggle for salvation. These models have striking cognitive components that encourage an awareness of permission-giving thoughts, an ascertainment of the sources of thoughts in terms of human rational faculties versus emotional reactions, the contextualization of thoughts within a continuum, and an appraisal of thoughts on the scale of short-term versus long-term consequences. The ancient ascetics also point out particular cognitive distortions such as mind-reading and fortune telling as well as the extremes of atheism and superstition. The patristic account of sinful thoughts is sophisticated, nuanced, and thoroughly practical.

Beck's Theory of Cognitive Distortions

Turning from a patristic anatomy of passionate thoughts culminating in sin to a cognitive anatomy of automatic thoughts leading to psychological dysfunction is like turning from a three-dimensional model to a two-dimensional diagram. With the loss of the spiritual dimension, linear relationships become clearer even as spatial relationships grow more illusory. According to the cognitive theory of psychopathology, "Although meanings are constructed by the person rather than being pre-existing components of reality, they are correct or incorrect in relation to a given context or goal. When cognitive distortion or bias occurs, meanings are dysfunctional or maladaptive (in terms of system's activation). The cognitive distortions include errors in cognitive context (meaning), cognitive processing (meaning elaboration), or both."[37] In other words, an individual's interpretation of a situation or the consequences of a particular action may be distorted or biased on account of pre-existing beliefs (schemata) that are irrational or counter-productive as well as on account of inferences that do not follow from all available information. This cognitive distortion prevents the person from responding in a reasonable manner and starts a chain reaction of maladaptive thoughts, emotions, and behaviors.

In life, to err is human; and according to the cognitive model, to make thinking errors is just part of being far from divine. Harry Stack Sullivan notes, "Almost everyone deals with other people with a wonderful blend of magic, illusions, and incoherent irrelevancy."[38] In psychopathology, this irrational "wonderful blend" becomes so potent that its inebriating influence overwhelms a person's way of processing information and assessing situations thus leaving the individual emotionally and behaviorally impaired. In particular, distorted thought processes that trigger psychopathology can be broken down into dysfunctional beliefs or schemata that are misapplied in a given situation and errors in logic that support dysfunctional beliefs and bias the conclusions that one reaches about that situation. These two aspects are related. Dysfunctional beliefs predispose a person to specific thinking errors, such as viewing a nuanced set of circumstances in black and white terms ("I am either a *total* success or an *absolute* failure").[39] Thinking errors in turn support dysfunctional beliefs by excluding other alternatives. Together, dysfunctional schemata and thinking errors lead to non-veridical assessments of a situation and restrict the number of options from which a person can choose. In plain, albeit flippant, terms, Ernest Becker sums up a cognitive understanding of psychopathology as follows: "Normal no longer can mean 'not ill'—it must mean 'not stupid.' And 'not stupid' means 'not coerced.'"[40]

Cognitive distortions describe the logical errors that people make on account of a negative bias that distorts the way they make sense of a situation and evaluate themselves. Often, the mistakes have to do with a restricted attention that focuses on supposedly negative data and ignores more positive aspects of a situation.[41] Beck's standard list of cognitive distortions includes: all-or-nothing thinking, catastrophizing, disqualifying the positive, emotional reasoning, labeling, magnification/minimization, mental filter, mind-reading, overgeneralization, personalization, "should" statements, and tunnel vision. Definitions of these errors and examples from a pastoral context are given in figure 4.1 where the relevancy of a given cognitive error vis-à-vis the eight bad thoughts is also indicated. When people become aware of how rigid their thinking can become and how wrong they can be when they evaluate themselves, others, and other people's motives, these thinking errors can be corrected and replaced by more flexible, veridical, and adaptive alternatives.[42] A few examples illustrating the role cognitive distortions play in psychological problems and disorders should flesh out our bare bones discussion.

---

1.   All-or-nothing thinking: You view a situation in only two categories instead of on a continuum. Example: "If I'm not perfectly virtuous, I'm totally vile." Observable in all the bad thoughts.

2.   Catastrophizing: You predict the future negatively without considering other more likely outcomes. Example: "I'll be so upset, I won't be able to respond with love." Observable primarily in despondency and as an auxiliary factor in gluttony (e.g., "If I don't eat now, I'll starve"), fornication, avarice, anger, and listlessness.

3.   Disqualifying the positive: You unreasonably tell yourself that positive experiences, deeds, or qualities do not count. Example: "He gave some alms, but that doesn't mean he's a good person." Observable primarily in despondency and as an auxiliary factor in gluttony, fornication (e.g., "It's irrelevant that I was able to be chaste in another situation"), avarice, anger, and listlessness.

4.   Emotional reasoning: You think something must be true because you "feel" (actually believe) it so strongly, ignoring or discounting evidence to the contrary. Example: "I know that God loves everyone, but I still feel as though he doesn't love me." Observable in all the bad thoughts.

5.   Labeling: You put a fixed global label on yourself or others without considering that the evidence might more reasonably lead to a less disastrous conclusion. Example: "I'm damned. He's a liar." Observable in anger, despondency, vainglory, and pride (e.g., "I'm amazing").

6.   Magnification/minimization: When you evaluate yourself, another person, or a situation, you unreasonably magnify the negative and/or minimize the positive. Converse example: "I fast twice a week. I am not a sinner like that publican." (See Lk 18:11) Observable in all the bad thoughts.

Continued on next page

7.   (*continued*) Mental filter: You pay undue attention to one negative detail instead of seeing the whole picture. Converse example: "Because I fulfilled a commandment, I am not an unprofitable servant." (See Lk 17:10) Observable in all the bad thoughts.

8.   Mind-reading: You believe you know what others are thinking, failing to consider other more likely possibilities. Example: "He's condemning me in his heart." Observable in anger, despondency, and vainglory.

9.   Overgeneralization: You make a sweeping negative conclusion that goes far beyond the current situation. Example: "Because my mind wanders during liturgical services, I don't get anything out of attending church." Observable in all the bad thoughts.

10.   Personalization: You believe others are behaving negatively because of you, without considering more plausible explanations for their behavior. Example: "The priest blessed me coldly, because I did something wrong." Observable in anger and despondency.

11.   "Should" and "must" statements: You have a precise, fixed idea of how you or others should behave and you overestimate how bad it is that these expectations are not met. Example: "It's terrible that my brother sins. A Christian should behave differently." Observable in gluttony, fornication, avarice (e.g., "I must have that new cell phone"), despondency, listlessness, and vainglory.

12.   Tunnel vision: You only see the negative aspects of a situation. Example: "She's mean, proud, and a lousy cook." Observable primarily in anger, listlessness, and dejection, but as an auxiliary factor in gluttony, fornication, and avarice.

Fig. 4.1. Common cognitive distortions with pastoral examples. Adapted from Judith S. Beck, *Cognitive Therapy* (New York: Guilford Press, 1995), fig. 8.2. Reprinted by permission of the publisher. All rights reserved.

In depression, the native environment in which cognitive therapy was first developed, a person makes a series of cognitive errors resulting in a distorted negative evaluation of himself, his world, and his future. For example, a depressed college student who receives a B on one examination and an A on another, may view the B as a failure (*all-or-nothing thinking*) that will prevent him from getting a job (*catastrophizing, overgeneralization*), and the A as insignificant (*minimization*) or a fluke (*disqualifying the positive*). In focusing solely on the B and ignoring the A, he also makes cognitive distortions such as *mental filter* by failing to take into account the entire situation and *tunnel vision* by only looking at the negative aspect. Finally, the depressed student will likely conclude that he is stupid or incompetent (*labeling*), because that is how he feels (*emotional reasoning*). If the instructor happens to frown, the student will assume that he is displeased with him (*personalization*), even though the instructor may simply have a headache. In order for the patient to see these cognitive distortions and alter his thinking, the therapist usually has to elicit further data to fill out the patient's understanding of his situation, so that the patient can then test his faulty inferences against the facts.[43]

In anxiety, a person's perceived vulnerability precipitates involuntary responses that sabotage his efforts to cope with a set of circumstances. Cognitive distortions magnify that sense of vulnerability and thus aggravate his condition. For example, a student with test anxiety about an upcoming exam may underestimate the amount of material he knows (*minimization*), view difficulties in answering a question on an examination as proof of his inadequacy (*magnification*), and construe each mistake as a confirmation of his pending failure (*overgeneralization*). The student may also recall all past defeats (*mental filter*) and imagine being expelled from college and unemployed (*catastrophizing*), even though one specific setback rarely leads to a ruined life. Since his scenario of pass or fail excludes the possibility of performing moderately well, he locks himself into *all-or-nothing* thinking. Finally, he interprets a cold sweat, a heightened heart rate, and other signs of physiological arousal induced by anxiety as proof that he will fail (*emotional reasoning*).[44]

In hostility, a number of cognitive distortions negatively bias and exacerbate people's interpretations of someone else's behavior. In a disturbing situation in which the motive is ambiguous, people tend to assume that the cause is deliberate rather than impersonal (*personalization*) and that they know what the other person intended (*mind-reading*). Aggrieved parties also assume that if the offender *could* have acted differently, he *should* have done so ("*should*" statement). Therefore, on the basis of counterfactual thinking the offender is at fault. Once blame is established, another set of cognitive distortions fans the flame of anger. If the offender is an acquaintance, the aggrieved will often recall all memories (which may or may not be accurate) of similar transgressions (*tunnel vision*) and conclude that the offender *always* or *never* acts in such a way (*overgeneralization*).[45] At this point, the provocation is usually inflated (*magnification*) and the provoker is characterized as bad (*labeling, mental filter, disqualifying the positive*), so that both anger and retaliation seem and feel (*emotional reasoning*) perfectly justified.[46]

The above survey of thinking errors as they present themselves in psychological problems might give the mistaken impression that cognitive therapy merely involves superficial lessons in logic. Thinking errors are simply the outward manifestations that the therapist and the patient can readily observe and correct. The sources of cognitive distortions such as *magnification, over-*

generalization, all-or-nothing thinking and so forth are the primitive and juvenile schemata that we introduced in the previous chapter.[47] Thus, a cognitive treatment of psychological disorders must not only correct cognitive distortions, but also identify and then modify those rigid, extreme beliefs, assumptions, and rules that generate those thinking errors. In personality disorders, negative maladaptive beliefs about the self ("I'm inept"), about others ("they're malevolent"), and about a situation ("it's awful") form an interconnecting matrix that locks the individual in a cage of distorted information processing and maladaptive strategies for coping with life.[48]

For example, someone with a dependent personality disorder has a core belief about himself—"I'm helpless and inadequate"—leading to *all-or-nothing thinking* with respect to independence. He only conceives of the possibility of complete helplessness or total self-sufficiency and thus concludes, "I've got to have someone to take care of me" (*"must" statement*), and proceeds to cripple his relationships by over-attachment. Someone with a paranoid personality disorder has beliefs about others—"people are dangerous"—and about himself—"I'm not able to cope with these dangers"—that lead to wariness and *all-or-nothing thinking* with respect to his being completely competent or totally incompetent and others being absolutely trustworthy or utterly unworthy of trust.[49]

In substance abuse, a series of dysfunctional beliefs trap the user in addictive behavior. For example, when maladaptive anticipatory beliefs such as "I'll feel amazing on drugs" are activated, the addict starts to crave using the drug. This urge triggers other maladaptive relief-oriented schemata such as "I can't stand the cravings," "these cravings are never going to stop," and "I've got to use the drugs." These relief-oriented beliefs in turn activate permission-giving schemata such as "it's all right to use just this once," inexorably leading to the development of a plan for acquiring and eventually using narcotics.[50] All these beliefs contain cognitive distortions: anticipatory beliefs exhibit *magnification, over-generalization* errors vis-à-vis how good one will feel; relief-oriented beliefs show the marks of *tunnel vision* and *"must" statements*; and permission-giving beliefs manifest the errors of *mental filter* and disqualifying the negative consequences of using drugs (a variation on the error *disqualifying the positive*).

The above examples not only illustrate the relationship among cognitive distortions, maladaptive schemata, and psychopathology, but also indicate that knowledge of cognitive distortions provide additional objective diagnostic tools for therapist and patient alike. Using the list of cognitive distortions, the patient can learn to identify his own thinking errors and thus make his first step toward therapeutic change.

Bad Thoughts and Cognitive Distortions: Discerning the Relationship

Having now dissected both the patristic and cognitive approaches to mistakes in judgment or cognitive distortions, we can now make some remarks about how the two approaches can be related. Comparative anatomy usually contrasts similar bodily structures whose differences in appearance and function are attributable to divergent environments to which those structures are adapted. Although the eight bad thoughts and twelve cognitive distortions involve mistakes in judgment and perspective, the two lists on the surface have as little in common as a psychologist's office and an ascetic's cell. If, however, we note that the eight bad thoughts are also considered the eight vices or passions and recall that we have established a relationship, however tenuous, between passions and dysfunctional schemata, a relationship between cognitive distortions and bad thoughts begins to emerge. Just as rigid dysfunctional beliefs tend to produce cognitive distortions, as seen in personality disorders, so the eight fundamental passions (eight bad thoughts) are accompanied by cognitive distortions (see figure 4.1). A cognitive examination of a few patristic specimens will make this connection clearer.

Someone given over to the thought of gluttony is in the grip of *emotional reasoning*, desiring to eat a great deal, because he feels as though he must do so ("*must*" *statement*). When "the heart of gluttons dreams only of food,"[51] they provide prime examples of *tunnel vision*. The desire to "devour a whole Egypt and drink a River Nile"[52] rather than starve supplies a graphic instance of *all-or-nothing thinking*. Viewing the glorious feast of Christ's resurrection in terms of what tasty dishes one will prepare in order to celebrate the Savior's victory over death is certainly a *mental filter* in which the importance of food has been magnified completely out of proportion (*magnification*).[53]

From the above example, we can see that accepting a bad thought entails several cognitive distortions, although a cognitive distortion per se does not correspond to any given bad thought. Consequently, the eight bad thoughts occupy a stratum of reality governed by spiritual laws that contains the lower level of cognitive distortions governed by psychological mechanisms, even as this sentence contains thirty-three words. This relationship is significant. Awareness of cognitive distortions as discrete cognitive mechanisms does not interfere with sensitivity to the eight bad thoughts as existential orientations, for the two sets of information exist on different hierarchical planes. Notwithstanding, knowledge of cognitive distortions can prove helpful in understanding why a bad thought is a mistake from a strictly human perspective. This additional information may be of use to a spiritual father guiding Christians whose reasoning resembles that of the Apostle Thomas before, rather than after, seeing the risen Lord. Similarly, a cognitive therapist working with a

Christian patient can provide examples that coincide with the eight bad thoughts and thereby reassure the patient that therapy is not proceeding at counter-purposes to the patient's faith.

The church fathers seem to have a tacit knowledge of these two hierarchical levels, since in addition to the eight bad thoughts they also identify some of the cognitive distortions similar to or identical with those in Beck's list. For example, patristic texts mention the human tendency to misjudge another's thought (*personalization, mind-reading*), to predict the future (*catastrophizing*), and to accept inaccurate thoughts stemming from desire or anger (*emotional reasoning*). The definition of virtue as a mean is not unrelated to viewing reality as a continuum and avoiding *all-or-nothing thinking*. In fact, Saint John Chrysostom's comment—"there is no righteous person without sin, but also no sinner bereft of goodness"[54]—can be seen as a tacit admonition to avoid *all-or-nothing thinking* and evaluations in general. Other examples of cognitive distortions can also be drawn from monastic literature. For example, when Abba Dorotheos of Gaza points out the difference between saying that someone told a lie and "drawing a conclusion about his whole life" by calling that person a liar, the saintly abbot provides a fine illustration of the cognitive errors of *overgeneralization* and *labeling*.[55] These examples should suffice to indicate that the identification of cognitive distortions is not inconsistent with patristic encouragement to lead the virtuous life.

Philautia and Egocentricity

Cognitive distortions make up the observable outer layer of psychopathology enveloping the more internal schemata that people use to make sense of their situation. If we cut a bit deeper, however, our metaphorical lancet will come across a subjective strand that runs through all schemata and cognitive distortions. That strand is egocentricity. Although everybody tends to view his life as his own private novel in which he is the hero around whom all the other characters revolve, Beck notes that such a subjective egocentric take on life becomes so overwhelming in psychiatric disorders that any semblance of objectivity is lost. In fact, in psychopathology, egocentricity colors every aspect of a patient's thought.[56] In like manner, the monastic fathers in general and Saint Maximus in particular view *philautia* or love of self (lit., friendship with self) as the "very essence of morbidity...and the root of all the passions."[57] In bare logical terms, bad thoughts are to philautia as cognitive distortions are to egocentricity. Philautia and egocentricity seem strikingly similar in meaning and function. In fact, they are too similar for any anatomist to let his probe rest idly on the counter.

Patristic Descriptions of *Philautia*

Saint Basil the Great provides the simplest definition of *philautia* [Lat., *amor suus*]. Someone with philautia "supposedly loves himself [*philautos oun estin ho heauton dēthen philōn*]. Whatever that person does, whether in accord or in conflict with God's commandment, is done for himself with disregard for others."[58] Philautia, thus, refers to self-centered motivation and intentionality. The word *supposedly* is significant. Philautia is not what it seems to be even to the person under its influence, presumably because it ultimately·fails to fulfill its intention of bringing benefit to the self. Elsewhere, the monk bishop of Caesarea contrasts philautia with not being concerned about oneself on account of a loving stance vis-à-vis Christ and one's brethren [*philochristou kai philadelphou diatheseōs*].[59] Although human beings are fashioned to be behaviorally active, mentally concerned, and temperamentally loving, they are also free to choose to direct that active concerned love in the wrong direction, that is, toward self rather than toward God and neighbor.

Saint Maximus the Confessor narrows Saint Basil's definition by describing philautia as an "irrational love for the body."[60] In Orthodox Christian theology and anthropology, the human body is indisputably good, for God not only created it in the beginning, but he also assumed it at the Incarnation. One might rightly ask how a loving disposition to this precious work of God's hand would become sickly. The answer is found in the key word in Saint Maximus's definition: irrational [*alogos*] meaning without reason, without purpose, like an animal or apart from the *Logos*, God the Word. For a human being created in the image of God to act contrary to the Logos entails acting contrary to his own nature.

Saint Theodore the Great Ascetic similarly defines philautia as "an impassioned disposition toward and love for the body and the fulfillment of carnal desires."[61] Based on our earlier discussion of the passions, we can see that an impassioned disposition will be both disorienting and irrational. Emphasis on fulfilling the desires implies that philautia sets the soul on a quest for pleasure. In fact, Saint Maximus notes that "pleasure is the dominating force" in philautia.[62]

In contemporary hedonistic society, it may not be immediately clear why the quest for pleasure is irrational. The Great Maximus offers an explanation: although experience teaches us that "every pleasure is inevitably followed by pain," people act as though this were not the case. Ignoring a plethora of disconfirming experiences, people irrationally believe that pleasure and pain can be kept apart. Thus, they continue to pursue pleasure, thereby generating passions that produce further pain in even greater measure.[63]

Although philautia involves an irrational attachment to the body, the person acting under the influence of philautia considers his thoughts and actions to be quite reasonable. Saint Peter of Damascus even defines philautia as "the love of one's own will and thoughts—which is equivalent to the love of pleasure and praise."[64] When someone affectionately coddles his preferences and opinions, he will quite naturally, albeit mistakenly, consider his will to be right and his thoughts to be accurate, because such a perspective is reinforced by the gratifying incentives of pleasure and increased self-esteem. From a cognitive point of view, philautia in this case justifies actions and desires by emotional reasoning. Often, intensely and passionately believing in one's thoughts is highly symptomatic of philautia.[65] Saint Theophan the Recluse likewise locates philautia in a person's deeply hidden thought about his own self-importance and insistence that everything be as he desires it.[66] Philautia thus operates below the conscious level in a peremptory fashion.

Consistently interpreting all things through the prism of love for one's will and thoughts gradually makes these abnormal interpretations seem perfectly normal,[67] especially when a person fails to ask others for feedback about the accuracy of his thoughts.[68] For example, someone living in the world will view his attempt to satisfy his various bodily desires as normal; the monk will consider his decision to overeat as proper care for his body.[69] In other words, philautia is an irrationality that is quite adept at appearing rational. Its logic, however, is at odds with the struggle for Christian virtue and leads the believer to ascetic sluggishness. Saint Gregory of Sinai notes that philautia "induces us to choose bodily ease rather than virtue-promoting hardship, or to regard it as positive good sense not willingly to burden ourselves with ascetic labor."[70] Philautia is a struggle not only for those dwelling in the world or for those beginning the ascetic life, but also for the spiritually advanced who must rebut the suggestion that they should discontinue their ascetic endeavor on account of possible illnesses that the soul sick with philautia imagines.[71] Irrational philautia thus has considerable persuasive power that appears reasonable to the individual, because it makes him forget the deeper eternal meaning of life beyond this transient world.[72]

Philautia not only obstructs the path toward virtue, but also opens up the road to vice. For this reason Saint John of Damascus calls philautia "the begetter of the vices" and thus the ultimate cause of the eight bad thoughts.[73] According to Saint Hesychius the Presbyter, its winged children are "self-praise, self-satisfaction, gluttony, unchastity, vain-glory, jealousy, and the crown of all these, pride."[74] These children of philautia "fly," for they alter the soul's state with the speed of a flying object and cause the soul to feel a sudden rush of exaltation as though she were swept off the ground by a gust of wind. Of course, the soul is no longer in control, and this again bespeaks irrationality. Saint Maximus the Confessor likewise notes that philautia begets the three core passions of gluttony, avarice, and vainglory while speciously justifying their existence.[75] Love of the body makes the soul strive to please the body by feeding it with a glut of food, by protecting it with a surplus of money, and by admiring it with an excess of praise.

Saint Gregory of Sinai points out that someone who is ensnared by his own philautia loses his freedom and becomes enslaved to sensual pleasure and vanity. This dependence on his own enjoyment and status in turn damages his relationships with others, since his philautia embitters him with envy over his neighbor's prosperity.[76] In a similar vein, Saint Maximus the Confessor observes that philautia makes use of sophistry to justify cutting up our single human nature into many fragments. Once philautia has casuistically convinced a person to view others as thoroughly different and separate from him, it makes him insensitive as well.[77] Insensitivity to others coupled with a hypersensitivity to satisfying one's own desires are two aspects of philautia that give the impression that it is reasonable to hate those who thwart one's plans.[78] According to Abba Isaiah, philautia twists man into an unsociable and even anti-social being bereft of friendship, justice, and piety.[79] The evils of philautia are truly legion.

Saint John Chrysostom notices that philautia blindfolds us with blinders that can only be removed by those who are hostile to us. "Under the influence of philautia we do not see our own failings, while those who are hostile to us often see them quite accurately."[80] Alongside of this subjective blindness caused by philautia, there is also a broader forgetfulness that "breeds philautia." Saint Peter of Damascus observes that concern with pleasing the body eventually "entangles us in worldly concerns and in this way leads us to complete unawareness of God's gifts and of our own faults."[81] In like manner, Saint Maximus locates the source of philautia in ignorance of God.[82]

Philautia is obviously contrary to God's purpose for humanity. In a passage of extraordinary beauty, Abba Isaiah writes,

> Nature did not fashion human beings to be like solitary beasts, but rather like a flock of gregarious animals who share the same pastures, so that each person would live not only for himself, but also for his father and mother, for his siblings, for his spouse, for his children, for his other relatives, for his friends, for his fellow townsmen, for his fellow countrymen, for those living in his part of the world, for all humanity, even for every aspect of all things, for the entire world, and foremost for his God and Maker.[83]

The tragedy of human philautia is the tragedy of the seed that never becomes a towering fruit-bearing tree, "so that the birds of the air come and lodge in the branches thereof."[84] Instead of growing into an ever-enlarging sphere of love that eventually encompasses all humanity even as Christ's love embraced all mankind on the Cross, the soul distorted by philautia shrivels up into a pitiful ball of lust, greed, and isolation. All the wonderful potential with which man has been endowed is smothered and distorted by being directed to an unworthy aim, thereby leaving him trapped in the very small, the very stifling, and utterly subjective world of his own body.

To overcome this abnormal state, the fathers advise fighting philautia by thinking sensibly and acting prudently.[85] Instead of mulling over how to receive pleasure and avoid pain, Saint Maximus suggests lifting up one's thoughts to a spiritual knowledge of the Creator. By changing the object of one's affection, the believer can replace philautia fixated on the body with a spiritual philautia concentrated on cultivating the virtues and thereby worshiping God.[86] Behaviorally speaking, this new focus manifests itself by the exercise of self-control instead of self-indulgence.[87] Cognitively speaking, it is guided by deep-rooted faith in God.[88] In unison, faith, love, and self-control bring about a transformation that leaves no room for philautia in the human soul.

For the holy ascetics, removing philautia transfigures the way a person reasons, desires, and struggles by allowing a worthy goal to be placed before each of the soul's faculties. Saint Maximus the Confessor writes, "By our intelligence we should be stimulated to overcome our ignorance and to seek the one and only God by means of spiritual knowledge; through desire— through a passion of self-love which has been purified—we should be drawn to longing for the one God; and with an incensive power divorced from all tyrannical propensity we should struggle to attain God alone. From these three powers of the soul we should actualize that divine and blessed love on account of which they exist."[89] Thus, fighting philautia is not a negative act, but a positive transfiguration of the entire man aimed at nothing less than God who is love. When all the soul's faculties function naturally, a person is then able to see and interpret reality as it truly is. As Elder Païsios puts it in one letter, "If we could come out of ourselves (from our love of self), we would also break free from the earth's gravity, and then we would see everything clearly as it really is with a pure, divine, and penetrating eye."[90] When philautia is absent, it becomes easy to conquer all the passions,[91] for "not the slightest trace or form of evil can exist in any way at all."[92] In place of the shifting emptiness of philautia, the new man in Christ "is filled with that goodness which is stable and permanent and always remains the same."[93]

Employing psychological idiom, we can define philautia as a barely conscious counterproductive state of irrationality in which motivation and intentionality are hedonistically linked to present and anticipated pleasurable sensations of a physical and symbolic nature. In this state, specious arguments for desired ends seem persuasive and even peremptory. Philautia is also a condition with moral, social, and theological ramifications. It should be resisted, because it breeds the passions that disorient man, strip him of his freedom, and make him forgetful of God's gifts. Philautia also poisons his relationships with others, since someone who is infected with philautia [*ho philautos*] becomes unfriendly, insensitive, anti-social, unjust, and hostile to others. To overcome philautia, a person who believes deeply will strive to widen his friendly concerns to embrace others, to learn self-control, to reject the pleasure-pain cycle, to seek God, to long for him, and to struggle for his sake. When this takes place, even philautia can become a "good philautia" in which one is truly friends with oneself by cultivating the virtues, primarily the virtue of love for God and love for neighbor.

A Cognitive Understanding of Egocentricity

Turning now an anatomical eye to the cognitive view of psychopathology, we observe that the concept of egocentricity appears to occupy roughly the same theoretical position as that of philautia in patristic thought. Divergent moral evaluations that we encountered earlier when comparing schemata and passions should resurface as we contrast philautia and egocentricity. For psychologists, egocentricity is just part of being human. Developmentally speaking, juvenile thought processes and behavior are egocentric, because children have to attract the attention of others in order to provide for their needs and protection.[94] Furthermore, they are not yet aware of the needs and limitations of other people.[95] In general, living organisms, including human beings, are compelled to be egocentric in terms of protecting themselves and promoting their best interests if they are to survive.[96] Emergency responses across the animal kingdom are necessarily egocentric reactions based on an interpretation of how a danger might affect the organism. Even in more cognitively advanced contexts, a personally meaningful interpretation of a situation is the egocentric interpretation of how a set of circumstances relates to the person as the center of that situation.[97]

Cognitive psychologists theoretically understand egocentricity as a constructivist perspective that Donald Meichenbaum defines as "the idea that humans actively construct their personal realities and create their own representational models of the world."[98] In layman's terms, everybody responds to life by forming his own personal frame of reference that makes connections between himself and whatever he experiences in his environment. These subjective connections coalesce into a person's understanding of what the world is and how it operates. What someone subjectively understands to be reality, however, is not the same as the objective state of things as they actually exist, and may even be radically out of kilter with the real world.[99]

Mature individuals are well aware of the distinction between objective reality that may have little to do with them and their subjective understanding of the world. They are also able to shift between egocentric, constructivist modes of interpretation and impartial, objective approaches. Those with psychological disorders, however, have difficulty both making that distinction and shifting to an objective frame of mind, because they live "in a purely constructivist state."[100] In other words, people with psychological disorders view impersonal reality as personal and irrelevant events as directly relevant to themselves. Psychotic patients provide the most dramatic cases of excessive egocentricity and abnormal constructivist states. For example, a schizophrenic patient may answer back to actors on a television screen, because he egocentrically believes that they must be talking to him. Similarly, a psychotic depressive may read in the newspaper about a disaster in a foreign land and egocentrically hold himself personally responsible.[101] These two examples indicate that it is a mistake to hastily identify egocentricity with philautia, for in these cases, the primary problem is not love of self, sensuality, or a lack of concern for others, but an attribution error concerning relatedness.

In personality disorders, egocentricity is also a major factor. For example, those suffering from an anti-social personality disorder are unable to take on another person's perspectives or predict the reactions of others, because they are chiefly focused on satisfying their own desires. For instance, an employee who secretly "borrows" money from the cash register to pay off some debts is unable to understand why his employer and the authorities do not share his egocentric perspective, but instead view his clandestine activity as theft.[102] Those with a narcissistic personality disorder are likewise unaware of the boundaries and perceptions of others. For instance, the young woman who demands that her sick and indigent grandmother provide her with money for purchasing designer clothes is unable to understand how her behavior creates hardship for her grandmother, because she egocentrically believes that "granny needs the satisfaction of spoiling her sweet little granddaughter."[103] In these cases, the concepts of egocentricity and philautia coincide to a greater degree, without fully overlapping. Cognitive therapeutic goals are still framed more in terms of relatedness rather than in terms of selflessness: that is, the aim is for the patient to learn to recognize and consider other perspectives.

Less extreme examples of egocentricity are encountered in anxiety and mood disorders. For example, a depressed person meets a friend—who happens to be in a hurry and cuts short their conversation—and immediately assumes that his friend does not care about him (this may be true, but is probably false). Someone with acrophobia approaches a balcony, and suddenly imagines himself falling over the side (something that could happen, but most likely will not take place).[104] In these cases, philautia may contribute to egocentricity, but again should not be identified with it. In cognitive therapy, the patient would learn to test his egocentric conclusions and then alter his assumptions (schemata) for coping with similar situations.

In all the above examples, the patient's thoughts and behavior are inexplicable and even mystifying outside his subjective world, but understandable and reasonable within it. The therapist's task is to enter the subjective egocentric world of the patient in order to relate to and communicate with him. The therapist then has to convince the patient about the existence of an outside objective world and lead the patient out into the light of objectivity[105] in a manner not unlike the illumined prisoner in Plato's famous allegory of the cave.[106] Although the concepts of egocentricity and philautia may not coincide, the notion of widening one's world of concern certainly does.

Aside from psychological syndromes and disorders, egocentricity is obviously a problem in interpersonal relationships. Beck notes, "Interestingly, very few of us think to look for egocentricity in ourselves, although we are dazzled by it in others."[107] In the case of hostility, our egocentricity leads us to mistakenly believe that other people interpret certain behaviors or words as we do. This egocentric assumption makes them seem even guiltier in our minds, since we believe that they "really" know that they are hurting us.[108] Thus, egocentricity justifies a hostile response. In expressing anger, egocentricity likewise makes us focus on the relief and satisfaction we will feel by letting the other party know how we feel. Unfortunately, we fail to consider what effect that expression of anger will have on the other person; and so we unwittingly set in motion the vicious cycle of hurt and retaliation.[109]

In marital relationships, egocentricity leads each partner to assume that his or her expectations are natural and universal.[110] Ironically, when the other partner does not fulfill those expectations, because he or she is unaware of them, that partner is labeled as selfish by the other spouse. Often, egocentricity leads both parties to view themselves as reasonable and justified and the other as selfish and stubborn. In this case, egocentricity is a self-serving form of self-deception.[111] Even in the case of domestic violence, the husband who beats his wife sometimes egocentrically views himself as a "victim" of her words and his use of force as a means to restore balance to a relationship spinning out of control.[112]

Philautia and Egocentricity: Contrasting Perspectives on the Self

From the above examples, it should be clear that the surface similarity between *philautia* and egocentricity is deceptive. The two concepts differ by more than the presence or absence of a moral valence. First of all, the two concepts differ in range. Philautia is necessarily egocentric, but egocentricity is not necessarily an expression of philautia. Egocentricity is therefore a logically broader conceptual category than philautia. Second, egocentricity is about subjective ways of relating events and persons to the self that may lead to psychopathology, whereas philautia involves a particular kind of affectionate relationship to the self that indubitably leads to enslavement to the passions. In other words, philautia is more nosogenic than egocentricity. Third, egocentricity is treated by teaching the patient to test his egocentric conclusions for accuracy and to consider the perspective of other people, whereas philautia is fought by adopting a new hierarchy of values that transfigures the believer's relationship to God, himself, and others. Finally, egocentricity is about a misguided perspective, whereas philautia is a matter of misdirected love.

Nevertheless, the two ailments do share common symptoms that can result in misdiagnosis. Egocentricity and philautia lead to conclusions and behavior that an outside observer may find irrational, but the individual himself finds reasonable and compelling. Furthermore, an outsider can see another person's egocentricity or philautia better than the individual can see his own. Both conditions restrict freedom, narrow one's world, and contribute to insensitivity and hostility. Finally, both egocentricity and philautia can be tempered by knowledge that alters a person's center of attention.

The two concepts are clearly not synonymous, but they usually refer to complementary and inter-related conditions. Most people struggle with their own egocentricity and philautia as well as with the egocentricity and philautia of others. Notwithstanding, it is important for both the therapist and spiritual father to distinguish between the two. After all, an exhortation to fight philautia or love one's neighbor is not particularly helpful for the acrophobic struggling to overcome his fear of heights, nor is the suggestion to increase objectivity the best remedy for the Christian lacking zeal in prayer. Someone with a psychological disorder "may be callously selfish or too unselfish....But he is always egocentric in the sense of being wrapped up in himself."[113] Someone in need of repentance may hold to objective standards or subjective whims, but he is always bound by philautia and unable to see "the boundless horizons of love commanded of us."[114] Combating egocentricity and philautia can be seen as dual goals on separate, but related planes of reality. Notwithstanding, the prize for each victory is utterly incommensurate. Overcoming egocentricity, one becomes noticeably objective, the mark of a genuine scientist. Conquering philautia, one learns to truly love, the mark of the Triune God.

The Relevance of Childhood for Church Fathers and Cognitive Therapists

As comparative anatomists often conclude their studies of related structures by considering the findings of comparative embryology, so we will conclude our comparative exploration of psychopathology with a brief examination of childhood as the period of forgivable egocentricity that incubates so many maladaptive schemata. The foray of cognitive therapists into childhood memories serves larger goals such as shedding light on the patient's subjective world and discovering why maladaptive schemata in the form of assumptions and core beliefs seem so true. By learning details about how schemata were formed in childhood, both patient and therapist are better able to evaluate their significance in the present.

In cognitive therapy, delving into the patient's childhood is often seen as a detour from the here-and-now, problem-solving emphasis that characterizes most therapeutic interventions, especially in the case of anxiety and depression. Nevertheless, childhood factors may be explored when work on current problems brings little relief, when an understanding of how the patient's current dysfunctional beliefs originated is important, and when the patient expresses the desire to investigate his formative years.[115] Knowledge about childhood experiences and perceptions is in fact necessary when treating patients with personality disorders.[116]

One could also characterize patristic responses to those seeking advice as here-and-now, problem-solving approaches. Ascetics do not usually ask about the believer's childhood experiences when proffering advice, but they are nevertheless aware of the impact of childhood on a person's later life and struggles. Furthermore, they do encourage repentance and confession that encompass one's entire life (see also chapters 6 and 9).[117] At least in terms of emphasis, cognitive therapists and church fathers seem to agree with respect to the present relevance of one's childhood past. Whether that agreement overlays other similarities beneath the surface, only a closer look at both approaches will tell.

Patristic Views on Children and Their Development

The fathers considered the love of parents for their children to be a given. This love, however, was meant to be more than natural affection; it was to be expressed in the purposeful formation of human beings worthy of the kingdom of heaven.[118] To that end, the church fathers encouraged parents to provide their offspring with a sacred education[119] in the fear of God,[120] whereas the sacred canons anathematized those who failed to do so, even under the most noble of pretexts.[121] According to patristic writings, the parents' task was to shape the souls of their children by teaching them to be good,[122] meek, forgiving, helpful, and charitable, so that they would be able to endure every trial[123] and make their entire life a preparation for eternity.[124] Parents were expected to advise their children to despise wealth, to avoid extravagance, to govern their appetites as well as to become pious, modest, and affectionate.[125] In psychological terms, parental instruction was to focus on two sets of behavior encouraging (1) healthy interpersonal relationships and (2) self-control. In turn, these good habits would discourage the development of *philautia*. In short, parents were to direct their offspring to look to Christ who as a child and as a youth was the perfect example of piety, righteousness, and submission.[126] To make their children receptive to these teachings, the fathers also indicate that parents were expected both to pray for God to assist their children[127] and to live righteously,[128] "for the effectual fervent prayer of a righteous man availeth much."[129]

Of course, parental instruction, like learning in school, was to be appropriate to the child's stage of development. In advising Gaudentius how to raise his infant daughter, Saint Jerome asks rhetorically, "Will she listen to the profound teachings of the apostle when her sole delight is in nursery tales? Will she pay attention to the enigmatic sayings of the prophets when her nurse can frighten her with a frown?"[130] Since such material is still too advanced for the child, he advises teaching her to sing the psalms and then rewarding her with bright flowers, a shiny trinket, or a cute doll. The psalter, furthermore, teaches the child how to turn to God in joys and in sorrows. In another letter to Laeta, Saint Jerome with the acumen of a modern learning theorist advises, "You should not scold her if she is a slow learner, but you should instead use praise to stimulate her mind...Above all, you must be careful not to make her lessons distasteful to her, lest a dislike for them conceived in childhood continue into her maturer years."[131] These passages indicate that the fathers were not only concerned with what was transmitted to children, but also with how it was done.

Long before Piaget's landmark investigation of cognitive development during childhood, the church fathers were also aware that children have limitations in terms of the type of information that they can assimilate. For example, Saint Gregory of Nyssa mentions that children's understanding is restricted in terms of spatial relationships and mathematical operations.[132] He also observes that small children with their imperfect and immature intelligence "do not accurately understand what they see."[133] These remarks indicate a patristic awareness of a special cognitive vulnerability during childhood. Saint Neilus the Ascetic in particular notes that from birth until the age of twelve, youngsters are not able to make distinctions beyond what they sense, and are thus subject to the influence of the passions. At the time of an attack by the passions, the child does not understand what damage has taken place, but later in life he will come to understand the harm that was done.[134] Given the relationship between passions and schemata, this patristic observation coincides nicely with the psychological observation that children are not aware of the formation of core schemata, although these schemata have a great influence on their behavior and thought in adult life.

According to patristic writings, children are not only vulnerable to misconceptions and a misuse of the senses on account of their stage of cognitive development, they are also quite impressionable. In fact, Saint John Chrysostom notes, "What children hear is impressed as a seal on the wax of their minds. Besides [childhood] is when their life begins to be inclined toward vice rather than toward virtue."[135] Elsewhere, he likewise observes that wrong beliefs are often formed during childhood and grow as a person matures.[136] For that reason, care is needed during the formative years, for as Saint Gregory the Dialogist observes, "The words of those who bring up children will be either milk, if they are good, or poison if they are evil."[137]

The ancient ascetics were quite aware that the quality of parenting has a decisive impact on children. Abba Dorotheos mentions the example of two slave girls: one was adopted by a dancing troop mistress, whereas the other by a pious virgin. And he asks, "Is it possible for God to demand the same of each?"[138] If God takes into account one's upbringing, should not a spiritual father do likewise? Saint John Chrysostom points out that children turn out badly because of parental incompetence and negligence.[139] Children are detrimentally affected especially by spouses who do not love each other,[140] by parents who are more concerned with their offspring's possessions than with their upbringing,[141] and by relatives who expose their little ones to the theaters.[142] It is noteworthy that such conditions would impede the development of healthy interpersonal relationships and self-control, the patristic aims of good parenting. Saint Jerome considers it to be unnatural for the young to be raised in a climate of fear rather than love. He recalls an ancient proverb, "Whom a man fears he hates; and whom he hates, he would fain see dead."[143]

Apart from bad parenting, childhood traumas also have an effect on a person's psychological and spiritual life. Saint Cyprian of Carthage relates the case of a small child, not yet able to speak, being present at a pagan sacrifice unbeknownst to his Christian parents and given bread mingled with wine from the sacrifice. Whenever the child was brought into church, he would tremble and weep. Once when the priest communed the infant, the child began to wail and vomited up the Holy Communion. For Saint Cyprian, although the child was not responsible for what he suffered, the trauma remained and would have to be cleansed through the grace of confession.[144] The fathers also recognize that some childhood traumas can leave a permanent scar on a child that can even prevent, for example, a young man from becoming a priest.[145] Notwithstanding God has a special love for children who have been harmed by their parents or others and will provide them with divine help.[146]

Thus, for the fathers, experiences during childhood are imprinted on the soul; traumas leave their mark. As Saint Jerome put it, "Early impressions are hard to eradicate from the mind. Once wool has been dyed purple, who can restore it to its previous whiteness? An unused jar long retains the taste and smell of that with which it was first filled."[147] When reviewing the entire process of human development, Saint John Chrysostom likens a person's life to a ship voyaging through the tempestuous seas of childish folly, youthful lust, and adult cares and greed. The traumas of each period make a lasting impact on the vessel of the soul and without correction lead to shipwreck in this life and the next.[148] Thus, the church fathers advise care at every stage of life. Regardless of upbringing and trauma, a human being is called to sanctification, which includes setting aside childish ways and acquiring a mature reasonable perspective.[149]

In summary, the ancient fathers view childhood as an impressionable stage of life in which cognitive immaturity leaves children vulnerable to misunderstandings about themselves, their worlds, and others, as well as open to the development of the passions when proper parental guidance is absent. Parents are therefore called to provide their offspring with a loving and discerning education in piety that will cultivate love for God and neighbor as well as self-control and abstinence. Without such favorable conditions, children are left open to be traumatized by others and by themselves. Notwithstanding, by the grace of God healing is always possible through repentance, confession, an ascetic way of life, and participation in the other mysteries of the Church.

The Cognitive Role of Childhood Experiences in Psychopathology

Cognitive psychologists also view childhood as a cognitively vulnerable and impressionable stage of life. According to cognitive theory, as children mature, they struggle to understand themselves, other people, and their worlds by inventing hypotheses (e.g., "If I get dirty, Mommy will yell at me") and theories (for instance, "Getting dirty is awful") that serve as organizing concepts as to what is very good and very bad. These early childhood interpretive attempts are often quite flawed and lead them to extreme conclusions and inadequate coping strategies. Nevertheless, people tend to cling to existing schemata and try to force new data through them, even if those schemata are as inappropriate as using a cup to strike the side of a crib rather than to drink a glass of water. Unfortunately, when children are exposed to harsh parenting or subjected to traumatic experiences, they attribute negative qualities to themselves and conclude that they are basically helpless, unlovable, or worthless. These developmental core schemata together with the rules, assumptions, and strategies that they generate can be as debilitating as the cognitive distortions discussed earlier.[150] For example, a person with a borderline personality disorder often views himself as worthless or unlovable and functions on the basis of rules such as "If I depend on someone, I will be abused," assumptions such as "I deserve punishment," and strategies such as relieving tension through self-mutilation.[151]

In order to bring to light schemata that were formed during early life, but continue to disturb the patient today, the therapist is sometimes obliged to explore "such significant events as continual or periodic strife among parents or other family members, parental divorce, negative interactions with parents or other family members, peers, or others in which the child felt blamed, criticized or otherwise devalued; illness, death of significant others, physical or sexual abuse and other conditions....The relevant childhood data may, however, be more subtle; for example, the child's perception (which may or may not be valid) that the parents favored a sibling over her; the child's continual self criticism."[152] In short, the therapist needs to examine troubling or painful memories that shape how the patient functions today.

When cognitive therapists examine these factors, they implicitly recognize the Freudian process of transference in which "a piece of unresolved history from past relationships gets projected onto people in the present."[153] Thus, one's interpretation of the present is biased by interference from the past. Harry Stack Sullivan noted the cognitive implications of transference when he wrote, "The principal handicap to alertness is that peculiar misidentification of events which arises from unresolved situations in the person's chronological past. The emotionally toned remnants of earlier difficulties complicate the present situation and befog the field of observation."[154] From this perspective, one can see that the befogging effects of childhood interpretations and earlier developmental experiences produce a particular kind of cognitive distortion that requires special interventions. In practical terms, this transference means a person will misread current life events as reinforcing his distress over being a failure, ugly, or bad, which ultimately stems from his underlying beliefs about helplessness, unlovability, or worthlessness, respectively. [155]

Beck explains that the purpose of reviewing childhood material is to "open up windows for understanding the origins of non-adaptive patterns. This approach can increase perspective and objectivity."[156] By way of illustration, in the case of substance abuse, childhood information can help both the patient and the therapist to understand how drug abuse is a continuation of juvenile ways of reacting to painful situations or escaping from them. For example, someone with the schema, "it's terrible to be left alone" might self-medicate by abusing drugs in response to deaths in the family. Thus, re-evaluating that schema can be helpful in preventing a relapse.[157] In paranoia, a lack of consistent parental love trains a person to expect sadistic treatment from others and to be unduly vigilant for the sake of self-protection.[158] In obsessive-compulsive personality disorder, contradictory parental messages lead to a need for certainty, thereby producing rigid thinking about what a person definitely should and should not do.[159]

Examining early life experiences, interpretations, and schemata in cognitive therapy is always more pragmatic than speculative. The ultimate goal is to correct present cognitive distortions and maladaptive schemata in order to produce less distressful emotional responses and more adaptive behavior. Cognitive distortions and maladaptive schemata formed by childhood interpretations and theories, like other thinking errors, *can* be corrected. As Harry Stack Sullivan puts it, "Unfortunate experience at any developmental phase may do great damage to one's possibilities of future interpersonal relations—and curiously enough, equally true—very fortunate experience at any developmental stage may do much to remedy the limitations already introduced by previous developmental misfortunes."[160] Cognitive therapy endeavors to offer such a fortunate experience. Of course, merely talking about childhood interpretations and traumas often fails to provide such a corrective experience, since discussion usually provides no more than an interesting insight into why a person has negative beliefs. It is therefore often necessary to recreate past situations through role-play and reverse role-play, so that the maladaptive schemata are emotionally activated and made accessible for re-evaluation using typical cognitive methods.[161] In other words, when a new, more accurate narrative is created, the traumatic past is separated from the present,[162] and cognitive restructuring can occur, enabling the memories to be stored differently, because the meaning assigned to those memories has been altered.[163] In some conditions, such as borderline personality disorder, a "re-parenting" approach is called for, in which caring acceptance provides the secure attachment missing in childhood.[164]

The Lingering Affects of Childhood

When I was a child, I spake as a child, I understood as a child, I thought
as a child: but when I became a man, I put away childish things.
—1 Corinthians 13:11

Contrasting patristic and cognitive conceptualizations of the role of childhood experiences in the growth of vice and in the development of psychopathology respectively, we note a common awareness that children's cognitive skills are limited and their inferences are often flawed. Both church fathers and cognitive therapists recognize that the effects of bad parenting and traumas linger into adult life. Both view the possibility of healing by altering the narrative in which childhood memories are stored. In the patristic case, this is done through confession that brings the presence of God's grace, love, and forgiveness into the believer's personal history (see chapters 6 and 9).

There are, however, differences in focus. Cognitive theory within Beck's works concentrates on the patient's negative schemata formed by bad parenting, without providing a prototype for good parenting.[165] Patristic teaching zeroes in on preventing bad parenting by advising mothers and fathers both what to teach their little ones and how to do so, so that their offspring might not remain infants, but develop into "the measure of the stature of the fullness of Christ."[166] The two sides of this equation, however, can be related. Cognitive theorists indicate that harsh parenting causes children to develop schemata revolving around the themes of helplessness, unlovability, and worthlessness. Church fathers point out that good parenting teaches children self-control by instructing them to despise wealth and to govern their appetites as well as to cultivate good interpersonal relationships by encouraging them to be forgiving, helpful, and charitable. It is unlikely that someone who learns to disdain riches and to control himself will be crippled by maladaptive schemata regarding helplessness. It is also improbable that someone who truly follows Christ's example and strives to be helpful, meek, and good will develop maladaptive schemata concerning worthlessness. Finally, someone who learns to be magnanimous will not likely be stricken with schemata about being unlovable, for he will have learned to forgive others and to love them by watching his parents both forgive him and love him at home as well as by experiencing God's forgiveness and love in Church.

Cognitive therapy introduces a number of useful concepts without parallel in patristic tradition. It explicitly refers to childhood theories and hypotheses that make sense out of life and result in the formation of schemata. It utilizes the originally psychoanalytic notion of transference to provide insight into the way in which the patient's unfortunate experiences in the past continue to influence how he interprets and reacts to events in the present. It employs techniques such as role-play and re-parenting in order to offer a new learning experience instrumental in altering those maladaptive schemata. Rich in tools, but necessarily poor in values, cognitive theory would be well served if it were supplemented by the fathers' counsel on parenting. It should also be noted that patristic advice to parents is also the advice given to all Christians in order to grow in virtue. In other words, when a person enters into the bosom of the Church, at any age, the Church provides that person with a new learning experience that naturally re-parents him in a world where reconciliation, forgiveness, and love can be found.

Comparative Anatomy: The Value of Divergence

When we looked back over our patristic voyage through the cognitive model at the close of chapter three, we concluded that church fathers and cognitive psychologists make similar observations concerning the way a person's interpretations shape his thoughts, mood, and behavior. We also noted that those ancient luminaries consistently pointed beyond those cognitive mechanisms to the spiritual dimension and eternal significance of those transitory processes. In this chapter, we have probed the anatomy of psychological and spiritual pathology, and encountered a similar patristic insistence that human dysfunction at the thought level stems from man's improper relationship with God as expressed by sins of thought, as described by philautia, and as first appearing during childhood. Via notions about good and bad parenting, we found some correlation between patristic and cognitive evaluations of childhood influences, but little correspondence in terms of understanding how those influences function in later life. In particular, psychologists offer a description of psychological mechanisms such as children's hypothesis formation and adult transference processes, whereas the fathers describe the prototype of healthy interpersonal relationships and self-control that Christian virtue and abstinence provide.

As for psychological notions of cognitive distortions and egocentricity, although they bear a functional similarity to ascetic notions of bad thoughts and *philautia*, they are in fact as anatomically related as are the wings of a swallow to those of a bumblebee. In terms of a one-to-one structural correspondence, there are no interchangeable parts. This lack of direct correspondence between the two sets of concepts, however, does not require the rejection of one set of concepts, but rather the appropriate use of both sets that can be understood as pertaining to distinct yet parallel planes of reality. Together, these concepts can bring much needed clarity to widespread muddled thought about a whole family of notions—such as philautia, selfishness, egotism, egoism, and egocentricity—that are unfortunately used more or less interchangeably. Knowledge of the difference between egocentricity and philautia can be applied diagnostically to determine whether a person is struggling primarily with a spiritual or a psychological condition, so that the appropriate help can be offered. Familiarity with cognitive distortions can provide the pastor with an additional tool for working with those who weigh their every decision in the balance of reason. An awareness of the eight bad thoughts can provide therapists with some sense of ethical direction in the unmarked moral desert of psychological advice. In unison, patristic wisdom and cognitive psychological findings can help us to understand those suffering with their thoughts and to assist them appropriately. Both approaches are useful. After all, the all-wise Creator has given wings to the bumblebee and the swallow alike, so that they both might fly.

The Fisherman's Art and the Scientist's Method: Two Images for Metacognition and Two Types of Education

If voyagers' memoirs are of interest to cartographers, if anatomical charts are useful to surgeons, the value of such knowledge lies in its preliminary guidance either for making a map to some destination or for locating an organ in need of surgical treatment. In the previous two chapters, we took a patristic look at analogous sources of information by exploring the cognitive model and the cognitive theory of psychopathology. Like voyagers' memoirs and anatomical charts, our exploration also provides preliminary guidance. The cognitive model suggests that psychological disorders may be treated by purposefully modifying the patients' thoughts in order to alter their emotional and behavioral responses. The cognitive understanding of psychopathology indicates that this can take place if patients learn to recognize cognitive distortions and acquire more objective perspectives on their situations. Cognitive theorists call this process *metacognition*. It is a mental skill that humans use as innately as peoples living by the sea learn to fish. And as inlanders can be trained in the fisherman's art, so patients can be coached in effective metacognition through patient education.

In cognitive theory, metacognition refers to "thought about thought" in which a person examines and evaluates his personal theories and hypotheses about himself, others, and his world, thereby regulating his core schemata, assumptions, and rules. Beck views metacognition as a cognitive system designed to consciously control and sometimes override primitive thinking that characterizes the rest of the animal kingdom.[1] In a strikingly similar vein, Saint Anastasius of Sinai once observed that man differs from beast by virtue of his ability to consider, to decide, and to will, thereby overruling the instinctual reactions that he shares with other living creatures.[2]

When the church fathers use these higher mental processes in order to carefully examine their thoughts, cognitive theorists would be inclined to label that activity in scientific terms as metacognition. In like manner, when cognitive therapists try to improve a person's metacognitive skills, the hesychastic fathers might see that attempt as akin to teaching someone the spiritual fisherman's art of catching the thoughts and weighing them in the balance of the heart. In both spiritual and psychotherapeutic contexts, we encounter an association between the use of higher mental faculties and the process of recovery or a state of health. In order to discern what this similarity means in frames of reference as unlike as a fresh water brook and the deep salt sea, both spiritual fishermen and cognitive scientists must look carefully beneath the surface of corresponding concepts.

The Rational Will, the Monarchy of the Mind, and the Tripartite Soul

In chapter three we noted that the ancient fathers often contrast a reasonable mode of responding to situations that is akin to metacognitive processes with an impulsive passionate mode akin to primitive reactions. Saint Paul made this distinction when he wrote to the Romans, "For I delight in the law of God after the inward man: But I see another law in my members, warring against the law of my mind, and bringing me into captivity to the law of sin which is in my members."[3] This same distinction can be seen in the Church's evaluation of the actions of saints and sinners. On the one hand, saints are lauded in the liturgical services for sagaciously enthroning a wise thought as the emperor of the mind ruling over the unreasonable passions of the body by means of the divine law.[4] On the other hand, unrepentant sinners are rebuked by their spiritual fathers for abandoning their wiser thoughts at the time of temptation.[5] These two ways of responding are often understood in terms of the will. Saint Nicodemos the Hagiorite refers to a higher logical will and a lower irrational will reacting to sense perceptions.[6] What is meant by a higher logical will?

The monothelite controversy of the seventh century obliged the church fathers to investigate the rational will as a faculty inherent in human nature. In Saint Maximus's disputation with Pyrrhos, the temporarily deposed monothelite patriarch of Constantinople, the saint observed that human nature has "a logical appetite that is also called the will of the noetic soul. By an act of will, we consider. By considering and willing, we take counsel. By an act of will, we inquire, deliberate, take counsel, judge, are disposed, choose, are moved to action, and act."[7] The ubiquity of the will in all these higher mental functions indicates that the person is actively present in a particularly conscious, particularly metacognitive way. In slightly more analytical terms, Saint John of Damascus delineates the cognitive processes involved in volition as follows: "After wish follows inquiry and speculation, and after these, if the object is within our power, comes counsel or deliberation: counsel is an appetite for investigating lines of action lying within our power. For one deliberates, whether or not to prosecute any matter, and then decides which is better, and this is called judgment."[8] In these passages, monastic theologians describe a logical, active, and incremental problem-solving approach that is built on self-conscious observation and linked to reflection in terms of feasibility, utility, and value. Such reflection is central to therapeutic metacognitive evaluations that we shall examine later.

Employing an atomistic approach to complex thought processes involved in volition, Saint Maximus the Confessor avails himself of the originally Stoic concept of a mental first movement that coalesces into a conception that can be articulated. For the saint, prudent understanding [phronēsis] occurs when that conception lingers and is cross-examined [basanisasa: lit., tortured], so that one's mental field of vision can be widened.[9] The notion of cross-examination coincides with the concept of metacognition as an attempt to understand one's thoughts; whereas the resultant altered perspective reflects the successful outcome of metacognitive insight. Prudence can thus be understood as a metacognitive process involving a refined use of common sense via the posing of questions. Prudence presupposes reliance on volition and right reason to define and to formulate a course of action. The saint contrasts prudence dealing with practical matters with wisdom construed as theoretical insight into the inner reasons of being.[10] This contrast is consistent with the conventional association of psychology with prudential discourse about practical matters and philosophy with theoretical discourse about wisdom.

According to patristic teachings, deliberative, prudent, common-sense processes that characterize the higher will are meant to illumine human decisions, guide human activity, and solve human problems. These processes include formal methods of logic and reasoning that many church fathers deployed so impressively in their disputations with heretics.[11] Notwithstanding, logic in the believer's hands is just a useful tool, not the philosopher's stone. Origen errs not by maintaining that no problem in ethics, or physics, or theology "can be properly conceived without accurately finding the meaning and without close regard to the clear rules of logic,"[12] but by making logic, rather than faith, the principle means for interpreting revelation.

With a masterly use of political imagery, Saint Gregory of Nyssa refers to "a praiseworthy tyranny allied with wisdom that transforms the democracy of the passions into a monarchy of the mind, bringing into subjection that which was wrongly let loose in liberty."[13] If we identify the monarchy of the mind [nous] with metacognition, this passage bespeaks the considerable effort [tyrannis: lit., tyranny] required for metacognition to prevail over primitive reactions as well as the way metacognitive processes introduce order and control to the mental life. Similar allusions are prevalent throughout patristic literature. For example, Saint Thalassius writes, "The true ruler is he who rules over himself and has subjected soul and body to reason [logos]."[14] Saint Maximus the Confessor additionally notes that reason is a skill that can be learned and applied to living and behavior: "Everyone should be taught to live and govern himself according to reason [logos] alone."[15]

For psychologists, the above passages call attention to the human ability to over-ride impulses by higher and more complex cognitive processes that a person can learn and use to shape how he reacts to situations. Although the above fathers commend a praiseworthy tyranny, rule, and governance, it is not the individual who is tyrannized, but his passions, which we earlier character-ized as dysfunctional schemata. The person is in fact free, for he follows the "true law of nature formed according to the image of God and true reason [ratio], the sign bearer of liberty."[16]

Being well versed in classical literature, some church fathers were wont to look through the lens of the platonic theory of the tripartite soul to discern the way in which reason [logos] rules over the passions in a healthy soul. On the surface, metacognition seems to correspond to the reasoning faculty [logistikon] and primitive thinking to the desiring [epithymētikon] and aggressive [thymitikon] faculties. Such surface resemblance, however, does not take into account how platonic theory changes in patristic hands.

For ancient ascetics, a prudent thought does not seek to quell all forms of yearning and zeal, but to prevent behavior stemming from improper desires or unjustified anger.[17] Maintaining that anger and desire have providentially been placed within human nature, Saint Macrina poses the following rhetorical questions: "If love is taken from us, how shall we be united to God? If anger is to be extinguished, what arms shall we possess against the adversary?"[18] Thus, a carefully formulated reasonable thought "is not the uprooter of the passions, but their opponent"[19] that aims at putting desire and anger to proper use.[20] According to Evagrius and Abba Dorotheos, the Christian objective is for "the desiring faculty to yearn for virtue, the aggressive faculty to struggle to attain virtue, and the reasoning faculty to behold created things."[21]

Such a state of spiritual health requires great effort to the point of spiritual warfare, since the devil uses the desiring and aggressive faculties together with the five senses to overcome the rational aspect, so that people will act unjustly, foolishly, licentiously, and cowardly.[22] Without this struggle to rebut passionate thoughts, the reasoning faculty is prone to "abandon its control and hand the reins over to the aggressive faculty, and so let the latter go unchecked."[23] When this happens, bad thoughts confuse the mind by clouding its mental vision so that it can no longer see properly,[24] and instead supposes that objects are much more worthy of love or hatred than they really are.[25] Thus, spiritual factors affect metacognitive processes and can make the effort required to engage in metacognition greater than psychologists might suspect.

The problem with identifying metacognition with the rational aspect of the tripartite soul is that such identification confuses the faculties as structural elements of the human soul with metacognition as a way of processing information. If we assume that metacognition takes place in or through the reasoning faculty, we do see a similar corrective function at work. In their ideal form, there is a harmony in the relationship between the faculties, whereas in their fallen form, they are at odds or sometimes cause dysfunctional thought and behavior, as is manifest in psychopathology.[26] It is noteworthy that for the church fathers, the faculties are healed not by imposing improved logic on an individual, but by opening up the way to more intimate communion with God through the ascetic and sacramental life.[27] For ancient ascetics, the *nous* or spiritual heart illumined by the grace of the Holy Spirit, ultimately, restores harmony to the other faculties. The illumined *nous*, however, has no analogue in cognitive theory. Rather than aligning theories that are not amenable to such alignment, it is more helpful to consider patristic examples of mental processes that can clearly be characterized as metacognitive.

Fishermen by the Sea: the Art of Spiritual Vigilance

The chief context in which the monastic fathers discuss the use of the rational faculty or the higher logical will is the Christian struggle to live according to the commandments of Christ. The virtuous life is far from the unexamined life, for it requires believers to attend strictly to themselves by paying heed to their thoughts.[28] This occurs in two basic situations: in their dealings with others and in solitary introspective prayer.

In the course of social interactions, believers need to be vigilant over their thoughts and ready to mentally step back and weigh their choices at times of uncertainty or temptation. This involves a stance of wariness vis-à-vis one's thoughts and interpretations, especially when one is inclined to judge or condemn others. In his characteristically whimsical manner, Elder Païsios advises a nun, "Is everything really the way it appears to you? Always put a question mark after every thought, since you usually look at things with a negative slant...If you put two question marks it is better. If you put three, it is better still."[29] The fathers knew full well that questioning a thought undermines its authority and decreases its influence. They also knew that such cross-examination requires effort. In the case of self-pity, Saint Barsanouphius remarked, "It is amazing how the human mind gets cloaked...not letting the person ask himself, why are you troubled? Why are you troubled, my soul, hope in the Lord."[30]

At times, the examination of a thought involves rapidly considering possible outcomes by weighing the hypothetical advantages and disadvantages of choices one can make or by recalling the real benefit and harm of similar decisions one has made in the past. For example, if a carnal desire is aroused after gazing upon a beautiful face, Saint Neilus the Ascetic suggests that the tempted individual make use of "the short period of time available for careful reflection, so that he can examine and discern what is harmful and what is beneficial as well as how sorrowful he will feel after engaging in illicit pleasure and how much satisfaction and joy he will have when good thoughts blossom forth."[31] Likewise, Saint John Climacus proposes that a person who has yielded to carnal pleasures reflect on his lost purity as a way of preventing further descent into the pit of sensuality.[32] In other words, when a similar situation arises, the good abbot of Sinai advises recalling a past fall in order to prevent its reoccurrence.

Of course, questions have been used to change another person's focus from time immemorial when Adam was in hiding and God asked him the question, "Where art thou?"[33] Patriarchs, prophets, apostles, and even Christ posed questions to open the minds of their listeners to truths as yet beyond their reach. Elder Païsios suggests that the best way to help someone who is indifferent is by making him blessedly uneasy, so that he will question himself.[34] There are abundant examples in patristic tradition of those blessed to encounter someone who could ask the right questions at the right time, thereby redirecting a person's thoughts in a proper direction (see chapter 9).

For example, once when a monk was tempted by a young maiden, the girl wisely asked him,

> "How may years have you been in the monastery?"
> "Seventeen years."
> And again she said to him, "Have you ever been with a woman before?"
> "No," he answered.

She then replied, "And you want to lose all your toils for one hour? How many tears have you shed so that your body would appear pure before Christ? Do you wish to lose all that labor for a little pleasure?"
In the end, the monk gratefully left the girl and went back to his monastery.[35]

In psychological terms, the appropriate questions convinced the monk to consider in detail the consequences of his behavioral choices, thereby shifting his mode from primitive desire to metacognitive re-evaluation that resulted in a quite different behavioral outcome.

The life of Saint Symeon the New Theologian narrates a similar use of questioning. Once when a sick monk was eating meat during the fast, another brother's countenance darkened from critical thoughts about the infirm brother. Saint Symeon then made use of questions to alter the judgmental brother's focus: "Arsenios, why don't you pay attention to yourself as you stoop over your bread instead of glancing furtively at your brother who is eating meat on account of illness? You wrestle with your thoughts and still think that you exceed him in piety, because you are eating vegetables. Didn't you hear Christ say that it is 'not that which goeth into the mouth that defileth a man?' Why don't you think sensibly?"[36] Thus, the appropriate questions wisely framed by the clairvoyant abbot opened up the critical brother's vision to a new perspective on the situation, leading him to compunction, humility, and compassion.

The other setting in which the fathers engage in "thought about thought" is solitary hesychastic prayer. In particular, monks remain in their cells in order to concentrate and to make their inner vision clearer.[37] They also benefit from the serenity of the night that lends itself to vigilance.[38] With this restriction of audial and visual stimuli, the mind becomes both calmer and more capable of self-examination. An ascetic way of life is consequently quite helpful for examining the thoughts. Calm conditions are so important that Kallistos Tilikoudis writes, "Repentance is not possible without stillness [hēsychia]."[39]

The ancient ascetics often liken this hesychastic [hēsychastikē] self-examination to the fisherman's art. "When the sea is calm, fishermen can scan its depths and therefore hardly any creature moving in the water escapes their notice."[40] According to this evocative metaphor, a person separates himself so thoroughly from his thoughts that they become like fish swimming in the sea and he comes to resemble a fisherman looking into its depths. This objectification of subjective thoughts requires a mind as calm as the sea on a windless day as well as the possession of knowledge about the thoughts and observational skills like unto those of a fisherman who knows the ways of fish in the deep. Above all, success in this endeavor requires a union with Christ in the heart through the invocation of his holy name that illumines the darkest reaches of the soul. In unison, the proper conditions, the appropriate skills, and the name of Christ enable the believer to distinguish good thoughts from bad ones. According to Saints John Climacus and John Cassian, a monk not only observes thoughts, like a fisherman spotting fish, but also catches them.

Saint Cassian, in particular, elaborates on the fisherman metaphor by describing the monk as "someone who keeps his body and soul continually shut up and enclosed within walls, so that he might eagerly and motionlessly catch the swarms of thoughts swimming in the calm depths of his heart. Like a splendid fisherman looking out for food for himself by the apostolic art, his inquisitive eye surveys the depths as though he were seated on a high rock from which he sagaciously and cunningly decides what he ought to lure to himself by his saving hook and what he can neglect and reject as bad and nasty fish."[41] For the saint, the hesychastic examination of the thoughts is a dynamic art that involves closely scrutinizing and dispassionately analyzing the contents of a collected mind in order to preserve thoughts that inspire the soul and to reject those that fail to do so.

For the ancient hesychasts, the spiritual fisherman's art hooks a natural alertness to careful discrimination. Saint Hesychius the Presbyter compares the alertness of the spiritual fisherman with the way people protect their eyes from any foreign object by rapidly shifting their gaze.[42] Saint John Cassian likens the discrimination of the spiritual fisherman to the act of placing a thought on the balance of the heart to determine "whether it be filled with the common good, heavy with the fear of God, and completely solid in meaning, or whether it be hollowed out by human display, the conceit of novelty, and the pride of foolish vainglory that diminishes and lessens the weight of its merit." With full awareness that one's personal scale may not be properly calibrated, the saint further suggests that this initial weighing of the thoughts be followed by "weighing them in the public balance, that is, testing them by the acts and proofs of the apostles and prophets."[43]

Just as a fisherman's desire to catch fish motivates him to learn where to go fishing, how to draw near his maritime prey, and what kind of bait to use, so the spiritual fisherman's yearning for the Lord motivates him to fully examine his thoughts by learning the causal relationships among them.[44] For Saint Maximus the Confessor, the believer pays close attention to any improper thoughts in order to recognize and eliminate their causes.[45] In fact, the spiritual fisherman is also a true philosopher who exercises self-control with respect to passionate impulses and studies how to rectify them.[46] To this end, he learns to detect the premonitory signs that make certain thoughts seem attractive and compares them with the ultimate results that are often repulsive.[47]

Evagrius Ponticus notes that when the believer scrutinizes a bad thought by determining what aspects of the thought are evil and what aspects are neutral, he saps the thought of its power.[48] Saint John Cassian advises analyzing thoughts in terms of their origin, cause, and author. During analysis, there are certain dangers of which the believer should be aware. An attractive style or philosophical sophistication can disguise a bad thought. Bad thoughts can even be formulated in scriptural or patristic terms, although they misinterpret the scriptures and the fathers' writings by suggesting inappropriate feats of piety or by justifying self-serving interpretations. Even thoughts cloaked with a veil of compassion and seeming godliness may be unsound.[49] Since the separation of style from substance is sometimes daunting, the believer needs recourse to a spiritual father when sorting out questionable thoughts.

From the above discussion, we can see that the ancient ascetics have an extensive and nuanced understanding of "thought about thought," that is, metacognition. For the church fathers, metacognition is associated with prudence involved in the higher mental processes of investigation, deliberation, and judgment that adjudicate the feasibility, utility, and value of a thought, opinion, or belief. Metacognition is both a control mechanism innate to human psychological makeup and a learned process like the fisherman's art that can be perfected. The tri-partite soul presupposes that reason can direct desire and anger to appropriate goals. The reality of wayward sensuality and volatile irascibility indicates that effort is required for those goals to be consistently reached. In the spiritual life, metacognition plays a vital role in the believer's struggle to live in accord with the commandments of Christ. In social interactions, metacognition occurs when the believer questions the validity of his thoughts and weighs the advantages and disadvantages of implementing them. In solitary prayer, it takes place when he observes the thoughts like a fisherman who watches for fish and then weighs them in the balance of Christ's teachings when his mind is in a calm and prayerful state.

Tertium Quid or *Sine Qua Non*: the Mode of Faith

Although our discussion of the fisherman's art, the rational will, the monarchy of the mind, and the rational faculty provides ample fodder for the comparative gristmill, we have not yet threshed out "the one thing needful"[50] that makes the patristic use of reason patristic: that is, the presence of the grace of God. In addition to a primitive mode of passion and a metacognitive mode of reason, the man of faith knows a third state in which he experiences divine grace through the spiritual heart that is also called the *nous*. Saint Mark the

Ascetic observes, "The nous changes from one to another of three different noetic states: that according to nature, above nature, and contrary to nature." He then notes both the behavioral and cognitive components of each condition. In the natural state, people can confess their sins and understand the cause of bad thoughts and passions. In a state contrary to nature, they fight with others and feel as though they have been mistreated. In the state above nature, they experience the fruits of the Holy Spirit such as love, peace, joy, warmth, compunction, and tears that bring divine illumination as well as noetic radiance revealing the will of God.[51]

Among the choir of the holy fathers, Saint Isaac the Syrian voiced the most detailed exploration of the mode of faith in contrast with the mode of reasoning. According to this master of the spiritual life, the mode of faith is "single, limpidly pure, and simple, far removed from any deviousness or invention of methods."[52] From this short description, we see that the mode of faith resembles the way in which people perceive external reality, rather than the mental process of conceiving an idea. In fact, the saint notes that the mode of faith involves a "perception of what is hidden" or initially invisible, that later by divine vision becomes visible as well.[53] Consequently, the mode of faith is more refined than the mode of reasoning, even as thought is subtler than action.[54] Through faith, believers see God's providence, protection, and care in their lives; they understand how thoughts are interrelated and perceive where bad thoughts lead. This in turn brings them to the realization that they must pray to God for all things, both great and small.[55] The mode of faith thus alters human awareness.

The mode of faith also affects how the believer evaluates situations. Saint Isaac writes, "When grace is abundant in man, he easily scorns the fear of death, because he longs for righteousness and finds in his soul many reasons why suffering tribulation is necessary for the sake of the fear of God." Thus, when grace is present in the soul, the believer can think and act independently of psychological rules or schemata for promoting personal safety and pleasure. However, when grace is absent, a person necessarily relies on his reason for investigating and solving problems instead of trusting in God.[56] In a passage capturing the meticulous calculations of knowledge and the incalculable possibilities of faith, Saint Isaac writes,

> Knowledge enjoins all those who journey on its path to investigate according to its laws the end result before making a beginning, and only then commence, lest labor be spent in vain, because the final state proves to be unachievable within the limit of human ability and difficult to realize. But what does faith say? "All things are possible to him that believeth," for to God nothing is impossible. O unspeakable wealth, O ocean rich in billows with marvelous treasures which abundantly spill forth by the power of faith.[57]

Faith and grace open up for the believer a world of possibilities unknown to reason on its own.

Although the states of metacognition and faith are distinct, they can work in unison. In fact, whereas reason alone may not be strong enough to overcome bad thoughts, reason united with the power of Christ can even extinguish the fire of the passions, the very source of such thoughts.[58] According to Saint Ilias the Presbyter, the best defense against bad thoughts is "the alliance of the nous with the reason and of the reason with sense-perception."[59] The nous here signifies the presence of active communion with God in the heart by faith. Saint John Cassian relates how the centurion in the gospel appropriately combined faith ("Speak the word only, and my servant shall be healed") and reason ("For I also am a man under authority") in approaching Christ. From this example, Saint Cassian concludes that the Christian can also be healed of bad thoughts by joining right reason to the power of the Cross.[60]

In general, the monastic fathers make use of this alliance of reason with the illumined heart when they advise, comfort, and exhort the faithful (see chapter 9). For example, Saint Maximus the Confessor advises those envious of their brethren's spiritual gifts to free themselves of envy by using their reason to consider two truths of the spiritual life: grace is given according to one's faith and how much a person believes depends on his own disposition.[61] Saint Basil the Great comforted his friend Nektarios over the loss of his son by inviting him to use "the gift which God has stored in our hearts," that is, the sobering thought that others also suffer, in order to confront his own trials in a more courageous way.[62] Saint Neilus exhorted Vindiki to use right reason to achieve appropriate regret over sins of the flesh, so that he might be freed from them.[63]

A final beneficial function of reasoning vis-à-vis faith is reason's role in the acquisition of knowledge. According to Saint Maximus the Confessor, the rational faculty is indispensable for knowledge, and knowledge is necessary for faith and hope.[64] Elsewhere, the saint notes that the right use of reason gives rise to prudence; prudence put into action begets virtue; and virtue opens the believer's eyes to faith that leads him to the Good itself.[65] Saint Isaac the Syrian likewise maintains that knowledge can be perfected by a heart that believes and employed as "a step whereby one can climb up to the heights of faith."[66]

Although the church fathers employed reason as an effective tool in the hands of faith, they were aware that others could misuse reason as an implement for undermining Christian beliefs. In this case, reason becomes the wisdom of the world that is foolishness with God, or even enmity against God.[67] The history of heresy is a tale of reason being misapplied to matters of faith. At the level of daily life, Elder Païsios observes how loving one's neighbor according to the gospel and acting in one's best interests according to society are rationales that are irreconcilable.[68] The logic of the gospel, which gives the same to the worker of the eleventh hour as to the first, will seem from a human perspective to be folly.[69] It is foolish, however, because reason is put to wrong use in order to judge a higher wisdom beyond reason's reach. According to Saint Neilus the Ascetic, such a misuse of reason is akin to an inexperienced apprentice judging a master craftsman's decisions on the grounds of what appears to be reasonable. The apprentice's reason has more in common with delusion than with rationality.[70]

For Saint Isaac the Syrian, people reason in a blameworthy manner when they attribute all success to human ability and methods instead of also recognizing God's providence. This attributional error makes people proud and presumptuous. In relationships with others, those who reason in this way will be more inclined to use their methods and abilities to investigate their neighbor's weaknesses rather than to love their brother or sister as a fellow child of God. In theory and in practice, blameworthy reasoning blinds people to the spiritual life[71] and "renders the soul cold to works that go in pursuit of God."[72] It should be clear why the hesychast bishop of Nineveh views human knowledge "with all the intricacies of its subtlety and all the convolutions of its method" as a potential obstacle for those who wish to reach the purity and simplicity of spiritual knowledge.[73]

In considering reason devoid of faith, Saint Isaac notes, "Knowledge everywhere sings the praises of fear....Fear is followed by doubt; doubt is followed by investigation; investigation is followed by ways and means; ways and means are followed by knowledge. Fear and doubt are always recognized in examination and investigation, for knowledge does not always succeed everywhere."[74] In other words, human reasoning cannot escape the limitations of the human condition besieged by manifold dangers and inexorable death. This is why the difference between reason bereft of faith and reason aligned with Christian beliefs becomes most apparent at the time of passing. Since human reasoning alone has no authority without investigation or examination,[75] the time of the soul's departure for someone relying solely on the reason is a time of sorrow, anxiety, shame, and regret.[76] However, since faith can enable the believer to "walk on the sea as on dry land,"[77] death itself can be greeted as a doorkeeper opening the gateway to eternal life.

The patristic understanding of metacognition is thus further nuanced by taking into account the role of grace, faith, and the illumined heart in cognitive processes. With the presence of grace, a person's awareness is altered; his choices multiply; and his freedom from the basic drives of pleasure and pain increases. With faith, metacognition can become a weapon for fighting bad thoughts, a tool for struggling for virtue, a map for acquiring edifying knowledge, and a pathway leading to Christ. When opposed to faith, however, metacognition can predispose an individual to selfishness, spiritual sloth, and ignorance of things divine. Consequently, for the Christian, faith and grace are significant factors that should be considered when evaluating the therapeutic value of metacognitive enhancement.

Socrates and Practical Scientists: the Science of Metacognition

Turning from the vast sea of patristic texts to the walled canal of cognitive theory, we find metacognition clearly defined in terms of higher regulatory mental processes that people use to navigate themselves through various situations in life. People observe regularities in how their actions affect their relationships with others and turn these observations into a hypothetical guide for future behavior.[78] Beck notes that this is a normal human aptitude when he writes, "In his approach to external problems, man is a practical scientist: he makes observations, sets up hypotheses, checks their validity, and eventually forms generalizations that will later serve as a guide for making rapid judgments of situations."[79] According to the cognitive model, "the metacognitive level (1) selects, (2) evaluates, and (3) monitors the further development of schemas."[80] For example, when a person suffering from social isolation considers whether the schema, "If I talk about myself, people will think that I'm conceited" is a good rule for social interactions,[81] he is making a metacognitive evaluation that can lead him to develop a new schema or rule for relating to others.

Theoretically, metacognition can be understood as a slow-paced rational system that examines causal relationships and is intended for delayed action. Cognitive theorists contrast this with the rapid experiential system of primal thinking that is based on past associations and aimed at an immediate response. Metacognition is a conscious analytic approach that can fine-tune the primal mode[82] and correct the cognitive distortions and maladaptive schemata that we discussed in previous chapters.

In both science and daily life, there are good theories and bad theories as well as competent and incompetent scientists. Some people go through demoralizing situations, but are not discouraged, because they are unusually alert to the manifold sides of a given situation and approach it in an objective and constructive manner.[83] Others are paralyzed by a difficult set of circumstances, because they are not able to clearly perceive, formulate, and weigh their choices.[84] This latter group has a deficit in metacognitive skills and provides prime candidates for cognitive therapy.

Cognitive therapy thus aims at alleviating psychological distress by enhancing a patient's metacognitive skills, so that he will be able to accurately perceive his situation, interpretations, choices, and best interests by correcting faulty conceptions and self-signals. To this end, cognitive therapy teaches the patient to approach his understanding of himself and his world in a rational, experimental, and active way. Intellectually, the patient learns to identify his misconceptions, to test their validity, and to substitute them with more appropriate concepts. Experimentally, he learns to put himself in situations that are salient enough tests to disconfirm his misconceptions. Behaviorally, he engages in activities that can alter the way he looks at himself and his world.[85]

For example, a mother suffering from depression may feel sad because her children are unruly, which she interprets as proof that she is a bad parent. A typical metacognitive intervention for this factor in depression would involve the therapist asking the patient to define good and bad parenthood in behavioral terms, to consider to what extent youthful unruliness is causally related to parenthood, and to devise experiments to test old suppositions and new hypotheses. After a successful metacognitive re-evaluation, the patient may recognize multiple causes for her children's misbehavior and view herself as a caring, but imperfect parent, if such is in fact the case.

The primary skill that patients are taught in order to enhance their metacognitive capabilities is how to evaluate their automatic thoughts and underlying schemata through Socratic questioning and guided discovery.[86] When patients' automatic thoughts produce emotional disturbances, they can question those thoughts in terms of their accuracy as a description, their logical consistency as a conclusion, and their utility as aids to human functioning. If a thought turns out to be a distortion of reality, an invalid inference, or counterproductive, patients can replace that thought with another more adaptive alternative.[87]

According to Beck, "Socratic questioning is used to bring information into the awareness of the *patient*....Questions should be phrased in such a way that stimulate thought and increase awareness, rather than requiring a correct answer."[88] In other words, Socratic questioning puts the patient in a metacognitive mode of logical, independent thought. Of course, Socrates' questions were framed to move his interlocutor to discover the truth that Socrates could already see. In cognitive therapy, however, therapists are not sure where their questions will lead.[89]

Standard questions for evaluating an automatic thought include:

1. What is the evidence? What is the evidence that supports this idea? What is the evidence against this idea?
2. Is there an alternative explanation?
3. What is the worst that could happen? Could I live through it? What is the best that could happen? What is the most realistic outcome?
4. What is the effect of my believing the automatic thought? What could be the effect of changing my thinking?
5. What should I do about it? What would I tell...(a friend) if he or she were in the same situation?[90]

Utilizing questions of this kind, the therapist prods the patient away from cognitive distortions—such as *all-or-nothing thinking, catastrophizing, disqualifying the positive,* and so forth—and toward a more realistic interpretation. For example, a person who labels someone else as a liar would be made to consider evidence for and against such a conclusion and thereby moderate his initially rigid thought. Of course, not all the above questions are relevant for the evaluation of a given thought or schema.

These questions can be altered according to the cognitive conceptualization of the particular syndrome or situation. For example, a lawyer suffering from anxiety may have the belief, "If I make a mistake in court, I'll pass out." The therapist can ask him questions such as: "Are you oversimplifying a causal relationship?...Are your interpretations of the situation too far removed from reality to be accurate?...Are you using words or phrases that are extreme or exaggerated?...Are you confusing a low probability with a high probability?"[91] Socratic questions thus compel the anxious lawyer to examine the evidence (e.g., has he passed out under other conditions? Do other lawyers pass out when they make mistakes?), to consider another way of looking at the situation (e.g., his pulse will increase; he will sweat profusely; and nothing else will happen), and to consider even the worse-case scenario (e.g., If he passes out, he will again regain consciousness, and continue with his life).[92]

Socratic questioning first encountered in the therapy session can also be used by the patient outside therapy in order to respond to a variety of situations in more adaptive ways. For example, someone prone to getting angry with a spouse might ask himself such questions as

1. What do I expect to gain by reproaching, punishing, or criticizing my spouse?
2. What do I lose by using these tactics? Even if there are good short-term results, are the long-term results likely to be bad?...
3. What is the point that I want to get across? What is the best way to make this point?...
4. Are there better ways than punishment to influence my spouse?[93]

These questions in turn lessen the impulse of the irritable husband to attack his spouse and open up more constructive ways for interacting with each other. Similarly, someone who is struggling with urges to use drugs might have recourse to questions such as the following to induce control beliefs:

1. What would you do if the drugs weren't available?
2. What are the disadvantages of using drugs?
3. How else can you look at this situation?
4. What else could you do to achieve the same end?[94]

Thus, when the patient learns how to question his thoughts, assumptions, interpretations, strategies, and rules in a systematic fashion, he begins the process of their evaluation. The primary skill of formulating questions that make the patient think about his thoughts is followed by self-observation and behavioral experimentation in order to test them and thereby complete the therapeutic pathway of metacognition. Questions guide the metacognitive process to a desired end, even as canal walls guide the flow of water back into the sea.

Imperial Fishermen and Practical Scientists

Having surveyed "thought about thought" as it appears in the ocean of patristic texts and as it is defined within the confines of cognitive therapy, we can now ask, "What do emperors, fishermen, and practical scientists have in common?" As metaphors for metacognition,...quite a bit. After all, the imperial mind pulling on the reins of analysis to keep in check the unruly steeds of desire and anger is but the church fathers' literary way of describing what cognitive theorists frame in sparse scientific terms: higher mental processes regulate lower impulsive reactions by a scientific approach that widens a person's perceptual field of vision and awareness. Both ancient ascetics and contemporary therapists characterize this slower rational system as a skill that can be perfected with effort by making thoughts the object of a person's scrutiny, even as swimming fish are the object of the fisherman's gaze. Both approaches recognize that posing questions as well as weighing advantages and disadvantages can induce this metacognitive mode in which the utility of a given thought can be evaluated.

Of course, there are differences. In contrast to broad patristic notions of the logical will, the rational faculty, and the monarchy of the mind from which notions of metacognition can be drawn, metacognition in cognitive theory is a straightforward and highly specific concept about the mechanics of cognitive change. As a concept, metacognition coincides with the standard hypothetico-deductive method of science: observation, hypothesis formation, experimentation/verification, and tentative conclusion. Although one can construe the ascetic practices of fasting, vigil, and prayer as behavioral experiments with cognitive ramifications, the selection of possible experiments is much more limited in a patristic setting than in the context of cognitive therapy (see chapter 7). Cognitive therapy, moreover, has a greater emphasis than ascetic tradition on determining the accuracy and logical consistency of a thought as well as on developing alternative explanations and interpretations. These differences, however, are not necessarily points of conflict.

Patristic tradition notes that the rule of reason goes hand in hand with sanctity and ascetic effort. The fathers observe that metacognition operates differently if a person is in a state of grace, because grace alters a person's awareness. With an experiential knowledge of Divine Providence, past and present, together with an assurance of God's care in the future, what a person considers to be a reasonable interpretation and a logical choice changes. Metacognition used with the faith can be a trusty staff for the wayfarer on the path toward sanctification. If, however, instruction in metacognition is turned against the faith, it can turn into harmful training in self-justification. One can imagine the standard cognitive question—"What is the worst that could happen?"—being used to quell the conscience's objections to engaging in sinful behavior, with spiritually regrettable consequences following thereafter.

Patristic Education: Training Spiritual Fishermen

The use of reason and metacognition in human society is usually honed in the context of education where knowledge and skills are imparted to budding students. Since the inception of psychoanalysis by Freud, therapy has been understood as a form of re-education.[95] Cognitive therapy not only follows this tradition of re-education, but also does so in a pedagogical format with which most school children will be familiar: namely, apprenticeship, instruction, and dialogue. Cognitive therapists help their patients to understand their emotional reactions, their particular syndrome, and the mechanisms of change in an educational process that is intrinsically therapeutic.[96] Likewise following in the footsteps of Christ, "the good teacher,"[97] and Saint Paul, "the teacher of the Gentiles,"[98] the church fathers provide the faithful with an education that brings relief to strugglers by teaching them about the spiritual life, including the discernment of the thoughts and the characteristics of the passions.[99] Ancient ascetics would hardly disagree with contemporary therapists concerning the role of learning in the healing process. In fact, Saint John of the Ladder makes the following comment about therapeutic knowledge in the life of the spirit: "I have seen physicians who did not inform their patients of the causes of their illness, and by so doing gave both themselves and their patients much toil and anguish."[100] Clearly, cognitive therapists and church fathers share an educational orientation, but the significance of this commonality can be discerned only by exploring the contents of both types of instruction.

A central tenet underlying patristic education concerning the thoughts is the principle of synergy between divine grace and the human will. On the one hand, someone in need of advice will never find a more reliable, more sensible, or more beneficial source than the teachings of Christ.[101] On the other hand, a person must have the will to recover from emotional disturbance in order to be healed.[102] In unison, the grace contained in the commandments of Christ and the believer's self-emptying struggle to fulfill them enable the believer to recognize the passions, the bad thoughts, and the soul's wounds of which he would otherwise remain ignorant.[103]

Monastic fathers acknowledge the difficulty of the struggle against the thoughts, but assure the believer that it is a struggle unto salvation. In fact, Abba Zosimas used to say that without the presence of temptations and thoughts, no one could become a saint.[104] Sometimes the fathers suggest a methodological approach to this struggle. For example, Saint John Chrysostom recommends working for one month on one set of virtues, and the next month on another set.[105] In psychological terms, this can be viewed as a scheduled approach to cognitive restructuring in which one emphasizes the development of alternative schemata consistent with the virtues in order to decrease the strength of schemata with which the passions are compatible. For instance, a person could conscientiously work on almsgiving to undermine avarice. A similar methodical approach can be seen in Saint Nicodemos the Hagiorite's advice about preparation for confession in terms of recalling sins committed in thought, word, and deed during the span of a month, a week, and a single day.[106] Such preparatory efforts surely increase a person's awareness of the cognitive and behavioral patterns of sin, an awareness that is the necessary first step for altering sinful habits.

The desert fathers stress a more streamlined approach in dealing with the thoughts by focusing primarily on becoming humble-minded. The virtue of humility is capable of protecting the believer from sundry thoughts that can damage his entire inner world.[107] For example, someone who feels humbled will avoid not only the appearance of critical thoughts, but also the temptation to weave such thoughts at the instigation of others. If that person happens to hear someone being criticized, he will use that criticism to humble himself even further.[108] As a help to avoid ranting about what others have done, the fathers suggest that the believer striving for humility recall that such inward tirades makes him resemble the demons who in this wise torment themselves and others.[109] To avoid acting with pride, the Christian should refrain from reacting before reflection and prayer.[110]

A further patristic counsel for acquiring a humble outlook, so crucial in the battle against the thoughts, consists in being skeptical about one's initial judgment regarding another person or situation. Elder Païsios suggests saying to oneself, "I don't always think correctly; I often make mistakes. How about when I had that thought, which turned out to be off the mark, and I misjudged my neighbor. Therefore, I shouldn't listen to my thoughts."[111] In monasticism where special opportunities for training in humility are available, the novice learns to distrust his thoughts by asking his elder about them. Abba Dorotheos relates how he would think about doing something, but at times be disinclined to bother his elder. In such cases, he would say to himself, "Curse you, your prudence, and your knowledge; whatever you know, you know from the demons," and then he would proceed to seek his elder's counsel. If his elder's advice coincided with his thoughts, he would tell himself, "Yes, now it is good and from the Holy Spirit, but earlier it was from your passionate state."[112] Obviously, the issue is not the truth value or utilitarian benefit of a given thought, but the acquisition of humility that can transfigure the entire thought process and open one's heart to the grace of God. Saints Barsanuphius and John situate this practice within biblical tradition by stating that to seek counsel before acting is to fulfill the law and the prophets, because by so doing, a person manifests in his life the humility of Christ who took on the form of a servant.[113]

Of course, questions call for answers; and certain answers regarding basic cognitive distinctions and processes are intrinsic to patristic instruction. The primary distinction is between thought as a temptation to sin and thought as a sinful state. Following Stoic tradition, Origen calls the initial response to temptation a prepassion, that is, an involuntary and hence sinless inclination toward an irritating stimulus.[114] Without prepassion, temptation would be an impossibility. For Didymus the Blind, the temptation of Christ demonstrates that prepassion is a sinless state. There is, however, a point when a sinless prepassion becomes a sin of thought.[115] Saint Jerome writes, "God does not punish the first and second stimuli [stimulos] of thoughts that the Greeks call propatheias and that no man can be without. But He does inflict punishment if someone decides to do what has been thought."[116] In his Commentary on Matthew, Saint Jerome notes that a person turns a thought [cogitatio] into an emotion [affectus] when he assents [consentire] to a thought and wills [voluntas] it. In this way, the neutral prepassion becómes a blameworthy passion.[117] Thus, for Saint Jerome sin begins with the use of the will in a mental act of decision [descerne] and judgment [judicium].[118]

This decision, however, may be less straightforward than the learned Latin ascetic suggests. According to Evagrius, a decision is made when a person lingers on a harmful thought.[119] Lingering implies immoderately indulging in a bad thought[120] that should be "spat out as soon as it touches the mind."[121] According to Saint Mark the Ascetic, if a person experiences pleasure or anger while dallying with a thought, then there also exists "an attachment that stems from one's free choice."[122] He also views the appearance of images accompanying thoughts as indicative of inner assent.[123] Since images often evoke emotional responses, these two observations are related. Perspicaciously, the saint discerns that being emotionally distressed over a bad thought, rather than being pleased by it, indicates that the thought was generated against the will and can be easily eradicated.[124]

After the distinction between temptation and sin in thought, the ancient ascetics instruct the faithful in the obvious, but crucial difference between sin in thought and sin in deed as well as in the need to prevent the former from slipping into the latter. Origen views sin in thought as tolerable and treatable, but sin in word and deed as dangerous and difficult to cure, if not incurable. For this reason, when a wise man is disturbed by a storm of thoughts, he keeps that tempest of the mind hemmed in, neither uttering a word, nor moving a muscle. The exemplary behavior of the wise demonstrates that an initial sinful thought can be arrested by an act of will.[125] Origen suggests that by some introspection anyone can come to see the possibility of such resistance. He writes, "If someone says that it is impossible to resist what comes from the outside, let him pay attention to his own passions and movements in order to see if his governing mind is somehow approving, consenting, or being inclined to that thing."[126]

As an aid to self-observation, the church fathers outlined in varying degrees of detail the cognitive processes whereby a temptation becomes a sin in thought and then in deed. Their ultimate aim was to help the faithful avoid sinful actions, acquire compunction, attain purity of heart, and discover the kingdom of heaven within them.[127] Saint Mark the Ascetic queries, "If someone has not perceived this general process of sinning, when will he pray about it and be cleansed from it?"[128]

The standard patristic account of the process of sin is enshrined in Balsamon's commentary on the fourth canon of the Council of Neocesarea (315): "The fathers say that there are four degrees of sin—provocation, struggle, assent, and the act [prosbolēn, palēn, synkatathesin kai praxin]; the first two of these are not subject to punishment, but the other two call for penance."[129] In psychological terms, there are three cognitive stages, apart from the behavioral enactment. Saints Augustine of Hippo and Gregory of Rome provide a slightly different description of the three stages: suggestion, pleasure, and assent [*suggestione, delecatione et consensione*] with pleasure replacing struggle [*palē*]. Actually, the Latin fathers simply focus on a different aspect of the central stage. Blessed Augustine gives the example of a person who is fasting. If that person suddenly sees food (the suggestion), his appetite will be aroused (the pleasure). He may then decide to go and eat it (the assent), unless reason holds the impulse back.[130] Saint Maximus the Confessor describes the three stages in almost cognitive terms as a memory bringing a thought into the mind, the arousal of a passion by lingering on that thought, and the mental assent to that passion.[131] His formulation construes the provocation/suggestion as a memory pre-existing in the mind and the second stage as a preconscious choice bringing pleasure to the person. Other fathers refer to these same stages, but emphasize the interaction between the devil who initiates the process and the individual who mingles or couples with the demonic provocation for the sake of self-indulgence or vainglory.[132] In psychological terms, there are both internal and external cues instigating the process of sin. Each stage deserves some attention in detail.

Saint John Climacus defines the first stage [*prosbolē, suggestio*] as "a simple conception or an image of something encountered for the first time in the heart."[133] Saint Philotheos of Sinai offers a similar definition, but he refers to a provocation as a thought, rather than a conception, and notes that it is engendered, rather than simply encountered in the heart.[134] In a text attributed to Saint John of Damascus, we are given a scriptural example: a provocation is "a suggestion coming from the enemy, like 'do this' or 'do that,' such as our Lord and God experienced when he heard the words 'Command that these stones become bread.'"[135] Saints Maximus the Confessor and Ilias the Presbyter note that the provocation takes place in the imagination.[136] Thus, the first stage involves the appearance of concepts, thoughts, images, and possible courses of action, real or imaginary. Appearing or being engendered in the heart, provocations touch the very core of the human person; being clothed in the imagination, they can do so where the heart is most vulnerable to attack.

Saint John, the abbot of Sinai, defines the next stage [*palē, delecatio*] as "a conversation with what has presented itself, accompanied by passion or dispassion."[137] In other words, an individual who converses with a thought will either couple with it by "deliberately dallying with it in a pleasurable manner" [*delecatio*] or wrestle [*palē*] with it by resisting it.[138] Although pleasure indicates an initial movement toward assent, whereas sorrow suggests an initial move-ment toward rejection, sometimes one's feelings are quite mixed.[139] As Saint Gregory the Dialogist puts it, "Often when the heart is tempted, it experiences delight in the sinfulness of the flesh, but resists this same sinfulness in its judgment. Thus, in one's secret thoughts, the heart is both saddened by what pleases it and pleased by what saddens it."[140] In other words, the tempted feels torn in opposite directions: self-indulgence and vainglory clamor for pleasure, whereas the wiser conscience exhorts the tempted to preserve his soul as the dwelling place of God.[141]

Remaining in this stage of struggling with a provocation for an extended interval is not without danger. Real time spent in an imaginary world sur-rounding the thought gives the thought a semblance of reality and grooves a channel in the mind through which similar thoughts will tend to flow. In this way, a habit-forming passion comes into existence.[142] At this point, the person's thought can become the person's tyrant in a process that the fathers call captivity, that is, "a forcible and involuntary rape of the heart."[143]

The final cognitive stage [synkatathesis, consensio] can be defined as an ap-proval of the passionate aspect of the thought in which the mind enjoys bending toward what it envisions.[144] At this point, a person plans how to commit the sin in practice and step-by-step transforms the thought into a deed.[145] Although detailed planning intimates decision-making and control, the person may well feel like a captive being dragged to the act.[146] Saint Gregory the Dialogist views this consent as a sin "not of thought, but of deed, for although circumstances bring a delay that outwardly defers the sin, the will has already accomplished it inwardly by the act of consent."[147] As thoughts become obsessional and habitual, so behaviors become addictive and unexam-ined, leading the unfortunate soul to a lack of repentance that paves the way to hell.[148]

Sometimes the fathers paint the above process with colorful metaphors so that the believer will better understand what is at stake. For example, Saint Ilias the Presbyter likens the provoking thoughts to marauding animals and a person's mind to a well-ordered vineyard. Repelling bad thoughts from the start is like driving out wild beasts, so that one's vineyard and the fruits thereof are protected. If a person converses with the thoughts, even without experienc-ing pleasure, the vineyard is placed at jeopardy. And although the fruit of the vineyard is still unharmed, wild boars have been allowed to enter therein. If the individual enjoys conversing with the thoughts, yet does not consent to them, the boars not only come into the vineyard, but also begin feeding on the grapes, those godly thoughts of humility, gratitude, and love that are the very aim of the spiritual vineyard of the mind. When assent takes place, the boars move about freely devouring at will.[149] Tito Colliander provides a more contemporary analogy for the stages before sin when he writes, "The impulse knocks like a salesman at the door. If one lets him in, he begins his sales talk about his wares, and it is hard to get rid of him even if one observes that his wares are not good. Thus follows consent and finally the purchase, often against one's own will."[150]

In terms of sin, according to the ecclesiastical canons, a person will not be tried for being provoked by a thought and struggling with it, but he will be judged for consenting to a thought and subject to punishment for putting it into practice.[151] Monastic literature seems to have a slightly higher standard regarding human responsibility within the stages. Saint John Climacus is of the opinion that converse with a thought may or may not be sinful, but assent to an ungodly thought always bears the mark of sin.[152] Saint Symeon the New Theologian teaches, moreover, that if someone remembers something apart from God's will and does not show regret immediately, he has sinned even if he eventually rejects the provocation.[153]

Given the detrimental effects of following a provocation on to its bitter end, the fathers advise cutting it off in the bud by rebutting it or viewing it dispassionately, as well as by invoking [epiklēsis] the Lord Jesus (see chapter 8).[154] Saint John Cassian suggests keeping watch over the head of the serpent, "the first inkling of the pernicious thoughts by which the serpent tries to creep into our soul," and striking it down.[155] The earlier a person rejects a bad thought, the less he will be harmed by it. Nevertheless, rejecting the thought at any stage before putting it into action has its value.[156] The corollary to this axiom is the principle that repentance should be in accord with how far one proceeds through the stages. Thus, Saint Gregory the Dialogist counsels, "Those who mourn over transgressions in thought are to be exhorted to consider carefully to what extent they have fallen into sin, so that they may be lifted up by an amount of weeping that is commensurate with their downfall that they are already inwardly aware of. Otherwise, if contemplated evils torment them too little, they will be led on to the perpetration of deeds."[157]

Patristic instruction concerning the thoughts is eminently practical, theoretically consistent, and readily understandable. It is also based on careful observations and time-tested approaches known to bring results. Obedience to Christ's commandments and the struggle to attain humility by reproaching oneself, questioning one's thoughts, and seeking advice are actions that weaken the hold that thoughts have over a person. Knowledge about when and how a provocation or suggestion becomes a sin of thought increases the believers' introspective awareness as well as their sense of responsibility for the development of their thoughts. Thus, this knowledge increases the probability that they will arrest a bad thought at an early stage of development. In patristic instruction, knowledge [gnōsis] and practice [praxis] are inseparable. One learns in order to do and in doing learns. Cognitive and behavioral components are as intertwined in patristic instruction as they are in life itself. And for the fathers, this education touches the very core of the Christian life. Even as a fisherman's livelihood relies on learning how to watch for fish in the sea, so the spiritual fisherman's life in Christ depends on learning how to watch for thoughts in the mind.

Cognitive Therapy: Educating Practical Scientists

Similarly in cognitive therapy, the patient as a practical scientist learns how to manage his thoughts. Much of the therapeutic process involves educating the patient regarding thoughts, emotions, behaviors, and metacognition as they relate to the particular psychological problem troubling him. A consistent explanation of the relationship between thoughts and emotions demystifies the patient's emotional and behavioral problems, thereby providing both relief and empowerment for change.[158] In clear-cut terms, the patient learns that certain people have cognitive vulnerabilities in terms of how they view themselves, their surroundings, and their future. These vulnerabilities make them susceptible to a given syndrome. For example, someone who views himself, his environment, and his future in negative terms will be prone to depression, whereas someone else who views herself as inadequate, her environment as threatening, and her future as uncertain will be predisposed to anxiety.[159]

At an early stage of therapy, the patient learns to distinguish between his feelings that are experienced as emotions and his thoughts that are ideas passing through his mind, so that he can target the thought in order to alter the emotion.[160] For example, an anxiety sufferer will learn to distinguish between fear rooted in the thought that something is dangerous and anxiety as an emotional response to that thought. When the patient understands this distinction, he can see that anxiety as an emotional response is neither rational nor irrational, but fear as a cognitive appraisal may be realistic or unrealistic.[161] This clarity of thought enhances the patient's metacognitive efforts and sense of being in control.

The patient also learns certain cognitive principles intrinsic to the therapeutic process. First, he learns that his beliefs about himself, his environment, and his future are ideas, often formed during childhood, which may or may not be true.[162] The patient then considers the logical and experimental consequences of this principle: since these beliefs are learned ideas, and not innate truths, they can be tested and changed.[163] In Beck's words, the patient learns to "be able to make the distinction between 'I believe' (an opinion that is subject to validation) and 'I know' (an irrefutable fact)."[164] Finally, the patient comes to understand how his system of beliefs functions as a filter allowing data that support those beliefs to freely enter, but preventing the entry of contradictory information without some modification. This helps the patient understand why he so strongly believes ideas supported by objectively inaccurate schemata.[165]

In addition to general instruction in the cognitive model, cognitive therapists also provide the patient with facts specific to the patient's particular psychological difficulty. This information is drawn from the verifiable results of biological, psychological, and sociological studies with bearing on the psychiatric disorders. A few examples will further disclose the nature and content of patient education in the context of cognitive therapy.

In the case of anxiety, instruction concerning the fight-flight-freeze response as well as information concerning symptoms stemming from the sympathetic (e.g., a rise in pulse rate) and parasympathetic (e.g., a drop in blood pressure) nervous systems can help the anxiety sufferer to become more objective about his bodily sensations, thereby altering his cognitive appraisal and subsequent emotional reaction.[166] By becoming aware of the psychological principle that "as long as a person has a firm belief in his competency, he is protected from sabotage of uncertainty, self-questioning, and concern about failure,"[167] the anxiety sufferer simultaneously receives guidance for the formulation of concrete cognitive goals. In particular, the patient learns that to neutralize the crippling vulnerability mode that characterizes anxiety, he should adopt a confident attitude that entails concentrating on the positive aspects of his situation, minimizing the dangers, and assuming a greater amount of control than he actually has.[168] Often, the therapist will provide the patient with concrete examples to make this process less abstract. For example, Beck notes that the difference between the reactions of a veteran soldier in a dangerous situation and those of an inexperienced private is that the veteran endeavors to solve the problem, while the inexperienced private tries to protect himself or escape.[169]

In marital counseling, couples learn about their unspoken rules and expectations concerning respect and caring that they read into their mate's words and actions. When a spouse's rules are symbolically violated, that spouse may have such feelings of loss and insecurity that he or she reacts like someone with a mood disorder such as depression or anxiety.[170] Given this principle of couple dynamics, both parties learn to make their rules and expectations explicit, to modify them if they are excessive, and to separate the reaction to the symbol from the intentions of the actor.[171] Couples also learn about real statistical differences between the sexes in terms of conversational styles that the opposite sex may erroneously ascribe to a lack of caring or respect. For example, whereas women tend to ask personal questions to express caring, men often interpret or misinterpret those queries as intrusive or meddlesome requests for information. Whereas men are prone to interrupt or not respond to their partner's comments, women usually interpret or misinterpret such interruptions or unresponsiveness as ill will or insensitivity.[172] Knowledge of these gender-related styles can help generate more objective and more benign interpretations of negative perceptions. Finally, couples learn to avoid jumping to negative conclusions because of ambiguous signals, to use non-accusatory language when communicating, and to avoid defeatist beliefs about their marriage in order to improve their relationship.[173]

In the case of substance abuse, the patient learns about the cognitive, affective, behavioral, and physiological aspects of craving, so that he will be able to label his experience more objectively and thereby weaken his subjective interpretation about how unbearable his cravings are.[174] For example, the patient enters an observer mode when he learns to distinguish between craving that is a visceral, appetitive state akin to hunger and control that is a cerebral, volitional state akin to the decision to tense a muscle. The patient also learns the principle that addictive behavior is a function of the ratio of control over urge: $b = f(c/u)$.[175] The logical implication of this principle is that treatment entails increasing the addict's ability to exercise control and decreasing the intensity of his urges, so that he does not succumb to drug use. With a clear-headed approach, cognitive therapy teaches the patient to formulate goals that are sufficient, realistic, and feasible. Rather than aiming for the discouragingly unrealistic ideal of absolute control or zero cravings, the patient simply aims at significantly shifting the balance between control and urges in a favorable direction, so that he will not resort to drugs.[176]

On account of the importance of cognitive changes involved in the decision to use drugs, the patient learns to be aware of his own sequence of beliefs in the form of automatic thoughts that cause increased craving and inevitable usage (see figure 5.1). That is, he learns to recognize how anticipatory beliefs that become progressively more romanticized ("This will feel so good") are followed by relief-oriented beliefs that grow increasingly imperative ("I've got to have the drug"), and terminate with permissive beliefs that justify otherwise unacceptable behavior ("Everything else is going wrong, I might as well use it"). When the patient connects his knowledge about the belief sequence with information about the nature of cravings, he comes to see that they become more intense during the interval preceding the appearance of permissive beliefs.[177] Consequently, he needs to learn to activate control beliefs ("I can say no to drugs") and coping responses in the interval between experiencing the craving and implementing the urge, or put differently, between the appearance of anticipatory/relief-oriented beliefs and the appearance of permissive beliefs. Often before therapy, the addict views willpower as a stoic, if not masochistic, passive endurance of discomfort. In therapy, he learns to define willpower as an active intervention by means of countering techniques such as the utilization of flashcards that list reasons why he should not use drugs when he is experiencing cravings (see chapter 8).[178]

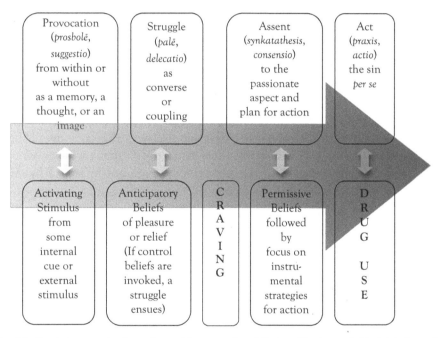

Fig. 5.1. Patristic stages in sin and cognitive stages in addiction. The lower half of this figure has been adapted from Aaron Beck, Fred Write, Cory Newman, and Bruce Liese, *Cognitive Therapy of Substance Abuse* (New York: The Guilford Press, 1993), 40, 46–47.

The similarity between the patristic stages for sin and the cognitive pathway in substance abuse is remarkable. The steps are identical, although the concepts and language differ. This independent discovery of the same pathway mutually corroborates the observational skills of clinical cognitive therapists and ancient church fathers alike. Each perspective has something to offer. If the tempted consider their anticipatory, control, and permissive beliefs, they may be able to refine their strategy for resistance and tailor it to their personal struggle. If users consider how they converse or couple with the desire to use drugs, their sense of personal responsibility may increase, thereby decreasing the likelihood of a lapse.

Fishing and Science: Some Meta-metacognitive Conclusions

Fishing and science are hardly interchangeable subjects, but in the right context the semantic overlap is surprisingly significant. In contrasting the views of fishermen of the spirit and scientists of the mind with respect to metacognition, they seem to be fishing in quite similar waters. Both describe mental functions that can be characterized as metacognitive in observational, evaluative, and regulatory ways. Both view metacognition as a natural control mechanism that can be perfected through appropriate training. Grounded in empirical observations, both ascetics and clinicians provide the learner with principles and descriptions of processes that enhance metacognition, increase awareness, and clarify thought.

Notwithstanding, spiritual fishermen and practical scientists do not look at the physical world, much less the cognitive sea, with the same eyes. Above all, the presence of grace and faith alters what the Christian sees and concludes. If a therapist's way of seeing and reasoning are not informed by faith, his understanding of healthy metacognitive functioning may be unhealthy from a Christian perspective. If he were to impose this understanding on a believing patient, the results could be spiritually devastating.

Even when church fathers and cognitive therapists agree, their rationales often differ markedly. For example, ancient ascetics propose distrusting one's judgment and avoiding critical thoughts, *so that* the believer may become humble. Cognitive therapists make a similar suggestion, *because* one's judgments may be false and one's criticisms based on the cognitive distortion of mind reading. The church fathers' instruction is moral, spiritual, and eschatological, whereas the instruction of cognitive therapists is factual and utilitarian with no aim beyond the presenting difficulty. Put differently, education in cognitive therapy empowers the patient and demystifies his reactions, because it brokers in the universally accepted currency of science. Patristic education encourages the believer and inspires hope, because it points beyond the narrow confines of science to the witness of those who have passed from death to life.

We have seen that the fathers maintain that reason in conjunction with faith can be used both to acquire spiritual knowledge and to grow in prudence, hope, and love for the Good. Metacognition in its cognitive therapeutic context can likewise be used in harmony with that blessed end. Many instructional principles in cognitive therapy mesh well with Orthodox Christianity. The cognitive understanding of willpower in terms of active interventions is consistent with the doctrine of active synergy as well as patristic advice concerning the active use of rebuttal and the invocation of Christ's name at the time of temptation. The cognitive understanding of addiction is remarkably similar to the monastic understanding of the stages leading to sin. Insights into anxiety, depression, and marital disturbances can certainly help Christians suffering with those problems. Again, both approaches have much to offer.

When all is said and done, however, we believe that the fishermen of the spirit have "chosen that good part, which shall not be taken away from them."[179] Elder Païsios once remarked, "Worldly logic is for a good person who doesn't believe."[180] The same could be said of the use of metacognitive enhancement via cognitive therapy. What of the good person who *does* believe? Such a person will discerningly use the logic of the gospel for faith-inspired metacognition in lieu of secular logic alone, as the situation requires. He truly dwells in the best of both worlds, scientific and piscine alike. As a scientist, he can calculate the number of fish remaining in an overfished sea, but as a spiritual fisherman, he lets down his net at the Master's command, and "draws the net to land full of great fishes, an hundred and fifty and three."[181]

✠ PART III ✠

Human Practitioners
and People in Need

Reflections from an Unlikely Portrait Gallery: Spiritual Fathers and Cognitive Therapists

Without theory, observations become as mute as statues and facts become as obscure as unintelligible inscriptions on the wall of a cave. In the past three chapters, we have discussed patristic and cognitive theories that give observations their voice and facts their Rosetta stone. In the language of psychology, both ways of understanding elucidate relationships between thoughts and emotion, thoughts and dysfunction, as well as thoughts and recovery. At some point, however, the models, metaphors, and formulae that constitute a given theory need to be put into practice, and this can only be done through the human practitioner.

The roles and ministries of the spiritual father (i.e., father confessor/spiritual director) and the cognitive therapist are so unmistakably different that their comparison may seem superfluous. And yet in day-to-day life, the unmistakably different are at times undeniably mistaken for each other.[1] Spiritual fathers may be tempted to act as amateur psychologists in the confessional. Therapists may be enticed into playing the part of quasi father confessors at the office. While it is helpful for spiritual fathers to be informed about psychological factors and for therapists to be knowledgeable about the spiritual life, clarity about role and function is necessary for the overall integrity of each ministry and the discerning utilization of what the corresponding profession offers. Moreover, both spiritual fathers and cognitive therapists who are uninformed about each other's work may be unduly suspicious about incompatibility or even encroachment.

In this chapter, we will leave the conceptual world of cognitive theory behind in order to step inside a rather unlikely portrait gallery consisting of icons of spiritual fathers alongside paintings of cognitive therapists. A thoughtful stroll through such a collection depicting their roles and ministries from a variety of angles should provide us with a clear and panoramic view of both figures. The subjects of our sketches include diptychs concerning how spiritual fathers and cognitive therapists become recognized, how they ply their trade, how their roles are characterized, what particular interpersonal skills they should possess, and whom they help. Of course, any collection of paintings will yield us its treasures only if we make a concerted effort to examine each sketch with the innocence of a child, with the sophistication of a connoisseur, and with the agility of a dancer ready to leap. With such ideals in mind, we will enter and strive to see.

An Ecclesiastical and Liturgical Sketch of a Spiritual Father

Our first image depicts the ministry of the spiritual father as it is quite legibly spelled out in the episcopal letter of mandate given to a hieromonk or priest when a bishop liturgically grants him the blessing to hear confessions. In this letter, the bishop instructs the spiritual father (1) to receive with kind-heartedness whoever comes for confession and (2) to investigate thoroughly his or her thoughts and actions. In so doing, the spiritual father is to enable his spiritual child to see how to remove the causes of sin and to take responsibility for its consequences. As the spiritual father becomes aware of the habits and tendencies of his spiritual child, he is (3) to make the necessary therapeutic interventions (e.g., encouragement, admonishment, or assignment of a penance) in order to lead him or her to salvation. Finally, he is (4) to bind what should be bound and to loose what ought to be loosed.[2] These responsibilities merge into an image of someone who unites in his person disparate roles: the spiritual father is a paternal investigator and a therapeutic judge.

Historically as priests in charge of penitents, spiritual fathers would assign the lapsed a penance and wait for its completion before granting them absolution.[3] Today, most spiritual fathers offer absolution to whoever sincerely repents and chooses to turn away from sinful acts and situations. Binding and loosing usually refers to permission to receive Holy Communion.[4] Although absolution is given, the priest may decide that the believer should be bound from approaching Holy Communion for some time because of the seriousness of certain sins.[5] In such a case, the penitent is like Lazarus who has been raised from the dead by the Master's voice, but not yet loosed from his binding clothes by the apostles' hands.[6]

The letter of mandate also indicates that the spiritual father will be answerable to God for what he looses and binds.[7] Saint Basil the Great stresses this responsibility at the conclusion of his canonical letter: "Keeping before our eyes the terrible day of the Lord's retribution, we will not consent to perish with the sins of others....Above all, let us pray that we may do them good, and rescue them from the snares of the evil one. If we cannot do this, let us in any event do our best to save our own souls from everlasting damnation."[8] Such accountability makes the spiritual father weigh every aspect of his encounter with his spiritual child in the balance of the fear of God.

Saint John the Faster has laid out a liturgical service for the mystery of confession that fills in the deft brushstrokes of the episcopal letter with the uniquely Christian shading of joyful-sorrow. Although this rite is not used today due to the exigencies of time-restraints, it adds painterly details relating to how a spiritual father should both guide the confessant in confession and send him back into the world. According to the saint's directives, the priest and the confessant begin by reading together the second, twenty-fourth and fiftieth psalms (LXX) as well as hymns of repentance. This both creates an appropriate atmosphere and provides models for how to express heartfelt confession to God. The priest then reads a prayer narrating how David, Ezekiel, Manasseh, Peter, the harlot, the publican, and the prodigal found mercy through repentance. While the priest addresses this prayer to the Master and Father of all, the precedent of very different people in diverse situations finding salvation through repentance encourages the confessant to identify himself with these biblical figures and to hope in a similar reconciliation with his exceedingly good Savior. The priest then admits his personal unworthiness and sinfulness, thus providing the confessant with a living example of humility, honesty, and confession. Afterward, the spiritual father explains that as a priest and in obedience to Christ's command, he receives the person coming to confession, so that the confessant will feel the assurance that through this mystery, both he and the spiritual father are being obedient to Christ. They then make three prostrations together, physically—and a psychologist might add, behaviorally—manifesting *their* repentance before God.

Having thus created an ambience of contrition, humility, and honesty, the spiritual father begins his instruction. He explains that it is not the priest who hears the confession and grants absolution, but it is God who lovingly borrows the priest's voice both to receive the person's repentance and to bestow on him divine forgiveness. The priest advises the confessant to hide nothing, reminds him that death comes swiftly, and exhorts him to turn to Christ who gives rest to those who labor and are heavy laden. He points out that if the confessant hesitates to confess some sin, he should keep in mind that by overcoming his present shame he can escape greater ignominy at the last judgment. Finally, the priest looks at the confessant with a kind and gracious countenance and asks about his sins in a calm and meek tone of voice.

After the confessant has opened up his heart, confessed his sins, and expressed a desire to change his ways, the spiritual father then absolves the penitent, prays for him to fulfill the commandments of Christ, has him rise, and embraces him. There follows a reading from the Prophet Ezekiel (Ez 18:21-28) encouraging the confessant to make a real effort at a new life by reminding him that God will not remember the lawlessness of those who turn away from their wrongdoing and fulfill his commandments. The spiritual father also reads the parable of the lost sheep (Lk 15:1-9), so that the confessant will be aware of the Master's love and be grateful to God who "leaves the ninety and nine in the wilderness, and goes after that which is lost, until he find it." Finally, the spiritual father tentatively proposes a penance that his spiritual child will be able to bear in order to gain not only the forgiveness of sin, but also a crown of virtue.[9]

The task of imposing penances in particular requires discernment in applying ecclesiastical canons. Saint John Chrysostom stresses this when he declares that the spiritual father needs "ten thousand eyes in order to observe the habits of the soul from every side."[10] The 102nd canon of the Council of Trullo similarly indicates that the spiritual father should have the discretion of a physician: that is, the spiritual father's therapeutic interventions should be based on "the nature of the sin and the readiness of the sinner for conversion,"[11] lest in the endeavor to completely transform the sinner into a saint, the spiritual father overwhelm the believer and cause him to relinquish his struggle.[12]

The liturgical service of Saint John the Faster superimposed on the letter of episcopal mandate forms an image that brings into high relief the chief duties of the spiritual father: questioning, instructing, listening, absolving, and assigning a penance. The saint's rubrics additionally illustrate how the spiritual father acts as a coach at the confessant's side preparing him or her for a humble confession and for a courageous return to the struggle for leading a virtuous life. Together, these two sources portray a symmetrical figure in which the finely controlled lines of investigation and judgment are balanced by the freely curved strokes of counsel and absolution. One might expect such a persona to both attract and repel, but in fact the spiritual father is wholly attractive, for his every gesture is saturated with the familiar earth tones of a sinner's honest humility and illumined with the gentle radiance of divine love.

A Procedural Sketch of a Certified Cognitive Therapist

Turning our gaze to the cognitive side of our first diptych, we encounter a depiction of a mental health professional who has expended time, effort, and financial resources in order to be trained in cognitive therapy. The particular therapist may be a psychiatrist, a nurse, a psychologist, a social worker, an occupational therapist, or a pastoral counselor.[13] Regardless of the individual's particular professional setting or preliminary training, he or she can be considered a cognitive therapist by virtue of employing the cognitive model as a conceptual tool for understanding the patient and his disorder as well as for designing a plan of treatment.

Beck's Academy of Cognitive Therapy, established in 1998, sets the requirements that candidates are obliged to fulfill in order to be certified as cognitive therapists. These prerequisites can also provide us with a preliminary sketch of the cognitive therapist. At present in the United States, someone certified in cognitive therapy must possess a graduate degree in the field of mental health, be licensed in his or her state to function as a mental health professional, complete forty hours of training in cognitive therapy, read a minimum of five approved books from a list provided by the academy, be recommended in writing by two professional cognitive therapists, use the cognitive model for one year, treat at least ten patients using that model, receive a positive assessment for a video-taped therapy session evaluated by trained cognitive therapist raters, and submit a positively rated written case history.[14] From the above list, we gather that becoming a certified cognitive therapist is a matter of education, experience, clinical training, and peer approval. Thus, our initial sketch portrays a scientist with a theoretical and experimental background placed at the service of others. Since re-certification is required every five years and re-licensing by state agencies is demanded regularly, a therapist is also someone who must take seriously his responsibility to maintain professional standards.

This sparse sketch of the cognitive therapist can be enlivened by an overlay of behavioral details of his or her work drawn from an outline for a standard therapy session. The structure of a typical session is as follows: "(1) Brief update and check on mood (and medication, alcohol and/or drug use, if applicable), (2) bridge from previous session, (3) setting the agenda, (4) review of homework, (5) discussion of issues on the agenda, setting new homework, and periodic summaries, and (6) final summary and feedback."[15] Even a cursory glance across this outline reveals that the therapist will collaborate with the patient in a logical fashion in order to make a maximum use of time and to avoid drifting from therapy goals.[16] If we allow our eye to more leisurely peruse this structure, other features also emerge.

The therapist begins the session (1) by asking the patient how he is feeling today and how was his week. While the patient responds, the therapist simultaneously looks over the patient's objective scores for anxiety or depression based on the evaluative tests (such as the *Beck Depression Inventory* or the

Beck Anxiety Inventory) that the patient filled out before the appointment. If the patient starts to digress or be excessively verbose, the therapist asks him to summarize the week in one sentence and to hold off the discussion of major issues such as a disagreement with an employer for later in the session. The therapist then briefly (2) makes a bridge with the previous consultation by exploring the patient's impressions about the last session and by asking him what he learned during that discussion. This exchange informs the patient that he will be responsible to review each session and to comment on it. Next, the therapist and the patient (3) set the agenda by deciding what issues they will discuss. To that end, the therapist not only asks the patient what problems he would like help solving, but also may suggest spending some time talking about the cognitive model and the cognitive formulation of the patient's disorder. After this, the therapist and the patient (4) review whatever assignments that the patient was to complete at home. In questioning the patient, the therapist avoids questions with yes or no answers. For example, instead of inquiring whether the patient has read an assigned booklet, the therapist would ask him how much time he spent reading it or what did he find to be important or valuable.

Having now completed the preliminary work, the therapist and patient (5) discuss the agenda items. This is the heart of the therapy session in which the therapist helps the patient solve his emotional, cognitive, and behavioral difficulties by the acquisition of new skills and strategies, the use of clear thinking, and the application of the scientific method. While engaging in collaborative problem-solving, the therapist also strives to relate the patient's problems to over-all therapy goals and to the cognitive model. When an agenda item is completed, the therapist may ask the patient to summarize their conclusions to verify the patient's understanding of their discussion. The therapist then suggests new homework to address the problems that they thrashed out. Finally, the therapist (6) summarizes the issues addressed and requests feedback from the patient about the session.[17]

Thus, our first portrait of a cognitive therapist depicts a scientist who efficiently gathers a maximum amount of data, fully engages the patient in the therapeutic process, and sensibly proposes relevant behavioral and cognitive interventions for the patient to test. The fine and even lines that form this portrait are perfectly aligned with the initial etchings of the education, clinical training, and experience necessary for certification.[18] There are no disparate elements to be held in unity. Everything is as clear and measured as the light emanating from a 100-watt bulb.

If we step back and look at our two sketches simultaneously, we are at first struck by an optical discord between the subjects. The spiritual father is a charismatic and ecclesiastical figure, a priest selected on account of his life of piety and given the bishop's blessing to hear confessions. The cognitive therapist is a psychologically educated and trained health professional approved by his peers to treat psychological disorders. The background in our portrayal of the spiritual father is a liturgical setting oriented toward restoring a proper relationship with God, whereas the backdrop in our depiction of the cognitive therapist is a clinical setting concentrated on symptom improvement. Furthermore, in terms of movement, the dénouement of confession clearly arrives at absolution, whereas the high-water mark of the cognitive therapy session comes sometime during the discussion of agenda items. If we alter the central subject, the background, or the overall movement of either painting, we irresponsibly destroy its integrity. If we interchange the structural, personal, or situational components of these pieces, our depictions portray neither cognitive therapists nor spiritual fathers, but instead foolish borrowers turned tragic debtors who in gaining little have lost everything.

If, however, we look more closely at the level of discrete brushstrokes, similarities resurface such as the importance of questioning and assigning remedial tasks in the form of penance or homework. Without altering either depiction, some sensible touch-up is possible. For example, the therapist's techniques of both framing questions in such a way as to receive a maximum amount of information and remaining focused on his therapeutic aim could be serviceable for the spiritual father questioning his spiritual child. The spiritual father's practice of gradually preparing the confessant before asking him about his struggles could also be employed by the therapist in order to foster a better relationship with his patient.

A Christological Icon of the Spiritual Father as Prophet and Priest

If we take a few steps down our imaginary gallery, we encounter our next depiction: a christological icon of the spiritual father. Saint Ignatius in his *Epistle to the Ephesians* writes, "There is one physician who is possessed both of flesh and spirit; both made and not made; God born in flesh; true life in death...even Jesus Christ our Lord."[19] For the church fathers, Christ is the unique physician, "the true shepherd and teacher"[20] who heals, shepherds, and teaches all Christians including spiritual fathers who look to Christ as their ultimate model. Consequently, a spiritual father properly exercises his ministry of healing, guiding, and teaching to the extent that he dwells in Christ and Christ in him.[21] As Blessed Augustine puts it, "Christ contains in himself all good shepherds. He establishes this by saying 'I am the good shepherd.' I alone am, and all the rest are one in unity with me."[22]

Indwelling in Christ transfigures spiritual fatherhood into a prophetic and priestly ministry rooted in the prophetic royal high priesthood of Christ whom the psalmist portrays as "king and priest, God and Lord, angel and man."[23] Exercising his prophetic ministry, the spiritual father brings to the repentant the *word* of God, "sharper than any two-edged sword, piercing even to the dividing asunder of soul and spirit."[24] Exercising his priestly ministry, he reads the *words* of absolution over the sincerely repentant, thereby closing the wound of sin with the remedy of Christ's grace.[25] Although the prophetic and sacerdotal aspects of spiritual fatherhood are meant to be united in a single person as they were unified in Christ, we can focus separately on these elements from this icon of the spiritual father in order to better appreciate the whole.

In his prophetic role of speaking forth the word of God, the spiritual father should be able to speak with the voice of scripture. Saint John Chrysostom writes, "After we have gone astray, there is but one technique and course of treatment: instruction by means of the word. This provides the finest surgical instrument, dietary regimen, and climate."[26] Instruction by means of the Word entails using "the medicine chest of the gospel, an antidote of sovereign power,"[27] as well as other "remedies derived from scripture."[28] These remedies, however, must be applied with understanding. As Saint John of the Ladder notes, "The guide ought not to tell all those who come to him that the way is strait and narrow, nor should he say to each that the yoke is easy and the burden is light. Rather, he should examine the case of each man and prescribe medicines which are suitable."[29] Consequently, it behooves the spiritual father to pray to God for the spiritual understanding necessary for discerning what kind of word is in his spiritual child's best interest.[30]

In accord with the pastoral theology of Archimandrite Sophrony [Sakharov], the spiritual father preparing for confession should earnestly beseech God not only to give him the appropriate word or counsel, but also to bless his encounter with his spiritual child. To touch the heart of the confessant, the spiritual father is not so much in need of exegetical expertise or rhetorical eloquence as he is in need of the grace of the Holy Spirit. Without the warmth of heartfelt prayer and the "seasoning of grace," the spiritual father's counsels can be reduced to mere opinions based on human reasoning, opinions that hardly differ from the advice of secular psychologists.[31]

By seeking a word from God, a spiritual father continues in the prophetic ministry of the Word of God at a personal level. Saint Ignatius of Antioch advises those who pastor the souls of others to "speak with every man according to the will of God."[32] This requires a dual sensitivity to the still small voice of the Lord and to the spiritual state of the person before him. As the prophets would pray and listen in order to discern God's will for the children of Israel, so the spiritual father prays and listens to discern God's will for his spiritual child. And only then does he offer him a word (see chapter 9 for further illustrations). As the prophets perceived the spiritual state of the people of Israel, so the spiritual father should learn to feel the inner world of the person before him.[33] Following the advice of Saint Paul, the spiritual father is to "rejoice with them that do rejoice, and weep with them that weep."[34] This may seem to correspond to the psychological notion of empathy, but it is not so much a kind of emotional sensitivity as knowledge of the spiritual child's state that the spiritual father acquires as he fervently prays for that person.[35]

Prayer is also at the heart of the priestly aspect of the spiritual father's ministry. As a priest providing the mystery of confession, the spiritual father represents both Christ and the community of the faithful in a living sacramental way. The spiritual father strives to restore the repentant to full communion of the Mysteries of Christ as well as to incorporate him into the Church, a community of love. From this perspective, "the spiritual father does not heal....The Church heals, not by what it says, but by what it is."[36] As a priest, the spiritual father also intercedes for his spiritual child praying for his growth in virtue and commemorating him at the Divine Liturgy. The French patristic scholar Jean-Claude Larchet notes, "All the saints when consulted in every case and before all, resort to prayer which is the fundamental principle of their treatment."[37] This certainly applies to the spiritual father as a priest of the Most High.

Together, the prophetic and priestly aspects of the spiritual father's ministry aim not only at leading the confessant to repentance and granting him absolution, but also at effecting a transfiguration of his entire life. The church fathers liken "the medicine of confession"[38] to a second baptism cleansing a person from sin and inaugurating a new life in Christ.[39] Even further, according to Archimandrite Sophrony, the spiritual father is called to collaborate in the ultimate aim of the incarnation: to create "gods for eternity in the uncreated Light."[40]

With colors that are both rich and deep, our christological icon of the spiritual father depicts a messenger from God and an intercessor for others, humbly following in the footsteps of the priests and prophets of old. The eye is naturally drawn to this vessel of clay that is transfigured into a monumental and numinous figure by the one "high priest, who is set on the right hand of the throne of the majesty in the heavens"[41] and the word of the Lord that "endureth for ever."[42]

An Occupational Mosaic of a Cognitive Therapist as a Conceptualizing Diagnostician, Educator, and Consultant

Shifting our attention to the cognitive side of our second diptych, we are confronted with an occupational mosaic of the cognitive therapist. If "cognitive conceptualization is the cornerstone of cognitive therapy,"[43] the cognitive therapist is first and foremost someone who can use the cognitive model to conceptualize a patient. The therapist does this by constructing a larger picture that logically connects the patient's automatic thoughts to his core-beliefs and schemata. For example, a patient seeking therapy will usually be upset about several situations that can be broken down into precipitants, understood as "large-scale events that may play a significant role in precipitating an episode of illness" (such as the death of a parent or a divorce) and activating situations, defined as "situations that stimulate negative moods or maladaptive bursts of cognitions and behaviors" (such as a critical remark by a friend).[44] To start conceptualizing the patient, the therapist asks him about the upsetting situation, the automatic thoughts that went through his mind at the time, the emotions that he experienced, how he reacted, and what the automatic thoughts meant to him. Like a detective, the therapist pieces together the clues offered by the patient's responses in order to form a working hypothesis about the patient's core schemata, conditional assumptions, and compensatory strategies. Then, utilizing this information, the therapist sets goals for therapeutic change and plans the appropriate interventions.[45]

An example from a case study can illustrate why it is so imperative for the successful cognitive therapist to be able to make an accurate cognitive conceptualization. Judith Beck refers to the case of a patient suffering from depression and reporting automatic thoughts such as "I'm a bad husband; my wife will probably leave me," and "My friend doesn't want to spend time with me; he thinks I'm a loser." According to the records, the therapist at first misconceptualized these automatic thoughts as indicating a strong unlovability schema. Based on this misconceptualization, the therapist suggested that the patient engage in activities that would promote positive social contact with others. When the patient's depression did not improve, the therapist sought the meaning of the patient's thoughts by asking him, "If your wife leaves you, why would that be so bad?" The patient did not answer, "No one will ever love me," but "I will have no one to help me." Hence, his main distressing schema was not unlovability, but helplessness. With a more accurate conceptualization of the patient in hand, the therapist then suggested activities that would give the patient a sense of mastery, which happily led to rapid improvement.[46]

In the process of therapy, the therapist's efforts at conceptualization can be distinguished into three inter-related roles that coalesce into an occupational mosaic of his or her work. The cognitive therapist acts "as a diagnostician, educator, and technical consultant who assesses maladaptive cognitive processes and works with the client to design learning experiences that may remediate these dysfunctional cognitions and the behavioral and affective patterns with which they correlate."[47] Adeptness at assuming each of these roles is essential to successful cognitive therapy.

As a diagnostician, the therapist begins with a tentative differential diagnosis on the basis of the patient's complaints and the results of psychometric tests that the patient has filled out. The therapist explores the vulnerabilities and life events that led to the patient's difficulties as well as coping strategies that the patient relies on, thereby perpetuating his problems. The therapist also tries to identify related dysfunctional thoughts and beliefs.[48] As the therapist gathers data about current difficulties, childhood experiences/traumas, core beliefs, conditional assumptions, and compensatory strategies, he rules out less plausible diagnoses and develops an integrated cognitive diagnosis or conceptualization of the patient that will guide him in selecting the appropriate therapeutic interventions.[49]

As an educator, the therapist teaches the patient about his or her disorder, about the cognitive model, and the process of therapy (see chapter 5). At the same time, he both normalizes the patient's difficulties and gives him realistic hope about overcoming them.[50] The therapist also clearly stresses that cognitive therapy aims at providing the patient with skills that he can use for dealing with life's problems after his course of treatment ends. For this reason, the therapist encourages the patient to actively participate in making clinical decisions and in developing a personal program of recovery. From the first encounter, the educational interaction is a collaboration between equals: between the therapist who is an expert in the cognitive model and therapeutic change, and the patient who is the authority concerning his own experience and the meaning he attaches to events.[51]

In his educational role, the therapist needs to be competent at Socratic questioning or guided discovery. When posing a question, the therapist always has in mind a clear therapeutic aim, but not a predetermined answer. Although questions have an initial diagnostic value for formulating a conceptualization, they later become pedagogical interventions based on that conceptualization. The cognitive therapist is neither a lawyer nor a high-pressure salesman trying to convince the patient of a given position,[52] but a teacher attempting to open up the patient's mind to other interpretations and possibilities. Keeping this objective in view, the therapist discerningly uses pauses between questions not only to gain an optimal amount of information from the patient, but also to give the patient an opportunity to think.[53] For the sake of practicability, the therapist keeps his questions specific and direct, rephrasing them if the patient seems confused.[54] Finally, since people have automatic learning blocks to avoid threatening material, the therapist remains alert to behaviors indicative of boredom, anger, or irritation, and may question the patient about them when observed.[55]

Lastly as a technical consultant, the therapist applies cognitive and behavioral techniques based on his conceptualization of the patient in order to address the target problems that he and the patient have already defined. It should again be noted, "the most effective techniques may be of little value if applied to the wrong individual or in an untimely manner."[56] In other words, conceptualization should always guide the selection of therapeutic interventions. Specific behavioral and cognitive techniques will be the subject matter of chapters seven through nine and be discussed in detail at that time.

Our occupational mosaic of the cognitive therapist uses clean lines to portray a fiercely intelligent and keenly perceptive figure engaged in a rationally conceived space of his own making. The roles of diagnostician, educator, and consultant blend so well, because they are all washed with the same silvery hue of clinical white and experimental grey. As a single entity, this mosaic exhibits all the confidence and competence of a scientist who firmly trusts in his method.

Stepping back to look at both our christological icon of a spiritual father and our occupational mosaic of a cognitive therapist, the differences between the two could not be more jolting. A competent therapist is an individual with highly developed conceptual and rational skills focused on restoring a person to normal life in society. A good spiritual father is a man of prayer and disciple of Christ who desires to see the lost sheep return to the green pastures of the Church. The cognitive therapist uses reason and the cognitive model to diagnose, to educate, and to advise his client. The spiritual father makes use of prayer to discern, to exhort, and to absolve his spiritual child. Whatever similarities exist between diagnosis and discernment, education and exhortation, advice and absolution, they are decidedly secondary to the particular focus and overall orientation of each approach. Altering these basic orientations and foci would fatally mar our depiction of either practitioner. At its core, the ministries of both the spiritual father and the cognitive therapist must remain utterly distinct.

A Depiction of the Pastoral Approach of a Spiritual Father

Our first two diptychs reveal incontrovertible differences between the spiritual father and the cognitive therapist. Our next diptych aims at capturing an underlying similarity between two people trying to help their fellow human beings, albeit in vastly differing settings and with quite distinct sources of inspiration. Our first depiction portrays the pastoral approach of the spiritual father. Although his stance may appear to have psychological or cognitive components, the church fathers view them as a natural extension of life in Christ.

First of all, the approach of a spiritual father is shaped by the sharp distinction between the sinner and the sin, a distinction that is embraced even by Albert Ellis, the atheist founder of rational-emotive therapy.[57] In his homilies, Saint John Chrysostom illustrates this principle with remarks such as "I hate the evil deed, not the human being,"[58] or "I do not turn away from the person, but I hate his delusion."[59] There is a clear dividing line between behavior and cognitions in the form of evil acts and delusions that can be evil and the person who is good by virtue of his or her creation in the image of God. This principle is firmly grounded in Orthodox Christian theology.

According to Saint Maximus the Confessor, "Evil is not substantial and cannot exist in any being, except through action" [*Hē kakia anypostatos estin kai en oudeni tōn ontōn hyparchousa ei mē monon en tō prattesthai*][60] or as Blessed Augustine more succinctly puts it, "Sin is an act, not a thing" [*Peccatum omne actum esse, non rem*].[61] In psychological terms, this means that problems, and hence solutions, are behavioral, not characterological. Elsewhere, Saint Maximus observes that "what is called evil is not necessarily evil, but is evil in relation to one thing, but not, however, in relation to something else."[62] In other words, sin is always relational and relative. It is a kind of behavior or cognition that exists on a continuum, in a context, and within a relationship. Outside these contextual and interpersonal factors, it can hardly be evaluated. The saint also explains that evil has no being by nature. Since everything shares in the good, which is in all things, even that which is called evil in a faint way participates in the good.[63] For Saint Maximus, evil is also "an irrational movement of the natural faculties toward something other than its real aim, because of a mistake in judgment."[64]

It should now be theologically clear why the church fathers advise the faithful to avoid evil deeds without accusing the essentially good person who commits them.[65] Although the spiritual father judges the seriousness of sins committed, he is obliged to remain non-judgmental with respect to the person before him. Moreover, by the grace of the Holy Spirit, the spiritual father should have such love and humility that if he could, he would make room in his heart for every human being, "without distinguishing the bad from the good."[66] If there is a distinction to be made, it is never between the good and the bad, but among those who are spiritually ill, those who are in the process of being healed, and those who are in a state of health.[67]

For the ancient ascetics, a non-judgmental stance then is not so much a cognitive decision based on a theoretical principle, as it is a natural response of the humble soul that has tasted the grace of the Holy Spirit and known the love of God. This state manifests itself in the very countenance of the spiritual father that is graced with a humility, a sweetness, and a hope that bear witness to divine love.[68]

The virtues of love, faith, and humility should be manifest in the way the spiritual father approaches his spiritual child. Without unfeigned love for the spiritually sick and a desire for their restoration to health, the spiritual father can hardly be considered a spiritual physician at all.[69] Without unshakable faith in God, he might be tempted to pronounce those who have been severely wounded in the Christian life to be dead, because he is blind to the fact that God can raise up both confessors and martyrs from those reckoned to be lost.[70] And without humility, he is in danger of resembling a physician who administers medicines to the sick and does not look after the poison of his own infection.[71]

Humility is especially important, because the Lord Christ trod along that most excellent way. The church fathers recommended various practices in order for the spiritual father to maintain a humble mindset. Elder Païsios suggested that those who advise others keep in mind how Christ humbly served his disciples and how Moses looked after the murmuring children of Israel.[72] Blessed Augustine would humble himself by recalling his own errors when he detected the mistakes of others.[73]

From a practical perspective, how a spiritual father speaks is obviously important, for as Saint John Chrysostom put it, "Better will the body bear unsuitable medicines than the soul unsuitable language."[74] The desert fathers knew from experience that a derogatory comment can cause a "good" person to react in a bad way and that an encouraging word can move a "bad" person to respond in a good way.[75] Thus, the spiritual father's words of guidance need to be pleasant enough to keep the attention and persuasive enough to subdue the will.[76] Perhaps since teaching is similar to reproving,[77] Elder Païsios suggested that the pastor should not speak like a teacher or a supervisor, but like a humble student who recalls the sayings of the holy fathers for similar situations.[78] Speaking like a student also means speaking with simplicity. Together, simplicity and humility are highly effective. Elder Païsios writes,

"Those with much discernment have noble love and humility. They even sweeten the bitter truth through their kindness and the great simplicity with which they speak."[79]

If a rebuke is necessary, it should be done "with great gentleness and great prudence."[80] In other words, when the spiritual father reprimands, he does so calmly, without any sign of indignation, in the proper way, and at the appropriate time.[81] Above all, the spiritual father's speech should be measured and properly seasoned. Speech "seasoned with salt" entails speaking in a way that is "agreeable, being neither wearisome nor frivolous. Instead, it should be both sharp and pleasant. For if someone is immoderately stern, he does more harm than good; but if someone is immoderately lighthearted, he brings more sorrow than happiness, so that everywhere there ought to be moderation."[82]

Finally, the spiritual father should be prepared for shocking disclosures, wearisome repetitions, and even insolent behavior. According to Saint Nicodemos the Hagiorite, when someone starts to recount his sins, the spiritual father "must take care to show neither amazement, nor to sigh, nor with any other display to indicate either disgust or boredom, because as a deer in labor can be hindered from giving birth by the mere rustling of a leaf, so the sinner in labor to confess his sins can be hindered in giving birth by a single gesture."[83] If a spiritual child insults his spiritual father, the spiritual father should try not to become distressed or irritated, but instead to respond like a physician dealing with those who are not in their right mind. In other words, he should give no thought to his own standing, but focus on how to heal the sick.[84] If his spiritual child does not conform to his advice, he should not treat him with contempt, but try other tactics to persuade him to do what is necessary for the cure,[85] "pointing out both the disease that is the consequence of negligence and good health that is the fruit of obedience."[86]

This last depiction thus portrays the spiritual father with measured brushwork as a non-judgmental judge who wisely distinguishes between the sinner and the sin and as a spiritual physician who is prepared for both timid and uncooperative patients. The edges of this composite figure are gently softened by the virtues of simplicity, humility, faith, and love that warmly color every word he utters, every gesture he makes, and every expression that appears on his face.

A Depiction of the General Therapeutic
Skills of a Cognitive Therapist

Emphasis on certification, structured sessions, patient conceptualization, pedagogical skills, and various techniques leads some to criticize cognitive therapists as cold logicians or mechanical technicians lacking in those personal qualities around which good relationships can be formed. As a point of fact, Beck repeatedly emphasizes the need for a warm empathetic relationship in order to build the therapeutic alliance required for therapy to move forward.[87] Our next depiction focuses on the traits and interpersonal skills that a competent cognitive therapist has cultivated in order to facilitate such a relationship.

Apart from competency and expertise in cognitive theory and research, the therapist needs to exhibit the simple courtesy of being punctual, available, and mindful of facts important to the patient.[88] The therapist also appears more approachable if he uses a minimum of psychological jargon and employs understandable metaphors.[89] Because the patient may interpret the terminology describing psychological disorders as pejorative, the therapist should also avoid psychological labels such as paranoid or schizoid and "think in terms of beliefs, predictable reactions, meanings, behaviors, and so forth."[90] For example, if a therapist diagnoses someone with a dependent personality disorder, he could tell the patient that he has "a strong belief in the value of attachment to others."[91]

In addition to these basic skills in social diplomacy, the competent therapist projects accurate empathy by carefully listening to the patient and making thoughtful comments and questions that indicate that the therapist understands why the patient's problems are so distressing.[92] To this end, the therapist focuses on how the patient views his world and then reports those views back to the patient and acknowledges how the patient probably feels.[93] In making comments, the therapist's tone of voice, facial expression, and body language should simultaneously convey a consistent message.[94] The therapist is also instructed to maintain eye contact and speak with a "mellow, soft, nonintrusive voice."[95] The therapist may need to adjust his overall style to the patient's dominant personality traits, emphasizing feelings with the more dependent patient and thoughts with someone who is more autonomous.[96]

The therapist can show that he cares about the patient's concerns by summarizing the patient's thought and feelings as well as by seeking feedback from the patient about these summaries.[97] Cognitive researchers have found evidence in their review of video-taped therapy sessions that when the therapist makes three concise summaries per session of the material presented by the patient, the patient considers that therapist to be warmer and more empathetic than therapists who neglect to do so.[98] Similarly, the therapist can forge a strong partnership with the patient by sincerely asking him for his views about their discussion, for his impressions about whether the therapist understood him, and for his ideas about how he would like the session to go differently next time.[99] Finally, the patient tends to conclude that cognitive therapy's problem-solving approach produces results and that the therapist understands him, when the patient experiences improvement in his symptoms and the resolution of some of his problems.[100]

Admittedly, the therapist may have difficulty remaining empathetic if the patient reacts to him in a childish or insulting way. At such times, the therapist is instructed to maintain empathy by viewing "the adult patient as a highly distressed child."[101] The therapist can also more easily remain objective if he realizes that "patients should be exactly how they are, given their genetic predisposition, experiences, beliefs, and strategies."[102] Beck formulates the cognitive principle underlying empathy as follows: "When we attribute somebody's distress to a factor beyond his control, we can empathize with that person. However, if we hold a person responsible for a harmful occurrence, especially if we attribute it to a moral or character defect, we are prone to disparage the sufferer."[103]

Even if a therapist considers an emotional reaction to be exaggerated or out of place, he will avoid characterizing it as such. Instead, he will empathize with the distress, struggle to find the truth in what the patient is saying, then focus on the dysfunctional thoughts and beliefs that are the source of the discomfort.[104] In other words, even when the therapist is obliged to confront the patient with information that may be upsetting for him, he will preface that presentation with an expression of empathy. For example, if a patient with a borderline personality disorder has a dysfunctional way of relating to other people (e.g., he physically mutilates himself to take revenge on others), the therapist will first indicate that he understands why the patient uses those tactics, and then have him consider some of the negative repercussions associated with them, as well as alternative strategies that the patient could adopt.[105]

In general, the therapist emphasizes solving problems, rather than correcting defects or bad habits, so that the patient will not feel inferior, ashamed, or defensive.[106] When a patient becomes uncooperative, the therapist needs to be sensitive to his own negative meaning assignment. In such instances, the therapist should focus on the patient's good qualities and on the goals that they have both agreed on. The therapist should also struggle not to respond like the patient, but to confront the patient with tact. For example, instead of saying, "You're lying to me," a therapist could say, "I have the feeling that you are struggling to try to tell me something, but you are not sure how to get out the words."[107] It is also important for the therapist to be honest and humble about any possible mistakes made in therapy. Difficult exchanges thus become opportunities for the therapist to model for the patient non-defensive interpersonal behavior, the use of accurate thinking, and an emphasis on problem-solving, thereby demonstrating the value of the cognitive therapeutic approach.[108]

Our depiction of the cognitive therapist in terms of general therapeutic skills presents an approachable figure in whom the angular patterns of rationality have been gently rounded by the human qualities of courtesy, consistency, and sensitivity. The lighting in this portrait comes closest to the shades of day-to-day life. The therapist appears quite human in the best sense of the word when he is seen making an effort to communicate psychological insights with everyday language and struggling to maintain empathy with the belligerent and uncooperative.

When we compare the two depictions in the last diptych, we find less similarity between them than we might have anticipated. Although the calm and gentle voice of the spiritual father might seem to resemble the mellow and non-intrusive voice of the cognitive therapist, the spiritual father's tone is softened by the peace of Christ, whereas the cognitive therapist's tone is technically muted in order to enable his patient to speak with candor. In like manner, although the simple words of the spiritual father may seem similar to the jargon-free language of the therapist, the spiritual father's simplicity is a reflection of his humility, whereas the therapist's plain talk is a *modus operandi* in order to avoid being irksome.

Even the non-judgmental attitude that characterizes both the spiritual father and the cognitive therapist are of a quite different hue. The spiritual father is non-judgmental, because he is humble, because he loves, and because he knows that whatever evil action the person before him has done, that person is good and by the grace of God can become holy as well. The cognitive therapist is non-judgmental, because being judgmental makes empathy impossible and because in a deterministic world each person is exactly as one would expect him or her to be. In terms of worldview, the spiritual father acts in harmony with his Christian faith, whereas the cognitive therapist acts in line with utilitarian and deterministic presuppositions. This motivational difference in non-judgmental stances partially explains why the cognitive therapist must sometimes trade off attributing responsibility to the exasperating patient to maintain empathy and why the spiritual father in a similar situation is able to face responsibility head-on in an empathetic way.

This being said, there is nothing incongruous about a spiritual father listening carefully to his spiritual child, making thoughtful comments, summarizing what has been said and seeking feedback, although these are traits of the empathetic cognitive therapist. In like manner, a cognitive therapist would hardly lose his certification for having Christian love for his patient, faith in God for his patient's recovery, and humility in his patient's presence, although he would share these characteristics with a good spiritual father. In other words, although the sources and aims of the two approaches differ, a prudent borrowing at this level need not be rejected if the borrowed trait is appropriate in the new context and not inconsistent with the ultimate source of inspiration in that setting. A spiritual father would be well advised to be honest and humble about mistakes and to respond in a non-defensive way to insults as a cognitive therapist is trained to behave. It would likewise be sensible for a cognitive therapist to keep in mind his own struggle with maladaptive thoughts and schemata as he relates to his patients, as the Blessed Augustine did when speaking with his opponents. Although similarities may not abound, this diptych is perhaps the richest in exchangeable materials.

A Portrait of a Spiritual Child
Reflected in the Spiritual Father's Eyes

Spiritual fathers and cognitive therapists are inconceivable outside their relationships with the people whom they serve. For this reason, our final diptych reverses perspectives as in an Escher lithograph indirectly depicting spiritual fathers and cognitive therapists through the direct portrayal of the persons reflected in their eyes. Our first portrait has as its primary subject a spiritual child, that is, an individual confessing to a spiritual father. In patristic literature, someone approaches a father confessor in much the same way as a patient approaches a physician—with a readiness for cooperation [synergeia].[109] Saint John Chrysostom stresses this requirement, asking the rhetorical question, "If the physician hates and flees from someone who is sick and if the sick individual turns away from the physician, when will the ailing ever be restored?"[110] In this relationship, the believer is responsible not only for taking the initiative to seek out a spiritual father, but also for implementing his advice.[111] Moreover, he or she must be honest and eager to become well, for a physician cannot cure someone who is sick "unless the patient first entreat him and urge him on by baring his wound with complete confidence."[112]

In this portrait, the person reflected in the spiritual father's eyes is built up out of three layers of differing brightness. A spiritual child is (1) a Christian, (2) a sinner, and (3) a penitent. Each layer requires separate consideration.

First of all, being a baptized Orthodox Christian ideally entails a knowledge and acceptance of the teachings of the Church that the believer manifests through a Christlike way of life.[113] Thus, the belief that "all hope of salvation should be put in Christ"[114] ought to lead the Christian to "pay close attention to the law of God,"[115] and to strive to fulfill Christ's commandments[116] by looking to the Sermon on the Mount (Mt 5-7) as the "perfect model for the Christian life."[117] This endeavor then adorns the believer with virtue, piety, and prayer. In terms of virtue, the Christian directs his thoughts in accord with his heavenly calling and seeks to make his conduct "worthy of the gospel of Christ."[118] In terms of piety, the Christian trusts in the power of the cross to sanctify every aspect of his daily life and accordingly makes the sign of the cross at important moments throughout the day.[119] In terms of prayer, the Christian not only turns to God in every season and in every hour, but also gives thanks to the Lord in times of rest and in times of struggle, ever striving for the gift of unceasing prayer.[120] Liturgically, the Christian chants the grace-filled words of the divine services and becomes a vessel of grace thereby.[121] Most importantly, the Christian is a person who is nourished by Holy Communion. Blessed Augustine in fact defines the faithful as "those to whom we distribute the Body of Christ."[122]

In our portrait of the spiritual child, the initially luminous outlines of the ideal Christian are darkened by the tenebrous stain of sin. The person who comes to a spiritual father for confession is also a sinner, that is, someone who fails to fulfill the commandments of Christ and lead that perfectly virtuous life. In practical terms, this includes all Christians, "for all have sinned and come short of the glory of God."[123] Even after holy baptism, "no one can be so prudent and so circumspect as never to slip at any time." For this reason, God gave us "the medicine of repentance "[124] as "a remedy for the sinner."[125] As Saint Leo, pope of Rome, puts it, "Is there anyone surrounded by the uncertainties of this life, who is exempt from temptation or free from fault? Is there anyone who does not desire for his virtue to grow or his vice to be removed?"[126] The conscientious Christian knows quite well which virtues to cultivate and which passions to fight as well as the character of his life and the secrets of his heart.[127] And since for the Christian, "nothing is more indecent than sin,"[128] awareness of sin both "pains the conscience and brings grief to the mind,"[129] making "the sinner a timid being trembling at a sound even when no one reproaches."[130] To leave this bruised and wounded state, there is but one path, that of repentance.

Hence, someone approaching a spiritual father will also be in a repentant state, for as Saint Ambrose put it, even the Lord himself "does not forgive anyone, except for those who repent."[131] Repentance adds new highlights to a darkened face. The repentant or penitent is someone who *accuses* his sins, rather than *excuses* them[132] or denies them.[133] This mark of genuine repentance, moreover, explains why the ancient ascetics considered self-reproach to be such a fundamental virtue in the Christian life (see chapter 9).

Patristic texts also describe the penitent as being concerned neither about his appearance nor about his diet, but only about his entreaty that God be merciful unto him.[134] This his supplication includes words of true penitence, sighs from the heart, tears of contrition, prostrations, patience, and almsgiving.[135] The repentant also refuse to condemn their brother for any sin.[136] Above all, the repentant are characterized by the meekness and humility necessary to submit to the divine will[137] as well as by "grief that springs from the love of God."[138]

When a person is in this state, he can come to his spiritual father, reveal his wound, be admonished, repent, obtain forgiveness and thereby be healed[139] by his restoration to the Body of the Church that takes up the sinner's burden.[140] Thus by repentance and confession, the Christian who has fallen into sin is restored to his rightful status as a child of God. From the perspective of the confessant, confession of sins is a confession of the truth about himself that makes his soul feel light and free.[141] By confession, the repentant leaves the dark world of dissimulation, denial,[142] and irresponsibility.[143] And as Blessed Augustine so eloquently comments on psalm 84:12, when truth, even the truthful confession of one's sinfulness, springs out of the earth, righteousness looks down from heaven.[144] By confessing one's sins, one already moves toward the truth who is light.[145] In fact, "the confession of evil works is the beginning of good works."[146] By a sincere confession, the soul is humbled.[147] And above all, the soul is given hope by her most compassionate Savior.

Saint Ambrose encourages the person preparing for confession with this exhortation: "The Lord knows all things, but he waits for your words, not in order to punish you, but to pardon you."[148] And that pardon opens the way for a new life that the confessant recognizes by the profound humility that enters his soul and by the grace of the Holy Spirit present in the mystery of confession.[149] This in turn leads to a second kind of confession, the praise of God for his abundant goodness.[150] Saint Cyprian's words about the martyrs who confessed Christ can be applied to the change possible for the sinner who confesses his sins: "At the confession of a single voice, adverse things give way, joyous things appear, kingdoms are opened, empires are prepared, suffering is overcome, death is subdued, life is preferred, and weapons for resistance by a mischievous enemy are broken asunder. If there is sin, it perishes; if there is crime, it is left behind."[151] For someone with faith, confession can change the very order of things, for when man confesses, God responds.

Thus, the eyes of the spiritual father look on a figure with the underlying radiance of the Christian calling, darkened by the fall into sin, and brightened again by the hope of reconciliation. The spiritual father who sees these traits is called upon to *enhance* them, so that his spiritual child will be drawn to the heavenly beauty of the Christian life, will come to a sobering awareness of the tragedy of his fall, and rejoice in the Lord's mercy to the repentant. The spiritual father does this with great compassion, for he is quite aware that as he looks upon his spiritual child he is also looking upon himself.

A Portrait of a Patient Reflected in the Therapist's Eyes

Our closing portrait depicts a patient reflected in the therapist's eyes. Just as someone coming to confession has certain characteristics, so a person having recourse to psychotherapy has specific traits that sociologists have been studying for over fifty years. They have isolated three sets of variables instrumental in a person's decision to turn to a mental health professional: (1) need indicated by clinical and subjective evaluations of mental health, (2) predisposition depending on factors such as sex, age, and education, and (3) resources in terms of factors such as income versus expenses.[152] These variables have different functions in the decision-making process. For example, neither predisposition nor resources cause a person to look for help. And even need is insufficient to lead someone to a therapist's office if that person is disinclined or without the necessary funds. When these factors are properly weighted, however, they form an accurate picture of the person who seeks help.

First of all, people usually decide to turn to a therapist because they subjectively perceive a disturbance in their mental health or a change in their overall mental condition. Those who experience the need for therapy also tend to exhibit behavior that objectively matches the symptoms that define the clinical (Axis I) and personality (Axis II) disorders.[153] From the clinician's perspective, patients are seen as people suffering from a wide variety of conditions such as dementia, psychotic disorders, substance-related disorders, mood disorders, anxiety disorders, somatoform disorders (characterized by physical symptoms without organic disease), factitious disorders (exhibiting self-induced symptoms), dissociative disorders (i.e., multiple personalities), sexual disorders, eating disorders, sleep disorders, impulse-control disorders, adjustment disorders (displaying inappropriate reaction to external stress), and personality disorders.[154] From the patients' perspective, however, they seek help because of real problems with themselves or others, not because of what a psychologist interprets as symptoms and designates with a diagnostic label.[155]

Given a need, there are also predisposing factors that make it more likely that someone will have recourse to therapy. In order to decide to look for psychological help, a person has "to define problems in mental health terms and to have favorable attitudes toward psychiatric treatment."[156] Favorable attitudes usually are derived from having friends with reassuring opinions about psychotherapy,[157] from reading books on psychology,[158] as well as from being exposed to social and psychological sciences.[159] This implies belonging to an informal community of "friends and supporters of psychotherapy," composed of users who share their experiences and even proselytize others.[160] Belonging to such a group turns seeking therapy into a normal decision and thereby makes it easier for a person to do so when the need arises.[161] In other words, someone with a psychological perspective about human behavior and mental functioning will find it easier to seek help from a therapist than someone without such a frame of reference.[162] If a person is not prepared by friends or readings, he or she may still be referred to a psychologist or psychiatrist by other health professionals, in which case adjustment to therapy is usually more difficult.[163]

Many studies have shown that women are more likely to turn to a mental health professional than men.[164] Patients also tend to be unreligious, to live in urban areas, to be divorced or separated, and to be better educated than the general population.[165] In terms of age, patients are usually between twenty-four and sixty-five with the majority of patients being young adults (25–45).[166] Often, patients lack the support of family and friends, and rapidly turn to a professional with relatively minor problems, because as patients often report, "they have no one to share their problem with."[167] Sociologists of religion view the absence of religious involvement as contributing to a sense of isolation. The unreligious lack the emotional support that a church community provides and are deprived of a source of hope that can ease stressful life events. Being outside a faith tradition also makes a person less likely to view the support received in a positive light.[168]

Those without the predisposing characteristics of the above population usually have to overcome a series of hurdles before seeking help from a health professional. These barriers include the innate human resistance to change,[169] objections from family members about seeking treatment,[170] the stigma of being labeled mentally ill,[171] the belief that "the clergy can adequately treat mental health problems,"[172] a value system and pattern of communication that does not mesh well with a psychological perspective,[173] and a lack of awareness that mental health services are an option. In general, patients try to find someone to help them that is acceptable to their general society and culture. It is then a matter of matching their problems with their attitudes about possible sources of assistance.[174] Nevertheless, if distress is severe and support from acceptable care providers insufficient, a person not predisposed to psychotherapy may still overcome existing obstacles and try to find help.[175]

Finally, a person with a psychological problem that is inclined to consider therapy also needs resources in terms of time and money in order to make therapy a viable option. It is not without reason that the patient is also referred to as a client, for the patient is a consumer in the market for health care who demands good mental health or services likely to improve his psychological condition. As a consumer, the patient weighs the cost of services against his own income,[176] considers the amount of time he can allot to therapy, and the geographical proximity of the therapist's office.[177] This means that the patient may do additional shopping before deciding on a particular therapist or type of therapy.

Statistics reveal that therapy in today's society is rarely a life-long engagement. Most patients "initially were high 'utilizers,' but...after psychotherapy their utilization declined significantly."[178] This is especially true for cognitive therapy users, given the long-term effectiveness of cognitive therapeutic approaches for most disorders.[179] For many, therapy is a matter of crisis intervention in which the patient meets with a psychologist acting as a counselor for a limited number of sessions in order to recover from a difficult period.[180] It is worth noting that as all sinners do not go to a spiritual father, so most individuals with a psychiatric disorder receive no mental health care.[181]

Our portrait of the patient in the eyes of the therapist is as clearly delineated as the behavioral criteria for the clinical disorders. It is, however, lacking in depth, perhaps because the person in need is also a nondescript customer prepared to pay for services rendered. Some color is added to the portrait by predisposing factors, such as belief in psychotherapy. Based on these traits in the average patient, the therapist can be described in terms of his abilities to make an accurate diagnosis, to socialize the patient to cognitive therapy, and to provide services commensurate with his fee.

Comparing the portraits in the final diptych of our series, we encounter some formal similarities, but essential differences. Both the individual seeking a mental health professional and the person resolved to go to confession make their decision by considering weighted factors such as need, predisposition, and resources. However, the values in these variables are quite different. The confessant has the predisposing factor of being a conscientious Christian, the need factor caused by the gnawing pain of a guilty conscience, and the enabling factor of sincere repentance. Since the needs are different, it is quite conceivable for someone to require therapy for an eating disorder, but also need spiritual direction about gluttony. How one frames one's problems (the predisposing factor) is a crucial consideration. It is of interest that those who seek therapy are not an indiscriminate general population, but usually members of a loosely knit "community" of believers, believers in therapy. And yet it is a community that offers little help other than a gentle nudge to the therapist's door. The analogous importance of both a value system and way of communicating is also thought-provoking. Admittedly, it is more harrowing for someone in society to view himself as mentally ill, than it is for a Christian to consider himself to be a sinner. On the other hand, it requires more courage and humility for a Christian to take responsibility for his sinful actions than for a secular individual to attribute his psychological problems to environmental and genetic factors beyond his control.

The contractual and short-term aspect of the therapeutic relationship also entails a weaker bond than the bond linking a spiritual father to his spiritual child. The therapist and patient come to a mutual agreement on the basis of exchange (fees for services rendered), whereas the spiritual father and spiritual child enter a covenantal long-term relationship of spiritual commitment before God[182] without any material gain for the spiritual father.[183] These two types of bonds have different standards. A contractual relationship is built on rationality and reliability. A covenantal relationship is based on spiritual sensitivity and commitment.[184]

Reflections from an Unlikely Portrait Gallery

Portraits and paintings aim at directing the eye of the observer to harmonies and tensions that may go unnoticed in a kaleidoscopic world where variations in lighting, design, and color are taken for granted. Our own unlikely portrait gallery brings into sharp relief the fundamental differences between the settings and the roles of both the spiritual father and the cognitive therapist. The harmony, the tone, and the logical perspective of each set of portraits would be grievously disrupted by even the slightest shift in the painted line.

Our icons of spiritual fathers are as rich in color as the frescos adorning the walls of an Orthodox temple. They are ideal images of calm spiritual beauty that bespeaks heavenly virtues adorning earthly men. Although the ideal may be rarely encountered in its fullness, by the grace of God, every spiritual father is able to do and to be far more than his human frailty and fallibility would predict. And this is because the primary agent effecting change is the Holy Spirit who draws sinners to repentance and can "turn their mourning into joy."[185]

Our portraits of cognitive therapists are all drawn with lines as straight and measured as a draftsman's ruler. Cognitive therapists are scientists in whatever role they assume. Regardless of whether they diagnose, teach, advise, or show empathy, their actions are guided by the findings of research and consistent with the scientific method. The high standards set for cognitive therapists are feasible for people with a keen intelligence and a good work ethic. Logically speaking in a secular setting, this achievement is entirely their own.

The indisputable differences in our portrayals of the roles and ministries of spiritual fathers and cognitive therapists may raise questions in the reader's mind about the practical utility of theoretical parallels between patristic approaches and the cognitive model. Although theoretical similarities can never sanction cognitive therapy in the confessional, they may permit both a believer with a psychological problem to consider cognitive therapy and a cognitive therapist working with a Christian patient to find acceptable ways to express cognitive concepts. Furthermore, spiritual fathers also pastorally counsel people with a variety of problems, such as marital difficulties, anxiety, and depression, *outside* the mystery of confession. Without taking on the role of a cognitive therapist, the spiritual father may at such times profitably complement patristic wisdom with insights from cognitive therapy in order to help those in need.

It is natural for the pious to wax lyrical about the quiet beauty of the warm light gently emanating from an oil lamp. It is easy for the caricaturist to exaggerate the calculated efficiency of the cool light shining brightly from a fluorescent bulb. And yet, both types of lighting have their role and functions in the worlds that human beings have both fashioned and occupy. Certainly, no one would praise the surgeon who prefers to operate by candlelight because of the pleasant atmosphere it creates. There is, however, something praiseworthy about integrity that remains true to its calling and recognizes its bounds. Singleness of focus is what enables a great painter to create a masterpiece. With such integrity and focus, both spiritual fathers and cognitive therapists should worthily practice their art, not with sable brushes on a pale canvas, but with calm voices on a troubled soul. And that soul, worth more than the entire world,[186] can surely hope to find the care she deserves from those who are fully devoted to their particular ministry, yet dare to be discerningly open to other worlds.

❧❧❧❧❧❧❧

✣ PART IV ✣

Strategies for Therapeutic Change

Following Ariadne's Thread: Problems, Goals, Experiments, and Behavioral Interventions

Comparing theories and contrasting portraits are suggestive exercises that clarify our vision and hone our judgment. The utility of ideas and the impact of individuals, however, are ultimately tested by their proven ability to solve problems or reach goals through the creative use or innovative development of methods and tools that are adopted by others. These tools and techniques may be as simple as Ariadne's thread attached to the door of a legendary labyrinth. What matters is that they enable any Theseus who employs them to emerge from an otherwise inextricable labyrinth unscathed.[1] Like unto the mythic Ariadne, both cognitive therapists and spiritual fathers proffer tools and techniques for the maze of problems and aspirations that drive a person to seek their aid. The continued use of patristic methods throughout the centuries and the established efficacy of psychotherapeutic techniques in contemporary clinical research indicate that we are dealing with practices that work. The question remains: Can "Ariadnian thread" spun in such divergent workshops be of use in both contexts? That is to say, to what extent are patristic and psychological techniques compatible and, even further, transplantable?

In our last chapter, we noted that people with problems seek help when they are unable to find satisfactory solutions on their own. Michael Mahoney puts it with admirable simplicity, "there are two kinds of solutions to problems: change the way things are or change what you need them to be."[2] In standard psychological parlance, therapists classify solutions to problems in terms of both behavioral interventions aimed at modifying a person's environment and cognitive interventions intended to alter the way an individual interprets events. In patristic tradition, solutions to spiritual problems can likewise be sorted into two classes: advice related to bodily asceticism and counsels concerning watchfulness.

There is, however, something artificial about strictly separating behavioral techniques from cognitive interventions as there is in detaching bodily asceticism from inward watchfulness. Modern learning theory has demonstrated that "people are neither driven by inner forces nor buffeted by environmental stimuli. Rather, psychological functioning is explained in terms of a continuous reciprocal interaction of personal and environmental determinants."[3] Both cognitive theorists and church fathers recognize this three-way relationship involving the environment, behavior, and cognition. Cognitive psychologists have found that altering beliefs can modify behavior and conversely that modifying behavior can alter beliefs.[4] Likewise, when ancient ascetics observe that repentance prepares the way for a virtuous life, they also affirm that a change in beliefs about past actions encourages behavior modification. And when they notice how obedience opens the heart to illumination, they also recognize that regulated behavior can bring about an expanded perspective. Consequently, outward behavior as a co-determinant with cognition in human functioning is a natural target for therapeutic interventions in both patristic and psychotherapeutic contexts. Put more simply, both church fathers and cognitive therapists encourage changes in behavior to correct unhealthy thought patterns, which the fathers view as bad thoughts originating in the passions and which therapists understand as cognitive distortions stemming from maladaptive schemata.

Just as some familiarity with the attributes of mazes can provide clues for someone entering a labyrinth and desiring to reach its end, so a preliminary knowledge of techniques in general can provide us with an illuminating context for discussing behavioral and cognitive strategies for change. In any field of human inquiry, techniques are experientially discovered or experimentally developed in order to solve problems and to achieve goals. Problem solving, goal setting, and experimentation also happen to be approaches explicitly taught in cognitive therapy and logically prior to the selection of behavioral or cognitive techniques. They can also be considered techniques in their own right. Hence, it seems only prudent to preface our examination of behavioral techniques in patristic and psychotherapeutic contexts with a more general exploration of how both church fathers and cognitive theorists solve problems, set goals, and perform experiments.

Solving Problems, Setting Goals, and
Running Experiments in Patristic Tradition

As we have already mentioned, people turn to spiritual fathers and therapists because they are unable to solve their problems on their own, in part because they fail to approach their predicament appropriately. The ancient fathers counsel the faithful to view life's reversals and afflictions as a whetstone to sharpen their minds, thereby keeping them active and making them wise. Saint John Chrysostom is even of the opinion that the presence of adversities has blessed humanity with the development of the arts.[5] Full of realistic optimism based on observed experience, patristic tradition regards problems as opportunities that can make people resourceful and even strong.[6] For example, the man married to a nagging wife is advised to consider this marital disturbance to be "a school and training ground" that provide him with the means to attain a crown.[7]

When monastic fathers approached problems, they would combine rigorous thought with fervent prayer.[8] Elder Païsios encouraged those at an impasse to examine all sides of a difficulty, to consider the potential positive and negative repercussions of each course of action, and then to select the best possible solution. Once the believer's human resources for solving a problem have been depleted, the elder then suggests prayerfully entrusting it to God's care.[9] In their exegetical, polemical, and apologetic works, the church fathers manifested what would today be called problem-solving skills in order to deal with whatever task was at hand. Their brief comments about resolving difficulties can be used to construct a patristic-based series of steps for the rational or metacognitive aspect of problem-solving in general.

According to the church fathers, to find a solution for a difficult situation, the problem-solver needs to *believe* that it can be solved in the first place.[10] Second, he should be knowledgeable about the wider context in which the problem is embedded in order to speak with precision.[11] This contextual knowledge entails gathering more data about matters related to the difficulty. The individual can then make use of this information to determine and articulate the pivotal issues at stake. As a rule, if someone coherently lays out a problem or lucidly formulates a question, the solution will also appear with clarity.[12] Third, the problem-solver needs to be thoroughly awake and alert in order to pay close attention to detail.[13] Fourth, he should make accurate distinctions, use neutral language,[14] be consistent, and consider possibilities that are manifest and clear.[15] Finally, if more than one solution has been generated, he should try to select the very best[16] by considering what brings him the most benefit and makes his soul feel at peace.[17]

Thus, the ancient fathers collectively teach that the labyrinthine chaos of a given problem can be ordered within a wider perspective by an observant eye. The patristic *modus operandi* for problem solving begins with optimistic faith and continues as a judicious investigative approach guided by attentiveness to detail, clear language, and consistent reasoning. The final results of this process are then set before the tribunal of a God-loving heart. This patristic methodology is as timely and practical now as it was then.

When ancient ascetics guided the faithful in the spiritual life, they effortlessly and automatically translated the problem of a particular passion into the goal of the virtue that opposes it. For example, Saint John of Sinai orients readers of *The Ladder* to the goal of freedom from anger [*aorgēsia*] when he discusses the problem of irascibility, to the goal of abstinence when he examines the problem of gluttony, and to the goal of purity when he considers the problem of fleshly desires.[18] Although the church fathers may not have *explicitly* spoken about the need to transform problems into goals, they did so in practice, because they realized that without spiritual goals people are doomed to wander endlessly in the trackless maze of human passions.

When Saint Paul wrote to the Philippians, he encouraged them in the spiritual life by sharing his own experience about the way a proper goal can sustain virtuous behavior: "Forgetting the things which are behind and stretching forward to the things which are before, I press on toward the *goal* unto the *prize* of the high calling of God in Christ Jesus."[19] Commenting on this passage, Saint John Chrysostom observes that in any contest, "the sight of the prize increases the determination of the will."[20] Elsewhere, he notes how people become resolute and roused for action by turning their thoughts to the future.[21] According to Saint Justin Martyr, this future hope is the secret that accounts for Christian heroism and martyric sacrifice.[22] Tertullian elaborates on the change brought about by goals when he remarks on how the martyr beholding an eternal crown at the final judgment finds his prison cell transfigured into a training ground and his trials into exercises in virtue.[23] Thus, a worthy goal can invigorate the soul, emboldening her to make lion-hearted decisions similar to those that set apart the apostles, martyrs, and all the saints.

Without proper goals, purposeful human activity languishes lamentably. Saint Ambrose of Milan vividly illustrates this state of stagnation as follows: "Deprive the pilot of the hope of reaching port, and he will wander with uncertainty here and there on the waves. Take away the crown from the athlete, and he will fail and lie down on the track....How, then, can someone whose soul is famished with hunger pray more earnestly to God, if he cannot hope to obtain the heavenly food?"[24] Thus, feasible goals, such as receiving Holy Communion in this case, provide motivation necessary for the active struggle for change. As a corollary to this principle, foolish goals are perhaps worse than no goals at all. *The Encheiridion* shared by Christians and philosophers alike notes that the desire for relatives to never die or for employees to make no mistakes is a fool's desire, for such goals lie beyond everyone's grasp. Goals should consequently be set for oneself and be attainable.[25]

Saint John Cassian observes that to succeed in any art or science, a person must possess both long-term and short-term goals, so that he can maintain diligence and persistence[26] in the face of unavoidable toils, imminent dangers, and unexpected losses.[27] Otherwise, his "mind will surely wander about from hour to hour, since it has no fixed point to which it may return and on which it may be primarily focused."[28] Even further, when the soul is fixated on worldly matters in the present, instead of concentrating on the ultimate goal of the kingdom of heaven in the future, it can also slip into all sorts of wickedness.[29]

Given the paramount importance of goals, the ancient fathers understandably provide a variety of comparable long-term aims designed to motivate Christians to follow the commandments of Christ. For example, Saint Gregory of Nyssa considers love [*agapē*] to be an ideal long-term goal, because it reflects divine perfection, encompasses all the virtues, and can thus guide Christian behavior at every stage in the spiritual life.[30] Elsewhere, he considers the vision of God [*ton Theon idein*] to be the unsurpassable aspiration for the believer.[31] For Saint John Cassian, the kingdom of heaven [*regnum coelorum*] is the final prize that the monk strives to attain.[32] When goals such as these underlie daily activities, even the lowliest and least of tasks become precious and meaningful steps in a lifelong pilgrimage to the Jerusalem on high.[33]

Although the fathers' eyes were fixed on heaven, their feet were planted firmly on the earth. The Gospels and the Lives of the Saints illustrate that it is not enough for the believer merely to set a worthy goal; he must also discover the way to secure it.[34] For instance, when the mother of Zebedee's children disclosed her sons' ambition to sit at Christ's right hand and at his left, the Lord instructed them in the way of humility whereby they could attain to the glory of God.[35] According to Saint Gregory of Nyssa, only a fool daydreams about goals without thinking about how they can be achieved.[36] For this reason, the church fathers both affirmed the necessity for short-term goals and detailed the particular steps required for a major goal to be reached.

For example, in order to attain the long-term objective of the kingdom of heaven, the monk is advised to make purity of heart [*puritas cordis*] his short-term goal on a daily basis.[37] Like Gregory of Nyssa, Blessed Augustine praises the aim of love [*dilectio*], emphasizing its immediate value as a guide for the believer's daily life: "Once and for all, a brief precept is given to you: Love, and do what you wish: if you hold your peace, out of love hold your peace; if you cry out, out of love cry out; if you correct, out of love correct; if you spare, out of love spare. Let the inner root be love, for from this root nothing else can shoot forth except for that which is good."[38] Thus, love as an immediate goal protects the believer from straying from Christian conduct and gives him a proper focus in the course of action.

Saint John Chrysostom suggests that the faithful consider how students in an ideal situation are not overburdened with many assignments or with one large project, but are given short tasks that they are capable of completing.[39] The saint concludes that the faithful should learn the Christian way of life in like manner. With respect to acquiring virtue, patristic consensus similarly advises taking one step at a time, since it is not possible to climb to the top of virtue's ladder by any other means.[40] For example, Saint Gregory of Sinai suggests that the believer can attain the goal of courage by first being patient in all his activities.[41] Saint Nicodemos the Hagiorite also indicates that the Christian struggler should acquire step by step the outward virtues such as fasting and vigils as well as inward virtues such as patience and humility. For example, if praying for an hour seems burdensome, the saint suggests starting one's prayer as though it would last for only fifteen minutes and repeating that step until the hour has been fulfilled.[42] In the same spirit, Saint Maximus the Confessor offers an incremental series of goals for the person desiring dispassion: (1) to stop committing sin in deed, (2) to reject bad thoughts, (3) to subdue passionate desires, and (4) to purge the mind of all imaginings.[43]

In summary, patristic tradition affirms the motivational necessity and metacognitive value of setting reasonable and feasible goals in order to sustain heroic behavior associated with holiness. The monastic fathers also stress the need for both long-term aspirations of an eschatological nature and short-term aims related to the daily life. These two sets of goals are intimately related and thoroughly interdependent, for short-term aims build toward long-term hopes, whereas long-term hopes provide incentive to fulfill short-term aims. Even short-term objectives can be broken down into a series of steps or subgoals required to reach them. Together, this diversity of goals shape a person's perspective, thereby facilitating purposeful and God-pleasing behavior.

When a person gathers more data in order to solve problems and engages in new activities in order to meet goals, he naturally acquires additional information and expanded perspectives drawn from experience. Although it is anachronistic to ascribe Baconian experimentalism to scriptural and patristic tradition, an experimental approach *qua* an experiential approach can be easily discerned. Philip's invitation to Nathanael, "Come and see," was in psychological terms an invitation to perform a behavioral experiment in order to acquire further data that would either verify or falsify Nathanael's beliefs.[44] In other words, it was a challenge to test the truth of an assertion by experience. Commenting on the psalm verse, "Be still and know that I am God" (45:11 [LXX]), Archimandrite Zacharias [Zacharou] writes, "If you try stillness, if you make your own experiment, then you will know. God is kind and wants us to carry out the experiment and prove it to ourselves and establish it as a law of our life."[45] Anachronistic or not, the scientific experimental paradigm works remarkably well as a description for the implicit invitation of scriptural tradition.

In the patristic context, the experimental aspect of experience is even more explicit. For example, Saint Gregory of Nyssa invokes an experimental approach to the truth when he refers to people determining whether a lethal drug is in fact poisonous by testing a small sample.[46] When Clement of Alexandria describes prudence as an offspring of experience, he defines experience in terms of establishing causality by observing similarities, altering contexts, and making new associations.[47] His definition provides a remarkably modern description of experimentation that also coincides nicely with comments by the Latin ecclesiastical writer Arnobius who views the arts as the logical consequence of observation, experimentation [experitur], as well as trial and error.[48] The church fathers also note that observation and experience enable people to believe assertions that would otherwise be unbelievable, such as the fact that an olive can mature into an olive tree[49] or that the soft seed of man can grow into a human being with flesh and bones.[50] Saint Basil the Great encapsulates the patristic consensus on the persuasive value of experience in one short sentence: "Experience seems better than reasoning about causation" [Kreittōn ephanē tou logou tēs aitias hē peira].[51]

Naturally, ancient ascetics directly apply these views on observation and experience to spiritual matters. Saint John Chrysostom considers mere words to be inadequate for conveying spiritual reality. For example, in order to understand what is meant by paradise, a person needs to experience it.[52] Saint John Cassian mentions that in the spiritual life the believer does not learn "by some previous verbal explanation, but rather by experience [experientia] and action leading the way."[53] The truth of ascetic counsels can be proved only through the test of experience or experimentation.[54] Saint John Chrysostom views such experimentation as a crucial element in the Christian life. In fact, unless it is demonstrated in practice that the virtues are attainable, discourse about virtue can be justifiably dismissed as brazenly far-fetched.[55]

Blessed Augustine takes the notion of experience/experiment into a recognizably cognitive context when he observes that "for the most part, the human mind cannot attain to self-knowledge except by testing its powers through temptation by some kind of experimental [*experimento*], and not merely verbal [*verbo*], self-interrogation."[56] In psychological terms, the learned bishop of Hippo links cognitive change at a schematic level with experimentation that necessarily involves behavioral or environmental modification. These modifications are more effective than cognitive approaches alone and can be understood as active ways of questioning the self and as paths leading the believer to more reliable self-knowledge than solitary introspection can offer.

In patristic tradition, experience is what can disprove deceitful thoughts as easily dismissible delusions, for thoughts are only as strong as the activity that undergirds them. According to Saint Neilus the Ascetic, "experience is the pathway to this kind of knowledge."[57] Blessed Augustine also made this point when he essayed to convince Vincentius Victor of his errors on the origin of the soul. In particular, the saint wrote, "But you can learn all of this with the greatest ease if you would simply prefer doing so, to stiffly maintaining your own statements for no reason other than that you have made them."[58] Without the purposeful action and observation that characterize experimentation, ideas remain untested and individuals grow obstinate and narrow-minded.

For this reason, the church fathers challenge the faithful to engage in behavioral experiments that can both transform their thoughts and improve their lives. For example, both Saint John Chrysostom and Blessed Augustine advise their flock to stop swearing experimentally and to observe the edifying results.[59] The holy archbishop of Constantinople additionally advises the person engaged in the experiment of overcoming a bad habit to ask others to correct him when he slips. This collaboration makes the experiment "official" and increases the prospect for success. "Just try it, if you doubt me,"[60] coaxes the saint.

Elder Païsios furnishes contemporary testimony to the power of behavioral experiments to alter cognition. He related that when people sought his advice about fears that they had contracted acquired immune deficiency syndrome, he would first question them about past behavior that might make them susceptible. Even if their behavior would not put them at risk, he would not only tell them to stop worrying, but also to be examined in order to put their minds at ease. Those who agreed to be tested and were clear would return to the elder with a relieved expression on their face, whereas those who apprehensively refused to do so would continue to be tormented by their thoughts.[61]

In summary, a diversity of patristic texts displays a clear understanding of what experimentation is, why it is necessary, and how it can be applied to benefit the believer's mental health and spiritual life. When we combine this knowledge with approaches to careful problem-solving and the use of goals, we can see that far from discouraging innovation and discovery, the ancient fathers encouraged such activities in the very arena where they can be of greatest value—in a person's relationship with God. Patristic tradition as a whole thus provides fertile soil not only for the development of what psychologists are wont to call "behavioral and cognitive techniques" in order to bring the soul closer to God, but also for the testing of new practices as well.[62]

Solving Problems, Setting Goals, and Running Experiments in Cognitive Therapy

Since people turn to therapists for help with their problems, it is hardly surprising that the very first session in cognitive therapy is usually devoted to defining a set of problems and considering strategies for solving them.[63] If the patient has a maladaptive approach to problems in general, the therapist must first demonstrate to the patient that they are a normal part of life and not catastrophes to be avoided. The therapist may also need to encourage the patient to view his difficulties as challenges that in time can be overcome with effort and careful planning.[64]

Once a patient views his problems in a realistic way, the therapist can then teach him four basic skills for approaching them as efficiently as a scientist would. The patient learns (1) how to clearly define a problem by gathering relevant information about it and its causes, (2) how to generate a large variety of potential solutions, (3) how to select the best choice on the basis of a rational cost-benefit analysis of the overall utility of each option, and (4) how to devise an experiment as a potential solution, to implement that experiment, and to revise it if it does not prove to be satisfactory.[65] As scientists do much of their work with pen and paper, so the patient is expected to keep a written record of the entire problem-solving process. This entails making lists of causes and potential courses of action, constructing charts with ratings for each prospective solution, and composing summaries in which the patient evaluates the degree of success for each solution that is implemented.[66]

For example, a widow diagnosed with breast cancer came to therapy on account of depression. In the first session, after the therapist and patient (1) considered various causes for depression such as her views about illness and fears of dying, they discovered that her primary concern was loneliness. They then (2) brainstormed a number of solutions to her problem such as buying a pet, visiting acquaintances, sending e-mails to friends, calling up others on the phone, asking family members to visit, and so forth. They afterward (3) evaluated each solution by assigning it a subjective numerical value [x] derived from its advantages and disadvantages. For instance, buying a pet has the

disadvantages of costing money [-2], requiring daily upkeep [-2], and increasing housekeeping tasks [-2], but the advantages of being always present [+4]
and available for petting [+3]. Thus, the desirability of obtaining a pet can be
assigned the cumulative value of +1. When this cost-benefit analysis was
completed for each of her options, the patient then (4) decided to implement
the highest rated solution by calling up a new friend every night and observing
how that would affect her overall mood.[67]

A related way of approaching problems in cognitive therapy is to focus on
goal-oriented behavior. In other words, the therapist takes the patient's
discouraging litany of negative problems and reformulates it as a promising
checklist of positive behavioral goals. For example, the problem of loneliness
can be changed into the goal of meeting new people.[68] Depressed patients will
often say that they simply want to feel happier. Such an abstract and general
goal needs to be reformulated, so that its attainment can be behaviorally
measured. Thus, "therapists often have to ask patients what they would be
doing differently if they were happier. The behaviors they state then become
the short-term goals, toward which the patients work at each session."[69]

Sometimes, patients list aims over which they have little control, such as
changing someone else's behavior. In such cases, therapists encourage them to
rework the goals that they set for others into behavioral goals for themselves.
For example, the teenager who complains about his mother constantly nagging
him can change his objective of making her stop finding fault with him, to
setting aside some quiet time for himself alone.[70]

In establishing goals, it is important for the therapist to make sure that
they are feasible and of moderate difficulty. To this end, the therapist may
have to break down a major objective in the future into smaller subgoals that
stepwise lead to its achievement.[71] It is also necessary for the therapist and
patient to establish a goal hierarchy by determining the most important
problem, so that they can address goals in their proper sequence. To help the
patient establish this hierarchy, the therapist can look over the list of problems
with the patient and ask him to imagine how he would feel if a given difficulty
would be eliminated. The problem whose elimination would bring him the
most relief is the most important.[72] The therapist and patient can also consider
how his troubles are related to one another and try to eliminate the first link
in a chain of difficulties.[73]

In cognitive therapy, solving problems and establishing goals become more
than an intellectual exercise through "small experiments designed to test the
validity of the patient's hypotheses or ideas about himself."[74] Although an
experiment may be justified as a means for gathering further data about a
problem,[75] the ultimate aim is usually to modify the patient's beliefs or

schemata through a disconfirming experience proving to the patient that his over-generalized conclusions are invalid.[76]

For example, someone who is depressed usually becomes inactive, because he views himself as ineffectual or worthless or both. He then construes his inactivity as proof of his worthlessness, leading him to even more pronounced passivity. To break out of this vicious cycle, the therapist urges the patient to modify behaviors such as inactivity or avoidance in order to demonstrate that his self-evaluations are biased.[77] Someone struggling with substance abuse, who believes that he will lose his friends if he does not smoke marijuana with them, can test his belief by experimentally participating with his friends in social activities, but without using drugs.[78] In general, patients with psychological problems stemming from a belief about unlovability are "encouraged to do behavioral experiments that involve taking steps toward connecting with others. Patients who believe that they are basically likable but are helpless or ineffective need to engage in a variety of mastery experiences."[79] These experiments can be as simple as going out to eat with a friend or taking up a new hobby; what is important is that they enable a person to test the validity of his beliefs, and thus emerge from his labyrinth of dysfunctional thoughts.

Therapists usually assign behavioral experiments to patients as homework to be completed before the next session. To reinforce the successful completion of homework, therapists make the point of praising the patient for a job well done and have the patient give himself credit for it as well.[80] In order to encourage the patient to comply with an assignment when motivational difficulties arise (as in the case of phobias and anxiety disorders), some therapists resort to contingency contracting: "The patient gives the therapist a fixed amount of money, which is returned only when the task is completed. If the task is not completed, the money can be disposed in a number of ways, such as being sent to a charity or a relative the patient dislikes."[81] Obviously, such arrangements are not far removed from Skinner's research on operant conditioning in which a laboratory rat learns to solve a maze with the prodding of reinforcing food pellets and discouraging electric shocks.

The patristic and cognitive approaches to solving problems, setting goals, and running experiments are remarkably consistent and compatible. Both approaches understand problems as a natural part of life and encourage people to face them head on. There is, however, a significant difference in the inner logic governing each approach. In a patristic context, faith in a loving God enables the believer to view problems as opportunities to grow in virtue, wisdom, and strength. In a psychotherapeutic context, empiricism and rationalism empower the patient to consider problems to be challenges that can be overcome with effort and planning. Nevertheless, it is certainly possible for someone to regard problems spiritually as opportunities for growth and rationally as challenges to be overcome.

In terms of problem-solving skills, both church fathers and cognitive therapists recognize the importance of gathering additional information about a given problem and of carefully determining the best possible solution. Both parties also have their own unique contribution to the art of resolving difficulties. For example, ancient fathers note that in order to solve a problem, a person needs to be alert, to pay attention to details, to formulate the question in clear, neutral language, and to make accurate distinctions. Contemporary therapists propose that problem solving can be facilitated if a person generates a large quantity and variety of potential solutions, if he systematically uses a utilitarian cost-benefit analysis, if he turns the potential solution into an experiment, and if he keeps records of the entire process. The church fathers, of course, affirm that prayer should accompany problem-solving efforts and that the intuitions of the God-loving heart should also be used to select the best course of action.

In terms of setting goals, both ancient ascetics and cognitive therapists view goal-oriented behavior as a crucial element in the therapeutic process. Both recognize that a person should establish feasible objectives for himself rather than for others and break down long-range complicated aspirations into subgoals and tasks of moderate difficulty. Although the monastic fathers tacitly turn problems into goals, cognitive therapists should be commended for making that process explicit. When the church fathers note that worthy aims can increase determination and motivation, thereby sustaining behavior and altering a person's perspective in a way that makes room for heroism and bravery, they provide cognitive therapists with an excellent rationale for setting goals. The cognitive practices of forming a goal hierarchy and looking for the first link in a chain of problems are also fine offerings for use in a pastoral context.

Finally, both church fathers and cognitive therapists view experience or experimentation as necessary in order for someone to be able to test the validity of his ideas, personal hypotheses, and convictions. They both recognize that mere words are too weak to persuade a person that a given practice is beneficial, harmful, or neutral. The ancient fathers note that without engaging in such experimentation, a person will have trouble gaining self-knowledge and an appreciation for the value of the virtues. He will, moreover, be in danger of growing obstinate and narrow-minded. Cognitive therapists would hardly disagree.

Thus, the time-tested approach of the fathers to problems, goals, and experimentation coincides nicely with the contemporary practice of cognitive therapists. Consequently, in theory, both patristic tradition and cognitive therapy should be open to techniques that are developed within the corresponding world. Cognitive therapy in particular makes a major contribution to the art of helping others by clearly linking problems to goals and goals to experimentation. This theoretical framework can also serve as a structure for patristic views on these subjects.

A Patristic Understanding of *Praxis* and a Sampling of Ascetic Practices

Throughout church history, the fathers have not only observed differences in the ways in which saints and sinners think and act, but also noted the close interrelationship between cognition and behavior, which they discuss in terms of noetic *theoria* and bodily *praxis* respectively. In patristic tradition, theoria and praxis refer to the inward and outward aspects of life in Christ. In classical literature, theoria meant seeing in general or the vision of the mind that in a patristic context came also to mean the spiritual and intellectual vision of a purified heart. Praxis referred to doing or moral action that in ecclesiastical usage came also to refer to Christian conduct and the cultivation of the virtues.[82]

In the spiritual life, theoria is meant to guide praxis, which at a bare minimum means that cognition should govern behavior. Thus, Saint Maximus the Confessor comments that in the saint, thoughts express true knowledge that regulates the body so that its actions are virtuous.[83] Hence, knowledge illumines the soul through theoria and right cognition, while virtue sanctifies the body through praxis and proper behavior.[84] In the sinner, the malady of ignorance is a spiritual blindness or lack of theoria that both darkens the thoughts and causes the body to be profaned by the sickness of vice or a lack of praxis. Thus, complete spiritual healing requires both changes in behavior by the practice/praxis of the virtues and in cognition by a spiritual vision / theoria that perceives divine reason (i.e., the *Logos*) woven into the very fabric of reality.[85]

Although praxis and theoria operate on distinct planes of human existence, they are not strictly separable, but rather mutually inhere in one another. The Christian life can be conceived of as a union of theoria and praxis that begets reasonable actions mentally defined and behaviorally activated by the commandments of the Lord.[86] The reciprocal interdependence of praxis and theoria has therapeutic import. Actions not only provide clues about thoughts,[87] but also can be purposefully altered in order to influence those thoughts, for "the soul is affected by what the body does"[88] and "becomes like its bodily occupations."[89]

When a father confessor guides his spiritual child, he usually first recommends behavioral change or praxis, such as fasting and a prayer rule, since such behavior leads to experiential knowledge that can transfigure the believer's way of life.[90] Furthermore, although both praxis and theoria are vital for all stages of the spiritual life,[91] the hesychastic fathers especially associate praxis with purification from the passions that readies the believer for theoria as illumination and deification in Christ. Praxis is thus "a prelude to a God-loving way of life"[92] and a blossom from which the fruit of theoria will grow.[93]

Praxis as a change in behavior, however, is never without its cognitive component, even if that component is intentionally disregarded, because it is spiritually unhealthy. For example, sometimes the ancient ascetics advise us to practice doing the opposite of what our thoughts dictate in order to weaken the passions,[94] so that new virtuous habits replace the former passionate ones,[95] thereby making "tranquility of character [morum tranquilitatis] our natural disposition by constant practice."[96] In terms of cognitive theory, behaviorally acting contrary to automatic thoughts weakens the strength of dysfunctional schemata and assists in the formation of new adaptive beliefs.

When the church fathers recommend making use of praxis, bodily asceticism, or bodily virtues as tools in order to become righteous,[97] cognitive therapists would be apt to view those tools as behavioral techniques in the service of cognitive change. The monastic fathers point out that bodily asceticism by itself is an insufficient means for the believer to attain spiritual perfection, but it is nevertheless a necessary supplement to more "cognitive" patristic approaches of humility and prayer.[98] Although lists of ascetic practices vary, they inevitably include the scriptural traditions of fasting and vigil.[99] One typical list of bodily virtues mentions "self-control, fasting, hunger, thirst, staying awake, keeping all-night vigils, constant kneeling, not washing, the wearing of a single garment, eating dry food, eating slowly, drinking nothing but water, sleeping on the ground...working with your own hands and every kind of hardship and bodily asceticism."[100]

The ascetic life has a number of aims, such as hindering thoughts of pleasure,[101] cutting off bodily passions,[102] and curbing habitual self-indulgence.[103] When these aims are met, corporal asceticism further prevents sins related to those passions from materializing,[104] while bringing a balance to the body's temperament,[105] a clear conscience to the mind,[106] contrition to the heart,[107] and purity to the nous.[108] In other words, the ascetic life makes it easier for the believer to acquire virtue and observe the commandments of Christ.[109] Abstinence also brings the grace of God in the form of spiritual nourishment, consolation,[110] joy, and experience,[111] for as Saint Thalassius puts it, "How God treats you depends upon how you treat your body."[112]

In order for bodily asceticism to bear good fruit, it must be appropriate, timely,[113] and within the boundaries established by the holy fathers and mothers.[114] Amma Syncletica refers to such asceticism as royal and divine by virtue of its symmetry or good proportion.[115] Any other kind of ascetic activity is demonic, for it harms the body instead of healing the soul.[116] Ideally, the spiritual father regulates the ascetic endeavor of his spiritual child and adjusts austerity in fasting according to physical endurance[117] and the overall emphasis on outward asceticism or noetic prayer according to mental aptitude.[118]

In the battle against lust and gluttony, the monastic fathers consider bodily asceticism to be indispensable.[119] They also note that a given ascetic practice can serve a variety of purposes. Fasting not only bridles gluttony, it also withers fleshly desire; vigil not only weakens lust, it also gives wings to prayer.[120] Sometimes, monks would employ one form of asceticism to discourage lapses from another. For example, Saint John Climacus refers to ascetics who would chastise lapses in fasting by standing throughout the night.[121]

In general, ascetic labor and hardship free the soul from bondage to physical pleasures and creature comforts.[122] Saint Gregory Palamas indicates that bodily hardship, fasting, and vigil are also conducive to prayer and compunction.[123] Even manual labor has its ascetic and therapeutic value, for as Abba Dorotheos observes, "Labor humbles the body, and when the body is humbled, the soul is humbled with it."[124] Physical work can act as an anchor that moors the mind otherwise endangered by the storm of bad thoughts,[125] whereas handcrafts can keep wind in the sail of the soul otherwise marooned on a desert isle of listlessness, idleness,[126] and sleepiness.[127] Simply keeping busy with tasks keeps the mind occupied and leaves less time for struggling with bad thoughts.[128]

Prostrations and a prayerful stance are behaviors frequently encountered and actively encouraged in Eastern Orthodox worship in order to bring about a proper "cognitive" approach to God and self.[129] Saint John Climacus gives a rationale for these practices when he advises beginners in prayer to adopt the stance of a person who prays with piety, since "in the case of the imperfect, the mind often conforms to the body."[130] Elsewhere, the author of *The Ladder* chronicles both how an illumined abbot ordered a formerly arrogant monk to make prostrations at the gate of the monastery and how that monk's inner sentiments grew more humble and contrite over time.[131] East and West, the church fathers note, "When the body is bent at a brother's feet, humble feelings are either awakened in the heart itself, or are strengthened if already present."[132] Even in solitude, the body's stance can be efficacious. For example,

Saint Gregory of Sinai suggests that those fighting thoughts of listlessness or lust imitate Moses by standing up with hands aloft and eyes turned toward heaven from whence help from the Lord will surely come.[133]

In addition to standard ascetic endeavors, patristic tradition recognizes the utility of other related practices and conditions with behavioral components such as the observation of self and others. For example, self-observation with respect to fasting and hunger can relativize the urgency of hunger pangs and demonstrate the value of abstaining from food.[134] Self-monitoring with respect to the thoughts can increase the believer's awareness of the particular passions that stir them up. Saint John Climacus thus advocated the monastic practice of keeping a notebook on one's person in order to record thoughts throughout the day for confession at a later time.[135] Observing the virtue and ascetic efforts of others can both keep one's own ascetic struggle in perspective and draw attention to models for imitation. The church fathers were well aware that living examples of virtue and ascetic endeavor are necessary, "for any discourse devoid of works is like a lifeless image, regardless of how attractively it happens to be presented."[136] Saint John Chrysostom encourages the faithful to consider how people have decided to venture overcoming a vice on observing the diligence of others attempting to do so.[137] Of course, the paragon of virtue that the believer should always keep in mind is the example of Christ.[138]

Since "we quickly get accustomed to what we hear and what we see,"[139] our surroundings have a direct effect on our thoughts. Consequently, our behavioral choice to place ourselves in a given environment is also an important ingredient in our ascetic struggle. The church fathers would heartily agree with Albert Bandura's observation: "Thoughts are partly governed by external stimuli. Thus, the cognitions elicited in a hospital differ markedly from those aroused in a night club."[140] With the observational acumen of a social learning theorist, Saint John Chrysostom suggests comparing the actions, demeanor, and conversations of people coming out of a theater with those leaving a prison.[141] Abba Dorotheos similarly observes, "The soul has one disposition when mounted on a horse, another when seated on an ass, yet another when installed on a throne, and another still when sitting on the ground."[142] Thus, one strategy in the battle for righteousness' sake involves learning to avoid situations conducive to sin and to seek out settings favorable to virtue. For example, the fathers often advise the faithful to avoid the theater, because the seamier side of the thespian arts, like television violence today, can operate as a school of corruption whose dramatizations train the young in vice and sin.[143]

Thus, environmental influences provide a partial psychological explanation for the therapeutic value of being present in church where God-pleasing thoughts are naturally evoked. Consistent attendance maintains these thoughts as a regular part of one's life. An account from *The Gerontikon* bears witness to the significant impact of the environment on cognitive and behavioral difficulties. There once was a certain monk who went to see an elder because the monk was troubled by the thought that he was incapable of fasting or working. In order to help the monk overcome both his present inactivity and his distressing thoughts, the elder designed a simple behavioral experiment: he told him to eat, drink, and sleep like everybody else, but to remain in his cell as befits a monastic. After a few days of boredom, the monk began his handiwork, then the reading of the Psalter, and finally fasting.[144]

The believer who remains in a monastic cell or attends church undergoes cognitive changes not only as a result of his passive presence, but also from his active—or to use behavioralist terminology, his operant—participation in prayer. Thus, Saint John Chrysostom likens church attendance to a soldier's drills and a wrestler's exercises, for the divine services and the pastor's instructions train the Christian to skillfully combat the spiritual adversary.[145]

Finally, some ascetics devised particularly physical behavioral interventions for dealing with the physiological and cognitive struggle with the lusts of the flesh. For example, Saint Hesychius the Presbyter suggests physically striking the body when under the influence of sensual pleasure, so that a change in physical sensation (viz., physical pain) will properly guide behavior and cognition to the way of chastity and purity.[146] In *The Gerontikon*, a certain father was troubled by the memory of a beautiful woman whom he had once seen in Egypt. When he had heard that the woman had died, he took a dishcloth and went to her grave and wiped it over her decaying remains. Then, when desires of the flesh would trouble him, he would smell the stench and say to himself, "Here is what you really desire, have your fill of it."[147] Although this example seems gruesome to modern sensibilities, disrespectful to the departed, and degrading to women, it does, nevertheless, demonstrate the power of experience to falsify and weaken otherwise compulsive bad thoughts.

In short, long before cognitive psychology appeared on the scene to correct one-sided behavioralism, patristic tradition had a unified understanding of human mental functioning in terms of theoria and praxis. Although theoria occupies a place of preeminence in patristic thought, even as cognition does in cognitive therapy, nevertheless, praxis is often addressed first in the spiritual life. Praxis takes the form of bodily asceticism, which is seen as a necessary supplement to an asceticism of the heart. Prudently directed ascetic activity is especially useful in breaking sinful habits and acquiring contrition and purity. Clearly defined behavioral practices—such as fasting, vigil, prostrations, standing, spending time in church and so forth—aim at fighting specific passions and acquiring distinct virtues. In cognitive terms, these practices can be understood as behavioral interventions that aim at altering spiritually maladaptive schemata and fostering new adaptive beliefs conducive to a virtuous life.

A Cognitive Understanding of Behavior and a Sampling of Behavioral Techniques

Behavioral techniques used in psychotherapy have their origin in Pavlovian studies and in Skinnerian research. In experimentation on classical conditioning, Ivan Pavlov (1849-1936) demonstrated how an unconditioned stimulus, such as salivation at the sight of food, and a conditioned stimulus, such as a tone sounded when food is presented, could be paired, so that an organism responds to the conditioned stimulus even when the unconditioned stimulus is absent. In studies on operant conditioning, B. F. Skinner (1904-1990) showed how positive and negative reinforcement following a behavioral act could alter the future probability of that behavior. Extrapolating from these kinds of studies, behavioral therapists began to apply techniques from operant conditioning such as the use of incentives as well as techniques from classical conditioning such as the threshold method that relies on a weak stimulus, the fatigue method that exhausts the organism with frequent stimuli, and the incompatible response method that simultaneously presents stimuli that are in conflict. All these procedures aimed at helping human beings in goal-directed activities such as breaking unwanted habits in the form of phobias and obsessive-compulsive behavior.[148]

Although cognitive therapy inherited a wealth of behavioral techniques from behavioral therapy, cognitive theorists quite differently appreciate the value of these techniques. For the behavioral therapist, when the undesirable behavior is modified, the patient has been cured. For cognitive therapists, however, behavioral modification is never an end in itself, but always a means to an end, which is a change in a person's way of thinking.[149] In other words, although both cognitive and behavioral therapists might prescribe the same methods to alter overt behavior, they interpret quite differently how that behavior has been altered and what that alteration means.[150] For example, a behavioral therapist views assertiveness training as a counter-conditioning response, whereas a cognitive therapist views it as an acquired skill that alters the patient's interpretation of himself and others.[151]

Cognitive therapists are keenly aware that changing the behavior of someone who is depressed will not necessarily free the sufferer from negative thoughts, but it will give him an opportunity "to evaluate empirically his ideas of inadequacy and incompetence."[152] Hence, behavioral techniques are employed in cognitive therapy in order to modify self-defeating conduct, to provide skills where deficiencies are apparent, and to gather information that can determine whether or not cognitions are valid.[153]

Cognitive therapists generally concentrate first on behavior, because "it is easier to change concrete actions or to introduce new ones, than it is to change patterns of thinking."[154] For example, with depressed patients, the therapist initially targets passivity, avoidance behavior, and lack of gratification, before directly challenging the patient's negative views about himself, his future, and his world.[155] In marriage counseling, the therapist at the outset helps the couple to develop new communication habits, before he attempts to alter the way they interpret each other's words.[156] As a rule, "the more severe a patient's problems are, the more important it is to use behavioral interventions to accomplish cognitive as well as behavioral change."[157] This is consistent with the findings of social learning theory, which indicates that "conversation is not an especially effective way of altering human behavior. In order to change, people need corrective learning experiences."[158]

Some of the more important behavioral techniques applied in cognitive therapy include: "(1) activity monitoring and scheduling...(2) scheduling mastery and pleasure activities...(3) behavioral rehearsal, modeling, assertiveness training, and role playing...(4) relaxation training and behavioral distraction techniques...(5) *in vivo* exposure...and (6) graded task assignments."[159] A brief examination of these behavioral techniques in the light of patristic tradition should clarify the relationship between the therapeutic uses of *praxis* or behavior in both approaches.

(1) Activity monitoring consists in keeping a daily record of activities by the hour. This documentation can help both patient and therapist to see more clearly how the patient's behavior relates over time to his particular psychological difficulty. From this information, they can then prepare (2) a new schedule aimed at modifying behavior and thereby cognition. For example, those struggling with substance abuse can discover how their daily activities have a bearing on drug use and then reschedule their week with pursuits that are less conducive to addictive behavior.[160] The depressed can learn how their immobility relates to their depression and plan activities that give them a sense of accomplishment or pleasant feelings, replacing pursuits that are no longer rewarding or enjoyable with satisfying or pleasurable ones.[161] The daily record requires depressed patients to rate on a five-point scale how much mastery or pleasure they associate with each activity, and then use this record to refine their schedule for the upcoming week. This technique can also be used to combat all-or-nothing thinking,[162] since the daily record usually demonstrates

that thoughts such as "nothing gives me pleasure," or "I don't accomplish anything" are not empirically true.

A structured day is not a novel idea for Orthodox Christians. Coenobitic monasticism involves a highly scheduled liturgical way of life that is favorable to growth in virtue. Furthermore, a detailed examination of how one has spent one's day in terms of actions pleasing or displeasing to God is a common monastic practice[163] that "illumines a man's hour by hour conduct."[164] Saint Theophan the Recluse even suggests that it be done with "the mathematical accuracy of a business ledger."[165] Although there is real similarity between corresponding forms of activity monitoring, the psychotherapeutic use of scheduling is far more personalized and amenable to quantitative evaluation.

Christians can certainly avail themselves of scheduling in order to see how their activities relate to virtue and sin as well as to reschedule their time in a more edifying manner. Nevertheless, believers may harbor misgivings about concentrating on pleasure and mastery, since such a focus can be construed as encouraging hedonism and pride. Observing and scheduling activities that bring pleasure or a sense of mastery, however, are not interventions aimed at those embroiled in sensuality or pridefully resting on the laurels of achievement, but at the depressed who find joy nowhere and view their every activity as insignificant and meaningless. Given patristic concerns about pleasure that results in pain and pride that engenders folly, this behavioral technique should, nevertheless, be applied with discernment.

A safer Christian application of this technique could involve scheduling time for wholesome joys, such as delighting in the beauty of God's creation, chanting or listening to spiritual hymns, and fulfilling the commandments of Christ.[166] Some Protestants are concerned about self-mastery being contrary to a passive resignation to the will of God.[167] The Orthodox Christian emphasis on salvation as synergy between God and man as well as on the ascetic life as an offering of man to God permit the downcast to reflect briefly on their accomplishments as long as this reflection also includes humble gratitude for the grace of God, whereby all human accomplishments are brought to fruition.

(3) Rehearsing behaviors, which means learning new ways to respond to others and to situations, is a useful technique commonly employed in cognitive therapy. Albert Bandura notes, "Behavior is modified far more effectively by providing better alternatives than by imposing prohibitions."[168] Those with personality disorders have a particularly small repertoire of coping behaviors and need help learning additional ones.[169] To this end, the therapist may teach behavioral skills such as active listening, assertiveness, and compromise by role-playing problematic interactions, so that the patient can "learn and practice

more effective interpersonal behaviors."[170] For example, someone with a passive-aggressive personality disorder may role-play conversations with his therapist in order to learn communication skills such as pausing for others to speak, respecting the boundaries of other people, and making eye contact during conversations.[171] A patient who feels psychological turmoil because he responds defensively or aggressively to those in authority may practice making assertive responses by role-playing conversations in which the therapist takes on the role of an authority figure.[172]

It would be a mistake to apply the fifty-first canon of the Council of Trullo forbidding acting and attendance at certain kinds of theater to the case of therapeutic role-playing.[173] The opposition of many church fathers to the theater was grounded in their objections to "immodesty of gesture and attire,"[174] "impure sights,"[175] and "offensive jokes."[176] Saint John Chrysostom opposed theatrical presentations on account of the "laughter, indecency, devilish displays, debauchery, the wasting of time, the useless spending of days, the planning for extravagant lust, the studying of adultery, the practical training for fornication, the schooling in intemperance, the encouragement to filthiness, the pretext for laughter, and the patterns for indecency."[177] None of these elements is present in therapeutic role-playing. Similarly, although some fathers reprove actors and the vainglorious for "wishing to seem what they are not"[178] and view sin as the cause for wearing masks,[179] therapeutic role-playing does not aim at teaching the patient to play someone else, but to learn how to behave and respond in a new way. The church fathers likewise recognized the importance of practice and working with a trainer and applied this observation to the struggle to live a virtuous life.[180] After all, monks are instructed to respond with the lines "may it be blessed" and "forgive me," rather than with whatever comes to mind after receiving an order or a reprimand. And those who manage to make this initial role-play a natural way of responding to others are considered especially blessed.

(4) Relaxation training is used as an adjunctive technique in treating children and adolescents with anger management difficulties,[181] as well as people struggling with anxiety, insomnia,[182] and symptoms associated with withdrawal from substance abuse.[183] When patients learn to methodically tense and relax their muscles and breathing, they also gain a sense of awareness and mastery over aggravating impulses and symptoms.[184] This technique might also be helpful for believers struggling with the passions of anger and desire.

(5) The "as if" technique involves defining a therapeutic goal and then acting as if that goal were already achieved. "For example, the patient who wishes to quit smoking might spend a week acting 'as if' he were a non-smoker. For example, he might ask others not to smoke around him, he might

exercise, or he might sit in the non-smoking sections of restaurants."[185] Someone with anxiety could try to act "as if" he had no fear in a situation that otherwise made him uneasy.[186] When Tertullian addressed Christians who were contemplating flight from the authorities in order to avoid denying Christ before a tribunal, he asked them, "*If* it is in our power to confess Christ or to deny him, why do we not *anticipate* the nobler deed, that is, that we shall confess him? If you are not willing to confess him, you are not willing to suffer, and to be unwilling to confess is denial. But *if* the matter is entirely in God's hands, why do we not leave it to his will by recognizing his might and power, for even as he can bring us back to trial when we try to escape, he is also able to screen us when we do not flee."[187] Tertullian's advice can thus be construed as a patristic precursor of the "as-if" technique in which faith in Providence endows the believer with the strength to act "as if" he already had the mindset of the saints.

Related to the "as-if" technique is the strategy of having patients get involved with activities that clash with their problems. For example, since substance abuse and sustained exercise are incompatible, the therapist might suggest that the addict begin a regular exercise program to heighten awareness of the disadvantages of substance abuse.[188] The church fathers were certainly aware that perceived incompatibility could spurn the believer away from sinful behavior, and toward virtuous conduct. After all, the Lord Christ taught that it is impossible to serve two masters, so that believers would not concern themselves solely with food and clothing. Saint Paul likewise observed that the desires of the flesh are contrary to those of the spirit, so that the Galatians would choose to occupy themselves with spiritual labors.[189] In a similar vein, Saint John Chrysostom suggests that those who are annoyed by his sermons on almsgiving and forgiveness try practicing those virtues, so that his homilies might become for them a source of delight, rather than irritation.[190]

Verbal self-instruction is an *in vivo* behavioral technique utilized to alter covert self-talk. For example, impulsive children and obese patients tell themselves what they are supposed to do as they are in the process of carrying out a task in order to increase self-control.[191] Anxiety sufferers give themselves directions out loud in order to maintain desired behavior and to override impulses caused by their symptoms. For example, someone with a social phobia can repeat a phrase such as "Don't run away," when he is in a situation from which he would otherwise flee. In this way, he remains there until his anxiety subsides and he discovers for himself that his initial fears were unfounded.[192] Saint John Chrysostom described the principle at the root of this technique as follows: "Words are the pathways to works. First we think, then we speak, then we act."[193]

Ascetics would use variations on this technique in order to avoid sinful conduct. For example, whenever Abba Agathon was tempted to judge something, he would say to himself, "No, Agathon, don't do that," and then he would be at peace.[194] *The Ladder* relates a similar instance of a certain monk who took delight in the joyful-sorrow that accompanied mourning over his sins. Whenever he could feel himself giving in to vainglory, anger, or over-eating, he would tell himself, as though the state of mourning could speak, "I am going to leave you." In this way, he was able to keep from falling into behaviors unbefitting to his monastic calling.[195] Other monks would likewise use the remembrance of death in order to maintain their ascetic endeavor.[196]

Therapists have other related techniques to help patients do what is ultimately in their best interest, even if they are unable to see that at the moment of difficulty. For example, the critical decision technique used with anxiety patients involves doing the exact opposite of what their instincts dictate in an anxiety situation. For instance, someone with social anxiety who instinctively backs away from people during a conversation forces himself to step forward.[197] Monastics apply this practice when they have an urge to talk back, but force themselves to remain silent or simply respond, "may it be blessed." The TIC/TOC technique is a similar technique in which the patient stays in a situation he fears by distinguishing between "task-interfering cognitions ('I've got to get out of here', 'I can't stand it') and task-oriented cognitions in which the focus is staying with a situation ('What do I have to do to get through this situation?')."[198] This technique could also be applied by the monk struggling with listlessness and the desire to leave his cell, by someone fighting against gluttony but desiring to fast, and so forth.

Finally, (6) the graded task assignment involves defining a problem and turning it into a project consisting of stepwise tasks that the patient will probably be able to fulfill and whose successful accomplishment he can directly observe. Beck relates the case of treating inactivity in a depressed woman who used to like to read. He suggested reading a short story. Although the patient demurred that she could not concentrate, she attempted to read one paragraph, and then another, eventually finishing the page on her own initiative.[199] In treating agoraphobia, the patient and therapist develop a hierarchy of anxiety-provoking situations, and then the patient sets for himself the task of remaining in the least stressful situation until the anxiety passes. When he has successfully completed this task, he tries the next level.[200] In a more strictly behavioralist paradigm, this is viewed as behavioral desensitization by increased exposure.[201] A cognitive therapist, however, would attribute success to the change in the way the patient interprets the situation, brought about by experience and the experiential knowledge that the situation is not as dangerous as he once thought it was.

Behavior and *Praxis*: Ariadne's Thread and the Person of Christ

We have already noted remarkable similarities between patristic and cognitive approaches to problems, goals, and experimentation as discrete entities, but not as a unified approach. That is, cognitive theorists explicitly integrate problems, goals, and experimentation, whereas the ancient fathers make no such attempt, because the heart of patristic thought is not human discovery, but divine revelation.[202] Likewise, behavioral techniques fit hand in glove with the cognitive theory of problems, goals, and experimentation. Since these three factors do not comprise an integrated theory in patristic thought, the church fathers' views on behavior or asceticism and an overarching psychological theory concerning problems, goals, and experimentation can only be tacitly related if that theory is kept in mind.[203] Notwithstanding, ascetic practices do conform nicely with the patristic model of theoria and praxis.

As in our earlier chapters on psychological theory, so now in this our first chapter on therapeutic technique, we have encountered a consensus of opinion on practical ways to help those in need. Both church fathers and cognitive therapists agree that healing requires both behavioral and cognitive interventions, that cognition can be altered by modifying behavior, that it is easier to change behavior than to change cognition, and that behavior should be addressed first in a course of treatment. Both ancient ascetics and contemporary therapists seem to use "techniques" that can be understood in terms of classical or operant conditioning and both would reject such models as being explanatorily deficient.

Both bodily asceticism and behavioral techniques inevitably aim at changing self-defeating behaviors and should be applied with moderation and in keeping with a person's natural strengths and weaknesses. Most behavioral techniques are compatible with patristic approaches, and some are even transplantable. For example, the daily activity record is not inconsistent with ascetic self-observation, nor is scheduling out of keeping with a life structured by the liturgical services of the Church. The verbal self-instruction technique has been used for ages by ascetics being tempted by the passions, and long ago Tertullian recommended a version of the "as-if" technique used today in treating anxiety disorders. Cognitive therapists may be inclined to understand the ascetic use of fasting, vigils, and standing to combat lust as an application of the incompatible activity technique, whereas church fathers might view the graded task assignment in the proper context as a description of the gradual ascent up the ladder of virtue. The above parallels tend to indicate that behavioral techniques are wider templates into which specific ascetic practices can be classified and interpreted as mechanisms for shaping thoughts and beliefs.

Obviously, ascetic practices and behavioral techniques also differ markedly, which is not particularly surprising, given that therapy patients are rarely ascetics and vice versa. Prostrations, vigils, and fasting are not behavioral techniques that the cognitive therapist would likely recommend. Likewise, some techniques in therapy, such as behavioral rehearsal through role-playing, have no equivalent in patristic tradition, although that does not necessarily indicate incompatibility. Other techniques, such as rating activities for mastery and pleasure, require additional caution in a Christian context.

At certain junctures, however, the two paths diverge. In cognitive therapy, behavioral techniques explicitly seek to supply the patient with further information and sometimes provide him with new skills. In the Christian struggle, God-pleasing asceticism is not intended to uncover unnoticed facts, but to help the believer to lead a life of virtue that can be a source of spiritual joy, consolation, and grace that are qualitatively and empirically different from worldly happiness, comfort, and pleasure.

Christian asceticism is never a gallimaufry of self-help techniques for problems of the moment, but is always and primarily an offering to God along the pilgrimage of human life. That life is in many ways like a labyrinth. At least, so say certain philosophers, psychologists, and saints.[204] And what matters most for those meandering through this labyrinth is to find their way out by making the right turns. On the one hand, psychologists have ingeniously extrapolated the results of laboratory rats scurrying through mazes into behavioral techniques that are offered as Ariadnian thread that can help those with problems experimentally reach new goals. On the other hand, the church fathers have transformed their observations on the life of prayer and obedience into a staff of ascetic praxis and a compass of spiritual theoria, so that those lost in a labyrinth of the passions can find the path of virtue and reach their final destination, the kingdom of heaven.

It should thus be clear that for the ancient fathers praxis does not mean reaching for some Ariadnian thread of their own spinning, but following the one who has passed from death to life. Saint Gregory of Nyssa puts it best:

> When people who are at a loss for how to thread the turns of mazes happen to meet someone experienced who knows how to get to the end of those various misleading turnings in the chambers, they follow closely behind their leader's footsteps, for

otherwise they could find no way out. Likewise, let it be understood that the labyrinth of this our life cannot be threaded by the faculties of human nature unless a person pursues the very path of the one who was once in this labyrinth, yet got beyond the difficulties which hemmed him in.[205]

In the case of behavioral techniques, we are handling Ariadnian thread, a marvel of human ingenuity and a precious gift to every Theseus who is lost. In the case of praxis and Christian asceticism, however, the gift received is from the very hand of Christ who reveals to all not only the way, but also "the truth and the life."[206]

To Survey the Thoughts is to Calm Them: *Theoria*, Watchfulness, and Preliminary Cognitive Skills

O Stillness! Scout of the thoughts
...calmness of the thoughts.

[John Chrysostom?], On Patience[1]

Before descending from the mountains of Ararat, Noah of old released a dove in order to ascertain whether "the waters were abated from the face of the earth."[2] Before departing from the wilderness of Paran, Moses, the greatest of prophets, sent forth scouts in order to survey the lay of the land.[3] In cognitive terms, these men of God attentively gathered reliable information as a means for making a judicious evaluation that would settle a future course of action. In spiritual terms, they sought to "discern the signs of the times"[4] before taking bold and blessed steps such as emerging from the confines of an ark or taking possession of "a land flowing with milk and honey."[5]

In like manner, both believers resisting temptations during their spiritual exodus from the land of Egypt and people struggling to stay afloat amidst a flood of psychological problems that disrupt their daily lives are obliged to reach out for various strategies to reconnoiter their inner worlds so that they might "lead a quiet and peaceable life."[6] Church fathers and cognitive therapists not only recommend active interventions in the form of asceticism or behavioral techniques that we examined in our previous chapter, they also provide instruction that can help people survey and respond to their thoughts via watchfulness and *theoria*[7] in the spiritual life or cognitive techniques for automatic thoughts in the course of therapy. For fathers and therapists alike, scouting the thoughts is the first step toward calming them.

Aaron Beck observes that the "techniques of psychotherapy overlap considerably with the process of therapy."[8] In other words, cognitive theory and cognitive techniques are distinguishable, but never inseparable. Accordingly, when we examined the theory of cognitive therapy and its patristic counterpart in chapters three through five, we necessarily had recourse to examples of specific cognitive interventions in order to elucidate discrete cognitive concepts. Consequently, we have already introduced many cognitive techniques and their patristic analogues. Notwithstanding, another foray into the distinct fields of patristic thought and cognitive therapy with an eye on preliminary cognitive techniques will afford us the opportunity not only to make a fresh reconnaissance of familiar terrain, but also to seek out new and valuable finds.

The Threefold Therapeutic Strategy of the Fathers: *Praxis, Nipsis,* and *Theoria*

In our previous chapter, *praxis* and *theoria* provided a conceptual framework for our therapeutic interpretation of bodily asceticism as a patristic form of behavioral intervention. The praxis-theoria dyad can also help us to discern more clearly the source, nature, and aim of the fathers' cognitive interventions. Hence, we will revisit this famed duo focusing, this time, on the patristic understanding of theoria that is born of stillness and begets the knowledge of the spiritual realm.[9]

In way of review, we remind the reader that although the wise rely on both praxis and theoria in order to be directly united with God,[10] ancient spiritual masters advise beginners to progress in praxis before attempting higher forms of theoria.[11] Saint Isaac the Syrian perceptively observes that believers engage in praxis by using their zeal and the human tendency to be aggressive, whereas they taste of theoria by yearning for God as their heart's true desire.[12] Thus, praxis is accomplished when believers push themselves on to virtuous action, whereas theoria is attained when their souls are enamored of their divine bridegroom. Significantly, the soul's ability to think rationally is not mentioned in this passage. For Saint Isaac, theoria is not an intellectual activity, but a gift bestowed on the soul who loves God. There is, however, a cognitive activity that is a prerequisite for divine theoria.[13] That activity is called *nipsis* or watchfulness.

In chapter five, the reader was acquainted with patristic counsel on watchfulness through a description of the spiritual fisherman's art and through an examination of the cognitive stages after the appearance of a bad thought. We noted that watchfulness not only prevents a sin of thought from developing into a sinful deed, but also keeps a person's inner world and outward life in a harmony that is pleasing to God.[14] Sincerely repentant and God-fearing Christians are naturally watchful.[15] They halt extraneous thoughts at the entrance of the heart[16] and humbly call out with the prayer, "Lord Jesus Christ, have mercy on me,"[17] thereby using watchfulness as a scout who detects bad thoughts and prayer as a soldier who then routs them out.[18]

For the ancient ascetics, watchfulness, like true philosophy, is "the science of sciences and art of arts."[19] They liken it to Jacob's ladder extending up into the heavens[20] and to a pathway leading to the kingdom within,[21] where the believer encounters "a spiritual world of God, splendid and vast, wrought from moral, natural, and theological forms of contemplation [theoria]."[22] The fathers refer to watchfulness as "stillness of heart,...attentiveness,...guarding the heart,...watchfulness and rebuttal,...the investigation of the thoughts and guarding of the intellect [nous]."[23] These synonyms denote distinct aspects of and approaches to watchfulness. Saint Hesychius the Presbyter distinguishes between four types of watchfulness: (1) calling out to Christ for help, (2) remaining silent and still in prayer, (3) ruminating on the thought of death, and (4) scrutinizing the thoughts for fanciful notions.[24] Saint Gregory Palamas likewise lists prayer, attention, remembrance of death, and mourning as means to repel the suggestions of the evil one.[25] In psychological terms, these forms of watchfulness can be construed as cognitive techniques, which we will examine later in this chapter and in the next.

Saint Nikitas Stithatos likens the contrast between watchfulness and theoria to the difference between the senses of touch and sight.[26] Both experientially impart knowledge, but through watchfulness, believers are only aware of what impinges on them directly, whereas through theoria, they also behold an entire panorama both near and far.

In patristic literature, the term theoria is understood primarily in two senses: as anamnesis or recollection and as vision. At a cognitive level, theoria means bringing to mind events or persons from the past. For example, ascetics who recall their sins in thought and deed as well as the virtues of others are engaging in theoria in order to foster a humble mindset.[27] The fathers also advise the faithful to ponder how God blesses them materially, spiritually, temporally, and eternally, so that they will be moved to gratitude and motivated to lead the God-pleasing life of virtue.[28] This kind of theoria alters people's perspective, their way of interpreting the world, and consequently their behavior. The centrality of this approach in Orthodox Christianity is evident in the placement of such a remembrance of the entire divine economy at the heart of the Divine Liturgy before the priest consecrates the holy gifts. From a psychological perspective, this theoria is a mental activity that therapists could call a cognitive technique. From a spiritual vantage point, however, it is a blessed and sanctifying use of the rational aspect of the soul and attracts the grace of God.

The holy hesychasts also refer to a second kind of theoria that is *not* the direct result of the mind's focus, but is rather a divine gift of revelation[29] in which the Holy Spirit overshadows the person engaged in prayer[30] or the reading of scripture.[31] The account of the transfiguration of Christ, Saint Peter's vision concerning the Gentiles, and Saint Paul's reference to "one caught up to the third heaven"[32] are early New Testament allusions to theoria in which God attracts the nous's vision and desire, illumining it with his light, so that it sees with an ignorance that surpasses all knowledge.[33] This "harvest of harvest"[34] is a revelation beyond the senses[35] and a divine vision "arrayed in luminous intuitions" that is so powerful that the person who experiences it will never again "gaze searchingly at the world nor will he cleave to his body."[36] In other words, the beauty of this divine vision slakes the soul's spiritual thirst even as a sumptuous banquet satisfies a hungry man's palate. Whoever has tasted this theoria despises the very remembrance of the passions as though it were the most unappetizing of gruels.[37]

The primarily spiritual state of divine theoria has tangible psychological consequences that become apparent when we recall the connection between the passions and maladaptive schemata made in chapter three, as well as the relationship between philautia and egocentricity established in chapter four. Divine theoria thoroughly heals the human person of philautia and the passions. In so doing, it fundamentally alters how believers view themselves by replacing egocentricity with theocentricity, even as it reshapes their core schemata or interpretations about their future in eternity and about their fellow human beings as children of God. Thus, the saints who have attained to divine theoria react dispassionately to difficult situations, which would bring maladaptive schemata to the surface in most people. For example, although Saint Dionysios of Zakinthos wept when he learned of his brother's murder from the killer's own mouth, the saint's immediate behavioral and cognitive reactions were neither egocentric nor based on his own idiosyncratic interpretation of the world. Instead, he automatically viewed the situation from the vantage point of eternity and divine love. Thus, he felt the need to comfort the murderer, to lead him to repentance, to give him absolution, to hide him from the authorities, and to arrange for his escape from the island.[38]

Divine theoria brings clarity and maturity to human cognition, for it equips the believer with a sure knowledge of the principles underlying ascetic practice, the created realm, and theology,[39] as well as "a partial understanding of the wisdom of God that governs all things."[40] Once theoria is attained, it can then serve as a wellspring of further guidance for praxis with the clear-sighted vision of spiritual knowledge.[41] Naturally, divine theoria also bears the mystical fruits of increased prayer and love for God.[42]

Our preliminary investigation of watchfulness and theoria indicate that patristic cognitive interventions are first and foremost living expressions of a multifaceted relationship between God and man. From a psychological perspective, watchfulness encompasses a diversity of patristic "cognitive techniques" for handling bad thoughts at an automatic level, whereas human theoria or recollection aims at cultivating God-pleasing thoughts at the level of core beliefs or schemata. Watchfulness and human theoria also prepare the soul for divine theoria, whenever the Holy Spirit so wills. Although divine theoria thoroughly heals the believer of the disease of bad thoughts, it is by no means a human technique, but a divine intervention like the rainbow God set in the post-diluvian sky. The person who has tasted divine theoria then becomes a sure guide for advising others in the struggle to be delivered from the noetic pharaoh and to take possession of their spiritual promised land.

Patristic "Cognitive Tools" for Coping with Bad Thoughts

According to Saint John Climacus, there are three basic approaches to the thoughts that correspond to the three stages of spiritual maturity: purification in which the believer prays for deliverance from bad thoughts by entreating God, illumination in which he contradicts them with passages from Holy Scripture, and deification in which he utterly prevails over them because his spiritual eyes are riveted on divine *theoria*.[43] For the first two stages, the ascetic fathers take into account practical considerations and furnish the believer with detailed instructions that in a psychological context are usually associated with cognitive techniques. For comparative purposes, we will embark on a brief expedition into those patristic meadows that are lush with advice given during those stages in order to help the believer fight and overcome bad thoughts. More concretely, we will consider the use of prayer, confession, disdain, rebuttal, and analysis as responses to malignant thoughts. Then from that vantage point, we will scout out preliminary cognitive techniques in psychotherapy for observing and responding to automatic thoughts that are maladaptive.

Prayer as a Response to Bad Thoughts

For the holy fathers, prayer is always an appropriate intervention regardless of whether a problem is cognitive, emotional, or behavioral. After all, prayer enables believers to entrust their human difficulties to God's care with the sure knowledge that "where God so wills, the order of nature is overcome."[44] With respect to temptations in the mind, prayer can repel thoughts that provoke sorrow, faintheartedness,[45] rancor,[46] anger, vainglory, and pride. It can also focus a wandering mind.[47] In fact, Saint Gregory Palamas affirms that prayer and the reading of psalms not only weaken the intensity of bad thoughts, but also transform them and redirect them.[48] For this reason, the texts of the Church's liturgical services encourage the believer to turn to Christ and to entreat him to calm the thoughts when they rage like a storm,[49] to bolster them when they waver in uncertainty, and to grant him reflections that inspire compunction, repentance, and renewed dedication to God.[50] Prayer thus treats the disease of bad thoughts in two ways: At the level of automatic thoughts, it weakens their intensity and metacognitively reframes them by placing them in the wider context of the spiritual life; at the schematic level, it transforms the passions by redirecting zeal and desire toward Christ, so that edifying thoughts blossom in their stead. The fifth prayer in preparation for Holy Communion concludes with a petition for just such a thorough cognitive transformation "unto the blotting out and utter destruction of bad thoughts, memories, predispositions, and dreams of the night."[51]

Monastic tradition enjoins beginners in the Christian life to turn to prayer whenever they are confronted with enticing, ambiguous, or deceitful thoughts. For example, Saint Nicodemos the Hagiorite advises those who are unable to resist or repel seductive bad thoughts to be silent and to flee to God for refuge.[52] Similarly, Abba Barsanuphius indicates that "there is no other way to humble our diverse passions more beneficial than invoking the name of God. To contradict a thought is not appropriate for everyone, but only for those who are strong in God."[53] What stands out in this advice is not the request for help, but the name of God that brings relief to the weak and his presence that does so for the strong. The minds of the strong are already focused on their Almighty Lord, but the weak need to actively turn toward Christ, the heart's true desire, so that those seductive thoughts lose their desirability. Moreover, when the weak contend with demonic thoughts, they are not in need of flimsy human arguments, but the sovereign power of God whereby the believer can do all things.[54]

Summarizing patristic tradition, Saint Nicodemos the Hagiorite enumerates three reasons why taking refuge in God through prayer is preferable to disputing bad thoughts: (1) believers are not always strong enough to fight their thoughts; (2) those who attempt to dispute them will still have to contend with impure images lingering in the mind, thereby further defiling it; and (3) those who admit their own weakness and inability to fight bad thoughts make their souls humble.[55]

In the case of a dubious thought, the ancient fathers advocate fleeing to God through prayer, fasting, tears, and vigil, rather than risking ensnarement by sinfully taking pleasure in the thought under the pretext of examining it in order to determine whether it is good or bad.[56] Saint Peter of Damascus proposed "saying to every thought that comes to us: I do not know who you are; God knows if you are good or not; for I have cast myself into his hands, as I shall continue to do so, and he looks after me."[57] For the pious, the appearance of an ambiguous thought becomes an opportunity for renewed trust in God. Likewise, Abba Dorotheos counseled a sorely tempted brother to call out, "'Lord, provide for this matter as thou desirest and as thou knowest,' for the providence of God arranges many things differently than what we suppose or anticipate."[58]

Turning to God in prayer should not be misconstrued as an abdication of human responsibility to judge a thought, but as a preparation for illumination before attempting to do so. The watchful fathers knew by experience that when the believer's mind is gathered in the heart and repeats the prayer, "Lord Jesus Christ, Son of God, have mercy on me,"[59] demonic thoughts, fantasies, and illusions are exposed as false and thus can be more easily rejected.[60] The correct application of this approach known as monologistic prayer entails "cognitively" paying attention to the words of prayer and "emotionally" feeling compunction in the presence of the Lord Jesus.[61] Attentive and compunctious prayer in turn augments the believer's yearning for Christ and watchfulness over the thoughts, thereby bringing him clarity of mind.[62] Although it requires much toil, humility, and even "assistance from heaven,"[63] the holy fathers consider this "cognitive method" to be as effective in bridling unruly thoughts as the behavioral technique of not voicing one's reaction to an insult is successful at stifling anger.[64]

When prayer illumines the soul, the believer can see well enough to take his place on the judgment seat of the heart and decide whether the thoughts belong to him or his enemies, so that he can then store good thoughts deep in the treasure chamber of his heart, but drive out bad ones with the whip of the rational thought.[65] In other words, the believer, who has reached the state of illumination, prays in his heart and then cross-examines the thought by asking it: "Are you on our side or that of our adversaries?"[66] If the thought seems good, but uncertain, the believer should neither accept it nor reject it, but instead remain in prayer and vigil until the Lord himself reveals whence it came.[67]

Exposure of Bad Thoughts

Since unconfessed thoughts are much like hen's eggs warmed by the dung of the passions and ready to hatch out with a noisy brood,[68] ancient ascetics sometimes advise the believer to expose them and not to let them nest in the mind undisturbed. This can be done mentally, orally, or in writing. The simple act of confessing the thoughts "to the Lord as to a human being"[69] can neutralize them and strengthen the believer in his efforts to observe his heart more closely.[70] Sometimes, however, the believer should also confess them to his spiritual father, so that "they would be destroyed by the shame felt in confessing them and by the hardship of the penance imposed."[71] Abba Dorotheos would write down his thoughts on a board in order to show them to his elder. And by simply doing so, he would experience relief and spiritual growth.[72] In like manner, Saint Anthony counseled his fellow monks to jot down the impulses of their souls as though they were going to show them to someone else, for that action would make them feel too ashamed to continue to harbor any bad thoughts.[73] In all these examples, the believer extracts the thought from his murky subjective world, so that he can examine it objectively in the clear light of Christ. Often, the act of extraction alone is sufficient to weaken the thought and decrease its hold over the believer.

Disdain for Bad Thoughts

The ancient fathers also recommend that believers in thrall to the passions disdain their bad thoughts by courageously closing off their senses and utterly rejecting impassioned images and memories.[74] This practice requires decisiveness and fortitude, because it opposes the path of least resistance, which is to allow sense impressions, imagination, and memory to feed the passions until they swell to unmanageable proportions. The desert fathers explain that when someone disdains bad thoughts instead of ruminating on them, they die like scorpions sealed in a jar.[75]

In patristic tradition, disdaining the thoughts encompasses diverse tactics ranging from vehement refusal to a knowing indifference. For example, Saint Dorotheos of Gaza suggested that the believer disdain bad thoughts as though they were merely barking dogs. This disinterest in them, however, is founded on the knowledge that the believer has God as his ally and that the devil's power was stripped at the crucifixion of Christ.[76] Elder Païsios viewed this tactic as better than rebuttal when dealing with unseemly or blasphemous thoughts.[77] This also happens to coincide with the advice of cognitive therapists for coping with obsessions.[78] Elder Païsios illustrated this approach when he counseled those troubled by thoughts of pride to step back and look at their own thoughts in the manner that one would look at someone else being ridiculously prideful, that is, with a good sense of humor and a hearty laugh.[79]

Another method for disdaining bad thoughts is to keep the mind occupied with other matters. This could entail studying scripture and the writings of the holy fathers. Those with spiritual vision note that as long as the monk is studying sacred books, he is not bothered by bad thoughts.[80] Abba Macarius advised an even more focused approach to fight the thoughts: the memorization of passages from the gospels and other parts of scripture.[81] Regardless of the level of cognitive intensity, the study and memorization of spiritual writings not only distract the mind from bad thoughts, but also provide material for rebuttal. Some fathers even engaged in purely intellectual pursuits such as language learning as a distraction technique in the struggle with the thoughts. For example, Saint Jerome admits that he studied Hebrew not only in order to learn how to read the Old Testament in the original, but also in order to keep his mind busy and to distract himself from the provocations of improper thoughts.[82]

Rebuttal of Bad Thoughts

Notwithstanding the patristic caveat to beginners concerning rebuttal as a way of coping with bad thoughts, rebuttal remains an important method in the believer's struggle. After all, on the very threshold of Christian life before the neophyte enters the nave for holy baptism, he is asked to renounce "Satan, and all his angels and all his works and all his service and all his pride."[83] Renunciation presupposes a readiness for rebuttal. Christ's temptation by Satan in the wilderness is the prototypical New Testament example of wisely responding to a bad thought disguised in the raiment of scripture by citing another biblical passage whose truth exposes the devil's wiles.[84] For the church fathers, Christ's responses were recorded in the gospels to teach the faithful how to reply to tempting thoughts.[85]

According to Saint John Cassian, it is God who provides the believer with the strength to reject tempting thoughts as well as the freedom to yield to them. Thus, the saint advises the believer, who is assaulted by bad thoughts, to reject and refute them in line with the scripture that says, "Resist the devil and he will flee from you."[86] Even though God alone can release a person from the struggle of wrestling with the thoughts, anyone can learn to rebut them, not take pleasure in them,[87] and not allow them to linger in the mind, regardless of whether the thoughts are impassioned or dispassionate.[88] This assertion both encourages the faithful and empowers them in their struggle with the thoughts.

When the church fathers elaborate on the art of rebuttal, they often mention psalm 136:8-9 (LXX): "O daughter of Babylon...happy shall he be that takes and dashes thy little ones against the rock." For ancient ascetics, rebuttal entails destroying those nasty little thoughts or desires by striking them against the Rock who is Christ.[89] This means placing those bad thoughts in the presence of the Lord Jesus, who as Almighty God can calm the sea and cast out the evil spirit. Other fathers suggest striking thoughts "against the firm and solid strength of reason and truth"[90] that Christ reveals.

Given the subjective and idiosyncratic nature of the thoughts passing through the mind, rebuking them sometimes takes the form of self-reproach (see chapter 9) in which the believer rebukes "the old man, which is corrupt according to the deceitful lusts."[91] The ancient fathers advise doing this "truthfully and objectively"[92] not only to exclude sickly self-pity or masochistic tendencies, but also to encourage honest humility. Although it may seem paradoxical, rebuking the thoughts by self-reproach actually increases the believer's personal interest in rejecting them even as he distances himself from those thoughts by placing himself in an observer mode. For example, when Abba Zosimas was agitated over something, he would place himself in an investigative state by saying, "Why are you upset, my soul?" and then motivate himself to reject his thoughts by adding, "Why are you disturbed like those frothing at the mouth?"[93]

In order for rebuttal to be successful, monastic luminaries advise the Christian struggler to rebuke bad thoughts piously, prayerfully,[94] swiftly,[95] "whenever they appear,"[96] with indignation,[97] and with a perfect hatred.[98] The holy fathers instruct the believer to strike a sinful thought quickly and resolutely as though it were the head of a serpent, because if the believer sluggishly allows that thought to linger, it will inject the venom of pleasure or anger that will then prod him on to irresponsible and regrettable acts.[99] As a means to increase response speed, Saint Gregory Palamas suggested to the nun Xenia that she view the very appearance of a bad thought as consent, for such a strategy can stir the soul to more vigorous action, more sensitive watchfulness, and more frequent compunction.[100] Saint John Chrysostom notes that prompt rebuttal not only prevents the believer from being harmed by malignant thoughts, but also clears the mind, so that it can receive thoughts that are salvific and inspire hope.[101] Angry rebuttal is especially useful in fighting thoughts of fornication, because anger can break through the focus on lust and thus deflect those flaming darts.[102]

Saint Nicodemos the Hagiorite outlines a multistage approach to indignant rebuttal that aims at strengthening a person's opposition to non-carnal bad thoughts. First, the believer firmly rebuts the thought when it initially appears. Second, once the mind grows calm, he rebukes the thought again with greater vehemence. Finally, the believer purposefully recalls the tempting thought and then drives it away with utter hatred and repugnance.[103] This patristic variation on rebuttal resembles forms of cognitive restructuring that we will examine in the next chapter.

When bad thoughts take the form of sinful images, it is helpful for rebuttal to be pictorial as well. Thus, the ascetics would advise those titillated by sensual images to imagine the body in the tomb in a state of corruption with "the skeleton stripped of flesh"[104] or the stomach cut open with its filth exposed.[105] For example, Amma Syncletica advised nuns tempted by sensual fantasies to alter those images by mentally gouging out the eyes of the person the enemy showed them, flaying his skin, and cutting his lips, so that nothing would remain of the initial image that tempted them except an ugly skeleton covered with a revolting mixture of blood and phlegm.[106] Such repulsive scenes are obviously incompatible with sensual images arousing carnal sensations.

Faithful to the example of Christ in the wilderness, the holy fathers advise the believer to employ scripture for rebuttal, that is, to cut off bad thoughts by invoking good ones inspired by God.[107] For example, when someone feels overwhelmed by past sins, Saint Macarius of Egypt advises saying, "I have God's written assurance, for he says, 'I desire not the sinner's death, but that he should return through repentance and live.'"[108] In general, the church fathers encourage the believer to chant the psalms to repel pernicious thoughts and calm the mind.[109] For example, Saint Ephraim the Syrian relates the case of a monastic who was struggling with desires of the flesh. When the monk had the thought—"how long are you going to be able to endure such labors?"— he rebuked that thought with a verse from the twenty-fourth psalm, until the Lord "looks down on mine humility and my labor, and forgives all my sins."[110] Such successful rebuttal undeniably changes one's entire interpretation of a situation.

So that the believer would have at his disposal the appropriate passage as a shield against the flaming arrows of tempting thoughts, Saint Jerome suggested that the struggling Christian frequently read Holy Scripture.[111] Evagrius even wrote an entire treatise preserved in Syriac that consists of a long list of possible scriptural responses for variations on each of the eight bad thoughts.[112]

Beyond the borders of the Orthodox Church, Protestant cognitive therapists are avidly touting scriptural rebuttal as a Christian technique for aiding patients in overcoming maladaptive automatic thoughts. For example, the depressed are taught to rebut thoughts such as "I am worthless" with the account of the repentant prodigal son being lovingly accepted by his father (Lk 15).[113] Those suffering from anxiety are taught to counter thoughts such as "What is going to happen to me now?" with 1 Peter 5:7—"Cast all your anxiety on him, because he cares for you."[114] Those who have relinquished their efforts because of thoughts such as "I'll never change" can counter that thought with the biblical fact that after denying his Lord three times Saint Peter changed enough to watch over Christ's sheep.[115] The above Protestant examples of biblical rebuttal are not inconsistent with the precedent of earlier patristic tradition that offers a veritable cornucopia of other possibilities.[116]

Analysis of Bad Thoughts

As noted in chapters three and five, some fathers recommend approaching the thoughts in an analytic or atomistic manner to determine whether a given thought is passionate and, if it is, to extract the passion by disentangling the passionate thought's external appearance to the senses from the principle that defines it.[117] In psychological terms, this means separating the subjective emotional connotations from the objective logical meaning. As a rule, thoughts or memories that provoke uncontrollable anger or improper desires are considered to be passionate or demonic.[118] Elsewhere, Saint Maximus the Confessor describes the distinctions that believers should make when they use this method. The saint writes, "A thing, a conceptual image, and a passion are all quite different one from the other. For example, a man, a woman, gold, and so forth are things; a conceptual image is a passion-free thought of one of these things; a passion is mindless affection or indiscriminate hatred for one of these same things. The monk's battle is therefore against passion."[119] Psychologically speaking, this patristic spiritual parsing can be seen as a cognitive technique for distancing oneself from one's thought.

This particular monastic strategy is not recommended for novices who may not be strong enough to resist the passionate aspect of the thought and consequently might misuse the attempt at analysis as an occasion for a fall. Those who have spiritual love, self-control, and a firm will, however, can avail themselves of this approach to gain experience that can strengthen their own convictions as well as to acquire knowledge with which they can help others who are struggling with inner warfare.[120]

A final analytical approach to the thoughts that is suitable for beginners and advanced alike consists of examining the behavioral and situational factors that contribute to the appearance and persistence of malignant thoughts. According to Saint Symeon the New Theologian, the faithful can gain much benefit by learning where they first had a bad thought, how they became aware of it, with whom they were interacting, and under what conditions.[121] This analysis requires believers to actively gather information about a specific thought that harms them, as well as to determine successful ways of expelling it.[122] Once they verify the causes, they are obliged to distance themselves from them. For example, a monk may have to fight carnal thoughts because he associates too much with women. In that case, he should quite simply reduce the amount of time spent in such interactions.[123]

In summation, under the heading of *theoria*, watchfulness, and hesychasm (the practice of stillness), the ancient fathers supply the faithful with a series of "cognitive techniques" that are useful for coping with harmful thoughts. These methods are tailored to the believers' spiritual maturity and intellectual capabilities as well as to the kind of thoughts troubling them. All the faculties of the tripartite soul are marshaled to action in the struggle for purity of the thoughts: desire in prayer, anger in rebuttal, and reason in analysis. And as always, the grace of God is present, healing, strengthening, and illumining those who strive to be vigilant over their thoughts.

Preliminary Cognitive Skills Required for Psychotherapy

Having inspected the basic weapons in the patristic armory, we can now make a brief incursion into the arsenal of cognitive techniques applied during therapy. In the preceding chapters, we investigated the vital cognitive therapeutic processes of patient education regarding the cognitive model and cognitive distortions; we examined the use of Socratic questioning to modify the patient's thinking; and we discussed the therapeutic development of behavioral experiments to induce cognitive change. Now, we will explore additional cognitive techniques that assist the therapist and patient in identifying automatic thoughts, emotions, and distress levels, as well as modifying the same. In other words, we will survey the preliminary cognitive skills designed for increasing awareness, facilitating evaluative processes, and changing transient thoughts. To borrow patristic terminology, these skills can be characterized as a form of "psychological watchfulness" aimed at treating the patient's particular disorder or presenting difficulty.

An Awareness of Automatic Thoughts and Their Relation to Emotion

According to Aaron Beck, "the most critical stage of cognitive therapy involves training the patient to observe and record his cognitions."[124] Without the ability to identify automatic thoughts, there can be no therapeutic change on a cognitive level, even as there can be no spiritual progress without watchfulness over the thoughts. Thus, after educating the patient on the importance of automatic thoughts and their relationship to emotion and behavior, the therapist empirically demonstrates this theory in practice. To this end, the therapist observes the patient as he speaks and remains particularly attentive during the session to "changes in facial expression, tightening of muscles, shifts in postures,...changes in tone, pitch, volume, or pace," which indicate that the patient's emotional frame of mind has changed.[125] When the therapist detects such a change, he asks the patient what was going through his mind.

This technique of identifying cognitions when affect is heightened is a skill that the patient will use throughout therapy and that will provide the therapist and patient with the data necessary to detect the source of psychological discomfort and to understand the patient's inner world. Another technique employed to illustrate to the patient how thoughts influence emotion is the induced imagery technique. This cognitive tool involves the patient imagining an unpleasant event in his past, observing how this makes him feel in the present, and then identifying the thoughts that passed through his mind. The same sequence is repeated for a pleasant memory. And so, the patient, as a practical scientist, verifies for himself the central tenet of cognitive theory: evaluative thoughts govern emotional responses.[126]

Given the importance of the patient's raw data about emotions and automatic thoughts, therapists sometimes need to apply additional techniques to help the patient accurately label emotions and cognitions that were present during past situations, which seemed to precipitate psychological distress. Of course, the therapist is responsible for determining whether the patient's problem in communication is because of hazy thinking, poor recall, or inexperience in talking about subjective states.

For example, patients with a limited emotional vocabulary can be instructed to consult a longer list of emotions in order to increase their fluency in speaking about them. In a spiritual context, Saint Peter of Damascus's list of the passions can likewise be construed as a useful tool for augmenting not only the believer's ease in conversing about the passions, but also his sensitivity to activities that are considered to be passionate.[127]

Therapists can show patients with difficulty labeling their emotions how to design a personalized basic emotion chart in order to not only clarify their understanding of emotion, but also to help them determine which emotion is prevalent in a disturbing situation. In practical terms, patients set up three columns for the three basic emotions of anger, sorrow, and anxiety. Next, they list in each column specific situations in which they clearly remember feeling the given emotion. Finally, they consult the chart when they are uncertain about the emotion they felt in response to a given situation and automatic thought.[128]

A variety of techniques is also available to offer assistance to patients with difficulty recalling and identifying their automatic thoughts. The therapist can request additional details about the circumstances, have the patient imagine that he is in the situation again and describe what happened using the present tense, or they can both role-play what took place when the patient felt distress.[129] The therapist can also vary his questions about automatic thoughts, have the patient choose between possible thoughts that might match the patient's emotional response, or suggest what kind of thoughts the therapist would have in a similar situation.[130]

Another preliminary skill that patients must acquire for the sake of gathering reliable cognitive and affective data is the ability to quantify numerically how much they believe an automatic thought and how much emotional distress they experience. This quantification will enable the therapist and patient to measure the degree of improvement after a given therapeutic intervention. The therapist can assist patients in a quandary about rating their emotions with percentages by developing a personalized emotional intensity scale. For example, the therapist can ask the anxiety sufferer to recall an experience that provoked the greatest amount of anxiety and to label that experience 100 percent. The patient then brings to mind a situation in which he was not at all anxious and marks it 0 percent. The patient subsequently fills in the chart with other circumstances of varying degrees of stress until he has a complete incremental scale that he can later use to more objectively evaluate how much anxiety he feels in a particular situation that troubles him.[131]

Although quantifying cognitive events may seem foreign to patristic literature, it is by no means unprecedented. After all, Blessed Augustine's exegetical remark—"the science of number [ratio numeri]...is quite valuable for the careful interpreter"[132]—is serviceable in many domains. In a treatise designed to elucidate the differences between a worldly and a monastic mindset, Saint Neilus the Ascetic mentions a monk who applied an empirical quantifiable approach to his thoughts. In order to determine with accuracy the ratio of good thoughts to bad remembrances per day, this monk would put a pebble on his right side for every good thought and on his left for every bad one. At the end of the day, he would count his stones and thus have a daily tally to measure his progress [kath' hekastēn epidosis].[133] In a similar vein, Saint Nicodemos the Hagiorite advised those preparing for confession to carefully reckon sins in thought, word, and deed on a monthly, weekly, and daily basis.[134] Quantification can thus be understood in a patristic context as an expression of exactitude [akribeia], which manifests the believer's love for God.

Once the patient has acquired the ability to speak clearly, objectively, and quantitatively about his thoughts and emotions, the therapist and patient can then begin to evaluate automatic thoughts that provoke emotional disturbances. David Clark notes, "Anyone who is at all distressed will have an enormous number of negative thoughts, most of which are totally irrelevant...They're not driving the system."[135] To select the most important automatic thoughts that *do* drive the system, the therapist needs to have an accurate understanding or conceptualization of the patient's world and disorder. A simple technique for weeding out peripheral automatic thoughts is for the therapist to ask the patient how much he believes the thought (0%–100%) and how strongly he feels the emotion (0%–100%). Obviously, thoughts and emotions with low ratings can be disregarded, while those with high ratings may call for further scrutiny.[136]

The Modification of Maladaptive Automatic Thoughts

In chapter five, we discussed the concept of metacognition and the way in which Socratic questioning is used to re-evaluate an automatic thought. Gathering data that support a cognition as well as looking for evidence that disproves it are pivotal metacognitive skills intrinsic to therapy and necessary for formulating an alternate realistic interpretation of a given situation. Cognitive techniques aimed at modifying thoughts are also designed for overcoming what Harry Stack Sullivan calls "selective inattention and wonderfully facile forgetting,"[137] that is, the tendency "to miss all sorts of things which would cause you embarrassment or, in many cases, great profit."[138]

When the patient learns the technique of paying attention to his automatic thoughts and viewing them as hypotheses that may or may not be correct, he often spontaneously re-evaluates them.[139] Sometimes, however, he requires some additional help in shifting focus and distancing himself from a thought so that he can weigh it on its own terms. To this end the patient must "challenge the basic belief that he is the focal point of all events"[140] and try to look at the thought from the perspective of an impartial third party.[141]

Although ideally the patient provides his own alternative adaptive response to an automatic thought, sometimes the therapist must help the patient by using techniques other than the standard Socratic questions. Dr. Judith Beck notes that the therapist can employ (1) persuasion, (2) alternate perspectives, (3) exaggeration, (4) self-disclosure, (5) diagrams, and (6) role-play to assist a patient in the evaluation of an automatic thought.[142] These techniques may also prove useful in a pastoral setting. For example, consider the spiritual father who has offered all the patristic advice that he can muster to help someone who tells lies. Unfortunately, the poor soul continues to justify himself with the thought—"If I am honest, others will be insulted and won't like me." At this point, the resourceful pastor may consider other approaches.

To help someone struggling with lying rebut the automatic thought that justifies his behavior, the spiritual father could (1) try to convince his spiritual child that his views are skewed, since most people find candor refreshing and hypocrisy irritating. He could (2) offer an alternative perspective by pointing out that being honest can open the way for sincere relationships and that honesty does not mean that we have to express everything that comes into our mind. He could (3) exaggerate the thought so that the distortion would be clearly seen by agreeing that the believer should not look for everything he dislikes about everyone else and then be rudely blunt about it. The spiritual father could then ask if that is really likely to happen. He could (4) use self-disclosure by mentioning that he respects those who are truthful with him and usually feels at peace with his conscience when he is sincere with others. He could (5) draw a diagram with the two extremes and note that according to the holy fathers the mean of virtue is always the most desirable choice:

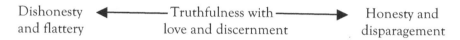

Dishonesty ◀——————Truthfulness with——————▶ Honesty and
and flattery   love and discernment   disparagement

Finally, they could (6) role-play the feared interaction in which the individual is honest in order to determine the accuracy of the automatic thought about the negative consequences of honesty.

When the patient has mastered the necessary skills for monitoring his automatic thoughts, for identifying cognitive distortions (see chapter 4) and for formulating an adaptive response (see chapter 5), he is introduced to the most important and effective cognitive tool for modifying maladaptive cognitions: a worksheet developed by Aaron Beck and today known as the dysfunctional thought record or DTR for short.[143] Its present form consists of six columns that are incrementally introduced in the course of a number of sessions.[144]

In column one, the patient enters the date and time; in column two, he briefly describes the situation and any physical sensation that he experienced; in column three, he reports his automatic thought and the extent to which he believes it (0%–100%); in column four, he records his disturbing emotion and the degree of intensity (0%–100%); in column five, he notes any cognitive distortion evident in the automatic thought and uses standard metacognitive questions to evaluate the validity of the thought and to compose an adaptive response; in column six, he then rerates how much he believes his automatic thought and how intensely he feels his emotion.[145]

For example, figure 8.1 presents a DTR filled out by someone who was asked to give a talk at a later date and suddenly felt anxious. After completing the exercise, the person not only experienced a significant decrease in emotional discomfort, but also empirically confirmed the efficacy of this technique and the relationship between the credibility of automatic thoughts and the intensity of emotions. Although the patient can also mentally fill out a dysfunctional thought record or review one that he has already completed for similar thoughts,[146] these techniques are not nearly as effective as active pen and paper methods that make automatic thoughts concrete and put the patient in an objective analytical mode.[147] Not without reason, writing down elicited cognitions is considered to be "one of the hallmarks of cognitive therapy."[148]

1. Date	2. Situation	3. Automatic thought	4. Emotion
Saturday evening	At home alone after a phone call about a talk.	"I will make a fool of myself!" — 80%	Anxiety — 90%
5. Cognitive distortions and adaptive response			6. Outcome
A. Catastrophizing, magnification distortions B. "I may be nervous at the beginning, BUT usually people respond well to my content and I calm down quickly." — 100%			A. "I will make a fool of myself!" — 10% B. Anxiety — 20%

Fig. 8.1. An example of a completed dysfunctional thought record.

Patients and therapists can also compose coping cards for responding to common dysfunctional automatic thoughts and problematic situations that generate them. This technique requires the patient to write out the common automatic thought or problematic situation on one side of a 3" x 5" note card and an adaptive response or strategy based on a careful metacognitive examination on the other side. The card is then read thrice daily and kept handy in a pocket or purse to be perused when relevant situations arise.[149] Evagrius provides a psychologically astute rationale for this technique: "When someone does not have a strong reasonable thought readily available for the swift rebuttal of a bad thought, he easily and quickly falls into sin....We are not able to rapidly search for sayings that oppose what the warring demons suggest at the time of battle."[150] In psychological parlance, people do not always have the luxury of being able to sit down and fill out a dysfunctional thought record, but need a prepared rational metacognitive response to common provoking automatic thoughts at the time of distress. Figure 8.2 illustrates how a Christian might compose a coping card employing Evagrius's list of biblical rebuttals to the classical list of bad thoughts.

Side 1. Type of Bad Thought: Sorrow

Common Automatic Thoughts:

1. *"The Lord doesn't see my suffering!"*

2. *"I'll never get better!"*

Side 2. Biblical Rebuttal:

1. *"The children of Israel sighed by reason of the bondage, and they cried, and their cry came up unto God" (Exodus 2:23).*
2. *"I am the LORD, and I will bring you out from under the burdens of the Egyptians, and I will rid you out of their bondage" (Exodus 6:6).*

Fig. 8.2. Two sides of a coping card with Evagrian example.

Interestingly enough, such a patristic application of the coping card technique is already in use by Protestant cognitive therapists who write apropos scriptural verses on index cards for their patients.[151] An Orthodox Christian therapist could also draw on the wealth of material available in patristic literature for developing such cards.

Recurrent thoughts that cause distress can also be dealt with by distraction or refocusing on something else. Using distraction or thought-stopping techniques, the patient "interrupts the stream of thoughts with a sudden stimulus, imagined or real, then switches to other thoughts before the stream of dysfunctional thoughts resume."[152] In practical terms, this means that the patient suddenly claps his hands and says, "Stop!" After distraction, the patient can then refocus on a pleasant memory or scene in order to calm down. Refocusing techniques are based on the finding that "aversive arousal generated by perturbing thoughts can be reduced by engaging in serene thoughts."[153] These techniques are more palliative than therapeutic, and hence used sparingly in cognitive therapy,[154] apart from initial difficulties with chronic worrying.

The Significance of Releasing a Dove and Sending Forth Scouts

Whoever scouts out the starkly divergent terrains of patristic literature and cognitive therapy will be struck by the remarkable similarity between respective preliminary techniques for troubling thoughts. Both fathers and therapists encourage those who seek their aid to begin the healing process by cultivating basic skills in watchfulness and active awareness in order to become conscious of the thoughts and thus no longer unwittingly subject to them. Both recognize the value of identifying the thoughts mentally, orally, and in writing, although therapists are clearly more cognizant of the advantages of written approaches. Both appreciate the use of number for assessing change, although therapists are more insistent on the necessity of refined quantitative methods. Both utilize lists to facilitate fluency in speaking about troubled areas as well as to expand awareness and sensitivity to those subjects. Both employ refocusing and distraction techniques for dealing with certain kinds of thoughts. Both make use of reason, persuasion, and rebuttal to provide an alternative to thoughts that are bad or maladaptive. Both suggest making cognitive preparations in advance to address common problematic cognitions. Both offer specific details to increase the effectiveness of a given cognitive tool, be it the use of speed and anger in rebuttal or the sequential utilization of the columns in the dysfunctional thought record.

And yet an honest scout will also have observed enormous differences in substance and in style that reflect the ultimate significance of these two sets of cognitive tools. Techniques involving percentiles, charts, scales, and diagrams do not exist on the same existential plane as practices encompassing humble self-reproach, hesychastic prayer, and divine theoria. As useful as charts and diagrams are for ordering information and clarifying thought about human difficulties, they are *never* more than techniques and make no pretensions to be so. Self-reproach, prayer, and theoria, however, are *always* more than "religious practices." They are facets of a relationship with the living God, who guided Noah to build an ark to escape the raging waters of the flood and Moses to lead the children of Israel on dry land in the midst of the sea. Faith in that guidance transfigures patristic "techniques" into expressions of obedience and love that cognitively accomplish far more than any short-range goal. They call forth a response from God.

And lo, the believer sees the dove return with an olive branch in its mouth; he follows the children of Israel as they enter a land flowing with milk and honey; and most importantly he beholds the hand of God at work in his life. At all levels, scouting the thoughts can prepare the way for calmness of the thoughts. But when it is accomplished for the sake of divine love, that calmness is borne aloft beyond the psychological horizon of human composure to "the peace of God, which passeth all understanding."[155]

Cultivating the Garden of the Heart: Patristic Counsel and Cognitive Techniques for Schema Reconstruction

A field of briars can be tilled into a bed of flowers, if gardeners but plan what they will plant, work the soil, and nurture their delicate seedlings. In the spiritual life, sinners can reach holiness, if they but clear the brambles of sinful thoughts by watchfulness, break up the hardened soil of sinful habits by bodily asceticism, and cultivate the fragrant blossoms of virtue through a life of repentance. In cognitive therapy, those with a psychological disorder can find some peace of mind, if they but uproot the weeds of distorted thinking with preliminary cognitive skills, reshape the landscape of self-defeating actions with behavioral techniques, and prune back their maladaptive beliefs through advanced techniques for schema change.

Cognitive therapy provides clearly defined and carefully designed cognitive techniques for identifying and restructuring deeply held maladaptive beliefs that perpetuate psychopathology. In the Orthodox Church, putting off the old man and putting on the new[1] entails a total immersion in a way of life that is guided by Sacred Scripture and Holy Tradition, nourished by the Divine Mysteries, and enlivened by the grace of God. In this context, the process of purification from the passions, illumination by the grace of the Holy Spirit, and deification in Christ also radically transfigure a person's basic beliefs or schemata. This process is a gradual one, like unto that of a seed that falls to the earth, then sprouts and grows.[2] Although spiritual fathers may plant and water, it is always God who gives the increase.[3]

For the believer, it is as clear as the noonday sun that the ineffable mystery of salvation is too vast and too divine to be compared with a finite number of psychological techniques that can induce enduring cognitive change. Notwithstanding, patristic advice aimed at shaping the way Christians look at the world can illustrate an alternative approach and provide a sense of meaning, a hierarchy of values, and a vision of the human person that can both direct Christian therapists who apply advanced techniques for restructuring their clients' core schemata and warn Christian patients of potential dangers in their quest for improved mental health.

In this chapter, we will consider how the garden of the human soul can be cultivated by the trusty spade of patristic counsel and the calibrated gauges of cognitive therapy. Initially, we will focus on ascetic advice to the faithful on the daily struggle for virtue, the cultivation of good thoughts, the reading of spiritual books, and new ways of looking at themselves, others, and the world. In psychological terms, implementing this advice undoubtedly shifts fundamental beliefs of the believer, but not in the highly calculated fashion of the techniques for schematic change that we shall survey at the close of this chapter. Rather, as warmth from the sun, moisture from the rains, and nutrients from the soil help a seed grow into a plant, so illumined patristic wisdom gradually and gently guides the blossoming souls of believers to turn their heads toward the Sun of Righteousness and send down their roots to the Wellspring of living water. And in the process, the believer is transformed: "first the blade, then the ear, after that the full corn in the ear."[4] Thus, advice of ancient fathers will form our gardener's standard for finally examining how the flora of the human mind is altered in cognitive therapy through the extended use of techniques for achieving schematic change such as cognitive continua, schema diaries, historical tests, and psychodrama. Of course, in examining these tools for growing the prized mental flowers of a manicured psychological garden, we will not forget the proverbial lily of the field.

Patristic Advice for Tending the Garden of the Soul

Counsel for Daily Training in the Virtues at Home

As teachers of the Christian faith and way of life, the fathers were well aware of basic pedagogical principles such as the necessity to practice learned material consistently in order to apply it in real-life situations.[5] Christian virtue, like every other art, requires daily practice[6] and the support of others. The faithful are encouraged to study throughout the day whatever they gather from the texts of the liturgical services, from sermons given by priests, or from the advice of spiritual fathers in confession. According to Saint John Chrysostom, it is fitting for the faithful to form study groups at home and review whatever they have gleaned in church before turning to the other tasks of day-to-day living.[7] The saint also advises the faithful to be creative in their effort to become proficient in virtue. For example, when he encouraged his flock to refrain from saying anything derogatory about anyone else, he suggested that they work at home as a family unit both exhorting and correcting one another as well as devising ways to make this God-pleasing practice permanent.[8] In general, he saw the home as "a training ground for virtue" [palaistra aretēs] where believers could experientially acquire the knowledge necessary for virtuous behavior in the marketplace of daily life.[9]

Orthodox monasticism likewise emphasizes the importance of spiritual training that takes place outside the·explicit contexts of private and corporate prayer. The ascetics repeatedly urge monks and nuns to practice cutting off their will [ekkopē thelēmatos] daily in order to grow in virtue, to become humble, and to acquire compunction.[10] Merely saying no to inquisitive thoughts about trivial matters cultivates a detachment from insignificant earthly concerns. Although it may not seem like a great accomplishment if a nun wonders what is for dinner, but refrains from asking the cook, over time this practice applied in a variety of situations establishes a proper hierarchy of values in her soul, shifting fundamental beliefs about her self and her world from the ephemeral to the eternal.[11]

Another example of patristic advice on planting precepts on virtue along the rolling hills of daily life is the practice of rehearsing in the mind how one would like to act in a troubling situation. For the fathers, this practice is scripturally rooted in psalm 118:60 (LXX): "I prepared myself and was not disturbed in keeping thy commandments," which they paraphrase as "I reviewed in advance how I would handle a chance encounter by considering my resources, and I was not disturbed by tribulations for Christ's sake."[12] According to the ancient ascetics, this previous preparation enabled the three holy youths to enter the Babylonian furnace and hosts of martyrs to face martyrdom without being flustered.[13] By anticipating and considering in advance what may take place, believers in the face of trials can likewise trim down excessive emotional reactions of fear or anger.[14]

For example, Saint John Cassian suggests that those who find themselves becoming impatient or angry should practice imagining that they are hindered, wronged or injured, but respond as the saints would—with perfect humility and gentleness of heart.[15] Saint Nicodemos the Hagiorite likewise recommends that believers prepare themselves before going somewhere or coming into contact with irritating and exasperating people by imagining that others curse them and dishonor them, but that they weather it all with thanksgiving and peace of mind.[16] Saint Theophan the Recluse expands this method to include all the conceivable encounters and imaginable feelings, desires, and reactions that a person might experience. He suggests reflecting on potential attacks at the beginning of the day and mentally planning how to react in a way that is in keeping with the commandments of Christ.[17]

This patristic practice also has classical antecedents. In the Christian redaction of Epictetus's *Encheiridion*, those who desire to become virtuous are advised to consider in advance the potential difficulties and obstacles that they might come across in any endeavor.[18] They also prepare themselves mentally for the irritating or demeaning actions of others, so that they can remain calm and composed when encountered in real life.[19] As an aid, they imagine how someone virtuous would behave in a similar situation.[20]

Given the Stoic pedigree for this practice, it predictably occupies a niche in cognitive therapy under the rubric of mental imagery techniques with the designation—cognitive rehearsal. In treating depression, it is used to help patients to identify potential obstacles that would prevent the completion of a therapy assignment.[21] In treatment for anxiety, patients are instructed to imagine in advance what they would do in order to respond calmly in a particular stressful situation that they dread facing.[22]

Struggling daily to attain virtue, conversing with others about living in a God-pleasing way, cutting off the will, and mentally rehearsing Christian responses to difficult situations are simple practices, like mulching newly hoed soil. Nevertheless, they can gradually uproot core beliefs and perspectives that incite sinful thoughts, "for virtue, when habitual, kills the passions,"[23] which is a theological way of saying that persistent, adaptive behavior dismantles maladaptive schemata. Most importantly, these exercises for righteousness' sake help the believer to keep the commandments of Christ, the heavenly Husbandman who further illumines the meadow of the heart with the sunshine of divine grace.

The Cultivation of Good Thoughts

In our previous two chapters, we discussed the concept of *theoria* or recollection in relation to *praxis* and watchfulness. For the ancient ascetics, theoria as the cultivation of good thoughts is an essential daily practice that brings order to the motley foliage of the human heart. It aims not at responding to specific thoughts, but rather at refashioning the overall way in which the faithful think by turning their attention to conceptual categories shaped by revelation. Saint Gregory Palamas defines the healthy thought-life in terms of thinking about the truths of revelation and the life in Christ in the same way as the prophets, apostles, and holy fathers did.[24] To this end, monks of old advised the faithful to cultivate good thoughts or to engage in theoria, whose ultimate planting, growth, and fruition come from the very hand of God.[25]

The Apostle Paul counseled the Philippians on the mental life writing, "Whatsoever things are true, whatsoever things are honest, whatsoever things are just, whatsoever things are pure, whatsoever things are lovely, whatsoever things are of good report; if there be any virtue, and if there be any praise, think on these things."[26] According to Saint John Chrysostom's commentary, this entails musing on virtue and on whatsoever is pleasing to the faithful and to God.[27] Saint Isaac the Syrian notes that this remembrance of the virtues is a better way to elude the passions than resistance.[28] This indicates that the cultivation of good thoughts works at a deeper schematic level than the methods for responding to individual bad thoughts that we examined in the previous chapter. Conscientious reflection on the virtues alters the way people interpret and thus respond to a variety of situations.

For example, if Christians, who often reflect on the virtue of speaking truthfully, encounter a situation in which a lie could help them save face, their previous reflections will nevertheless lead them to admit the truth.[29] In like manner, those who frequently ruminate on patristic advice about fighting anger will be more apt to apply that advice in time of need.[30] In psychological terms, the cultivation of good thoughts has developed new schemata that alter the faithful's perception of a situation and the value they assign to potential choices. This practice can exert a powerful influence on people's lives. By daily recalling the zeal with which they first chose the way of repentance, monks acquire new wings with which to continue their flight.[31] By reflecting on the "bold deeds done by their fathers,"[32] the martyrs discover within themselves the courage to fight in like manner, for "the brave and steadfast mind riveted to religious meditations [*religiosis meditationibus*] endures."[33]

Thus, the active cultivation of good thoughts provides the believer with a corrective lens for properly viewing the world, even as the passions distort what a person sees. According to Saint Barsanuphius, good thoughts are like pigments that the believer applies to the painting of the heart and thereby makes it difficult for clashing colors to be knowingly added.[34] In addition to the psychological and moral benefit of this practice, the cultivation of godly thoughts also increases faith[35] and brings the promise of consolation after death.[36]

Together with musing on the beauty of virtue, the cultivation of good thoughts also entails pondering on the basic truths of revelation and the human predicament. Saint John Chrysostom points out that the value of this kind of theoria is not merely intellectual and didactic. Those who unremittingly remember God not only choose to do what is right, but are also remembered by God who then gives them the strength to accomplish it.[37]

As an aid to the faithful, the ancient ascetics prepared lists of edifying topics to be sown in the soil of the believers' hearts. For example, Saint Gregory of Sinai advises cultivating thoughts about God, the angelic ranks, created being, the incarnation, the universal resurrection, the second coming, eternal punishment, and the kingdom of heaven.[38] Saint Peter of Damascus mentions the above subjects in his list, but also adds other more philosophical and personal topics such as the flux of time, the trials of human life, the soul's plight after death, our faults, and God's bounty toward us.[39] The irrevocability and finality of these considerations form a layer of bedrock that stabilizes the human mind.[40] They, moreover, establish firm beliefs about human finitude, value, and responsibility that powerfully shape the way that people view themselves, their world, and their future. In psychological terms, these concerns can prevent or modify those maladaptive forms of the cognitive triad (i.e., negative ways of viewing self, the world, and the future) that leave people particularly vulnerable to depression and anxiety.

Although all the subjects on these patristic lists are worthy of cultivation, the particular needs and spiritual maturity of the individual Christian dictate which topics should be emphasized. For example, Saint John Cassian prefers love of virtue and love for God to the fear of hell as motives for the life in Christ.[41] Consequently, he advises keeping the love of the Lord at the immovable center of the mind.[42] Saint John Climacus likewise praises the sublimity of thinking about love for God, the kingdom of heaven, and the zeal of the martyrs, but he also notes the universal effectiveness of reflecting on one's departure, the last judgment, and eternal retribution.[43]

In other words, although the love of God is the most exalted of subjects, the harsh reality of death can soften even the most insensitive souls,[44] encouraging them to turn away from arrogance, vain thoughts, and inordinate desires,[45] as well as to follow an ascetic way of life.[46] Such a radical reconsideration of basic priorities naturally entails a shifting of core beliefs. Saint Theophan the Recluse advises the believer to reflect on the above subjects upon wakening from sleep and to repeat a scriptural verse such as "Where shall I go? It is appointed unto men once to die, but after this the judgment."[47]

The daily cultivation of good thoughts or *theoria* complements the everyday practice of the virtues by further altering the faithful's interpretation of the world around them. When people ponder on virtue, patristic advice for fighting the passions, the achievements of the saints, and the history of salvation, as well as their own future death and judgment, they domesticate the wilderness of their souls with fruit-bearing trees. Not only is their inner life nourished by the truth of the gospel, but also their inner vision is clarified by the light of Christ that exposes the falsehood of the passions as well as the treachery of dysfunctional beliefs stemming from selfishness, irresponsibility, and ingratitude.

The Careful Reading of Sacred Writings and Spiritual Texts

The reading and study of spiritual books are essential patristic tools for the cultivation of good thoughts throughout the day, even as bibliotherapy (i.e., the reading of appropriate books on the cognitive approach to a particular psychological disorder) is instrumental in sustaining therapeutic progress by enabling therapy to continue outside the office.[48] Furthermore, as bibliotherapy continuously reinforces important points made during therapy sessions,[49] so spiritual reading consolidates what the believer learns during the divine services and mystery of confession.

Spiritual reading [lectio divina, theio anagnōsma] is such an important facet of both the Christian life and the health of the soul that Saint Ignatius Brianchaninov begins his advice to monks with an exhortation on studying the gospels and engraining the commandments of Christ in the mind, so that monastics might put them into practice.[50] Saint Theophan the Recluse likewise emphasizes this practical and purpose-laden aspect of reading when he advises the believer who has finished perusing a text to "persuade himself not only to think exactly like that, but also to feel and act so."[51]

For the holy fathers, the spiritual benefits of reading sacred texts are manifold. The reading of scripture protects the faithful from sin,[52] for it both makes them more sensitive to spiritual matters[53] and arms them with expertise about how to withstand and overcome temptations.[54] In psychological terms, reading increases awareness and provides additional choices for coping strategies. It also strengthens faith,[55] steadies a wandering mind,[56] gives rise to pious thoughts,[57] illumines the heart, and guides believers to virtuous behavior.[58]

Saint Athanasius the Great notes that constant rumination on the law of the Lord is a necessary form of spiritual exercise that should be practiced regularly, so that good thoughts might lead a person to acts of virtue.[59] When believers daily read familiar teachings with the same eagerness and thirst for sanctifying knowledge that they had when they encountered those teachings for the first time, then even the purposes of their hearts and the wanderings of their imagination are sanctified.[60]

Even as the cultivation of good thoughts shapes a person's core schemata, so do daily spiritual readings, for as Saint Neilus the Ascetic notes, "Frequent reminders of good examples carve similar images within the soul."[61] The ascetic fathers even maintain that extensive spiritual reading can heal a person's evil memories by imprinting in the mind the remembrance of the good,[62] thereby purifying the memories of the passions,[63] and distancing the soul from distressing recollections.[64] Spiritual readings moreover "fill the soul with incomprehensible wonder and divine gladness."[65]

When a cognitive therapist assigns psychology books for the purpose of bibliotherapy, patients are expected to take notes on the material and their reaction to it.[66] In like manner, ancient monastics recommend that the therapeutic reading of the saints' writings be done with the diligence of zealous students[67] who pay attention to every word. The primary aim of such careful reading, however, is neither effective reinforcement, nor the inducement of a metacognitive analytical state for schema modification, but the discovery of spiritual treasures embedded in sacred texts. As Saint John Chrysostom notes, "One sentence often supplies those who receive it with ample provisions for their entire life."[68] Consequently, spiritual reading should have greater potential for schema modification than standard bibliotherapy on account of the greater faith, trust, and hope with which believers approach inspired writings as well as on account of the grace of God that inheres therein.

Since the faithful read scripture and the writings of the saints with an awareness that through these texts God may be speaking to them, it follows that they will also read humbly and prayerfully.[69] In terms of practical instruction, Saint Theophan the Recluse advises believers to empty their minds, open their hearts, and pray to God before attentively and slowly reading sacred texts.[70]

Of course, devotional reading should be commensurate with the believers' spiritual maturity, which means that they can feasibly put into practice the teachings contained in the books they read.[71] Saint Ignatius Brianchaninov advises monks to study works written for those living in community such as *The Discourses* of Abba Dorotheos, *The Catechetical Homilies* of Saint Theodore the Studite, and *The Ladder* of Saint John of Sinai, before reading texts written for solitaries such as *The Ascetical Homilies* of Saint Isaac and *The Philokalia* of Saints Nicodemos the Hagiorite and Makarios of Corinth.[72] Saint Nicodemos himself advises those sick with the thoughts to read "sacred books, especially Saint Ephraim, *The Ladder*, *The Evergetinos*, *The Philokalia*, and other similar books."[73] Although their advice differs, both monastic masters emphasize that the selection of spiritual books is neither a haphazard process, nor an academic exercise, but a purposeful and practical endeavor that should ideally be under the direction of the believer's spiritual father.

Appropriate devotional reading thus fertilizes the garden of the soul with the spiritual nutrients she needs. At a psychological level, new memories are formed, virtuous approaches to the world are learned, and godly schemata are made available for adoption. Thus, in addition to the sacramental life and the life of prayer, the church fathers also recommend concerted work on the virtues, the cultivation of good thoughts, and spiritual reading as practical daily methods for transfiguring the soul into another Eden where the Lord God walks in the cool of the day and guides her in naming her world.[74] These are indeed powerful tools when used consistently over a lifetime, for like unto the rivers of paradise they water the soul with the grace and truth of the gospel of Christ.

Insight from the Inspired Words of the Saints

In chapter six, we discussed the prophetic aspect of spiritual fatherhood. When an elder, a priest, or a monk offers a word from God to a soul in need, that word can potentially transfigure the way that soul sees God, herself, and her world, thus bringing about what cognitive theorists would call schema restructuring. The tradition of seeking a prophetic word is especially evident in *The Sayings of the Desert Fathers* that frequently recount tales of a sojourner entreating an elder: "Give me a word."[75] With a fatherly word comes a flash of insight, and suddenly the struggler finds himself deftly grafted onto Christ the True Vine and in a position to bring forth much fruit.[76] We will thus complete our pastoral description of the tools the fathers employ to tend the garden of the soul by considering the form and content of some of the God-given words present in the tool shed of patristic correspondence, homilies, and sayings.

God's love, providence, and ultimate designs for humanity. Every human being is precious in God's sight and greatly loved. The church fathers never tire of sowing this fundamental Christian truth in the hearts of those who turn to them. It is a truth that expands the outlook of believers to encompass their ultimate destiny and God's providential care for their salvation.[77] In cognitive terms, this certainty instills new core beliefs about self, others, and the future that act as a corrective lens for viewing the ills to which flesh is heir.

For example, Saint Basil the Great once told a discouraged soul, "Everything is governed by the Lord's goodness. We do not have to be distressed by anything that befalls us, even if it currently affects us in our weakness. Even if we are ignorant of the reasons why trials come and are sent as blessings from the Lord, we should be convinced that all things happen to us for our own good, either to reward our patience or to preserve our soul lest she linger too long in this life and be filled with wickedness."[78] Although people may not be able to understand the wisdom that governs individual struggles, by patiently enduring them they can gain a crown.[79] Saint John Chrysostom similarly suggests that believers give thanks to God for whatever happens, even if they do not fathom why it occurs, for the Lord loves us even more than our parents do.[80] From this perspective, one can understand why the holy fathers believe that "trial is profitable for every man."[81] Thus, ancient ascetics would guide the faithful to interpret whatever happens to them through their trust in God's providence, wisdom, and love that looks after their growth in virtue and aims at their eternal well-being. This humble trust then shapes or reshapes their innermost thoughts about themselves and their world, leaving little room for impatient demands stemming from sickly self-pity. Knowledge of God's justice and tenderhearted compassion, moreover, endows believers with the courage to brave adversity, for this knowledge assures them that trials will prove that they are good or make them better.[82]

Trust in God's providence and love is not nebulous optimism, but rock-hard faith in the personal significance of Christ's salvific work as a means for overcoming life's trials and tribulations as well as sickness and death. Saint John Chrysostom beautifully illustrates how profound faith can transfigure one's interpretation of the most grievous tragedies. To parents who lost their beloved son, he advised, "When you see the eyes closed, the lips shut, and the body motionless, do not have thoughts like these: 'These lips no longer speak; these eyes no longer see; these feet no longer walk; but will all fall into corruption!' Do not say such things, but the very opposite: 'These lips shall speak of better things; these eyes shall see things greater still; these feet shall mount on the clouds; and this body that now rots away shall put on immortality. And I shall receive my son back again even more glorious.'"[83] Faith in the Resurrection of Christ gives the Christian the strength and courage to view life and death from another perspective that brings acceptance of trials, healing of wounds, and ultimately the hope of the saints.

As a general approach to encounters with others, Saint Isaac advises the faithful to keep in mind that they "receive help from every man by God's secret command."[84] They can even view distressing or insulting individuals as physicians [hōs iatrou] and their actions as healing medicines [hōs pharmaka therapeutika] sent by Christ for their purification from the passions and spiritual health.[85] Saint Philotheus of Sinai likewise suggests that believers turn their thoughts from the injury or distress that others provoke to the deeper purpose cloaked by the affront.[86] From a cognitive perspective, patristic advice on looking through unpleasant situations to God's providence and the soul's health provides new categories (schemata) for interpreting reality.

The value of self-reproach. Alongside recalling Divine Providence, ancient monastics also advise the faithful to use self-reproach as a basic interpretive principle in order to avoid judging others who sin as well as to prevent agitation, anger,[87] and pride.[88] For example, when Saint Dorotheos would notice a brother failing in some way to lead a Christian life, he would say to himself, "Woe is me, him today and surely me tomorrow."[89] Thus, whenever observation would bring harm rather than benefit, the saint would deftly switch from a critical observer mode to a repentant introspective frame of mind. He formulated a rather simple algorithm for interpreting life's vicissitudes: "If something good takes place, it is by God's providence [*oikonomia*]; if something bad happens, it is on account of our sins."[90] As in other instances in the works of Abba Dorotheos, the aim of this rubric is not to provide simplistic answers to life's complexities, but to encourage traits of gratitude and humility at all times through what cognitive theorists would describe as a fundamental change in core beliefs or schemata about the self and the outside world.

In the case of insults and perceived wrongs, Abba Isaiah would tell monks to search their conscience whenever a brother speaks unkindly to them, for somewhere in God's eyes they have sinned.[91] As a rule of thumb, Elder Païsios counsels believers to always consider how much they are at fault, rather than how much their neighbor has wronged them.[92] Saint John Cassian suggests that the irritated ascetic remind himself how he had planned to get the better of all his bad qualities and how a gentle breeze caused by a troubling word shook his entire house of virtue.[93] In other words, the disturbing word becomes an opportunity for humble honesty that is the foundation of genuine self-knowledge. Abba Dorotheos likewise enjoins the grieved to stop brooding over their grievances and refocus on silence, heartfelt repentance, and prayer.[94]

Of course, it can be challenging for people to reproach themselves when a reasonable assessment of a situation clearly indicates that they are innocent. Saint Nicodemos the Hagiorite offers a number of aids for self-reproach in such instances. For example, he suggests that believers bring to mind other faults where they were clearly responsible and to view the present difficulty as a penance imposed for them. Alternatively, they can recall that tribulations form the entryway to the kingdom of heaven, that adversities line the path of Christ and his friends, and that everything that happens on life's journey is permitted by God.[95]

Consideration of the opposite point of view. Sometimes in lieu of self-reproach, the church fathers try to help the faithful to cultivate a Christian perspective by exhaustively examining an alternative point of view or the other side of an argument. Citing a saying attributed to Hippocrates, Saint Jerome notes, "Opposites are the remedies for opposites."[96] This principle lies at the root of the patristic practice of listing a plurality of counter-arguments so that believers might be persuaded that their misguided convictions or conclusions are mistaken. For example, in the case of thoughts of despair, Saint Nicodemos the Hagiorite arms the spiritual father with the following arguments to counter despondent ruminations: (1) despair over sins ignores the existence of God and in Manichean fashion elevates vice to the rank of deity; (2) it fails to draw the conclusion that the Lord still accepts the sinner from the fact that the sinner is still alive; (3) despair is a trait of the devil, not of a struggling Christian; and (4) it is inconsistent with the witness of scripture that clearly narrates how the Lord accepted sinners of every ilk.[97] In the case of a lack of contrition over sins, the spiritual father counsels the hard-hearted to consider their own responsibility for the loss of grace, for their exile from the blessedness of paradise, and for the decision to follow the path that leads to perdition.[98] In the case of vain thoughts, he advises the careless to consider that one day they will give an account for every idle thought, that vain musings crowd out salvific reflections, and that pointless reverie often harbors bad thoughts in nascent form.[99]

Consideration of the perspective and plight of others. At other times, the holy fathers assist believers in acquiring a new way of interpreting painful situations by having them step back from their own problems and consider the plight of others. This basically Stoic approach naturally undercuts egocentric beliefs and tendencies. The Christian redaction of *The Encheiridion* provides a classic example: "If someone else's servant breaks a cup, the answer is ready: those things happen. When you break your own cup, you should likewise respond as though someone else's cup were broken, and then react in like manner with more important things."[100] Detachment and distancing from sources of distress naturally moderate emotional reactions and allow for a rational and objective response to problems.

Although the church fathers do not reject this humanistic philosophical approach, they always supplement it with faith in Divine Providence. For example, Saint Basil the Great comforted a friend whose son had died by urging him stoically to remind himself that "life is full of similar misfortunes" and as a Christian to believe that "earth has not hidden our beloved, but heaven has received him."[101] Later, the saint instructed his friend's wife to think about others who have passed through such trials victoriously, on the inevitable mortality of all human beings, and the shining example of the grieving who comfort those who mourn.[102] In a similar vein, Saint Ambrose advised those who lament the loss of a loved one to remind themselves not only that death is common to all and often a release from the miseries of this world, but also that the grace of the Resurrection together with the assurance that nothing perishes in death, can assuage every grief and dispel every sorrow.[103] Saint Theodore the Studite similarly counseled his banished friend Thomas to consider how all humanity is exiled from paradise into these withering lands [thanatēphoron chōrion], but, nevertheless, the believer like the psalmist dares to hope that the Lord will lead his soul out of prison to confess his name.[104] Finally, Elder Païsios masterfully combined both Stoic distancing and Christian trust in Providence when he noted that the best medicine for our troubles is to consider the greater trials of our neighbor, so that we will thank God for sparing us and have compassion for others.[105]

Reflecting on the last judgment and eternity. Occasionally, some fathers attempt to open believers' minds to consider the long-term future repercussions of current choices. Although we have already examined this approach in our discussion of goals, we should note its importance in the acquisition of a Christian perspective on reality that affects people's values and hence their core beliefs about themselves and their world. Cognitive psychologists are not unaware of this fact, for even secular therapists may invoke religious beliefs about the future and the sanctity of life in order to counter suicidal ideation.[106] Saint John Chrysostom repeatedly enjoins believers bravely to endure every trial "and soar above the attack of human ills by the hope in future blessings."[107] In other words, the faithful are to reframe their interpretation of their situation in eschatological terms. This interpretative framework recasts almsgiving and chastity, so that the balance is tipped away from greed and lust.[108] In the struggle against temptations, the saint suggests that believers picture the judgment seat and repeat to themselves, "There is a resurrection, a judgment, and a scrutiny of our deeds."[109] This practice not only bridles sinful impulses, it also bolsters beliefs such as "I am responsible for my actions." Other ascetics also suggest turning to God and bringing to mind the Last Judgment as a way of enfeebling bad thoughts.[110] If the hope of eternal blessings does not provide sufficient motivation, sometimes the threat of punishment can be used to rouse the believer to contend more earnestly.[111] At the very least, such prospects discourage the slothful from looking to death as a release from afflictions,[112] for eternal suffering makes transitory anguish appear milder by comparison.[113]

Considering the future as though it were already the past. At times, the church fathers would help believers to overcome troubling thoughts about the future by suggesting that they mentally project themselves to the time after the feared or desired event has already occurred. For example, Saint Maximus the Confessor approvingly quotes the Sophist Libanius's axiom as a valuable antidote to sorrow and boredom: "If you wish to live a life without sorrow, regard those things that are going to happen as though they have already taken place."[114] Saint John Chrysostom makes a similar recommendation when he notes that the believer can douse the desire for glory by imagining that the envied position has already been attained, for afterward it loses its allure.[115] In terms of schema reconstruction, this approach can help a person who defines his worth in terms of acquiring recognition ("If I become a lawyer, a doctor, or teacher, then I will be worthwhile") to redefine value in theological terms ("All human beings are precious, because they are created in the image of God"). A variation on this approach can also be applied to encourage those in despair after a fall. In that case, however, the fallen are instructed to take courage by reflecting on how, after their restoration to health, they will one day use their experience to rescue others in danger of falling. Thus, they replace their present image of themselves as failures with an image of what they can still become by the grace of God, namely, physicians, beacons, and lamps.[116]

Interestingly, cognitive therapists employ similar tactics to decrease the emotional distress of patients tormented by images of impending danger or failure. For example, anxiety sufferers often imagine a fiasco taking place, such as making a fool of themselves while giving a talk, and stop their fantasy at the point of embarrassment without going any further. The therapist can instruct such patients to imagine how they will feel a month or even a year after the mishap, so that they might gain enough detachment to put their fears in perspective and to see the extent to which they are exaggerating how terrible are the consequences of the worst-case scenario actually transpiring.[117]

Cognitive therapists have an arsenal of imagery techniques for dealing with their patients' images of a feared crisis or terminal condition. In addition to techniques that involve patients jumping ahead in time and coping in their image that we also encounter in patristic texts, therapists also advise their patients to change the way an imagined scene ends, to question what they imagine as though it were an automatic thought, and to follow the imaginary chain of events to their ultimate conclusion.[118]

Protestant cognitive therapists sometimes enrich imaging techniques by having their patients imagine that the Lord Jesus is in an imagined scene. For example, people who are facing a difficult task are told to visualize themselves accomplishing the undertaking with Christ by their side.[119] One therapist instructed a patient trying to cope with a tragedy to envision herself as a branch in reference to Christ's words "I am the true vine, and my Father is the husbandman...I am the vine, ye are the branches." After this exercise, the patient reported feeling at peace.[120]

The use of imagery. In the Orthodox Church, the holy icons purify the spiritual vision of those who venerate them with faith and love. Quite naturally, the church fathers would also use verbal icons or metaphors in order to alter spiritually unhealthy perspectives and to foster a Christian outlook. This practice can be traced back to Christ's sayings and parables in which he employed metaphor and visual imagery to inspire the faithful to keep the commandments. Those who live according to the beatitudes are commended not as "good people," but as "the salt of the earth" and "light of the world."[121] Saint Theophan the Recluse recommended, "If possible, do not leave a thought naked in reasoned form as it were, but robe it in some sort of image and then carry it into the head as a constant reminder."[122] This practice is consistent with the psychological finding that images can directly introduce new patterns into the network of schemata that guide a person's responses to various situations.[123] The homilies and correspondence of the holy fathers abound with a forest of images that aim at altering the way believers approach various tasks and sets of circumstances.

For instance, Saint John Chrysostom advised those sluggish at prayer to picture the awesome scene of the sacrifice of Abraham, complete with details like the wood, the fire, the knife, and the gates of heaven thrown open.[124] Such images are emotionally and cognitively effective. They not only reshape the faithful's understanding of the vital significance of prayer and their relation-ship to God, but also motivate them to strive to make their own prayerful supplications into a living sacrifice to the most High. This same image can also be used to rally those weary in fighting a host of temptations. For example, the saint also noted that although legions of thoughts rose up against Abraham when he was told to sacrifice his beloved son, the patriarch withstood them all and "God from heaven proclaimed him conqueror...the Olympic victor...not in this theater but in the theater of the universe, in the assembly of angels."[125] Although believers' lives may seem to be worlds away from Abraham's sacri-fice, Olympic contests, and the angelic hosts, by faith they find something equally noble in their attempt to draw nigh unto God and thus dare to imitate what their physical eyes have never seen.

Images reminiscent of prophetic visions are especially apt at inspiring zeal for spiritual undertakings. For example, Saint Theodore the Studite advised those weary with fighting the thoughts to reframe their view of spiritual warfare by picturing the man of prayer as a fiery cherubim or a many-eyed seraphim who bravely wields the sword of rebuttal against every sinful provocation.[126] Thus, by associating captivating images with spiritual activities, the ancient ascetics could enhance the believer's convictions about the significance of those activities and thereby ignite zeal for undertaking them.

With full awareness of the leverage that anticipated reward and punishment exert on behavior, the holy fathers also used threatening and enticing images to favorably influence people's judgment about alternative courses of action. For example, Saint Theophan the Recluse prods negligent believers to behave in a Christian fashion by having them form the threatening image of the sword of truth hanging above them and the chasm of death gaping in front of them.[127] To stir his listeners to almsgiving, Saint John Chrysostom paints an evocative image of the splendors of an earthly ruler and then describes the awe-inspiring magnificence of the King of kings and Lord of lords, so that a desire for unfailing wealth and unfading beauty might become an incentive for virtuous behavior that enriches the soul.[128]

Often the images, which the ancient fathers would devise to portray vice, are far from flattering. Saint John Chrysostom once compared people who seek money, rather than the kingdom of heaven, to souls "exceedingly full of stupidity, no different from flies and gnats," since in their short-sightedness they desire material lead in the presence of spiritual gold.[129] Obviously, to avoid such characterizations, the avaricious believer must rethink basic priorities and aspirations.

With similarly vivid depictions, Saint John Chrysostom tried to cultivate self-control in those prone to anger. On the one hand, he portrayed the enraged individual in repugnant terms as a "drunk with protruded eyes in the act of retching, vomiting, erupting, and covering the table with filth avoided by all."[130] On the other hand, he glowingly depicted the insulted person who keeps silent as a mighty warrior who slays the beast within and is proclaimed victor in the civil war for his heart.[131] Frequent reflection on such images may serve as deterrents to anger by altering the faithful's assessment of the impression their anger makes on others and the personal significance of their controlling it. In other words, these images tend to reverse false beliefs about the strength and superiority that angry people dream they possess. If believers can accustom themselves to bring those images to mind at the time of irritation, they can shift their focus and strive to be on guard like sailors who save their ship from sinking by lowering the sails when they feel the winds blustering against their faces[132] or like housekeepers who use fire for cooking and lighting the lamps, but never for setting their homes ablaze.[133] This variety of images gradually restructures believers' understanding about the use of anger as a response to thwarted desires, unforeseen difficulties, and perceived disparagement by making virtue's victory over anger their primary desire, objective, and source of self-esteem.

The application of biblical parallels to personal experience. One final characteristic method that the fathers so effectively use to reshape an individual's perspective on his situation is to locate a parallel to his experience in Holy Scripture and consider how the biblical figure responded. For example, the fathers remind the infirm of the much suffering apostles, the sorely tried righteous, and the blessed Timothy who had sickness as a constant companion. As the sick person already resembles the saints in affliction, he needs but their courage and patience in order to resemble them in their virtuous response to suffering as well.[134] Elder Païsios likewise recommended that those going through a trial recall the tribulations of the righteous and how we have made greater mistakes than they did, but suffer far less.[135] Saint John Chrysostom explicitly refers to the therapeutic value of drawing biblical associations when he comments, "Remember your Master, and by the remembrance, you have immediately applied the remedy. Remember Paul, reflect that you who are beaten has conquered and the beater is defeated, and in so doing you have completed the cure."[136] This cure is a new perspective on a familiar situation or in cognitive terms, the modification of schema about the self and the world.

This scriptural approach is especially well suited to encourage those sensitive souls in despair over their sins. For example, Amma Syncletica would remind her nuns that Rahab the prostitute was saved by faith, that Paul the persecutor became an elect vessel, that Matthew the tax collector became an evangelist, and that the murderous thief was the first to open the gates of paradise.[137] Since someone in despair can easily identify with the failures of others, such examples mesh perfectly with his despondent state, and yet they introduce to that state the miracle of repentance and the presence of God that break it wide open by directly modifying core beliefs about the meaning of a person's view of the past and resolve for the future in terms of his relationship to his Creator and Redeemer.

In *The Spiritual Meadow*, John Moschus relates the account of a monk who was distressed by his struggle with the thoughts and came to the conclusion that he had made a mistake in renouncing the world and that he would not find salvation. He came to an elder who did not directly dispute his thoughts, but had him look back to the time of the exodus and told him, "Know, my brother, that even if we cannot enter the promised land, it is better to let our carcasses fall in the desert, rather than to return to Egypt."[138] Finding meaning for his experience in the example from scripture, the brother acquired a new perspective and a more comprehensive schema for understanding his situation, so that he was able to accept his weaknesses, to set more humble goals, and to return to his own struggle with calm determination.

In the case of despondency over sins, believers not only have wrong beliefs about the irreversibility of their lapses, but also about God's disposition toward them. For this reason, Saint John Climacus reminds the repentant that the Lord gave Peter the command to forgive a person who sins seventy times seven, and adds, "He who gave this command to another will himself do far more."[139] This assurance in turn counters disbelief in God's forgiveness. Saint Theodore the Studite likewise suggests that the distraught recall that the Lord loves every human soul and always stretches out his hand toward those who repent.[140] Saint Symeon the New Theologian advises the downcast to remember that they are not saved by their own accomplishments, but by the grace of God.[141] Thus, with the assurance of God's love, with faith in divine forgiveness, and the hope of true repentance, the despondent can acquire the courage to emerge from their slough of despond.

In summary, within the believers' rich and variegated life of ascetic struggle and participation in the Holy Mysteries, they are initiated into teachings and practices that can transfigure their basic perspective vis-à-vis themselves, others, and their world. In particular, the daily struggle for virtue, the practice of cutting off the will, and the prior rehearsal of virtuous responses behaviorally reshape their values and their views about significant details of their lives. The cultivation of good thoughts concerning the beauties of virtue, the truths of revelation, and the inevitabilities of death and change together with spiritual reading cognitively instill both powerful categories of thought for appraising their situation and inspiring models for imitation. Finally, salvific words from the pulpit (ambon) or the confessional on God's love and providence, the value of self-reproach, the plight of others, and the Last Judgment as well as the use of imagery and parallels from scripture can provide an epiphany that enables believers to see and interpret their lives in the clear light of Christ. Thus, the faithful who struggle to follow Christ entrust themselves to the Church's care, and collaborates with the Husbandman of their souls to transform the wilderness of their hearts into gardens where virtue ever blooms. Beholding the change wrought in their souls, they exclaim with the psalmist's voice, "This is the Lord's doing; it is marvelous in our eyes."[142]

Working with Beliefs in Cognitive Therapy

Having considered *some* representative ways in which the believer's conscientious participation in the life of the Church prunes back self-centered, irresponsible perspectives and nurtures a virtuous response to life, we can turn now to the highly focused and interactive way in which cognitive therapy identifies, modifies, and replaces maladaptive schemata that perpetuate psychological disorders.

Techniques for Identifying Schemata

In chapter four, we noted that the cognitive theory of psychopathology maintains that maladaptive schemata or beliefs are the templates for the production of distorted automatic thoughts that precipitate emotional distress. Consequently, the therapist starts searching for relevant schemata from his very first session with the patient. At the time of crisis when the patient is highly disturbed emotionally, automatic thoughts such as "I'm a failure" often express schemata directly.[143] As the therapist garners data about the patient's automatic thoughts in various situations, he tries to detect patterns and reoccurrences that reflect the patient's views about self and rules for living, and thereby to make intelligent hypotheses about potential maladaptive schemata.[144] To verify his conjectures, the therapist can employ a variety of techniques to ferret out the patient's silent assumptions and tacit beliefs that form his "psychological Achilles' heel."[145]

The simplest identification technique is for therapists to question patients about the personal meaning of those automatic thoughts that provoke the strongest emotional responses. To access self-schemata, therapists can ask, "What does this thought say about you?" To elicit beliefs about others, they can inquire, "What does this say about other people?" To draw out schemata about the patient's world, they can pose the question, "What does this say about life in general?"[146] Christine Padesky also suggests using the sentence completion technique in which therapist begin—"I am____"; "People are____"; "The world is____"—and the patient finishes the phrase, usually with a single word.[147] For example, someone with an obsessive-compulsive disorder might fill in the blanks as follows: "I am *a perfectionist*"; "People are *expected to do things my way*"; and "The world is *supposed to be ordered*."[148]

Another useful identification technique requires patients to complete questionnaires such as *Weissman's Dysfunctional Attitude Scale, Beck's Schema Checklist,* or *Young's Schema Questionnaire.*[149] These psychometric tests facilitate the identification of a variety of typical maladaptive beliefs. Patients read a series of statements such as "I need other people's approval in order to be happy," and rate how much they agree or disagree with each statement. The tallied scores then provide the therapist with a schematic profile of their patients and a good indication of their psychological strengths and emotional vulnerabilities stemming from beliefs about approval, love, achievement, perfectionism, entitlement, omnipotence, and autonomy.[150]

The third and most important method for the identification of problematic schemata is the downward arrow technique. Using this approach, the therapist asks the patient what it would mean if his upsetting cognition were true. The patient answers with another automatic thought that is then examined in the same way. They repeat this process, pealing off the layers and following the downward arrow until they reach a core belief. Although the downward arrow technique might appear to be prone to infinite regress, in practice the core belief is reached rather quickly. In particular, the therapist can infer that he has arrived at a core belief when the patient exhibits a noticeable shift in mood or starts repeating the same statement.[151]

For example, a depressed mother might taste some soup she made and feel sad after thinking to herself—"This soup is awful!" The downward arrow technique for this ostensibly insignificant automatic thought, illustrated in figure 9.1, reveals that beneath this typical evaluation lies a more problematic core schema about the self.

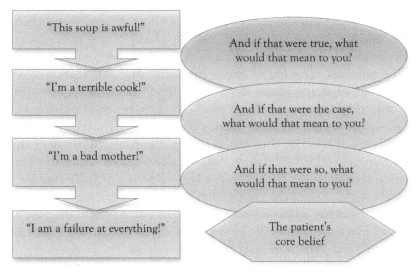

Fig. 9.1. An example of the downward arrow technique.

Dr. David Burns astutely observes that the downward arrow technique guides the patient in a direction that is diametrically opposite to the dysfunctional thought record in which the patient tries to distance himself from an automatic thought and objectively evaluate it. Instead of invalidating the cognition with a rational response, the patient assumes what he subjectively feels to be true: namely, that his thought is 100 percent valid. He is then asked what it means to him or what is so bad about its being true.[152] If the patient strongly believes in a given dysfunctional belief that has a broad impact on his life, the therapist then begins to utilize techniques for modifying that belief.[153]

Techniques for Modifying Maladaptive Schemata

Once pervasive maladaptive schemata have been identified and the patient recognizes both how they contribute to his psychological distress and leave him vulnerable to future relapses, the therapist and the patient usually decide to work on replacing, modifying, or reinterpreting those schemata.[154] Their first step is to identify an alternative belief that is more desirable. For example, the patient who believes she is unlovable would be asked, "If you weren't unlovable, how would you like to be?" The patient's answer (e.g., "I would be lovable") would then be the goal for schema work through techniques aimed at weakening the currently held maladaptive belief and strengthening the newly defined alterative.[155]

An Orthodox Christian has reason for concern about the values used to determine the maladaptive schema and especially its ideal replacement. There has to be a better criterion for altering the way a person interprets reality than the hollow subjectivity of wishful thinking that fails to consider the human being holistically as a spiritual, moral, and psychological entity. Although most of the examples given in cognitive therapy manuals for clinicians are reasonable and result in an improvement in the patient's quality of life, it is certainly conceivable for some suggestions for schematic replacement to clash with the Christian virtues of humility, chastity, patience, and self-sacrifice for the sake of the love of God.

Since schemata can be expressed in propositional form, many of the techniques that the patient has already learned to use for evaluating and responding to distorted automatic thoughts can be applied in order to gradually chip away at more deeply ingrained maladaptive schemata. Techniques include many behavioral approaches examined in chapter seven, as well as preliminary cognitive skills discussed in chapter eight. For instance, alternate perspectives, cost-benefit analyses, and Socratic questioning provide tools for re-evaluating old schemata, whereas behavioral experiments, acting "as if," graded task assignments, and activity monitoring impart additional data for strengthening new beliefs. Rather than review all these techniques, we will just consider two representative examples in order to illustrate how they can be applied for the sake of schema change.

First, we have seen how patients used an advantage-disadvantage analysis in chapter seven to determine the best solution to a given problem. This same technique can also be employed to undermine a maladaptive belief that minimizes the consequences of harmful behavior. For example, someone fighting drug addiction may have a whole set of schemata that collectively make drug use seem desirable (e.g., "It's just some harmless fun"). With the therapist's guidance, the patient can fill out a 2 x 2 chart in which the patient tries to make an exhaustive list of the advantages of quitting and the benefits of not quitting as well as the drawbacks of quitting and the disadvantages of not quitting. Looking squarely at this diagram, the patient is no longer able to avoid noticing that the stark reality of drug abuse differs markedly from his Pollyannaish beliefs about recreational drugs.[156]

Our second example is taken from the various techniques in chapter eight for distancing oneself from automatic thoughts and acquiring a new perspective in order to evaluate them. When the patient applies these techniques to schema modification, the contrast is not with a rational response to a given thought, but with a more functional approach that stems from a more adaptive core belief. By taking into consideration the beliefs of others, the individual can often step back from his own beliefs and then re-examine them more objectively. For example, the perfectionist patient may recurrently become anxious or depressed, because of a schema such as "If I don't perform perfectly, I am a failure." Such a patient could consider what he would tell a friend or imagine what he would tell his children, if they had the same dysfunctional belief causing them distress.[157] The inconsistency between what the patient subjectively believes about himself and what he objectively holds to be the case for others then gives him enough distance to re-evaluate his belief.[158]

Christian therapists sometimes endeavor to help their patients distance themselves from maladaptive beliefs by asking them questions such as "What would God think? What would Jesus do?"[159] In the West, such pietistic questions are acceptable, especially given the emphasis of the Latin tradition on the humanity of Christ since the early Christian era.[160] In fact, in his homilies, Blessed Augustine would find a present-day parallel to a situation described in scripture and ask, "What would the Lord do?"[161] or elsewhere, "What would he have us do?"[162] Likewise, Tertullian in his efforts to defend the gospel against various heretical groups asked questions such as "How would Christ speak?"[163] or even "How would their own Christ act?"[164]

Although Orthodox Christians might understandably balk at the tone of the above questions out of deep reverence for the Second Person of the Most Holy Consubstantial Trinity, such questions can be reformulated in a more humble spirit and still have the same effect. Furthermore, Saint Paul did instruct the Romans to "prove what is that good, and acceptable, and perfect, will of God."[165] Based on this passage, Saint John Chrysostom asked, "What exactly is God's will [for us]? [His will is for us] to live as the poor with a humble mindset and disdain for glory, in abstinence rather than self-indulgence, in hardship rather than in ease, in mourning rather than in dissipation and laughter, and in all the other points that he has laid down for us."[166] Thus, Orthodox Christians could, and in fact should, ask themselves, "Given the divine commandments, what would a follower of Christ do?"

As we saw in chapters three and four, core schemata are formed during childhood, reinforced over a lifetime, and consequently resistant to change. Therefore, schema modification requires considerable time, persistent effort, and special techniques both in session and at home. Among the more important cognitive instruments for schema change are cognitive continua techniques, positive data logs, core belief worksheets, the historical test technique, and psychodrama. If we liken these highly versatile tools to modern farming equipment and patristic methods to handcrafted plowshares and pruning hooks, our present examination of the above schema modification techniques should highlight yet again the functional similarities and worldview differences that have been the subtext of our study.

First of all, the cognitive continuum technique is employed to modify dichotomous schemata by placing the problematic belief and its opposite, or alternative, on a scale with other specific examples that visually demonstrate the existence of gradations.[167] When patients come to realize that a given issue is not just black or white, their evaluation of themselves or others often shifts to a more moderate position.[168] In practice, this approach requires the therapist and the patient to draw a line, to define the two extreme forms of the belief, to place them at the two endpoints of the line, to list relevant examples from the patient's life experience, to assign their relative placement on the line, and then after examining the scale they have just constructed, to reconsider the initial belief.

As an example of the cognitive continuum technique, Christine Padesky relates the case study of someone with chronic anxiety that was maintained on account of the belief "I will be punished for my faults" (See figures 9.2-9.5). With the therapist's help, the patient formulated an alternative desirable schema: "I am safe, even if others see my faults." In order to weaken the old belief and strengthen the new one, they constructed a safety scale on which the patient put an X to indicate how safe he felt when others noticed his faults:

Fig. 9.2. Step 1 of the cognitive continuum technique: constructing a scale.

The patient was then asked to define 0 percent safety and 100 percent safety and to write down those definitions beneath the two endpoints on the scale:

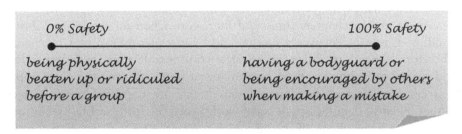

Fig. 9.3. Step 2 of the cognitive continuum technique: defining extremes.

The therapist then asked the patient to define 50 percent safety and to put that at the midpoint:

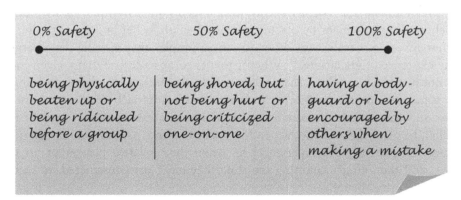

Fig. 9.4. Step 3 of the cognitive continuum technique: defining the midpoint.

Next, the therapist asked the patient to call to mind three recent experiences in which someone noticed a fault, to rate how safe he was in reality, and to place those responses on the continuum. The patient recalled his boss making fun of him when he was unable to figure out the sales tax, his son being disappointed when the patient could not fix his son's toy, and the therapist responding with understanding when the patient failed to complete his therapy assignment. The final form of this patient's cognitive continuum is given below:

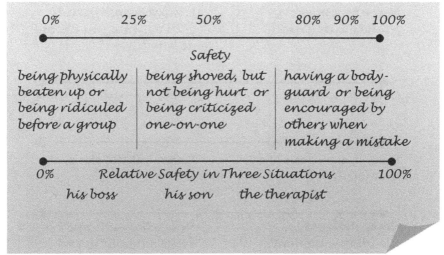

Fig. 9.5. Step 4 of the cognitive continuum technique: applying the scale.

Finally, the therapist has the patient compare how safe he expects to feel if someone notices his faults with how safe he actually felt when this happened. This process is than repeated throughout the week with new experiences.[169]

There are dozens of other useful variations to this technique for schema change. For instance, the criteria continua technique has the patient make a continuum for an important schema and its opposite, and then place himself on that scale. Next, the patient lists the qualities that define that schema, turns those qualities into continua, and rates himself separately on each derivative continuum. For example, in figure 9.6 a patient who viewed himself as weird made a continuum for normality and ranked himself as 0 percent normal. When the therapist asked the patient what are the qualities of someone who is normal, the patient answered, "having friends, holding a job, and being happy." With the therapist's help, the patient laid out his criteria for normality as a series of personal continua that he separately evaluated. Looking at the criteria, the patient could see that his ratings based on his own criteria for normality did not add up to his belief that he is 0 percent normal.[170]

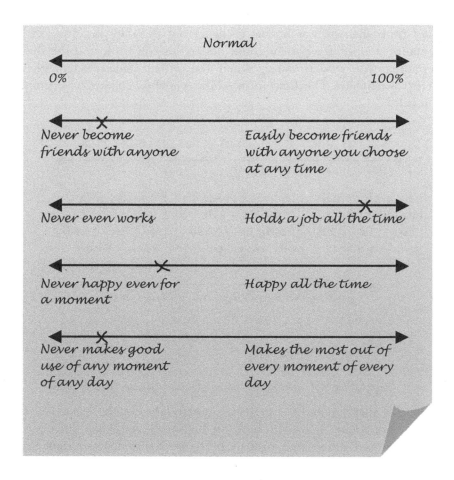

Fig. 9.6. A patient's global continuum of normality and criteria continua. Taken from Christine A. Padesky, "Schema change processes in cognitive therapy," *Clinical Psychology and Psychotherapy* vol. 1 (5), fig. 1. Reprinted by permission of the publisher. All rights reserved.

The therapist and patient usually apply continua techniques on a regular basis over the course of six months. As the patient's accumulated experiences supply additional data related to his new beliefs, his old schema is weakened and his new schema is reinforced, leading to an enduring change in perspective.[171] Other continua techniques include two-dimensional charting of continua for schemata that correlate interrelated variables (e.g., "Getting close to people is painful") and two-dimensional continuum graphs that contrast schema predictions with reality (e.g., "Perfection is a measure of worth").[172]

In chapter four, we noted that the church fathers' understanding of virtue as a mean between two extremes also counters dichotomous thinking. Continua techniques can also reinforce this patristic position. However, a therapist who is uninformed about certain Christian values and virtues could conceivably use these techniques with a Christian patient to bring about psychological improvement, but unwittingly harm the believer's spiritual life. For example, if the Christian, who believes like Saint Paul that he is the chief of sinners,[173] were instructed to make a sin continuum in order to prove that he is not really so sinful, the exercise could dry up his tears of compunction and cool his zeal for repentance. In like manner, a therapist, who is oblivious to the spiritual value, grace, and joy of wholesome self-sacrifice for the love of God, could suggest that someone who sacrifices himself for the sake of others construct an assertiveness continuum that could promote more psychologically adaptive, but less Christian responses to life.

Furthermore, when a created being approaches the uncreated, no language from the created realm is adequate. One can simply apophatically point toward the divine with absolute negations such as infinite and unoriginate, while referring to the human reality via cataphatic appellations such as "I am but dust and ashes."[174] In other words, in the spiritual life, there is room for certain kinds of dichotomous schemata, as basic as the sacred and the profane,[175] that should not be modified or restructured for the sake of illusory psychological gain.

Another important set of techniques for schema modification involves the use of diaries, journals, and positive data logs. These techniques help the patient to organize and to store new observations that demonstrate the inadequacy of older maladaptive schemata as well as the value of new ones.[176] Patients usually find these techniques to be discouragingly difficult, because the facts that they are being asked to observe and write down are automatically filtered out, distorted, or disqualified by their present maladaptive schemata. In other words, the therapist is requesting that patients record data whose very existence they strongly doubt.[177]

For example, a therapist may suggest to a depressed patient with the belief, "I don't accomplish anything," that he keep a notebook divided into sections for work experiences, social interactions, parenting, and being alone. Under each heading, the patient is instructed to list anything that he did or tried to do, for which he deserves some credit,[178] and to review this log daily. Protestant therapists sometimes try to increase the impact of such logs by having the patient imagine how Christ would react to even the smallest of his accomplishments.[179]

In general, the type of diary selected can be modified according to the psychological disorder or maladaptive schema that causes problems. For example, a woman who expected to encounter awful and unmanageable catastrophes every day was told to keep a diary in which every morning she would list in one column predicted catastrophes and every evening she would write down what actually occurred. At the end of a month, she found that one out of five "catastrophes" actually took place.[180] In marital counseling, couples are advised to make lists of enjoyable time spent together each day as well as any pleasing actions or words by the other spouse (that are rated in terms of importance), and then to review these lists at the close of the day and the end of the week. As they discover pleasant times spent with each other, they begin to actually look at each other as persons, rather than as the vilified images that they have in their minds.[181]

In patristic tradition, Blessed Augustine's *Confessions* stands out as a singular example of autobiographical journaling. In his equally unique *Reconsiderations*, he notes that the process of writing down observations about his life and thought increased his fervor to approach God at the level of thinking and feeling.[182] This observation is psychologically quite significant, since when both cognitive and affective systems are activated, deeper schemata become more accessible for modification. In other words, Blessed Augustine implicitly affirms the value of journaling for schematic change. In wider patristic tradition, many fathers collected, recorded, and organized sayings of elders and saints for their own personal edification and the spiritual enrichment of others.[183]

The above examples indicate that the proper use of the psychological technique of keeping diaries or positive data logs is not inconsistent with Orthodox Christianity. Significantly, Russian luminaries such as Saint John of Kronstadt and Father Alexander Elchaninov have availed themselves of diaries and memoirs for the sake of their own spiritual profit and the spiritual benefit of the faithful.[184] Properly handled, journaling, together with the more widespread patristic practice of making collections of inspiring advice, can contribute to the cultivation of good thoughts that we examined earlier in this chapter.

Another important tool for schema change is the core belief worksheet developed by Dr. Judith Beck. This worksheet calls for the patient to deploy rating and rational responding skills already honed by the dysfunctional thought record, but now employed weekly for the sake of schema change. At the top of the worksheet, the patient jots down his old core belief (e.g., "I am inadequate"), estimates how much he believes it at present (0%–100%), and rates how much he believed it during the week whenever he accepted it as probably true (0%–100%) as well as whenever he dismissed it as likely false (0%–100%). The patient then writes out an adaptive replacement for his core belief (e.g., "I am adequate, but human") and reckons how much he currently believes it. Below this line there are two columns for the patient to record experiences during the week that confirm or disconfirm his core belief. In the first column, he lists data that contradict the old core belief and support the new one. In the second column, he records evidence that seems to support the old core belief, and then makes a rational response to it that interprets the evidence consistently with the new schema.[185]

Old core belief: *Others can't be trusted.*

How much do you believe the old core belief right now (0–100): *70%*

What is the most you've believed it this week (0–100): *100%*

What is the least you've believed it this week (0–100): *40%*

New belief: *Many people are trustworthy, but even they make mistakes.*

How much do you believe the new belief right now? (0–100): *50%*

Evidence that contradicts old core belief and supports new belief	Evidence that supports old core belief with reframe
1. My friend gave me back the pen I loaned him. 2. My co-worker covered for me when I was late for work. Etc. ...	1. Another friend did not return my call, BUT he may have just been too busy at the time. 2. A group of colleagues were whispering when I came into the room, BUT they may not have been talking about me. Etc. ...

Fig. 9.7. Core belief worksheet. Format taken from Judith S. Beck, *Cognitive Therapy* (New York: Guilford Publications Inc., 1993), fig. 11.3. Reprinted by permission of the publisher. All rights reserved.

In figure 9.7, we provide an example of how the core belief worksheet could be used with someone suffering from paranoid personality disorder. Core belief worksheets, like schema journals, are tangible ways to help the patient recall and see new patterns. With time, the alternative schema will be strengthened to the point that the patient spontaneously uses it to interpret unfamiliar situations and thus acquires a broader range of choices for his interactions with others, along with more moderate emotional responses.[186]

In chapter four, we discussed the crucial role that childhood experiences play in the development of global maladaptive schemata about self and others. Although a person's life history is an unalterable fact, his interpretation of that history is subject to change. Not only does a person's schemata skew and affect what that person remembers, but efforts at recalling experiences incompatible with a belief can weaken it and strengthen a new belief. One formidable technique based on these principles and developed by Jeffrey Young is the historical test of schema, in which the patient examines evidence supporting both the old and new schema over his entire life history.

First, the patient breaks down his life into segments that make sense to him, such as early childhood, elementary school, middle school, high school, college, employment, and so forth. Second, the patient begins to think about the first segment of his life: he brings to mind any negative memories that support his maladaptive schema (e.g., "I am unlovable") and writes them down. Third, the patient struggles to recall positive memories that can bolster up his new more adaptive schema ("I am loved") and records that evidence in the next column. Fourth, he tries to reinterpret and rationally respond to each memory that appeared to support his old schema, so that it will now be in harmony with his new one. Fifth, he writes down a summary for that segment of his life. In the course of therapy, the patient repeats this process for each period until he reaches the present, and then he makes a summary covering his entire life history.[187]

Although patristic tradition may not offer such a systematic approach to the reinterpretation of one's past, Blessed Augustine did have a quite sophisticated theory of memory, which even today retains its psychological value. The erudite bishop of Hippo was well aware of the benefit of entering "the fields and roomy chambers of memory where are the treasures of countless images,"[188] for by so doing new memories can also be formed.[189] He also perceptively noted that the individual's understanding of his past is the basis for facing the future.[190] In reviewing one's personal history, it is important to recognize that memories are not the events themselves, but "footprints of the senses made in the mind by the images of things."[191] Some memories may be exaggerated by the mind;[192] other remembrances may be out of focus, because at the time the will was concerned with other objectives.[193]

If a person possesses a good mind [bona mens], which is more important than an admirable memory,[194] reviewing the past can help the believer see how God's guidance prevented his downfall[195] and that the Lord has not requited him with punishment that was his due, but has bestowed on him forgiveness and eternal life.[196] From an Orthodox Christian perspective, associating God's mercy, compassion, and love with past memories can both heal the soul's wounds and encourage the believer "to fight the good fight."[197] For example, when Saint Anthony the Great realized by divine revelation that Christ was invisibly present with him during his trials, he could look at them differently and thereby acquire increased vigor to struggle.[198]

A contemporary Greek Orthodox practice that can be seen as a spiritual historical review is the life confession [genikē exomologēsē]. Elder Porphyrios used to advise believers with psychological traumas or unresolved issues in the past to confess their entire life to a priest. While the person recounts pleasant and unpleasant experiences, the priest simultaneously prays for the person's release from painful memories and asks questions from time to time as God leads him. The clairvoyant elder noted that when he would use this approach, he could see the grace of God enter and heal the wounded soul, releasing the person from the chains of the past and enabling him to begin life anew.[199]

A final set of strategies for schema change in cognitive therapy has its origins in the emotionally charged techniques of Moreno's psychodrama. In cognitive therapy, however, the aim of re-enacting schema-related incidents is not abreactive catharsis, but schema re-evaluation in its original context.[200] During the re-enactment of a past event, other techniques such as Socratic questioning, as well as identifying automatic thoughts, emotions, and beliefs, can also be used to modify schemata that role-play brings closer to the surface.[201]

Sometimes early memories can be restructured by re-enacting traumatic experiences. First, the patient recalls the experience and relates it to the therapist. Second, they role-play the situation with the therapist taking on the role of the patient and the patient playing the part of the other significant figure. Finally, they switch parts and discuss what they have learned from the exercise. For example, Christine Padesky and Judith Beck relate the case of Jane, a woman with avoidant personality disorder who held the belief "I'm unlikable" from childhood. She recalled her mother yelling at her, "You're so bad! I wish you were never born." Using role-play, the therapist took the role of Jane's mother and Jane played herself at the age of six. After the memory enactment, Jane reported her thoughts and emotions to the therapist. Next, they switched roles and Jane played her mother. At this point, Jane began to understand that her mother was very unhappy about her father's desertion and that her mother's comments were a reaction to her own unhappiness rather than an unalterable pronouncement that Jane was "unlikeable." This was an important first step to altering this maladaptive schema.[202]

Less emotionally intense role-plays can also contribute to schema modification. For example, rational-emotional role-play can help a patient who intellectually realizes that his maladaptive belief is irrational, but emotionally feels as though it were true. With this technique, the therapist argues against the belief, playing the rational side of the patient, while the patient argues for it, playing his own emotional side. When the arguments have been exhausted, they then switch roles and repeat the exercise.[203] Protestant therapists sometimes do this kind of role-play between the sin-loving and God-loving aspects of the believer.[204]

The Art of Gardening and Schema Modification

To make a garden out of a barren wasteland requires careful planning, hard work, and some insight into the quality of the soil and the temper of the seasons. The same could be said about engendering lasting change in the way in which a person views himself and others. Both church fathers and cognitive therapists utilize the same universal tools of work, thought, and insight to cultivate new growth in the human soul. With the exception of the common method of considering the future as past, the content and form of the particular tools employed vary dramatically, even where surface similarities crop up.

For example, both bibliotherapy and the study of spiritual books as methods require active attentive reading and provide continuity, reinforcement, and practical assistance for dealing with life's problems. However, the content of spiritual books also sanctifies the mind, protects the soul from sin, and increases faith. Cognitive rehearsal is found in both contexts, but for the ancient fathers the aim is virtue, whereas for contemporary therapists the objective is task completion for the sake of therapeutic change. Although an eager taxonomist might place data logs in the same genre as collecting edifying sayings and the historical test of schema with the autobiographical exploration of God's presence in one's life, the content of the data collected, and the importance of introspection differ markedly. Cognitive therapists are concerned with the accuracy of introspective data for psychological improvement; the holy fathers are prepared to die for the Truth of God that is their salvation.

Cognitive techniques for schema modification provide effective tools for systematically evaluating beliefs through the empirical collection of data about those beliefs and the rational analysis of their development in the past and functional utility in the present. In effect, these tools uncover information that can only be processed by new cognitive structures. Fresh information thus gives rise to insight that exposes undesirable undergrowth and in the process begins to clear the field of the mind for planting more functional beliefs. Although relapse prevention and the personal wishes of the patient may seem to be reasonable guides for selecting new schemata, such criteria can hardly guarantee human wholeness and fulfillment. For such an aim, a higher order of values is necessary.

In the Church, "schema-modification" is *always* a value-driven process aimed at nothing less than the very likeness of God revealed in Christ Jesus. Patristic measures provide the believer with far more than additional tools. The fathers offer both true life that can resurrect the soul dead in sin and the ultimate meaning of existence that can infuse the believer's life with hope, purpose, and significance. Insight is not merely an idiosyncratic discovery about self, but a deeper understanding of human nature and the human person as revealed by the light of divine revelation and the experience of God. For the church fathers, even the praiseworthy goal of self-knowledge is secondary to "the knowledge of the truth."

Obviously, it is a noble endeavor to free someone from the chains of depression, anxiety, and other psychological disorders. The long-term effects of cognitive therapy highly recommend techniques for schema modification such as cognitive continua, diaries, core belief work sheets, historical tests of schema, and psychodrama. Without rejecting such useful tools in a psycho-therapeutic context, Christians should be concerned about what kinds of seeds are being planted and what kind of garden is being fashioned in the human soul. If Christian therapists would adopt patristic teachings on the virtuous life, the eight bad thoughts, and the Sermon on Mount, these tools could be employed in a way that is psychologically healthy, existentially fulfilling, and spiritually salvific.

In secular cognitive therapy, human rationality, observation, and intro-spection design a personalized garden defined as much by the absence of weeds as the presence of new shrubs. It may be an objectively better garden than the present conditions, but without some higher standard for the seeds that are planted, it can hardly be the very best that every human soul deserves. In patristic tradition, the garden of the heart is a patient work of faith and love in which believers do not labor alone. Rather, they unceasingly invite God "to come and abide in them" and be the sun, the rain, and tiller of the soil. Not only are the seeds planted completely trustworthy, but with faith, "there is such a thing as rocky soil changing and becoming a fertile land."[205] For the fathers, the gardening of the soul is a lifelong endeavor undertaken, not only for the believers' sake, but also for God's sake. The ancient ascetics affirm in their writings and by their lives that it is possible by the grace of the Holy Spirit for the soul to become, in the words of Saint Cyril of Alexandria, "a well-watered garden rich in flowers, abounding in fair trees, adorned by all manner of blossoms and bearing every kind of fruit."[206]

For the church fathers, every movement toward virtue, wholeness, and truth is commendable. Certainly cognitive restructuring of beliefs that aims at restoring a person to normal functioning at home and in the workplace may plant some elements of virtuous behavior, psychological wholeness, and an accurate understanding of the self, but these elements will be undoubtedly mixed with the tares already present in a fallen world. The Truth of Christ that critiques human society can also offer constructive help to those providing cognitive therapy by setting forth another prototype and an alternative goal higher than normal functioning within an abnormal society. With the practical patristic tools we have outlined in the last three chapters, the holy fathers reveal how to fashion a garden of virtue in the soul that will be a source of joy for angels and the children of Eve. Such a garden "in the likeness of paradise"[207] is the hope of every believer. It would also be a worthy aim for any patient undergoing therapy and, for that matter, for anyone who longs for the perennial health of the soul.

≪↔⊱↔⊱≫≪↔≪↔⊱

CHAPTER TEN

Final Coda: The Chorus of the Fathers and the Harmonies of Cognitive Therapy

The choir of the church fathers forever raise their voices in song to hymn the Celestial Word who leads sinners to holiness and brings the dead back to life.[1] "Neither the notes of the nightingale nor the flute of the Muses"[2] can equal the beauty of their melody whose echoes sweeten the air with the grace of the Holy Spirit.[3] In the introduction to this work, we made the following statement: "Cognitive therapists echo patristic findings in a noticeably altered key and in an ontologically thin, but theoretically elegant form." Having now heard both the captivating music of the ancient fathers and the measured harmonies of cognitive therapy, we are at last in a position to offer an Orthodox Christian critique of this significant offering from contemporary culture and to substantiate our claim that a dialogue can be beneficial for theologians and cognitive therapists alike.

In our patristic review of the worldview, theory, practice, and techniques of cognitive therapy, we have respectfully tried to let church fathers chant and cognitive therapists speak with their own voices, although from time to time we have modulated between sacred and scientific keys. Naturally, we lose something significant when we translate the poetic, metaphorical, and theological language of spiritual texts into the sparse, precise, and mathematical jargon of science. For this very reason, we have clothed each chapter in its own over-arching metaphor as testimony to our conviction that patristic thought can encompass and elevate the best of modern culture and science, but that scientific approaches are ill equipped for grasping the depths and heights of faith.

In chapter one, we considered the historic alliance between patristic counsel and the practice of medicine as well as the relationship between early Christian thought and ancient Greek philosophy. Based on historical precedent, we concluded that the best approach to the findings of cognitive therapy involves neither dismissive rejection, nor superficial merger, but discerning openness. Such an approach not only filters out and rejects incompatible elements, but also selects, incorporates, and transfigures whatever is congruent by placing it within a conception of the world and system of values that can infuse modern concepts and techniques with a higher purpose. In this study, we have discovered not only extraordinary harmonies at the level of theory and technique, but also significant dissonance with respect to worldviews and practitioners. In fact, our examination of patristic counsel and cognitive therapy begins and ends with the leitmotif of values that are inherent in overall worldviews (see chapter 2) and necessary for the modification of maladaptive beliefs that guide people's interpretations of themselves and their world (see chapter 9).

In chapter two, we explored the worldview implicit in an Orthodox Christian understanding of revelation and in the philosophies intrinsic to modern science. On the one hand, the prophets, apostles, and saints reveal that man is a theological being who is loved by God, gifted with rationality and freedom, but easily deceived, forgetful of his Maker, and susceptible to pride, irrationality, and a lack of self-control. These luminaries testify that human beings live in a world that is dependent on God, subject to change, and saturated with meaning. They can overcome their brokenness by the remembrance of God, participation in the mysteries of the Church, the adoption of an ascetic life of virtue, and obedience to the divine commandments.

On the other hand, philosophies inherent in the scientific *Weltanschauung* maintain that human beings are living organisms determined solely by the interplay between learning experiences and genetic material. They live in a fragile world understood in materialist, mechanistic, and atomistic terms. In the process of evolution and for the sake of survival, these organisms happened to develop powerful observational and rational skills that can override less adaptive instinctual reactions. Psychological disorders are descriptions of maladaptive cognitive, affective, and behavioral responses to a person's environment that can be remedied by using human metacognitive skills in order to provide more adaptive interpretations and behaviors, which in turn improve emotion as well.

An Orthodox Christian is obliged to reject certain assumptions present in a scientific worldview, such as the beliefs that God is not active in history, that Divine Providence is not present in the life of the individual, and that the human being can be understood sufficiently without reference to the Maker. In lieu of the myths of man the computer and man the evolved animal, the believer affirms that every human person is a free and responsible being who is fashioned in the divine image and called to attain to the very likeness of God by humbly, obediently, and gratefully using reason, observational skills, and all the other gifts with which human nature is endowed.

Notwithstanding such discordance between patristic and scientific cosmologies and anthropologies, the main tools of cognitive therapy and axioms of cognitive theory are derived from empiricism, rationalism, atomism, and pragmatism, which are not only philosophical movements, but also practical methods that are employed daily by the Christian and non-Christian alike. These tools and axioms can be harmonized with patristic teachings if we approach them in a spirit of discerning openness. In this way, we can place them within a larger hierarchy of values and virtues, so that spiritual fathers can have access to valuable supplemental information about human thought and behavior and so that therapists can find guidance for providing cognitive therapy that is in harmony with Christian beliefs.

In chapters three through five, we explored the cognitive theory of thought, emotion, behavior, psychopathology, and therapy. A significant passage in Epictetus's *Encheiridion* affirms that people are disturbed by their judgments about things and not by the things themselves. This passage, which was ostensibly preserved in the Church by Saint Neilus the Ascetic and repeatedly cited by Aaron Beck, began the first movement in our examination of the counterpoint between patristic and cognitive theories of human emotion and behavior.

In chapter three, we considered the three pivotal concepts of meaning assignment, automatic thoughts, and schemata. Ancient ascetics and cognitive theorists both recognize that healthy meaning assignment is of utmost importance for successful human functioning. They both note that the interpretation of a situation or action triggers an emotional response, influences behavior, affects interpersonal relationships, and contributes to the formation of characteriological traits. Patristic observations about the role of the imagination in meaning assignment, as well as remarks by psychologists about the way in which meaning assignment activates attentional and memory systems make valuable contributions to our understanding. The church fathers also point out that meaning assignment plays a crucial role in the faithful's efforts to lead a virtuous life and in their relationship with God.

With respect to automatic thoughts, ancient fathers and cognitive theorists both recognize the importance of rapid thoughts that are difficult to identify and hard to control. Cognitive psychologists explicitly state that these automatic thoughts involve evaluations about self, others, and consequences. Patristic recognition of inner speeches, which serve as motives for action, indicates a tacit awareness of the cognitive concept of evaluative self-monitoring. The fathers' understanding of thought as the product of logic and imagination offers therapists a cogent explanation for the persuasiveness and inaccuracy of automatic thoughts.

Intriguingly, the notion of dysfunctional schemata and the patristic understanding of the passions have a common tonality. Both passions and dysfunctional schemata can be viewed as pathological mental states that are habitual, inflexible, idiosyncratic, and biased. Under the influence of both passions and schemata involving danger or pleasure, thinking becomes simplistic, dualistic, and causally un-nuanced. Both passions and schemata are dependent on concrete situations in which some object or information serves as a trigger activating the schema or enflaming the passion. Once activated, both unleash a flood of related thoughts and block the flow of incompatible ones.

The two notions, however, differ on moral, theological, and spiritual grounds. For the church fathers, the brutish and childish passions are inconsistent with the divine image in man and damage his relationship with God. For cognitive therapists, primitive and juvenile schemata are simply cognitive manifestations of biological and developmental factors that as such are morally and spiritually neutral.

An awareness of the spiritual aspects of meaning assignment, automatic thoughts, and schemata enriches these psychological concepts with an ultimate sense of purpose and meaning that can increase their existential significance. Moreover, this spiritual sensitivity gives rise to alternative solutions to psychological problems by treating the human being holistically as a spiritual and biological entity. For example, we proposed regarding avarice and vainglory as misguided strategies for coping with a sense of helplessness and viewing the love of pleasure as an improper means of dealing with unlovability. In both cases, the consistent cultivation of the memory of God can both spiritually redirect the believers' passions and psychologically restructure their schemata. For example, if people recall that God is their helper, amassing wealth and attracting fame no longer offer additional security. If they recall that God loves them, sensual pleasure in no way increases their sense of being loved.

In chapter four, we examined the central cognitive concepts of psychopathology, namely, cognitive distortions, egocentricity, and childhood factors. Both church fathers and cognitive therapists recognize the existence of thoughts that are mistakes in judgment and interfere with a person's ability to cope and to remain calm. In particular, the ancient ascetics encourage the believer to become aware of permission-giving thoughts, to discern the sources of thoughts in terms of rational versus emotional reactions, to place thoughts within a continuum defined by two extremes, and to evaluate thoughts by considering short-term versus long-term consequences.

Although the fathers identified at least five of the twelve cognitive distortions on the standard list used in cognitive therapy, they would insist that a real transfiguration in a person's relationship with God and others takes place by rejecting the eight bad thoughts. We noted that accepting a bad thought entails several cognitive distortions, but that a given cognitive distortion does not correspond to any particular bad thought. The two lists refer to two distinct, yet related, hierarchal planes of human mental functioning. The list of bad thoughts corresponds to an overall existential orientation to God, neighbor, and creation, whereas the list of cognitive distortions corresponds to discrete psychological mechanisms of faulty information processing.

The corresponding notions of philautia and egocentricity occupy the same theoretical position in patristic thought and cognitive theory respectively. Although both conditions restrict freedom, narrow one's world, and contribute to insensitivity and hostility, they are by no means interchangeable terms. Egocentricity is a natural way of relating events and persons to the self that in an exaggerated form may lead to psychopathology. Philautia refers to an affectionate relationship to the self that can be characterized as fallen and inevitably leads to enslavement to the passions. Although egocentricity is not necessarily an expression of philautia, philautia is always egocentric. In simplest terms, egocentricity is about the self and an inaccurate perspective, whereas philautia concerns the self and misdirected love. Octaves apart with divergent chord progressions, patristic and cognitive views correspond to two related, but distinctly unique hierarchal planes of human functioning.

Similar findings on the relationships among cognitive distortions and bad thoughts as well as between egocentricity and philautia are quite significant. It logically means that mental illness does not necessarily stem from personal sin, but sinfulness does carry the trappings of mental illness. Nevertheless, sin can be conceptualized as a particular strain of "mental illness" that develops within the broader domain of egocentricity, that is supported by a number of clearly-defined cognitive distortions, but whose particular constellation of symptoms manifests not only ruptured communion with others, but also moral brokenness, a loss of grace, and existential alienation from God. Consequently, Christian therapists and spiritual fathers should be cautious about drawing hasty conclusions based on their preferred mode for interpreting the disturbing words and actions of others. To avoid making a misdiagnosis, both therapists and pastors would be well advised to broaden their hermeneutical framework to include both sets of parallel concepts. Moreover, someone may conceivably need help on both the level of psychological mechanisms for processing information and the spiritual level of genuine love for God and neighbor. Responsible care can be assisted by dual knowledge of both realms.

In chapter four, we also investigated the rich resonances between patristic and psychotherapeutic views on childhood factors. Both church fathers and cognitive theorists are aware that children's cognitive skills are noticeably limited and their inferences are often flawed. Both recognize that the effects of bad parenting and traumas linger on into adult life, like a sustained flat in an all-natural key. Both maintain that healing is possible if the traumatized can alter the narrative in which childhood memories are stored. When we consider patristic advice on parenting in light of schema theory, the preventive value of patristic teaching becomes apparent. When parents train their offspring to disdain wealth, to control their appetites, to forgive others, and to love their neighbor, the young form healthy schemata, making it less likely for maladaptive beliefs concerning helplessness, worthlessness, or unlovability to develop in later life. The patristic prototype for healthy parenting as well as the fathers' teachings on the eight bad thoughts can give moral guidance to the work of cognitive therapy. Knowledge of childhood hypothesis formation and cognitive distortions can also provide spiritual fathers with additional tools for guiding those who rely more on logic than on faith.

In chapter five, we considered the patristic use of reason and the cognitive emphasis on metacognition as comparable vehicles for therapeutic change. Both ancient fathers and cognitive theorists recognize higher mental processes that regulate lower impulsive reactions by an analytic approach that widens a person's field of vision and awareness. Both approaches characterize this slower rational system as a skill that can be perfected by making the thoughts the object of a person's scrutiny. Both provide the learner with principles and descriptions of mental processes that enhance metacognition, increase awareness, and clarify thought. In particular, the cognitive understanding of addiction is remarkably similar to the patristic description of the stages leading to sin.

In terms of differences, cognitive therapy has a greater emphasis than patristic tradition on determining the accuracy and logical consistency of the thoughts as well as on developing alternative explanations and interpretations. The holy fathers stress that the presence of grace alters the believers' awareness, multiplies their choices, and increases their freedom from the basic drives of pleasure and pain. Moreover, an experiential knowledge of God's providence, past and present, together with an assurance of God's care in the future, significantly changes what people consider to be a logical interpretation of their situation and available choices. The fathers also warn us that when instruction in reasoning is turned against the faith, it can turn into harmful training in self-justification.

In this chapter, we also noted a prime example of the way in which world-views subtly influence overall approaches and shape the basic character of ostensible similarities. For example, both ancient monastics and cognitive therapists propose that people distrust their judgments and avoid critical thoughts. The fathers offer this advice so that the believer may become humble and enjoy the moral, spiritual, and eschatological benefits that humility brings. Cognitive therapists offer their advice because of two pragmatic considerations: people's interpretations are frequently false, and critical thoughts are often based on cognitive distortions such as mind-reading. In this case, the resounding tone of a seeming similarity can deafen the inattentive to a significant difference in existential orientation.

In chapter six, we took a closer look at the role and function of the spiritual father and the cognitive therapist. Although both ask questions, try to discern major problems, offer advice, and assign remedial tasks, the differences in selection, training, context, tools, and aims of both figures are frankly unbridgeable. Notwithstanding, insights from cognitive therapy can still be used by the spiritual father outside of the confessional when counseling people with problems such as anxiety and depression. Patristic teachings can also provide a cognitive therapist with acceptable ways to express psychological concepts to a patient who is a pious Christian.

In this chapter, we also considered how outward resemblances can obscure divergent conceptions of the world. For example, both spiritual fathers and cognitive therapists speak calmly and gently. The spiritual father's tone of voice is softened by a state of prayer that attracts the peace of Christ, whereas the cognitive therapist intentionally uses a mellow tone in order to help the patient speak with candor. Both figures are likewise non-judgmental, but for quite different reasons. The spiritual father's non-judgmental stance stems from humility, love, and the knowledge that whatever evil action the person before him may have done, that person is by nature good and by the grace of God can become holy as well. The therapist's non-judgmental stance is based first on the utilitarian fact that a judgmental attitude makes empathy impossible and second on the philosophical position of environmental and genetic determinism: that is, given the person's developmental history and genetic limitations, it would be illogical to expect him to be otherwise or to behave in any other way.

In chapters seven through nine, we explored the techniques of cognitive therapy in the light of patristic tradition. In chapter seven, we noted that patristic and cognitive approaches to problem-solving, goal-setting, and experimentation are externally quite consistent and compatible. Both recognize the importance of gathering additional information about a given problem and determining the best possible solution. Both view goal-oriented behavior and the use of subgoals as crucial elements in the therapeutic process. Both view experience or experimentation as necessary to test the validity of ideas, personal hypotheses, and convictions. Cognitive therapists characteristically link problems to goals and goals to experimentation. The church fathers understandably affirm that prayer should accompany problem-solving efforts and that the intuitions of the God-loving heart should be used to select the best solution.

Although the two approaches often dovetail nicely, underlying worldviews do affect the way a person construes problems. In the patristic context, faith in a loving God enables the believer to view problems as opportunities for growth in virtue, wisdom, and strength. In a cognitive context, empiricism and rationalism are what empower the patient to consider problems to be challenges that can be overcome with effort and planning. Of course, it is possible to regard problems both spiritually as opportunities for growth and rationally as challenges to be overcome.

Both ancient ascetics and cognitive therapists agree that healing requires both behavioral and cognitive interventions, that cognition can be altered by modifying behavior, that it is easier to change behavior than to change cognition, and that behavior should be addressed first in a course of treatment. Both bodily asceticism and behavioral techniques inevitably aim at changing self-defeating behaviors and should be applied with moderation and in keeping with a person's natural strengths and weaknesses.

Most behavioral techniques are consonant with patristic approaches. For example, the daily thought record is not inconsistent with ascetic self-observation, nor is scheduling out of keeping with a life structured by the Church's liturgical services. The verbal self-instruction technique has been used for ages by monks being tempted by the passions, and Tertullian recommended a version of the "as-if" technique used today in treating anxiety disorders.

The analogy of two hierarchal planes encountered in our examination of cognitive theory and patristic thought applies to the subject of techniques. Behavioral techniques are wider templates into which specific ascetic practices can be classified. Of course, there are significant differences that again reflect respective worldviews. Behavioral interventions in cognitive therapy explicitly seek to provide further information and sometimes provide the patient with new skills, whereas Christian asceticism is always and primarily an offering to God.

In chapter eight, we examined preliminary cognitive techniques. Both fathers and therapists encourage those who seek their aid to begin the healing process by cultivating basic skills in watchfulness and active awareness in order to become conscious of the thoughts and no longer unwittingly subject to them. In terms of techniques, both recognize the value of identifying the thoughts mentally, orally, and in writing. Both appreciate the use of number for assessing change. Both utilize lists to facilitate fluency in speaking about troubled areas. Both employ refocusing and distraction techniques for dealing with certain kinds of thoughts. Both make use of reason, persuasion, and rebuttal to provide alternatives to thoughts that are evil or maladaptive. Both suggest making cognitive preparations in advance in order to address common problematic concerns. Again, however, we must note that cognitive techniques and patristic practices do not exist on the same existential level and are not directed toward the same ultimate goal.

In chapter nine, we investigated how church fathers and cognitive therapists use the universal tools of hard work, structured thought, and penetrating insight in order to redirect the passions and restructure core schemata. Apart from broad similarities between bibliotherapy and the study of spiritual books, apart from a taxonomic likeness between the historical test of schema and the autobiographical exploration of God's presence in one's life, the two sets of approaches are dissimilar in form and substance on account of differences in focus and aim. For the holy fathers, insight is not an idiosyncratic discovery about self, but a deeper understanding of human nature and the human person as revealed by the light of divine revelation. The believer's goal is not relapse prevention or the realization of personal wishes, but the attainment of nothing less than the likeness of God.

In summary, the chorale of the ancient fathers offers a robust and informative approach to the problem of the thoughts and consistently provides wise commentary on the chief theoretical and practical aspects of cognitive therapy, viz., the cognitive theory of human mental functioning, the cognitive conceptualization of psychopathology, the metacognitive approach to recovery, the therapeutic relationship, behavioral interventions, and cognitive techniques. While both patristic and cognitive approaches have great value in their own right and their own domain, knowledge about "the other side" is always helpful, and in the case of patristic thought, salvific. In other words, knowledge of cognitive therapy can help the spiritual father communicate with those who approach human problems with the psychological mindset that is prevalent in contemporary culture. Knowledge of patristic teachings can infuse the work of the cognitive therapists with meaning, purpose, and moral direction, especially when treating Christian patients.

Some knowledge of the two different worldviews is necessary to make sense of the similarities and differences between patristic thought and cognitive therapy recounted in the preceding pages. It is often pointed out that the saints were human beings with weaknesses like the rest of us.[4] We can add that they used the native talents of the human mind like the rest of us as well. In particular, the church fathers methodologically utilized reason, experience, analysis, and practical considerations to solve problems and reach goals, long before those methods were formalized by the modern philosophies of rationalism, empiricism, atomism, and pragmatism. Consequently, on the one hand, core human methodological similarities between ancient ascetics and cognitive theorists have led to theoretically comparable observations about thoughts, dysfunction, and restoration to health. On the other hand, deeper commitments at a theological or philosophical level alter the tone of these observations and at times reveal that surface resemblances conceal underlying disparities.

In terms of techniques, there are striking similarities for discrete transient problems in thought and behavior. However, as one approaches the core of the human person and his interpretation of reality, significant differences begin to resurface. This too is to be expected. The fathers wisely rely more on faith and the grace of God than reason alone when they enter the depths of the human heart, that mysterious meeting place between God and man.

Cognitive therapists, furthermore, use rationalism, empiricism, atomism, and pragmatism with all the intellectual rigor of their modern philosophical manifestations. When the church fathers employ these tools, they do so as acting under the inspiration of the Holy Spirit who subtly moves pure hearts who love Christ. This transforms these earth-born tools into interventions of heavenly wisdom that do far more than overcome a particular problem with thoughts, emotions, or behaviors. The fathers' words re-align the soul to God even as a musician adjusts the strings of a harp in order to produce a soothing melody. The attentive reader will have heard this realignment in every chapter that consistently stressed the universal importance of the truth of revelation, man's relationship with God, the life of virtue, and the experience of grace.

Perennial patristic teachings on the spiritual aspect of human life will continue to offer a viable alternative and necessary supplementation to cognitive therapy as the latter continues to change with the passage of time. Today in this "the golden age of cognitive therapy,"[5] the restless human spirit is driving therapists in divergent directions. On the one hand, Aaron Beck's legacy, his daughter Judith Beck, and their many colleagues continue to diversify therapeutic applications and to expand theory.[6] On the other hand, there is "a psychoanalytic drift in the practice of cognitive therapy,"[7] which means that cognitive therapists are increasingly interested in the growth and transformation of their patients. From a theological perspective, this latter interest expresses the spiritual thirst for perfection stemming from the creation of humanity in the image of God. Spiritual thirst, however, can hardly be quenched by the avowedly non-spiritual waters of modern science, a fact that many therapists fully recognize.

For example, constructive psychotherapy, an offshoot of cognitive therapy, seeks transformation by supplementing behavioral interventions with beginner's yoga, cognitive techniques with *vipassana* meditation (mindfulness meditation), and cognitive theory with concepts from Buddhism and Taoism.[8] Constructive therapy may be a helpful way for treating Buddhist and Hindu patients. For an Orthodox Christian, however, participation in such syncretic therapy is fraught with spiritual danger, since many of the practices it employs entail, often in a subtle or covert manner, underlying beliefs that are incompatible with traditional Christianity.

In addition to increased interest in psychological growth, cognitive therapists are also becoming more aware of the importance of respect for the religious beliefs of their patients. In the United States, cultural competence is an ethical requirement for responsible psychotherapy and entails sensitivity to the patient's religious view of the world.[9] Christine Padesky, one of Beck's students who currently specializes in training cognitive therapists, mentions that for the treatment of a wary Christian patient, it was helpful for the therapist to consider examples from the New Testament, to endorse prayer as a means for coping with anxiety, and to encourage consultation with religious leaders.[10] Such respect for a person's religious beliefs is certainly commendable. Other therapists from a variety of religious traditions have also developed forms of cognitive therapy modified for Christian, Muslim, and Taoist populations. Empirically, these spiritually modified cognitive therapies have been at least as successful as standard treatments.[11]

Our study demonstrates that cognitive therapy can be richly supplemented by patristic wisdom and used in a manner consistent with Orthodox Christianity. It also testifies to the potential for cognitive therapy as it stands to precipitate subtle, but highly significant, changes in the mindsets of Christian therapists and patients alike. Cognitive therapists maintain that it is "very difficult to do any harm with cognitive therapy," because the data are the patient's thoughts and because feedback is frequently requested.[12] This is certainly the case if one's mindset matches the wider culture of modernity or post-modernity. Conscientious Christians, however, must struggle to maintain a Christian identity within a secular society that espouses an ideology, epistemology, set of prescriptions, ethical assumptions, and vision of reality in conflict with Christianity. It is not inconceivable for patients who once were centered on God and strived to understand events in terms of the larger divine purpose intended for their lives to become in the process of therapy "autono-mous, self-regulated, rationally oriented individuals"[13] at home in the world, but estranged from the Church.

There is, however, another possibility. The patristic edifice for helping people afflicted by their thoughts does stand on its own. One could further develop an Orthodox therapy based on the teachings of the fathers and informed by the findings of cognitive therapy. In other words, the approach of discerning openness that guided our study can be used for the development of a Christian form of therapy. More specifically, it would be a worthwhile endeavor if someone trained in both psychology and Orthodox theology were to analyze the cognitive conceptualization and treatment protocols for each disorder in terms of both methodological and metaphysical rationalism, empiricism, atomism, and pragmatism. In addition to philosophical sensitivity, a proper analysis also requires the cultivation of a good patristic ear by carefully and regularly listening to the fathers' teachings so that the analyst might quickly detect any jarring note in cognitive treatment manuals.[14] Thus, useful data gathered from methodological applications of human inquiry can then serve as scaffolding on which related patristic teachings can be attached. The end result of this process would be a patristic approach to psychological disorders similar to the earlier patristic adaptation and utilization of classical philosophy.

Long ago, during the golden age of the great Cappadocian fathers, a cer-tain erudite musician named Harmonius disseminated erroneous teachings about the soul through the lyrics of songs with enchanting rhythms and elegant melodies.[15] In response to that situation, Saint Ephraim the Syrian "adopted the music of the songs, but set them to piety, and so gave the hearers at once great delight and healing medicine."[16] A similar adaptation of the music of cognitive therapy as counterpoint to the magnificent hymn of the fathers is certainly possible. By the grace of the Holy Spirit, the notes sounded can also be a "great delight and healing medicine," arousing the depressed with the silvery tones of a heavenly trumpet, calming the anxious with the golden strains of a spiritual lyre,[17] and improving the lives of those who have ears to hear with the tidings of great joy brought by the angelic voices of those who ever keep festival in the eternal kingdom of Christ.[18] Such is the trans-figurational power of the Orthodox Christian faith and the heavenly hope she extends to all dwellers on earth.

✠ Notes ✠

Introduction

1. Tertullian *Prescription against Heretics* 7 (*PL* 2.20). Unless otherwise noted, all translations are mine own. For patristic titles in their original languages, see the corresponding author, volume, and column range in the series *Patrologia graeca*, *Patrologia latina*, or *Sources chrétiennes*, as noted in the bibliography.

2. Jn 1:14 KJV (italics mine). All New Testament citations are taken from this version.

3. In brief, purification refers to the believer's struggle to purify his heart of the passions, the thoughts, and deceitful desires; illumination refers to the Holy Spirit illumining the heart of the believer who is thereby moved to pray without ceasing; deification refers to the vision of Christ that likewise transfigures the one who sees him. These stages assume an ecclesial life of ascetic striving guided by the Christian virtues and nourished by the Holy Mysteries.

4. Beyond this, there is a degree of success in treating certain limited realms of problems, most prominently infantile autism and certain forms of phobic reaction.

5. In the clinical literature and in Dr. Beck's own works, his therapy is called *cognitive-behavioral therapy*. Beck explains that his original term was *cognitive insight therapy*, but as behavioral therapists started to adopt his treatment protocols, they would use the label *cognitive-behavioral therapy* and that term has remained, although the therapy is strictly speaking cognitive with some behavioral components used for their cognitive effects. Cf. Aaron Beck, interview by Sidney Block, May 4, 2004, Philadelphia, PA, http://www.academyofct.org/Library/InfoManage/Guide.asp?FolderID=1169.

6. Albert Ellis, PhD and Robert Harper, PhD, *A Guide to Rational Living* (Chatsworth: Melvin Powers Wilshire Book Company, 1997), 213–214; Judith S. Beck, *Cognitive Therapy: Basics and Beyond* (New York: The Guilford Press, 1995), 1. For a fine overview of cognitive-behavioral therapies, see Keith Dobson, ed., *Handbook of Cognitive-Behavioral Therapies* (New York: The Guilford Press, 2001), 11–27.

7. Beck has written 17 books and co-authored over 480 professional books and scholarly journal articles as of 2010. Dr. Salkovskis notes, "When those involved in psychological treatment refer to cognitive therapy, they almost invariably mean Beck's cognitive therapy." See Paul Salkovskis, "Cognitive Therapy and Aaron T. Beck," in P. Salkovskis, ed., *Frontiers of Cognitive Therapy* (New York: The Guilford Press, 1996), 533.

8. Stanton L. Jones and Richard E. Butman, *Modern Psychotherapies: A Comprehensive Christian Appraisal* (Downers Grove, IL: Intervarsity Press, 1991), 198. R. L. Wessler describes rational-emotive therapy as "a set of non-empirical assertions masquerading as scientific therapy." See his "Idiosyncratic Definitions and Unsupported Hypothe-

ses: Rational-Emotive Behavior Therapy as Pseudoscience," *Journal of Rational-Emotive and Cognitive-Behavior Therapy* 14 (1996), 52.

9. Ellis and Harper, *Guide to Rational Living*, 57.

10. Mark R. McMinn and Clark D. Campbell, *Integrative Therapy: Toward a Comprehensive Christian Approach* (Downers Grove, IL: Intervarsity Press, 2007), 82–83.

11. Cf. *Journal of Rational-Emotive and Cognitive-Behavior Therapy*, vol. 19, no. 1 (2001) that is dedicated to this issue.

12. Jones and Butman, *Modern Psychotherapies*, 174–175.

13. Aaron T. Beck, Fred D. Wright, Cory F. Newman, and Bruce S. Liese, *Cognitive Therapy of Substance Abuse* (New York: The Guilford Press, 1993), 27.

14. Andrew Butler, Jason Chapman, and coworkers in meta-analyses of 332 studies with 9,995 subjects indicated that cognitive therapy "is highly effective for adult uni-polar depression, generalized anxiety disorder, panic disorder with or without agoraphobia, social phobia, PTSD, childhood depressive and anxiety order....Across many disorders the effects of CT are maintained for substantial periods beyond the cessation of treatment." "The Empirical Status of Cognitive-Behavioral Therapy: A Review of Meta-analyses," *Clinical Psychology Review* 26 (2006): 28.

15. McMinn and Campbell, *Integrative Therapy*, 71, 72–78.

16. Ibid., 385. Jeffrey H. Boyd notes in his article "Self-Concept: In Defense of the Word Soul," "Today theology is considered irrelevant to the American people, but secular psychology is a required subject on every campus." Mark R. McMinn and Timothy R. Phillips, eds., *Care for the Soul: Exploring the Intersection of Psychology and Theology* (Downers Grove, IL: Intervarsity Press, 2001), 115.

17. Both the advertising industry and marketing practices revolve around the findings of psychological research. Cf. Ellen T. Charry, "Theology After Psychology," in McMinn and Phillips, eds., *Care for the Soul*, 119.

18. Nichos Matsoukas, *Dogmatikē kai symbolikē theologia: eisagōgē stē theologikē gnōsiologia* [Dogmatic and symbolic theology: introduction to theological epistemology], vol. 1 (Thessaloniki, Greece: Pournara, 1985), 62, 96.

19. Ibid., 160.

20. Fr. Vasilios Thermos, *Anthrōpos ston horizonta! Proseggizontas tē synantēsē orthodoxēs theologias kai epistēmōn psychismou* [Man on the horizon! Approaching an encounter between orthodox theology and sciences of the mind] (Athens: Gregore, 2006), 200.

21. David N. Entwistle, *Integrative Approaches to Psychology and Christianity: An Introduction to Worldview Issues, Philosophical Foundations, and Models of Integration* (Eugene, OR: Wipf & Stock Publishers, 2004), 137.

22. Jones and Butman, *Modern Psychotherapies*, 202.

23. Entwistle, *Integrative Approaches*, 90. Cf. Dorotheos of Gaza *Discourses* 6.73 (SC 92.274–276).

24. Entwistle, *Integrative Approaches*, 140.

25. Theodore the Studite *Catechetical Discourses* 22 (HPE 18.427): "Speaking about things on high leads us each time to application."

26. Brad A. Alford and Aaron T. Beck, *The Integrative Power of Cognitive Therapy* (New York: The Guilford Press, 1997), 15. In like manner, Fr. Anthony M. Coniaris re-

marks, "Everything we do begins in the nous or mind with the thoughts." *Confronting and Controlling Thoughts According to the Fathers of the Philokalia* (Minneapolis, MN: Light & Life Publishing Company, 2004), 1.

27.   Alford and Beck, *Integrative Power*, 16. Elder Païsios the Hagiorite writes that "there is no greater sickness in the world than the thought." *Epistoles* [Letters] (Souroti-Thessaloniki, Greece: Hieron Hēsychastērion Evangelistēs Iōannēs ho Theologos, 1994), 103. See Elder Païsios the Hagiorite, *Logoi, pneymatikos agōnas* [Discourses: spiritual struggle], vol. 3 (Souroti-Thessaloniki, Greece: Hieron Hēsychastērion Evangelistēs Iōannēs ho Theologos, 2001), 22.

28.   Cf. Prayer of the hours in *Ōrologion to mega* [The great book of hours] (Athens: Phōs-Xeen, 1992), 20.

29.   Maximus the Confessor *Centuries on Love* 1.92 (PG 90.981).

30.   Entwistle, *Integrative Approaches*, 91.

31.   Fr. Adamantios Augoustidis notes how St. John of the Ladder uses a cognitive imagining technique, the remembrance of the Divine Passion to heal bitterness toward others, while Fr. Vasilios Thermos notes that "the technique of good thoughts essentially consists of a cognitive approach." See Augoustidis, *Hē anthrōpinē epithetikotēta* [Human aggression] (New Smyrna, Greece: Akritas, 1999), 233-234; Thermos, *Anthrōpos ston horizonta!*, 193.

32.   Fr. George Morelli, "Christian Asceticism and Cognitive Psychology," in Stephen Muse, ed., *Raising Lazarus: Integral Healing in Orthodox Christianity* (Brookline, MA: Holy Cross Press, 2004), 120.

33.   Fr. George Morelli, "Internet Continuing Education Course in Christian Spirituality and Therapy" (n.d.): 2.4, http://www.ocampr.org/CCC_course.asp.

34.   1 Cor 13:5.

35.   Entwistle, *Integrative Approaches*, 162; cf. ibid., 5-6n2.

36.   Ibid., 161.

37.   See J. N. Spencer, John F. Trader, et al., "Hydrogen bond equilibria of phenol-pyridine in cyclohexane, carbon tetrachloride, and benzene solvents," *J. Phys. Chem.*, 91, no. 6 (1987): 1673-1674; J. N. Spencer, John F. Trader, et al., "Linear solvation energy relationships for the hydrogen-bonded complexes of m-cresol," *J. Phys. Chem.*, 91, no. 11 (1987): 2959-2962.

38.   Ex 3:22; 12:25; 32:4; 40:5.

39.   Mt 24:15.

Chapter One

1.   Augustine *On Christian Doctrine* 2.40.60 (PL 34.65). Origen makes a similar analogy in his *Letter to Gregory* (PG 11.87-92).

2.   For a cogent substantiation of the proposition that therapy is not a value-free endeavor, see Allen Bergin, "Values and Religious Issues in Therapy and Mental Health," *American Psychologist*, 46 (1991): 394-403; Alan Tjelveit, "The Ethics of Value Conversion in Therapy: Appropriate and Inappropriate Therapist Influence on Client Values," *Clinical Psychology Review*, 6 (1986): 515-537.

3. Basil of Caesarea *Longer Rule* 55 (PG 31.1048b-d).

4. John Demakis, "Historical Precedents for Synergia and Combining Medicine, Diaconia, and Sacrament in Byzantine Times," in Muse, ed., *Raising Lazarus*, 16.

5. Jean-Claude Larchet, *Mental Disorders and Spiritual Healing*, trans. G. John Champoux and Rama P. Coomaraswamy (Hillsdale, NY: Sophia Perennis, 2005), 40.

6. See Demakis, "Historical Precedents for Synergia," in Muse, ed., *Raising Lazarus*, 23.

7. See Larchet, *Mental Disorders*, 36. Cf. *Who Must be Purified, Clavdii Galeni Opera Omnia*, vol. 11, (Heildesheim, Germany: Georg Olms Verlagsbuchhandlung, 1965), 344.

8. John Chrysostom *Exhortation to Stageirus* 1.1 (PG 47.449). The saint further adds, "*Ouk ho daimōn estin ho tēn athymian kinōn, alla ekeinē hē poiousa ton daimona ischyron kai tous logismous hypoballoua tous ponērous.*"

9. See Larchet, *Mental Disorders*, 8.

10. For example, in *The Constitutions of the Apostles* 2.41 (PG 1.697b), pastors are advised to be compassionate physicians. John Climacus counsels, "Acquire, O wondrous man, plasters, potions, razors, eye salves, sponges, instruments for blood-letting and cauterizations, ointments, sleeping draughts, a knife, bandages, and freedom from nausea. If we have none of these how can we prove our medical knowledge?" *To the Shepherd* 11 (PG 88.1168-1169). Translated by Holy Transfiguration as *The Ladder of Divine Ascent* (Holy Transfiguration Monastery: Boston, 1991), 232. Similarly, Symeon the New Theologian writes, "As we have heard doctors practice...dismembering corpses in order to study them...so the spiritual father must work." *Ethical Discourses* 6.12 (SC 129.138-140).

11. According to the second canon of the Council in the Troullo, the canons are "for healing [*therapeia*] of souls and medical treatment [*iatreia*] of passions." See Theodore Balsamon *Council of Trullo* 2 (PG 137.520d-521a). Cf. Agapios the Monk, ed., *Hieron pēdalion* [Sacred rudder] (Athens: Blastou Barbareggou, 1886), 183; G. Ralli and M. Potli, eds., *Syntagma tōn theiōn kai hierōn canonōn* [Constitution of the divine and sacred canons], vol. 2 (Athens: G. Chartophylakos, 1852), 308.

12. E.g., Archimandrite Hierotheos [Vlachos], *Orthodoxē psychotherapeia kai paterikē therapeutikē agōgē* [Orthodox psychotherapy and patristic therapeutic practice] (Odessa, Greece: Hiera Monē Timiou Staurou, 1986), 21, 26.

13. Fr. John Romanides, *Romaioi ē romēoi pateres tēs ekklēsias* [Romans or romeoi fathers of the church], vol. 1 (Thessaloniki, Greece: Pournara, 1984), 22-23.

14. See the dispute between St. Gregory Palamas and Barlaam in which St. Gregory refers to Barlaam as "the philosopher." *On behalf of the Hesychasts* 2.2.22-23. *Syngramata*, vol. 1, ed. P. Christou (Thessaloniki, Greece: P. Christou, 1962), 529-531.

15. A contemporary example of this friendship is afforded by the saintly Elder Porphyrios who relates, "I bought medical books, anatomy books, and physiology books in order to study and keep abreast. Once, I even attended lectures at the medical school for better instruction." Elder Porphyrios, *Bios kai logoi* [Life and discourses] (Chania, Greece: Hiera Monē Zōodochou Pēgēs, 2003), 137.

16. See Joseph Miller, "Reflections on Science and Belief," *Science and Orthodox Christianity: Two Orthodox Psychologists Offer Their Views, Monographic Supplement Series*, vol. 34, (Etna, CA: Center for Traditionalist Orthodox Studies, 1998), 7-8.

17. Michael Polanyi, *The Tacit Dimension* (Glouchester, MA: Peter Smith, 1983), 71.

18. Fr. Michael Pomazansky, "Talks on the Six Days by Basil the Great," *Pravoslavnyj put'* [The orthodox path] (1958): 39, 41. Translation taken from Monk Damascene Christensen, *Not of This World: The Life and Teachings of Fr. Seraphim Rose* (Forestville, CA: Fr. Seraphim Rose Foundation, 1993), 521.

19. See H. Richard Niebuhr, *Christ and Culture* (New York: Harper & Row, 1951), 40-43.

20. See Entwistle, *Integrative Approaches*, 164.

21. See James R. Beck, "The Integration of Psychology and Theology: An Enterprise out of Balance," *Journal of Psychology and Christianity* 22, no. 1 (2003): 22.

22. See *Epistle of Barnabas* 2 (SC 172.78-80); *Shepherd of Hermes* 3.1 (PG 2.953a).

23. See Niebuhr, *Christ and Culture*, 45, 49, 65, 66.

24. See Fr. Justin Popovich, *Philosophie de la vérité: dogmatique de l'église orthodoxe* [Philosophy of the truth: dogmatic theology of the orthodox church], vol. 4, trans. Jean Louis Palierne (Paris: L'Age d'Homme, 1997), 127-130.

25. Tertullian *Prescription against Heretics* 7 (PL 2.20-21).

26. David Powlison, "Questions at the Crossroads," in McMinn and Phillips, eds., *Care for the Soul*, 41.

27. Robert Roberts, "Outline of Pauline Therapy," in McMinn and Phillips, eds., *Care for the Soul*, 134-135.

28. See Niebuhr, *Christ and Culture*, 72. For example, Tertullian writes, "We go from it, not like troops of mischief-doers, nor bands of vagabonds, nor to break out into licentious acts, but to watch over our modesty and chastity as if we had been at a school of virtue rather than at a banquet." *Apology against the Nations* 39 (PL 1.477ab).

29. Acts 17:28.

30. See Thermos, *Anthrōpos ston horizonta!*, 244.

31. See Entwistle, *Integrative Approaches*, 167.

32. James R. Beck, "Integration of Psychology and Theology," 22-23. See Martin Bobgan and Deidre Bobgan, *Psychoheresy: The Psychological Seduction of Christianity* (Santa Barbara, CA: East Gate Publishers, 1987).

33. John Chrysostom *Homily on Humility* (PG 51.312).

34. Niebuhr, *Christ and Culture*, 81.

35. Tertullian refers to Valentinus as "the apostate, and heretic, and Platonist." *On the Flesh of Christ* 20 (PL 2.786).

36. Niebuhr, *Christ and Culture*, 86-87.

37. See Fr. Justin Popovich, *Philosophie de la vérité: dogmatique de l'église orthodoxe* [Philosophy of the truth: dogmatic theology of the orthodox church] vol. 1, trans. Jean Louis Palierne (Paris: L'Age d'Homme, 1992), 212; idem., *Philosophie de la vérité: dogmatique de l'église orthodoxe*, vol. 2, trans. Jean Louis Palierne (Paris: L'Age d'Homme, 1993), 214, 216-217.

38. Hippolytus, *Refutatio omnium haeresium*, Patristische texte und studien, vol. 25, ed. Miroslav Marcovich (Berlin: Walter de Gruyter, 1986), 237.

39. Matsoukas, *Dogmatikē kai symbolikē theologia*, vol. 1, 141.

40. Irenaeus of Lyons *Against Heresies* 5.26 (PG 7.1194).

41. See Popovich, *Philosophie de la vérité*, vol. 1, 211.

42. Niebuhr, *Christ and Culture*, 109.

43. McMinn and Campbell, *Integrative Therapy*, 388.

44. Gal 1:8.

45. Niebuhr, *Christ and Culture*, 103–107. Whereas Orthodox theologians would be hard pressed to characterize the God-man as a great psychologist, some are tempted to label the fathers as great psychologists, resulting in a distorted image of who the fathers were and giving psychology a perhaps unwarranted patristic authority.

46. See Gary Collins, *Christian Counseling* (Dallas, TX: Word Publishing, 1988), 127.

47. See Entwistle, *Integrative Approaches*, 236; McMinn and Campbell, *Integrative Therapy*, 386.

48. The writer of St. Maximus's life notes how the saint studied the science and knowledge of his day, but "not haphazardly or without discernment, but having set aside the sophistic part and whatever was related to deception and absurdity, he accepted whatever referred to reason, dogma, logical methods, and proofs." *Life of Maximus* (PG 90.69–72).

49. Entwistle, *Integrative Approaches*, 273.

50. Niebuhr, *Christ and Culture*, 143–144.

51. Clement of Alexandria *Who is the Rich Man that Shall be Saved* 37 (PG 9.641).

52. Basil of Caesarea *Address to Young Men* (PG 31.568).

53. See Augoustidis, *Hē anthrōpinē epithetikotēta*, 58.

54. Maximus the Confessor *Selections from Diverse Books* (PG 91.721–1017).

55. See Matsoukas, *Dogmatikē kai symbolikē theologia*, vol. 1, 200.

56. See Nikos Matsoukas, *Dogmatikē kai symbolikē theologia: ekthesē tēs orthodoxēs pistēs se antiparathesē me tē dutikē christianosunē* [Dogmatic and symbolic theology: presentation of the orthodox faith in contrajuxtaposition with western Christianity], vol. 2 (Thessaloniki, Greece: Pournara, 1985), 49–50.

57. Ibid., 366, 381.

58. 1 Cor 2:16.

59. See Basil of Caesarea *Address to Young Men* (PG 4.31). Cf. Heb 5:14.

60. Deborah Van Deusen Hunsinger, "An Interdisciplinary Map for Christian Counselors, Theology, and Psychology in Pastoral Counseling," in McMinn and Phillips, eds., *Care for the Soul*, 225, 230.

61. *Pace* Entwistle, *Integrative Approaches*, 261.

62. See Polanyi, *Tacit Dimension*, 35–36.

63. Matsoukas, *Dogmatikē kai symbolikē theologia*, vol. 1, 140.

64. See Panagiotis Nellas, *Zōon theoumenon: prooptikes gia mia orthodoxē katanoēsē tou anthrōpou* [Deified life: perspectives on an orthodox understanding of man] (Athens: Armos, 1979), 113; Matsoukas, *Dogmatikē kai symbolikē theologia*, vol. 1, 236–237.

65. See Matsoukas, *Dogmatikē kai symbolikē theologia*, vol. 1, 144.

66. See Entwistle, *Integrative Approaches*, 174–176, 253, 257.

67. Stephen Moroney, "Thinking of Ourselves More Highly than We Ought: A Psychological and Theological Analysis," in McMinn and Phillips, eds., *Care for the Soul*, 324–325.

68. See Entwistle, *Integrative Approaches*, 172.

69. Ibid., 214.

70. Lk 6:44.

71. See Thermos, *Anthrōpos ston horizonta!*, 230; Paul Tillich, *The Courage to Be* (New Haven: Yale University Press, 1952), 41.

72. For example, Dr. Judith S. Beck in a clinical vignette notes that humans struggle with existential questions, but that mental issues such as depression need to be tackled first for a person to be in a position to answer them. Her approach is pragmatic and reasonable, but it is also noteworthy that no answer is given, perhaps because the sources of modern science offer none. See her *Cognitive Therapy for Challenging Problems: What to do When the Basics Don't Work* (New York: The Guilford Press, 2005), 148-149.

73. Elder Païsios the Hagiorite, *Logoi: me pono kai agapē gia ton synchron anthrōpo* [Discourses: with compassion and love for contemporary man], vol. 1 (Souroti-Thessaloniki, Greece: Hieron Hēsychastērion Evangelistēs Iōannēs ho Theologos, 1998), 78 and *Logoi: pneumatikē aphypnisē* [Discourses: spiritual awakening], vol. 2. (Souroti-Thessaloniki, Greece: Hieron Hēsychastērion Evangelistēs Iōannēs ho Theologos, 1999), 346.

74. See Paul C. Vitz, "Beyond Psychology" (lecture, New Westminster, British Columbia, September 29, 1995, http://catholiceducation.org/articles/civilization/cc0004.html).

75. See Augoustidis, *Hē anthrōpinē epithetikotēta*, 143.

76. See Moroney, "Thinking of Ourselves More Highly than We Ought," in McMinn and Phillips, eds., *Care for the Soul*, 323; Entwistle, *Integrative Approaches*, 118.

77. Albert Bandura, *Social Learning Theory* (Upper Saddle River, NJ: Prentice Hall, 1977), 213.

78. See Miller, "Reflections on Science and Belief," 13.

79. See Thermos, *Anthrōpos ston horizonta!*, 60.

80. See Morelli, "Christian Ascetics and Cognitive Psychology," 122, 124.

81. Elder Païsios the Hagiorite, *Logoi*, vol. 1, 212.

82. See Nicholas Wolterstorff, *Reason within the Bounds of Religion* (Grand Rapids, MI: William B. Eerdmans Publishing Company, 1984), 68, 76, 108.

83. Glory at vespers for the feast of the holy fathers of the Seventh Ecumenical Council in the plagal of the second tone. (*MEN* 10.64).

84. Mk 9:23.

Chapter Two

1. See Gregory Palamas *On behalf of the Hesychasts* 1.20-21, 383-385.

2. Nikos Matsoukas, *Dogmatikē kai symbolikē theologia: anakephalaiōsē kai agathotopia, ekthesē tou oikoumenikou charaktēra tēs christianikēs didaskalias* [Dogmatic and symbolic theology: recapitulation and utopia, an essay on the ecumenical character of Christian teaching], vol. 3 (Thessaloniki, Greece: Pournara, 2005), 12.

3. See Entwistle, *Integrative Approaches*, 76; Mary Stewart Van Leeuwen, *The Person in Psychology: A Contemporary Christian Appraisal* (Grand Rapids, MI: William B. Eerdmans Publishing Company, 1985), 46.

4. Ps 116:10 (MT); 115:1 (LXX); 2 Cor 4:13.

5. See Cyril of Alexandria *Commentary on John* 4.4 (PG 73.628–629) and Augustine *Tractates on John* 40.9 (PL 35.1689).

6. Meaning "on the authority of no one." This was the motto of the Royal Society of London for the promotion of natural knowledge, founded in 1660.

7. Of course, no scientist can go back and check the results of all previous experimentation. Every scientist must necessarily rely by good faith on the authority of other scientists. See Polanyi, *Tacit Dimension*, 63–64.

8. See John Chrysostom *On the Saying by Whose Authority Doest Thou These Things* (PG 56.416).

9. See Fr. Justin Popovich, *Philosophie de la vérité: dogmatique de l'église orthodoxe* [Philosophy of the truth: dogmatic theology of the orthodox church], vol. 5, trans. Jean Louis Palierne (Paris: L'Age d'homme, 1997), 19.

10. See Popovich, *Philosophie de la vérité*, vol. 1, 76, 104–105.

11. See Matsoukas, *Dogmatikē kai symbolikē theologia*, vol. 1, 176.

12. Ibid., 73.

13. See Johann Goethe's *Farbenleher* where he argued that the Newtonian theory of light explains everything except what we see. See idem, introduction to *Theory of Colours* trans. Charles Eastlake (London: John Murray, 1840), xviii–xxiiv, xliv–xlviii.

14. Athanasius the Great *Letter to Serapion* 3.5 (PG 26.632b).

15. See Popovich, *Philosophie de la vérité*, vol. 1, 248–249.

16. See Matsoukas, *Dogmatikē kai symbolikē theologia*, vol. 3, 107–109.

17. See ibid., 111.

18. See Matsoukas, *Dogmatikē kai symbolikē theologia*, vol. 2, 182; idem, vol. 3, 62.

19. See Matsoukas, *Dogmatikē kai symbolikē theologia*, vol. 2, 181, 188. Cf. Dionysius the Areopagite [pseud.] *On the Divine Names* 4 (PG 3.697c–700a).

20. See Matsoukas, *Dogmatikē kai symbolikē theologia*, vol. 3, 165.

21. See Nellas, *Zōon theoumenon*, 45; Matsoukas *Dogmatikē kai symbolikē theologia*, vol. 3, 192–194.

22. See Popovich, *Philosophie de la vérité*, vol. 1, 280, 285.

23. See Nellas, *Zōon theoumenon*, 33–34.

24. See Matsoukas, *Dogmatikē kai symbolikē theologia*, vol. 2, 196.

25. See Matsoukas, *Dogmatikē kai symbolikē theologia*, vol. 3, 195

26. See Nellas, *Zōon theoumenon*, 26–27.

27. See Popovich, *Philosophie de la vérité*, vol. 1, 282.

28. See Nellas, *Zōon theoumenon*, 29.

29. John of Damascus *Exact Exposition on the Orthodox Faith* 2.12 (PG 94.920b, 924a).

30. See Matsoukas, *Dogmatikē kai symbolikē theologia*, vol. 2, 197; Larchet, *Mental Disorders*, 28–29; Popovich, *Philosophie de la vérité*, vol. 1, 290.

31. Nellas, *Zōon theoumenon*, 23. Cf. Col 1:15.

32. See Matsoukas, *Dogmatikē kai symbolikē theologia*, vol. 2, 42–43; Nellas, *Zōon theoumenon*, 133.

33. Nellas, *Zōon theoumenon*, 24–26.

34. See Matsoukas, *Dogmatikē kai symbolikē theologia*, vol. 3, 97–98.

35. See Popovich, *Philosophie de la vérité*, vol. 5, 51.

36. Gregory of Nyssa *On the Creation of Man* 16 (PG 44.180c).

37. See Matsoukas, *Dogmatikē kai symbolikē theologia*, vol. 2, 176–177.

38. See Matsoukas, *Dogmatikē kai symbolikē theologia*, vol. 3, 207, 213–214, 232–233.

39. See Popovich, *Philosophie de la vérité*, vol. 5, 96.

40. See Popovich, *Philosophie de la vérité*, vol. 1, 270.

41. See Matsoukas, *Dogmatikē kai symbolikē theologia*, vol. 2, 205–206.

42. See Popovich, *Philosophie de la vérité*, vol. 1, 304, 306, 319; Cf. Matsoukas, *Dogmatikē kai symbolikē theologia*, vol. 2, 191.

43. See Metropolitan Ioannis [Zizioulas], "Nosos kai therapeia stēn orthodoxē theologia," [Sickness and healing in orthodox theology] in idem, *Orthodoxia kai synchronos kosmos* [Orthodoxy and the contemporary world] (Leukosia, Cyprus: Kentro Meletōn Kukkou, 2006), 67–68.

44. See Nellas, *Zōon theoumenon*, 49–50, 52–53, 62.

45. See Popovich, *Philosophie de la vérité*, vol. 1, 330.

46. See Popovich, *Philosophie de la vérité*, vol. 2, 10; Fr. Justin Popovich, *Philosophie de la vérité: dogmatique de l'église orthodoxe*, vol. 3, trans. Jean Louis Palierne (Paris: L'Age d' Homme, 1995), 28.

47. See Popovich, *Philosophie de la vérité*, vol. 3, 9, 12, 20; idem, *Philosophie de la vérité*, vol. 4, 76; idem, *Philosophie de la vérité*, vol. 5, 55.

48. Athanasius the Great *Commentary on the Psalms* 44.8 (PG 27.209cd).

49. Irenaeus of Lyons *Against all Heresy* 3.19.1 (PG 7.939).

50. See Popovich, *Philosophie de la vérité*, vol. 2, 13.

51. Gregory of Nazianzus *Letter to Kledonion the Presbyter* 101 (PG 37.180a).

52. See Popovich, *Philosophie de la vérité*, vol. 3, 76–77.

53. See ibid., 12–13.

54. Gregory of Nazianzus *Orations* 2.25 (PG 35.436a).

55. Augustine *The Encheiridion* 1.53 (PL 40.257).

56. See Popovich, *Philosophie de la vérité*, vol. 3, 96.

57. See Athanasius the Great *Against the Arians* 1.47 (PG 26.108c–109c).

58. See Popovich, *Philosophie de la vérité*, vol. 3, 99, 103, 109, 116, 134.

59. See ibid., 291.

60. See Popovich, *Philosophie de la vérité*, vol. 5, 12.

61. See Jn 11:1; Lk 8:52; Mt 9:24; Mk 5:39.

62. Popovich, *Philosophie de la vérité*, vol. 3, 260.

63. See Gregory Palamas *Homilies* 21 (PG 151.276ab).

64. See Nellas, *Zōon theoumenon*, 125.

65. See Popovich, *Philosophie de la vérité*, vol. 4, 38, 74, 166.

66. See Popovich, *Philosophie de la vérité*, vol. 5, 49, 220, 250.

67. See ibid., 234.

68. See Met. Ioannis [Zizioulas], "Nosos kai therapeia stēn orthodoxē theologia," 79–80.

69. 1 Cor 12:6.

70. See Plato *Cratylus* 385e (*LCL* 167.385). Of course, the modern interpretation of this saying does not include the original connotation that all knowledge is merely opinion.

71. See Nikos Matsoukas, *Historia tēs philosophias me syntomē eisagōgē stē philosophia* [History of philosophy with a short introduction to philosophy] (Thessaloniki, Greece: Pournara, 2001), 325.

72. See William James, *Some Problems of Philosophy* (New York: Longman's Green & Company, 1911), 35; Cornelius G. Hunter, *Science's Blind Spot: The Unseen Religion of Scientific Naturalism* (Grand Rapids: Brazos Press, 2007), 14, 35.

73. See Renée Descartes, *Rules for Direction of Mind, Great Books of the Western World*, vol. 31, ed. Robert Hutchins, trans. Elizabeth Haldane and G. R. Ross (Chicago: Encyclopedia Britannica, 1952), 7–27; A. T. Beck, *Cognitive Therapy and Emotional Disorders*, 226–227, 261.

74. See Bertrand Russell, *A History of Western Philosophy* (New York: Simon & Schuster, 1945), 542.

75. See Hunter, *Science's Blind Spot*, 14.

76. See ibid., 18.

77. See Matsoukas, *Historia tēs philosophias*, 325–326.

78. See Jones and Butman, *Modern Psychotherapies*, 198–199; J. S. Beck, *Cognitive Therapy*, 139, 194–195.

79. See Evagrius *On Diverse Thoughts* 7 (*PG* 79.1209a–1209b); Maximus the Confessor *Centuries on Love* 3.41 (*PG* 90.1028d–1029a).

80. See Frederick Copleston, *A History of Philosophy: Descartes to Leibniz* (New York: Image Books, 1985), vol. 4, 33–34.

81. See ibid., 36. The primary source in Locke's corpus is his *The Reasonableness of Christianity*.

82. Frederick Copleston, *A History of Philosophy: Bentham to Russell* (New York: Image Books, 1985), vol. 8, 120.

83. See Hunter, *Science's Blind Spot*, 11–12, 47.

84. Sir Francis Bacon writes, "My first admonition (which was also my prayer) is that men confine the sense within the limits of duty in respect of things divine: for the sense is like the sun, which reveals the face of earth, but seals and shuts up the face of heaven." Quoted in Hunter's *Science's Blind Spot*, 16.

85. Frederick Copleston, *A History of Philosophy: Maine de Biran to Sartre* (New York: Image Books, 1985), vol. 9, 79, 83.

86. See Auguste Compte, *Système de Politique Positive* (Paris: Carilian Goeury et Vᵒʳ Dalmont, 1851), vol. 2, 65.

87. See A. J. Ayers, *Language, Truth and Logic* (New York: Dover Publications, 1952).

88. See Van Leeuwen, *Person in Psychology*, 7.

89. See Julien de La Mettrie, *L'homme machine* and *L'homme plante* respectively.

90. Frederick Copleston, *A History of Philosophy: Wolff to Kant* (New York: Image Books, 1985), vol. 6, 41, 47, 48.

91. From his *Rapports du physique et du moral de l'homme* noted in Copleston, *A History of Philosophy*, vol. 4, 39.

92. See J. S. Beck, *Cognitive Therapy for Challenging Problems*, 272–282; Alford and Beck, *Integrative Power*, 11; Beck, Freeman, Davis and Associates, *Cognitive Therapy of Personality Disorders*, 25–26, 29–30.

93. Gardner Linzey, Calvin S. Hall, and Richard F. Thompson, *Psychology* (New York: Worth, 1975), 31.

94. See the thought of John Dewey (1859–1952) and John Tyndall (1820–1893) as well as the concerns of William James (1842–1910). See Copleston, *A History of Philosophy*, vol. 8, 357, 108, 343 respectively.

95. See Copleston, *A History of Philosophy*, vol. 8, 323, 377. See the philosophies of C. S. Pierce and John Dewey.

96. See Aaron T. Beck, *Prisoners of Hate: The Cognitive Basis of Anger, Hostility, and Violence* (New York: Harper Collins Publishers, 1999), 37; Aaron T. Beck and Gary Emery with Ruth Greenberg, *Anxiety Disorders and Phobias: A Cognitive Perspective* (New York: Basic Books, 1985), 13; Aaron T. Beck, Arthur Freeman, Denise D. Davis and Associates, *Cognitive Therapy of Personality Disorders*, 19; Marjorie E. Weishaar, *Aaron T. Beck* (London: Sage, 1993), 147.

97. See Beck and Emery, *Anxiety Disorders and Phobias*, 13, 19.

98. Beck et al., *Cognitive Therapy of Personality Disorders*, 19–21.

99. Alford and Beck, *Integrative Power*, 27.

100. See Gayle Woloschak, *Beauty and Unity in Creation: The Evolution of Life* (Minneapolis, MN: Light & Life Press, 1996), and George and Elizabeth Theokritoff, "Genesis and Creation: Towards a Debate," Review of Seraphim Rose, *Genesis, Creation and Early Man: The Orthodox Christian Vision*, St. Vladimir's Theological Quarterly 46, no. 2 (2002).

101. See William James, *The Varieties of Religious Experience* (New York: Penguin Books, 1982), 501–503.

102. See Jones and Butman, *Modern Psychotherapies*, 146–147.

103. Miracles in themselves do not abrogate scientifically established laws, since those laws adequately describe the order in *created* reality, but not the action of God's *uncreated* energies acting within and upon that reality. See Matsoukas, *Dogmatikē kai symbolikē theologia*, vol. 2, 163–164; Entwistle, *Integrative Approaches*, 117.

104. See Van Leeuwen, *Person in Psychology*, 45.

105. Ibid., 64, 66.

106. *Journal of Counseling Psychology* 7 (1960): 188–192.

107. Alvin C. Dueck and Kevin Reimer, "Religious Discourse in Psychotherapy," *International Journal of Existential Psychology and Psychotherapy* 1, no. 1 (July 2004): 6–7.

108. See Ellis and Harper, *Guide to Rational Living*, 245–246.

109. See ibid., 39.

110. See ibid., 230, 250, 252.

111. See ibid., 46–49.

112. See ibid., 74, 164.

113. Albert Ellis, "Therapy and Atheistic Values: A Response to A Bergin's Therapy and Religious Issues," *Journal of Consulting and Clinical Psychology* 48 (1980): 635; idem, *The Case against Religion: A Psychotherapist's View and the Case against Religiosity* (Austin, TX: American Atheist Press, 1980), 15; Ellis and Harper, *Guide to Rational Living*, 51, 53. In order to avoid appearing unscientific, Ellis was forced to modify his position on religion in response to a large body of research indicating that no positive correlation exists between religious commitment and psychological disturbance. Notwithstanding, a basically anti-religious orientation can be detected even in his later works. See W. Brad Johnson and Stevan Lars Nielsen, "Rational-Emotive Assessment with Religious Clients," *Journal of Rational-Emotive and Cognitive-Behavior Therapy* 16, no. 2 (Summer, 1998): 102, 103, 113

114. See Van Leeuwen, *Person in Psychology*, 48–49.

115. See Entwistle, *Integrative Approaches*, 115n13.

116. See Rediger, "Psychiatric Considerations" in Muse, ed., *Raising Lazarus*, 65.

117. Pss 14:1 (MT); 13:1 (LXX); 53:1 (MT); 52:1 (LXX).

118. James R. Beck, "Integration of Psychology and Theology," 23.

119. See Hunter, *Science's Blind Spot*, 74, 98.

120. Alford and Beck, *Integrative Power*, 86.

121. See Van Leeuwen, *Person in Psychology*, 115, 138–139.

122. See McMinn and Campbell, *Integrative Therapy*, 113, 120, 124.

123. See Russell, *A History of Western Philosophy*, 816.

124. Copleston, *A History of Philosophy*, vol. 8, 355.

125. Copleston, *A History of Philosophy*, vol. 8, 308.

126. See McMinn and Campbell, *Integrative Therapy*, 100–103.

127. Significant psychological theories would include Sigmund Freud's theory of psychoanalysis, B. F. Skinner's behavioralism, E. C. Tolman's cognitive map theory, Wolfgang Köhler's insight gestalt theory, Karen Horney's theory of social psychoanalysis, Jean Piaget's stage theory, and Albert Bandura's social learning theory. Beck himself notes his use of the cognitive constructs of George Kelly as well as the vocabulary of Sir Frederic Bartlett and Jean Piaget. See A. T. Beck, "Beyond Belief: A Theory of Modes, Personality and Psychopathology," in Salkovskis, ed., *Frontiers of Cognitive Therapy*, 1 (see intro, n. 7).

128. See Van Leeuwen, *Person in Psychology*, xi–xii, 143.

129. Macarius of Egypt [pseud.] *Homilies* 22.2 (PG 34.664d).

130. Aaron Beck, interview by Sidney Block, May 4, 2004, Philadelphia, PA.

131. Thermos, *Anthrōpos ston horizonta!*, 39.

132. Aaron T. Beck, "Reflections on my Public Dialogue with the Dalai Lama," June 13, 2005, Göteborg, Sweeden.

133. See Met. John [Zizioulas], "Nosos kai therapeia stēn orthodoxē theologia," 66, 80.

134. Demetra Jacquet, "Pastoral Psychological Response: An Orthodox Expression of Pastoral Counseling" in Muse, ed., *Raising Lazarus*, 111.

135. See Siang-Yang Tan, "Cognitive Behavior Therapy: A Biblical Approach and Critique," *Journal of Psychology and Theology* 15, no. 2 (1987): 107.

136. C. S. Lewis, *The Abolition of Man* (San Francisco: Harper Press, 2001), 76.

137. See Ellis and Harper, *Guide to Rational Living*, 47–49.
138. See Thermos, *Anthrōpos ston horizonta!*, 18, 55–56. Cf. Maximus the Confessor *To Thalassius* 42 (PG 90.405).
139. Jones and Butman, *Modern Psychotherapies*, 218.
140. Ps 8:5 (MT); 8:6 (LXX).
141. Ps 49:20 (MT): 48:21 (LXX).
142. Gregory Palamas *On Behalf of the Hesychasts* 1.1.21, 383–385.

Chapter Three

1. See McMinn and Campbell, *Integrative Therapy*, 80.
2. See Elder Païsios the Hagiorite, *Logoi: pathē kai aretes* [Discourses: passions and virtues], vol. 5 (Souroti-Thessaloniki, Greece: Hieron Hēsychastērion Evangelistēs Iōannēs ho Theologos, 2006), 171.
3. See Aaron T. Beck, A. John Rush, Brian F. Shaw, and Gary Emery, *Cognitive Therapy of Depression* (New York: The Guilford Press, 1979), 3.
4. See J. S. Beck, *Cognitive Therapy*, 1.
5. See L. Rebecca Propst, *Therapy in a Religious Framework: Spirituality in the Emotional Healing Process* (New York: Human Sciences Press, 1988), 41; J. S. Beck, *Cognitive Therapy*, 2.
6. Beck, Shaw, and Emery, *Cognitive Therapy of Depression*, 4.
7. See Entwistle, *Integrative Approaches*, 220, 225 (see intro., n. 17).
8. See Bryan N. Maier and Phillip G. Monroe, "Biblical Hermeneutics and Christian Psychology," in McMinn and Phillips, eds., *Care for the Soul*, 291.
9. Polanyi, *Tacit Dimension*, 4.
10. See ibid., 10.
11. See J. S. Beck, *Cognitive Therapy*, 14, 75.
12. Bandura, *Social Learning Theory*, 59 (see chap. 2, n. 74).
13. *The Encheiridion* 5.1.4 (LCL 218.486–488). See references to this quotation in Beck, Shaw, and Emery, *Cognitive Therapy of Depression*, 8; A. T. Beck, *Love is Never Enough* (New York: Harper & Row Publishers, 1988) 38; A. T. Beck, *Cognitive Therapy and Emotional Disorders*, 47; and Ellis, *Guide to Rational Living*, 39.
14. See Neilus the Ascetic [pseud.] *The Encheiridion of Epictetus* 10 (PG 79.1289b). The full text is found in PG 79.1279b–1312c.
15. Ambrose of Milan *Letter to Simplicanus* 1.37.30 (PL 16.1091b).
16. John Cassian *Institutes* 9.7 (PL 49.356).
17. See Dorotheos of Gaza *To Those in the Cells* 182 (SC 92.492–494).
18. Elder Païsios the Hagiorite, *Logoi: pneumatikos agōnas* [Discourses: spiritual struggle], vol. 3 (Souroti-Thessaloniki, Greece: Hieron Hēsychastērion Evangelistēs Iōannēs ho Theologos, 2001), 31–32.
19. Elder Païsios the Hagiorite, *Epistoles*, 110.
20. Jn 13:34.

21. Mt 7:1.

22. 1 Cor 15:28.

23. John Chrysostom *Commentary on First Corinthians* 38.7 (*PG* 61.331–332).

24. For example, the Christian redactor completely omits chapter fifty-two about division in philosophy and chapter fifty-three with its invocation of Zeus and Fate. It is also worth noting that St. Gregory the Theologian openly admires Epictetus in his *Letter to Philargius* 32 (*PG* 37.72ab); St. Basil the Great quotes from him in his *On the Hexameron* 2 (*PG* 29b.40bc); and Blessed Augustine sets forth some of the philosopher's more important teachings in his *City of God* 9.4 (*PL* 41.259–260).

25. See Neilus the Ascetic [pseud.] *Encheiridion of Epictetus* 24 (*PG* 79.1293c).

26. Ibid. 27 (*PG* 79.1296a). Cf. *Encheiridion* 20 (*LCL* 218.498).

27. John Chrysostom *Commentary on Ephesians* 1.3 (*PG* 62.92).

28. Theodore the Studite *Catechetical Discourses* 100 (*HPE* 18a.368–370). Cf. Latin translation in *PG* 99.638d.

29. See Theodore the Studite *Letter to Naukratius* 2.36 (*PG* 99.1220d).

30. See Symeon the New Theologian *Catechetical Discourses* 4 (*SC* 96.320–328).

31. Alford and Beck, *Integrative Power*, 15.

32. See Beck et al., *Cognitive Therapy of Personality Disorders*, 18.

33. See A. T. Beck, *Prisoners of Hate*, 25.

34. See Beck et al., *Cognitive Therapy of Depression*, 58–59.

35. See Beck et al., *Cognitive Therapy of Personality Disorders*, 18.

36. See A. T. Beck, *Love is Never Enough*, 30, 121–121, 335–336.

37. A. T. Beck, *Prisoners of Hate*, 43. Elder Païsios the Hagiorite likewise locates the source of anger in the assignment of blame to others. See *Logoi*, vol. 5, 131.

38. See ibid., 81–82.

39. Ibid., 8.

40. See ibid., 74–76.

41. For example, Beck notes that cognitive therapy reveals the power of *realistic* thinking, rather than *positive* thinking. He even warns that unrealistically positive thoughts that are repeatedly falsified can lead a person to disillusionment. See his *Cognitive Therapy of Depression*, 298–299.

42. Beck et al., *Cognitive Therapy of Personality Disorders*, 30.

43. See John Cassian *Conferences* 1.10 (*PL* 49.538).

44. See Beck and Emery with Greenberg, *Anxiety Disorders and Phobias*, 192. Merely the awareness of automatic thoughts qua automatic thoughts relativizes their previous status as absolute personal truths.

45. Dt 6:5.

46. Mt 22:37.

47. For the thoughts and the heart, see Gn 6:5; Jgs 5:15; 1 Chr 29:18; Mt 15:9. For thoughts and the soul, see 1 Sm 20:4; Ps 42:5 (MT); 41:6 (LXX).

48. Mt 15:19.

49. E.g., Origen *On First Principles* 3.2.4 (*PG* 11.308d).

50. See Nicodemos the Hagiorite, *Exomologētarion* [Book for confession] (Athens: Ho Hagios Nikodimos, 1868), 6.

51. See Gregory of Sinai *Chapters* 69 (*PG* 150.1257b).

52. See Methodius *Discourse on the Resurrection* 3.2 (*PG* 18.304d–305b).

53. John of Karpathos *To the Monks in India* 55 (*PHIL* 1.287). See also Latin version 52 (*PG* 85.801c). Translated by G. Palmer, P. Sherrard, and K. Ware as *Philokalia*, vol. 1 (London: Faber & Faber, 1979), 311.

54. See John Cassian *Conferences* 1.19 (*PL* 49.508c–510a).

55. See Isaac the Syrian, *Ta eurethenta askētika* [Extant ascetic homilies], ed. N. Theotokis, (Thessaloniki, Greece: B Rēgopoulou, 1985), hom. 73, 284; Ilias the Presbyter *Gnostic Chapters* 28 (*PG* 127.1153b).

56. John Cassian *Conferences* 1.19 (*PL* 49.510a).

57. See Maximus the Confessor *Centuries on Love* 2.84 (*PG* 90.1009d).

58. Peter of Damascus *Book One on the Sixth Stage of Contemplation* (*PHIL* 3.53). Translated by G. Palmer, P. Sherrard, and K. Ware as *Philokalia*, vol. 3 (London: Faber & Faber, 1984), 134 [translation modified].

59. See Evagrius *On Diverse Thoughts* 27.7 (*PG* 79.1209a–1209b).

60. See Peter of Damascus *Book One on the Sixth Stage of Contemplation* (*PHIL* 3.52–53).

61. Gregory Palamas *Natural and Theological Chapters* 17 (*PG* 150.1132d). Translated by G. Palmer, P. Sherrard, and K. Ware as *Philokalia*, vol. 4 (London: Faber & Faber, 1995) 353.

62. See Methodius *Discourse on the Resurrection* 3.2 (*PG* 18.300c).

63. See John of Damascus [pseud.] *On Virtues and Vices* (*PG* 95.93a).

64. See Macarius of Egypt [pseud.] *Homilies* 27 (*PG* 34.709b).

65. See Nikitas Stithatos *Natural Chapters* 2.37 (*PG* 120.916d).

66. Nicodemos the Hagiorite, *Aortatos polemos* [Unseen warfare] (Athens: Phōs-Xeen, 2002), 54.

67. See Macarius of Egypt [pseud.] *Freedom of the Intellect* 3 (*PG* 34.937c).

68. Jerome *Letter to Demetra* 4.130.8 (*PL* 22.1115).

69. Gregory of Sinai *Chapters* 67 (*PG* 150.1257a). Palmer, Sherrard, and Ware, *Philokalia*, vol. 4, 223.

70. Mark the Ascetic *On the Spiritual Law* 1.120 (*PG* 65.920).

71. Augustine *On the Psalms* 148.2 (*PL* 37.1958).

72. See Ibid.

73. Irenaeus of Lyons *Against All Heresies* 4.16 (*PG* 7.1019).

74. See Neilus the Ascetic *Discourse on Non-acquisitiveness* 7 (*PG* 79.977d).

75. See Theodore of Edessa *Century of Spiritual Texts* 9 (*PHIL* 1.305).

76. See Tertullian *On the Soul* 58 (*PL* 2.751b).

77. See Isaac the Syrian, *Ta askētika*, hom. 54, 216–217.

78. See Elder Païsios the Hagiorite, *Logoi*, vol. 2, 108.

79. See Isaac the Syrian, *Ta askētika*, hom. 34, 138.

80. Dorotheos of Gaza *Discourses* 12.137 (SC 92.400). See also Abba Olympios *Sayings of the Fathers* O.1 (PG 65.313d).

81. See Hesychius the Presbyter *On Watchfulness and Holiness* 2.91 (PG 93.1541b).

82. See Mark the Ascetic *On Divine Baptism* 4 (PG 65.992b)

83. See John Cassian *Conferences* 1.17 (PL 49.506–507).

84. Elder Païsios the Hagiorite, *Logoi: pneumatikos agōnas* [Discourses: spiritual struggle], vol. 3 (Souroti-Thessaloniki, Greece: Hieron Hēsychastērion Evangelistēs Iōannēs ho Theologos, 2001), 20.

85. Ibid., 56.

86. For example, see the eirmos for the fifth ode for the Wednesday ferial canon in the first tone. *Paraklētikē* [*Ferial service-book of consolation/invocation*] (Athens: Apostolikēs Diakonias tēs Ekklēsias tēs Hellados, 1984), 35.

87. Clement of Alexandria *Stromateis* 7.7 (PG 9.453b).

88. John of Karpathos *To the Monks in India* 66 (PHIL 1.287–277). Cf. the Latin translation numbered 53 (PG 85.801c). See also Lk 8:43–44.

89. See Mark the Ascetic *On the Spiritual Law* 1.160 (PG 65.925a).

90. Augustine *On the Trinity* 15.10.18 (PL 42.1070–1071).

91. Maximus the Confessor *Letter to Marinus* (PG 91.277d).

92. See Augustine *City of God* 7.14 (PL 41.205).

93. See Gregory of Sinai *Chapters* 66 (PG 150.1257a).

94. See Jerome *Against John of Jerusalem* 1.1 (PL 23.371a).

95. Cyril of Jerusalem *Catechetical Discourses* 6.2 (PG 33.540b).

96. Neilus the Ascetic *Chapters* 70 (PG 79.1255a).

97. John Cassian *Conferences* 1.7.4 (PL 49.672). See also ibid. 1.1.18 (PL 49.508a).

98. Theodore of Edessa *Century of Spiritual Texts* 16 (PHIL 1.17). See Theophan the Recluse, *Put' ko spaseniju* [The path to salvation] (Moscow: Tipo-litografija I. Efimova, 1908), 275.

99. John of Damascus *Exact Exposition of the Orthodox Faith* 3.15 (PG 94.1048c).

100. Theophan the Recluse, *The Art of Prayer*, 183.

101. *Ladder* 15.75 (PG 88.897bc). Holy Transfiguration Monastery, 116

102. Illias the Presbyter *A Gnomic Anthology* 28 (PG 127.153c). Palmer, Sherrard, and Ware, *The Philokalia*, vol. 3, 50.

103. Theophan the Recluse, *Put' ko spaseniju*, 285. Translated by Fr. Seraphim Rose as *The Path to Salvation* (Platina, CA: Saint Herman of Alaska Brotherhood, 1996), 298.

104. See Tertullian *On the Resurrection of the Flesh* 15 (PL 2.814a).

105. See Gregory Palamas *To the Nun Xenia* (PG 150.1081a).

106. Maximus the Confessor *Other Chapters* 1.131 (PG 90.1432a). For a modern description of the production of deductively valid inferences from factually erroneous suppositions, see A. Bandura, *Social Learning Theory*, 185.

107. See Isaac the Syrian, *Ta askētika*, hom. 83, 319; Nicodemos the Hagiorite, *Exomologētarion*, 39–41.

108. See Maximus the Confessor *Centuries on Love* 2.74 (PG 90.1003b).

109.   See Thalassius *On Love and Self-control* 1.46 (*PG* 91.1432c).

110.   See A. T. Beck, introduction to *Prisoners of Hate*, xi.

111.   See Ellis and Harper, *Guide to Rational Living*, 172–173.

112.   See A. T. Beck, *Cognitive Therapy and Emotional Disorders*, 34.

113.   See A. T. Beck, *Love is Never Enough*, 145; J. S. Beck, *Cognitive Therapy*, 88.

114.   See J. S. Beck, *Cognitive Therapy*, 14–15.

115.   See Beck and Emery with Greenberg, *Anxiety Disorders and Phobias*, 192.

116.   See J. S. Beck, *Cognitive Therapy*, 10, 76.

117.   See ibid., 82–84.

118.   See ibid., 105–106.

119.   See Alford and Beck, *Integrative Power*, 15.

120.   See Beck et al., *Cognitive Therapy of Depression*, 14–15.

121.   See A. T. Beck, preface to *Anxiety Disorders and Phobias*, xvi.

122.   See John Chrysostom *Commentary on Second Corinthians* 29 (*PG* 61.604).

123.   For example, see matins for St. Thekla (24 Sept.), first troparion of the ninth ode (*MEN* 9.148).

124.   St. Gregory of Sinai gives a rather extensive list likening the passions/demons to pigs, donkeys, stallions, lions, wolves, foxes, snakes, dogs, cats, crows, and jackdaws. *Chapters* 71 (*PG* 150.1257d–1260a). St. Isaac the Syrian notes that the passions resemble dogs in a butcher shop or attacking lions. (*Ta askētika*, hom. 55, 220). Evagrius compares one of the passions to a viper. *On Various Bad Thoughts* 13 (*PG* 79.1216a). St. John Chrysostom likewise makes an analogy between passions in human beings and the behaviors of bulls, horses, bears, mules, wolves, serpents, scorpions, and foxes. *Commentary on Matthew* 4.8 (*PG* 57.48). St. Theodore of Edessa also notes that "animals signify the various shameful passions," *Century of Spiritual Texts* 7 (*PHIL* 1.305). See also Ilias the Presbyter *Gnostic Anthology* 59 (*PG* 127.1160b).

125.   Joseph Miller, "Reflections on Science and Belief," 13.

126.   Dorotheos of Gaza *Discourses* 1.6 (*SC* 92.154). See also Plato *Republic* 589b (*LCL* 237.402) where he also refers to the inner man [*ho entos anthrōpos*].

127.   Gregory Palamas *Homily* 20 (*PG* 151.273a).

128.   John Climacus *Ladder* 15.74 (*PG* 88.897a). Translation by Holy Transfiguration Monastery, 116.

129.   See Dorotheos of Gaza *Discourses* 11.115 (*SC* 92.360).

130.   See Maximus the Confessor *To Thalassius* 16 (*PG* 90.301d).

131.   See Maximus the Confessor *Centuries on Love* 3.78 (*PG* 90.1041).

132.   See Neilus the Ascetic *Untitled Letter* 3.293 (*PG* 79.529a) and *Ascetic Discourse* 72 (*PG* 79.808c).

133.   See Maximus the Confessor *Centuries on Love* 1.14 (*PG* 90.964c).

134.   See Matsoukas, *Dogmatikē kai symbolikē theologia*, vol. 2, 506–507.

135.   See Neilus the Ascetic *Ascetic Discourse* 50 (*PG* 79.781b).

136.   Dorotheos of Gaza *Discourses* 1.6 (*SC* 92.154) and 1.5 (*SC* 92.154).

137.   For example, St. Peter of Damascus enumerates 298 passions. *Book One A List of the Passions* (*PHIL* 3.107–108).

138. See Dorotheos of Gaza *Discourses* 12.31 (*SC* 92.392).

139. See Anastasius of Sinai *Questions and Answers* 8 (*PG* 79.781b).

140. See Neilus the Ascetic *Letter to Monk Eulesius* 2.125 (*PG* 79.253b).

141. Neilus the Ascetic *Ascetic Discourse* 75 (*PG* 79.809b).

142. *Homily* 51, Sophokles Oikonomos, 114–115.

143. See Maximus the Confessor *Diverse Theological Chapters* 2.24 (*PG* 90.1233b).

144. See Maximus the Confessor *To Thalassius* 58 (*PG* 90.596b).

145. See ibid., *Introductory Comments* (*PG* 90.256c).

146. See Antiochus the Monk *Discourse for Eustathius* 23 (*PG* 89.1504d–1505a).

147. See Neilus the Ascetic *Discourses* 50 (*PG* 79.1177b).

148. See Maximus the Confessor *Diverse Theological Chapters* 1.26 (*PG* 90.1200).

149. See Maximus the Confessor *Commentary on the Divine Names* (*PG* 4.281a).

150. See Maximus the Confessor *To Marinus* (*PG* 91.20b).

151. See Neilus the Ascetic *On Prayer* 63 (*PG* 79.1180d).

152. Evagrius *On Various Bad Thoughts* 21 (*PG* 79.1224c).

153. See Maximus the Confessor *To Thalassius* 56 (*PG* 90.585d).

154. See John Chrysostom *Commentary on Acts* 41.5 (*PG* 60.295).

155. See Jean Piaget, *La representation du monde chez l'enfant* [Representation of the world in the child] (Paris: Presses Universitaires de France, 1926).

156. See Beck et al., *Cognitive Therapy of Depression*, 12; J. S. Beck, *Cognitive Therapy*, 16.

157. See J. S. Beck, *Cognitive Therapy*, 15.

158. See J. S. Beck, *Cognitive Therapy for Challenging Problems*, 270; J. S. Beck, *Cognitive Therapy*, 167; Beck and Emery with Greenberg, *Anxiety Disorders and Phobias*, 130–132.

159. See Beck and Emery with Greenberg, *Anxiety Disorders and Phobias*, xvi, 15–16.

160. A. T. Beck, *Prisoners of Hate*, 72. See also Beck and Emery with Greenberg, *Anxiety Disorders and Phobias*, 61.

161. See Beck and Emery with Greenberg, *Anxiety Disorders and Phobias*, xvi, 15–16, 25–26.

162. See ibid., 13.

163. See ibid., 58. A. T. Beck, *Prisoners of Hate*, 42.

164. Ibid., 54,56–57.

165. See A. T. Beck, *Love is Never Enough*, 42. Blessed Theodoret of Cyrus makes a similar observation about fathers considering their unattractive children to be attractive under the influence of affection for them. *Letter to Someone Anonymous* 2 (*PG* 83.1176a).

166. See Beck et al., *Cognitive Therapy of Personality Disorders*, 27.

167. See A. T. Beck, *Cognitive Therapy and Emotional Disorders*, 247.

168. See J. S. Beck, *Cognitive Therapy*, 137.

169. See J. S. Beck, *Cognitive Therapy*, 166; Beck and Emery with Greenberg, *Anxiety Disorders and Phobias*, 293.

170. See Beck and Emery with Greenberg, *Anxiety Disorders and Phobias*, 62.

171. See J. S. Beck, *Cognitive Therapy*, 15.

172. See Beck, Emery with Greenberg, *Anxiety Disorders and Phobias*, 59–60, 65.

173. A. T. Beck, *Love is Never Enough*, 73–75.

174. See A. T. Beck, *Prisoners of Hate*, 73.

175. See ibid., 38, 39.

176. Ibid., 83.

177. Beck and Emery with Greenberg, *Anxiety Disorders and Phobias*, 31. See also ibid., 14–15, 40, 41.

178. See Beck et al., *Cognitive Therapy of Substance Abuse*, 50.

179. See Beck et al., *Cognitive Therapy of Personality Disorders*, 6.

180. See J. S. Beck, *Cognitive Therapy for Challenging Problems*, 268–269.

181. See Beck et al., *Cognitive Therapy of Personality Disorders*, 81–83. A. T. Beck, *Cognitive Therapy and Emotional Disorders*, 246.

182. See Keselopoulos, *Pathē kai aretes*, 177; cf. Gregory Palamas *On behalf of the Hesychasts* 2.2.22–23.

183. Gordon W. Allport, *Becoming: Basic Considerations for a Psychology of Personality* (New Haven: Yale University Press, 1955), 28–29. Blessed Augustine likewise comments, "We have to bear in little children so many things which we punish in older persons, that we cannot enumerate them." *On the Merits and Forgiveness of Sins* 1.67 (*PL* 44.149).

184. See McMinn and Campell, *Integrative Therapy*, 232–233 for reference to G. Stavros, "An Empirical Study of the Impact of Contemplative Prayer on Psychological, Relational, and Spiritual Well-being" (PhD diss., Boston University, 1998).

185. Rom 8:21.

Chapter Four

1. A. T. Beck, *Cognitive Therapy and Emotional Disorders*, 235.

2. John Chrysostom *On the Earthquake* 7 (*PG* 48.1037–1038).

3. See A. T. Beck, *Cognitive Therapy and Emotional Disorders*, 218–219.

4. See Hesychius the Presbyter *On Watchfulness and Holiness* 75 (*PG* 93.1536d); Evagrius *On the Eight Thoughts* (*PG* 40.1272).

5. See Evagrius *On the Eight Thoughts* 1 (*PG* 40.1272): "*Prōtos ho tēs gastrimargias, kai met auton ho tēs porneias; tritos ho tēs philargyrias; tetartos ho tēs lypēs; pemptos ho tēs orgēs; hektos ho tēs akēdias; hebdomos ho tēs kenodoxias; ogdoos ho tēs hyperēphanias.*" The same list can also be found in his *On Various Thoughts* (*PG* 79.1200d–1201a), *On the Eight Spirits of Wickedness* (*PG* 79.1145–1163d), *On the Eight Thoughts of Wickedness* (*PG* 79.1436a) as well as in [St. Athanasius the Great?] *Letter to Kastora* (*PG* 28.872d) and *Discernment of the Tripartite Soul* (*PG* 28.1397a). See also St. John of Damascus *On the Eight Spirits of Wickedness* 1 (*PG* 95.80a). St. Macarius of Egypt [pseud.] has another list of six bad thoughts (*porneia, philargyria, kenodoxia, typhos, zēlos kai thymos*) that was not generally adopted by the patristic consensus. *Homilies* 15.50 (*PG* 34.609c). In the West, Pope St. Gregory the Great turned Evagrius's eight bad thoughts into the seven cardinal sins (*principalia vitia: inanis gloria, invidia, ira, tristitia, avaritia, ventris ingluvies et luxuria*) in his *On Job* 31.45.87 (*PL* 76.620d–621a), a simplification that St. John Climacus congratulated in his *Ladder* 29.10 (*PG* 88.949a).

6. Maximus the Confessor *Centuries on Love* 3.53 (*PG* 90.1032d). Translated by G. Palmer, P. Sherrard, and K. Ware as *The Philokalia*, vol. 2 (London: Faber & Faber, 1981), 91 [translation modified].

7. John of Damascus [pseud.] *On Virtues and Vices* 1 (*PG* 95.93d). Palmer, Sherrard, and Ware, *Philokalia*, vol. 2, 338 [translation modified].

8. See J. S. Beck, *Cognitive Therapy for Challenging Problems*, 15.

9. Maximus the Confessor *Centuries on Love* 2.17 (*PG* 90.989b).

10. See Evagrius *On Diverse Evil Thoughts* (*PG* 79.1201c and *PG* 79.1213d).

11. William Backus, *The Hidden Rift with God* (Minneapolis, MN: Bethany House Publishers, 1990), 86–87.

12. See Evagrius *On the Eight Thoughts* (*PG* 40.1272b–1272c).

13. Mutual exclusivity in set theory designates the irreducible distinctness of each member of the set without denying the inter-relatedness between the members in the set.

14. Anastasius of Sinai *Questions and Answers* (*PG* 89.400a).

15. Mt 7:14.

16. Basil of Caesarea *On the Seventh Psalm* 7 (*PG* 29b.244d). Cf. Dorotheos of Gaza *Discourses* 10.106 (*SC* 92.340).

17. See G. Manzaridis, "Aristotelikē ēthikē kai christianismos" [Aristotelian ethics and Christianity], reprint from *Aristotelika* (Thessaloniki, Greece: Panepistēmio Thessalonikēs 1980), 166–167; A. Keselopoulos, *Pathē kai aretes*, 116; cf. Gregory of Nyssa *Commentary on the Song of Songs* 9 (*PG* 44.972a) and *On Virginity* 8 (*PG* 46.356bc).

18. Dorotheos of Gaza *Discourses* 10.106 (*SC* 92.342). See also Aristotle *Nicomachean Ethics* 1107ab (*LCL* 73.98).

19. See Maximus the Confessor *To Thalassius* 64 (*PG* 90.709a).

20. Clement of Alexandria *Exhortation to Heathen* 2 (*PG* 8.93b) and 10 (*PG* 8.240b).

21. Gregory of Nyssa *On Virginity* 8 (*PG* 46.353c).

22. See Gregory of Nazianzus *Orations* 27.10 (*PG* 36.24c).

23. Theodore Balsamon *Council of Ancyra* 24 (*PG* 137.1190d–1192a), *Council of Carthage* 86 (*PG* 138.301c). Cf. canons 24 and 91, Agapios Monachos, ed., *Pēdalion*, 312, 413–414. Cf. also canons 24 and 93, G. Ralli and M. Polti, eds., *Syntagma tōn theiōn kai hierōn kanonōn*, vol. 3, (Athens: G Chartophylakos, 1853) 66–68, 413–414. See also John Chrysostom *Commentary on Colossians* 8.5 (*PG* 62.358) and Augustine *On Christian Doctrine* 2.23.36 (*PL* 34.53) and 2.29.45 (*PL* 34.56).

24. Maximus the Confessor *Letter to Constantine* 5 (*PG* 91.421c).

25. John of Damascus [pseud.] *On the Virtues and the Vices* (*PG* 95.92b). See also Plato *Republic* 4.12–17 (*LCL* 237.435–443).

26. Hesychius the Presbyter *On Watchfulness and Holiness* 2.24 (*PG* 93.1520b).

27. Maximus the Confessor *Commentary on the Divine Names* 4 (*PG* 4.281b).

28. Jerome *Against John of Jerusalem* 1.1 (*PL* 23.371a).

29. Augustine *Tractates on John* 77.4 (*PL* 35.1834).

30. See ibid. 90.3 (*PL* 35.1859).

31. See Kallistos Aggelikoudis *Chapters on Prayer* 62 (*HPE* 21a.177).

32. For example, Mt 9:4; 12:25; Lk 5:22, 6:8 in which Christ perceived the thoughts [enthymēseis, dialogismous, dianoēmata] of those around him.

33. See Elder Païsios the Hagiorite, Logoi, vol. 3, 84.

34. See Kallistos Aggelikoudis Chapters on Prayer 62 (HPE 21a.183). The author, of course, wrote before the age of Louis Braille.

35. See John of Damascus Exact Exposition on the Orthodox Faith 3.21 (PG 94.1084b,1085a).

36. Gregory the Wonderworker Interpretation of Ecclesiastes 1.10 (PG 10.1013c).

37. Alford and Beck, Integrative Power, 16.

38. Harry Stack Sullivan, The Fusion of Psychiatry and Social Science (New York: W. W. Norton & Company, 1964), 20. Sullivan (1892-1949) was an American psychiatrist and theorist whose works Beck respects. See Weishaar, Aaron T. Beck, 21.

39. See Beck et al., Cognitive Therapy of Substance Abuse, 115.

40. Ernest Becker, The Revolution in Psychiatry: The New Understanding of Man (New York: The Free Press of Glencoe, 1964), 209.

41. See J. S. Beck, Cognitive Therapy, 224-225.

42. See A. T. Beck, Prisoners of Hate, 22-23.

43. See Beck et al., Cognitive Therapy of Depression, 153-154.

44. See Beck and Emery with Greenberg, Anxiety Disorders and Phobias, 33, 67-68, 151.

45. See A. T. Beck, Prisoners of Hate, 44, 74, 80, 93, 99; David Burns, Feeling Good, 142.

46. See Burns, Feeling Good, 142-143.

47. See Beck et al., Cognitive Therapy of Substance Abuse, 115.

48. See Beck et al., Cognitive Therapy of Personality Disorders, 47-51; J. S. Beck, Cognitive Therapy, 168.

49. See Beck et al., Cognitive Therapy of Personality Disorders, 21, 121-123, 131, 133, 268, 275.

50. See Beck et al., Cognitive Therapy of Substance Abuse, 38, 45-46.

51. John Climacus Ladder 14.16 (PG 88.865d). Holy Transfiguration Monastery, 100.

52. Ibid. 14.17 (PG 88.868c). Holy Transfiguration Monastery, 101.

53. See ibid. 14.4 (PG 88.864d).

54. John Chrysostom Homily on Lazarus 6.9 (PG 48.1041-1042).

55. Dorotheos of Gaza Discourses 6.70 (SC 92.270).

56. A. T. Beck, Cognitive Therapy and Emotional Disorders, 91-92.

57. Metropolitan John [Zizioulas], "Nosos kai therapeia stēn orthodoxē theologia," 70-71.

58. Basil of Caesarea Shorter Rules 54 (PG 31.1120a).

59. See Basil of Caesarea On Teaching and Admonition 2.5 (PG 32.1141c).

60. Maximus the Confessor Centuries on Love 2.59 (PG 90.1004b), 3.8 (PG 90.1020b), 3.57 (PG 90.1033d). Cf. also Thalassius Centuries on Love and Self-control 3.86 (PG 91.1456d) and John of Damascus On the Eight Spirits of Wickedness (PG 95.89a).

61. Theodore of Edessa A Century of Spiritual Texts 93 (PHIL 1.322). Palmer, Sherrard, and Ware, Philokalia, vol. 2, 35. See also Maximus the Confessor Centuries on Love 2.8 (PG 90.958c).

62. Maximus the Confessor *Various Texts on Theology* 1.53 (PG 90.1200a). Palmer, Sherrard, and Ware, *Philokalia*, vol. 2, 175.

63. See ibid.

64. Peter of Damascus, *Book One Introduction* (PHIL 3.9). Palmer, Sherrard, and Ware, *Philokalia*, vol. 3, 79.

65. See Elder Païsios the Hagiorite, *Logoi*, vol. 3, 51.

66. See Theophan the Recluse, as quoted in *The Art of Prayer: An Orthodox Anthology* compiled by Igumen Chariton of Valamo, trans. E. Kadloubovky and E. M. Palmer (London: Faber & Faber, 1966), 225.

67. See Elder Païsios the Hagiorite, *Logoi*, vol. 3, 24.

68. See ibid., 53–54.

69. See Maximus the Confessor *Centuries on Love* 2.60 (PG 90.1004c).

70. Gregory of Sinai *Chapters* 106 (PG 150.1276b). Palmer, Sherrard, and Ware, *Philokalia*, vol. 4, 235.

71. See Nikitas Stithatos *Practical Chapters* 1.28 (PG 120.804d).

72. See Elder Païsios the Hagiorite, *Logoi*, vol. 1, 76.

73. John of Damascus *On the Eight Spirits of Wickedness* (PG 95.88c).

74. Hesychius the Presbyter *On Watchfulness and Virtue* 2.100 (PG 93.1541d). Palmer, Sherrard, and Ware, *Philokalia*, vol. 1, 198 [translation modified].

75. Maximus the Confessor *Centuries on Love* 2.59 (PG 90.1004b); see also Thalassius *Centuries on Love and Abstinence* 3.87 (PG 91.1456d).

76. Gregory of Sinai *Chapters* 126 (PG 150.1289c).

77. Maximus the Confessor *Letter to John Koubikoularius* 3 (PG 91.408d–409a); See also *Diverse Theological Chapters* 1.46 (PG 90.1196b).

78. Theodore of Edessa *A Century of Spiritual Texts* 65 (PHIL 1.315). See Maximus the Confessor *Centuries on Love* 2.8 (PG 90.985c).

79. Abba Isaiah, passage cited by John of Damascus in his *Sacred Parallels* Φ.13 (PG 96.420d). Cf. also *Fragments* (PG 40.1213b).

80. John Chrysostom *On Saul and David* 3.4 (PG 54.700).

81. Peter of Damascus *Book One Introduction* (PHIL 3.9). Palmer, Sherrard, and Ware, *Philokalia*, vol. 3, 79.

82. Maximus the Confessor *Diverse Theological Chapters* 1.31 (PG 90.1192b).

83. Abba Isaiah, passage cited by John of Damascus in his *Sacred Parallels* Φ.13 (PG 96.420d–421a). Cf. also *Fragments* (PG 40.1213b).

84. Mt 13:32.

85. See Maximus the Confessor *Letter to John Koubikoularius* 3 (PG 91.409a); See also his *Various Texts on Theology* 1.46 (PG 90.1196b).

86. Maximus the Confessor *To Thalassius, Introduction* (PG 90.260d). See also his *Various Texts on Theology* 1.50 (PG 90.1197b).

87. Maximus the Confessor *Centuries on Love* 3.8 (PG 90.1020b).

88. Nikitas Stithatos *Practical Chapters* 1.28 (PG 120.864d).

89. Maximus the Confessor *Various Texts on Theology* 1.32 (PG 90.1192c). Palmer, Sherrard, and Ware, *Philokalia*, vol. 2, 171. See also *Letter to John Koubikoularius* 2 (PG 91.397b).

90. Elder Païsios the Hagiorite, *Epistoles*, 130.

91. Theodore of Edessa *A Century of Spiritual Texts* 93 (PHIL 1.321). See also Maximus the Confessor *Centuries on Love* 2.8 (PG 90.958c) and 3.57 (PG 90.1033d).

92. Maximus the Confessor *Various Texts on Theology* 1.33 (PG 90.1192c). Palmer, Sherrard, and Ware, *Philokalia*, vol. 2, 172.

93. Ibid. 1.51 (PG 90.1197c). Palmer, Sherrard, and Ware, *Philokalia*, vol. 2, 175.

94. See Harry Emerson Fosdick, *On Being a Real Person* (New York: Harper & Brothers, 1943), 80.

95. See Karen Horney, *Neurosis and Human Growth* (New York: W. W. Norton & Company, 1950), 48.

96. See A. T. Beck, *Prisoners of Hate*, 5.

97. See Beck and Emery with Greenberg, *Anxiety Disorders and Phobias*, 39.

98. Donald H. Meichenbaum, "Changing Conceptions of Cognitive Behavior Modification: Retrospect and Prospect," *Journal of Consulting and Clinical Psychology* 61, no. 2 (1993): 203.

99. See Beck and Emery with Greenberg, *Anxiety Disorders and Phobias*, 303.

100. Alford and Beck, *Integrative Power*, 24.

101. See A. T. Beck, *Cognitive Therapy and Emotional Disorders*, 91–92.

102. See Beck et al., *Cognitive Therapy of Personality Disorders*, 167.

103. See ibid., 258. See the case study of Misty, ibid., 253.

104. See J. S. Beck, *Cognitive Therapy*, 108–109; A. T. Beck, *Cognitive Therapy and Emotional Disorders*, 92.

105. See Beck and Emery with Greenberg, *Anxiety Disorders and Phobias*, 29.

106. See Plato *Republic* 7.514–517b (LCL 276.119–129).

107. A. T. Beck, *Prisoners of Hate*, 6.

108. See ibid., 27.

109. See A. T. Beck, *Love is Never Enough*, 183, 205.

110. See ibid., 76.

111. See A. T. Beck, *Prisoners of Hate*, 107.

112. See ibid., 128.

113. Horney, *Neurosis and Human Growth*, 291–292.

114. Archimandrite Sophrony [Sakharov], *We Shall See Him as He is*, trans. Rosemary Edmonds (Essex, UK: Stavropegic Monastery of St. John the Baptist, 1988), 145.

115. See J. S. Beck, *Cognitive Therapy*, 7.

116. See Beck et al., *Cognitive Therapy of Personality Disorders*, 88.

117. See John the Faster *Service and Rubrics for Confessants* (PG 88.1892ab).

118. See Basil of Caesarea *Letter to Athanasius* 1.24 (PG 32.297b).

119. See Ignatius of Antioch *Letter to the Antiochians* (PG 5.905b).

120. See Polycarp *Epistle to the Philippians* (PG 5.1009a).

121. *Council of Gangra* 15 (PG 137.1257d-1260a). Cf. also Agapios Monachos, ed., *Pēdalion*, 327 as well as G. Ralli and M. Polti, eds., *Syntagma*, vol. 3, 110-112.

122. See John Chrysostom *Commentary on First Timothy* 9.2 (PG 62.547).

123. See John Chrysostom *Commentary on Ephesians* 21.4 (PG 62.154).

124. See Gregory of Nazianzus *Orations* 7.18 (PG 35.777a).

125. See John Chrysostom *Commentary on First Timothy* 9.2 (PG 62.547-548).

126. See Irenaeus of Lyons *Against All Heresies* 2.22.4 (PG 7.784ab).

127. See John Chrysostom *Commentary on Romans* 27.1 (PG 60.643). See also his *Commentary on Philippians* 3.4 (PG 62.204).

128. See Cyprian of Carthage *On Works and Alms* 18 (PL 4.616).

129. Jas 6:16.

130. Jerome *Letter to Gaudentius* 4.128.1 (PL 22.1096).

131. Jerome *Letter to Laetus* 3.107.4 (PL 22.871).

132. Gregory of Nyssa *Against Eunomius* 1 (PG 45.301c): "*Oudeis gar outō pais tēn dianoian hōs epi tēs noeras te kai asōmatou physeōs, tēn kata topon diaphoran ennoein.*" See also ibid. 6 (PG 45.736b): "*Tis outō pais tēn dianoian hōs oiesthai to theion ek prosthēkēs epi to teleion pheresthai?*"

133. Ibid. 6 (PG 45.745d): "*Tauton epathe tois nēpiois tōn paidōn ois to ateles kai aōron tēs dianoias kai to tōn aisthētēriōn agymnaston ouk akribē didōsi tōn phainomenōn tēn katanoēsin.*"

134. Neilus the Ascetic *Ascetic Discourse* 52 (PG 79.784b-c).

135. John Chrysostom *Commentary on John* 3.1 (PG 59.37).

136. John Chrysostom *Commentary on Second Thessalonians* 1.1 (PG 62.470).

137. Gregory the Great *Letter to Theoctistus the Patrician* 7.27 (PL 77.881).

138. Dorotheos of Gaza *Discourses* 6.73 (SC 92.276). Cf. Basil of Caesarea *On Proverbs* 12.9 (PG 31.404ab).

139. John Chrysostom *Commentary on Titus* 2.1 (PG 62.672).

140. John Chrysostom *Commentary on Ephesians* 20.1 (PG 62.135-136).

141. John Chrysostom *Commentary on Matthew* 59.7 (PG 58.583-584).

142. John Chrysostom *Commentary on John* 3.1 (PG 59.37).

143. Jerome *Letter to Theophilus* 3.82.3 (PL 22.757). Cf. Cicero *De Officiis* 2.23.4 (LCL 30.190).

144. Cyprian of Carthage *On the Lapsed* (PL 4.484-486).

145. For example, canon nineteen of St. John the Faster does not permit a child who has been sodomized to become a priest. See PG 88.1933d; cf. Agapios Monachos, ed., *Pēdalion*, 571 as well as G. Ralli and M. Polti, eds., *Syntagma tōn theiōn kai hierōn kanonōn*, vol. 4 (Athens: G. Chartophylakos, 1854), 442.

146. Elder Païsios the Hagiorite, *Logoi: oikogeneiakē zōē* [Discourses: family life], vol. 4 (Souroti-Thessaloniki, Greece: Hieron Hēsychastērion Evangelistēs Iōannēs ho Theologos, 2002), 9.

147. Jerome *Letter to Laetus* 107 (PL 22.872).

148. See John Chrysostom *Commentary on Matthew* 81.5 (PG 58.738).

149. Neilus the Ascetic *Ascetic Discourse* 63 (PG 79.796b).

150.   See J. S. Beck, *Cognitive Therapy for Challenging Problems*, 21; A. T. Beck, *Prisoners of Hate*, 134; Backus, *Hidden Rift with God*, 112–113.

151.   See Beck et al., *Cognitive Therapy of Personality Disorders*, 48.

152.   J. S. Beck, *Cognitive Therapy*, 141.

153.   Tian Dayton, *Trauma and Addiction: Ending the Cycle of Pain Through Emotional Literacy* (Dearfield Beach, FL: Health Communications, 2000), 75. See also Sigmund Freud, *Introductory Lectures on Psychoanalysis*, trans. J. Strachey (New York: Penguin Books, 1982), 496.

154.   Sullivan, *Fusion of Psychiatry and Social Science*, 119.

155.   See Dayton, *Trauma and Addiction*, 102; J. S. Beck, *Cognitive Therapy for Challenging Problems*, 22.

156.   Beck et al., *Cognitive Therapy of Personality Disorders*, 88.

157.   See Beck et al., *Cognitive Therapy of Substance Abuse*, 188–189.

158.   See Beck et al., *Cognitive Therapy of Personality Disorders*, 117.

159.   See ibid., 323–324.

160.   Sullivan, *Fusion of Psychiatry and Social Science*, 266.

161.   See Beck et al., *Cognitive Therapy of Personality Disorders*, 88. In classical therapeutic role-play, a traumatic scene is re-enacted with the patient taking the role of parent and the therapist taking the role of the patient as child.

162.   See ibid., 89 and Dayton, *Trauma and Addiction*, 191.

163.   See Dayton, *Trauma and Addiction*, 113.

164.   See Beck et al., *Cognitive Therapy of Personality Disorders*, 201–202.

165.   However, Phillip Kendall does suggest that cognitive principles could be used for the purpose of parental training. See Phillip Kendall and Melissa Warman, "Emotional Disorders in Youth," in Salkovskis, ed., *Frontiers of Cognitive Therapy*, 525.

166.   Eph 4:13–14.

Chapter Five

1.   See Alford and Beck, *Integrative Power*, 66, 68.

2.   See Anastasius of Sinai *Discourses* 3 (PG 89.1165d): "*Kata gar to noeron, kai logistikon, hētoi bouleutikon kai thelētikon, kai monon tōn alogōn diapherei ho anthrōpos· schedon en pasi tois loipois, kai malista tois tou sōmatos koinōnikos kai homoios kai homousios tōn alogōn katheseke· kai gar ek tēs autēs gēs onta, hothen kai to hēmeteron sōma gegone kai thymon echousi, kai kinēsin echousin.*" Blessed Augustine also notes, "*Animal est enim, sed rationale.*" *On the Soul and its Origin* 4.6 (PL 33.727). Similarly in *Against Celsus* 3.69 (PG 11.1012b), Origen refers to man as a *logiko zōo*, a phrase also used in the liturgical services of the Church. See Sunday evening vespers verses in tone one. *Paraklētikē*, 18.

3.   Rom 7:22–23.

4.   For example, in the vespers for St. Basileus (26 Apr.), the hymnographer writes, "*Tōn pathōn ebasileusas, nomōi theiōi, megiste kratynomenos kai logismon autokratora.*" (MEN 4.105). See similar examples in liturgical services for the Prophet Isaiah (MEN 5.37) and the Martyr Mamas (MEN 9.17).

5. For example, St. Ambrose of Milan writes, "Where were your thoughts and advice with the strength of which you might have protected yourself from unrighteousness and warded off transgression?" *Letter to Horontianum* 2.70.5 (PL 16.1288c).

6. See Nicodemos the Hagiorite, *Aoratos polemos*, 43.

7. Maximus the Confessor *Disputation with Pyrrhus* (PG 91.293c).

8. John of Damascus *Exact Exposition of the Orthodox Faith* 2.22 (PG 94.945b).

9. See Maximus the Confessor *Letter to Marinus* 8 (PG 91.21a). For the Stoic background on first movements, see Richard Sorabji, *Emotion and Peace of Mind: From Stoic Agitation to Christian Temptation* (London: Oxford University Press, 2000).

10. See Maximus the Confessor *On Various Difficult Passages* (PG 91.1109b).

11. E.g., Maximus the Confessor *Disputaton with Pyrrhus* (PG 91.237-354) and Photius *Mystagogia of the Holy Spirit* (PG 102.279-392).

12. Origen *Commentary on Genesis* 3 (PG 12.89a).

13. Gregory of Nyssa *Against Eunomius* 3.2 (PG 45.576c).

14. Thalassius *Centuries on Love* 1.20 (PG 91.1429b). Palmer, Sherrard, and Ware, *Philokalia*, vol. 2, 308 [translation slightly modified].

15. Maximus the Confessor *Various Texts on Theology* 4.73 (PG 90.1336d). Palmer, Sherrard, and Ware, *Philokalia*, vol. 2, 254 [translation slightly modified].

16. Ambrose of Milan *Letter to Simplicianus* 37.31 (PL 16.1092a).

17. See Anastasius of Sinai *Questions and Answers* 8 (PG 89.408b).

18. Gregory of Nyssa *On the Soul and the Resurrection* (PG 46.65b).

19. Anastasius of Sinai *Questions and Answers* 8 (PG 89.408b).

20. See Gregory of Nyssa *On the Soul and the Resurrection* (PG 46.65c-68a).

21. Dorotheos of Gaza *Discourses* 17.176 (SC 92.480). See also Evagrius *Practicos* 1.58 (PG 40.1233-1236) and Maximus the Confessor *To Thalassius* 1 (PG 90.269b-c).

22. See Philotheus of Sinai *Forty Texts on Watchfulness* 18 (PHIL 2.280).

23. Ibid. 16 (PHIL 2.279). Palmer, Sherrard, and Ware, *Philokalia*, vol. 3, 22 [translation slightly modified].

24. See John Chrysostom *Commentary on Galatians* 1.7 (PG 61.622).

25. See Nicodemos Hagioritis, *Aoratos polemos*, 33.

26. In a fallen state, the soul's faculties can be considered dysfunctional when they are under the influence of harmful thoughts: distracting thoughts befog the reasoning faculty in its ability to reason; irritating thoughts disturb the faculty for aggression and incite it to violence; and sensual thoughts stimulate the desiring faculty to satisfy its bestial appetites. See Gregory of Sinai *Chapters* 63 (PG 150.1256d); Maximus the Confessor *Centuries on Love* 3.20 (PG 90.1021c).

27. The temptation of Christ in the wilderness provides a model for how the ascetic life for the sake of union with God can heal the tripartite soul: "By fasting, he healed the desiring aspect; by vigil and hesychastic prayer, he healed the rational aspect, and by rebuttal the aggressive aspect." Kallistos Kataphygiotou *On Union with God* 36 (PG 147.873c).

28. See Symeon the New Theologian *Catechetical Discourses* 9.2 (SC 104.106). See also Maximus the Confessor *Centuries on Love* 3.20 (PG 90.1021c).

29. Elder Païsios the Hagiorite, *Logoi*, vol. 3, 62.

30. Barsanuphius, *Keimena diakritika kai hēsychastika* [Texts on discernment and stillness], vol. 3 (Kareas, Greece: Etoimasia, 1997), no. 692, 306–308.

31. Neilus the Ascetic *Letter to Prisko* 3.294 (PG 79.529c). NB how much this advice resembles the counsel found in the Christian redaction of *The Encheiridion* that is spuriously attributed to the same author.

32. See John Climacus *Ladder* 15.49 (PG 88.901b).

33. Gn 3:9.

34. See Elder Païsios the Hagiorite, *Logoi*, vol. 3, 40.

35. John Moschus *Spiritual Meadow* 39 (PG 87c.2892ac). A similar example is related later in the same work. A monk suffering from a snake-bite was tempted by fleshly desires while being treated by a pious woman. The woman told him, "Far be it, Father, you have Christ. Think about the sorrow and regret you will later feel when you return to your cell. Think about the sighs you will utter and the tears you will shed. After hearing such, the warfare of the flesh ceased." John Moschus *Spiritual Meadow* 204 (PG 87c.3093d–3096a). The Christian redactor of the *Encheiridion of Epictetus* provides a rationale for this practice in 53 (PG 79.1305c) as does St. Neilus the Ascetic in his undisputed work, *Ascetic Discourse* 40 (PG 79.769b).

36. Nikitas Stithatos *Life of Saint Symeon* 50–51 (HPE 19.115–117). Cf. *Orientalia Christiana* 12, no. 45, (1928).

37. See John Cassian *Conferences* 3.24.3 (PL 49.1287b).

38. See John Climacus *Ladder* 20.5 (PG 88.940d).

39. Kallistos Tilikoudis *On the Practice of Stillness* (PG 147.817b).

40. Diadochos of Photiki *On Spiritual Knowledge* 26 (SC 5bis.97–98). Palmer, Sherrard, and Ware, *Philokalia*, vol. 1, 259–260. See also John Climacus *Ladder* 20.5 (PG 88.940d).

41. John Cassian *Conferences* 3.24.3 (PL 49.1288a). See also John Climacus *Ladder* 20.5 (PG 88.940d).

42. See Hesychius the Presbyter *On Watchfulness and Holiness* 2.19 (PG 93.1517b).

43. John Cassian *Conferences* 1.1.21 (PL 49.518b–519a). Symeon the New Theologian offers the same advice for judging the thoughts. See his *Catechetical Discourses* 3.9 (SC 96.302). See also Gregory of Sinai *On Deception* (PG 150.1341bc).

44. See Macarius of Egypt [pseud.] *On Prayer* 4 (PG 3.856c).

45. See Maximus the Confessor *Centuries on Love* 3.20 (PG 90.1021c).

46. See ibid. 2.56 (PG 90.1001d).

47. See Neilus the Ascetic *Ascetic Discourse* 39 (PG 79.768d).

48. See Evagrius *On Various Evil Thoughts* 20 (PG 79.1221d–1224ab).

49. See John Cassian *Conferences* 1.1.20 (PL 49.510b–518a); Dorotheos of Gaza *Discourses* 7.85 (SC 92.298–299).

50. Lk 10:42.

51. See Mark the Ascetic *On Those Who Think They Are Made Righteous by Works* 2.83 (PG 65.941d). See also Nicodemos the Hagiorite, *Aoratos polemos*, 38–39.

52. Isaac the Syrian, *Ta askētika*, hom. 62, 251. Translated by Holy Transfiguration Monastery as *The Ascetical Homilies of Saint Isaac the Syrian* (Boston, MA: Holy Transfigura-

tion Monastery 1984), hom. 52, 254. NB the Greek Theotokis text and the English Holy Transfiguration Monastery translation number the homilies differently. For a table of homily equivalences, see introduction to *Ascetical Homilies*, cxiii–cxv.

53. See ibid., hom. 18, 65.
54. See ibid., hom. 65, 261.
55. See ibid., hom. 19, 71–72.
56. Ibid. hom. 1, 2–3.
57. Ibid., hom. 62, 253. *Ascetical Homilies*, hom. 52, 256 [translation modified].
58. See Ambrose of Milan *On Repentance* 2.11.105 (*PL* 16.524a).
59. Ilias the Presbyter *Gnomic Anthology* 71 (*PG* 127.1161b). Palmer, Sherrard, and Ware, *Philokalia*, vol. 3, 56 [translation slightly modified].
60. See John Cassian *Conferences* 1.2.5 (*PL* 49.673c–674b). Cf. Mt 8:5–13 and Lk 7:2–10.
61. See Maximus the Confessor *Other Chapters* 3.34 (*PG* 90.1273d).
62. See Basil of Caesarea *Letter to Nektarius* 1.5.2 (*PG* 32.240b).
63. See Neilus the Ascetic *Letter to Vindike Martyrio* 2.282 (*PG* 79.341a).
64. See Maximus the Confessor *Other Chapters* 2.74 (*PG* 90.1248c).
65. See Maximus the Confessor *Mystagogy* 5 (*PG* 91.681c). See also ibid. 5 (*PG* 91.673b).
66. Isaac the Syrian, *Ta askētika*, hom. 72, 254. *Ascetical Homilies* hom. 52, 257
67. See 1 Cor 3:19 and Rom 8:7.
68. See Elder Païsios the Hagiorite, *Logoi*, vol. 1, 233.
69. See Elder Païsios the Hagiorite, *Epistoles*, 218.
70. See Neilus the Ascetic *Letter to Monk Theodorus* 2.65 (*PG* 79.229b).
71. Isaac the Syrian, *Ta askētika*, hom. 73, 256–257.
72. Ibid., hom. 75, 260. *Ascetical Homilies*, hom. 52, 261.
73. Ibid., hom. 19, 69–70. *Ascetical Homilies*, hom. 72, 353.
74. Ibid., hom. 72, 252–253. *Ascetical Homilies*, hom. 52, 255–256.
75. See ibid., hom. 72, 251.
76. See ibid., hom. 18, 66.
77. Ibid., hom. 72, 252.
78. See Bandura, *Social Learning Theory*, 17–18, 180 (see chap. 1, n. 77).
79. A. T. Beck, *Cognitive Therapy and Emotional Disorders*, 12, 216.
80. Alford and Beck, *Integrative Power*, 66.
81. See example in J. S. Beck, *Cognitive Therapy for Challenging Problems*, 237–239.
82. See Alford and Beck, *Integrative Power*, 67–69.
83. See Sullivan, *Fusion of Psychiatry and Social Science*, 187 (see chap. 4, n. 38).
84. See Becker, *Revolution in Psychiatry*, 206 (see chap. 4, n. 40).
85. See A. T. Beck, *Cognitive Therapy and Emotional Disorders*, 213–215.
86. See J. S. Beck, *Cognitive Therapy*, 8. Beck developed this emphasis under the influence of Carl Roger's client-centered therapy and Albert Ellis's use of Socratic questioning. See Aaron Beck, "Cognitive Therapy as the Integrative Therapy: Comments on Alford and Norcross," *Journal of Psychotherapy Integration* 1 (1991): 191–198.

87. See ibid., 77.
88. Beck et al., *Cognitive Therapy of Substance Abuse*, 103 (italics in the original).
89. See Dobson, ed., *Handbook of Cognitive-Behavioral Therapies*, 363; J. Overholser, "Elements of the Socratic Method," *Therapy* 30 (1993): 67–85. For example, see Socrates' dialogue with the uneducated boy in Plato *Meno* 82b.10–85b.5 (*LCL* 201.304–318).
90. J. S. Beck, *Cognitive Therapy*, 109, fig. 8.1.
91. Beck and Emery with Greenberg, *Anxiety Disorders and Phobias*, 197–198.
92. See ibid., 201.
93. A. T. Beck, *Love is Never Enough*, 343.
94. Beck et al., *Cognitive Therapy of Substance Abuse*, 179.
95. See Sigmund Freud, *Introductory Lectures on Psychoanalysis*, 504.
96. See Beck and Emery with Greenberg, *Anxiety Disorders and Phobias*, 168–169.
97. See Lk 18:18.
98. See 1 Tm 2:7; 2 Tm 1:11.
99. For example, in *Sayings of the Fathers* Π.149 (PG 65.360a), Abba Poimen instructs "*Hē akēdia stēkei epi pasēi archēi kai ouk esti cheiron autēs pathos· all' ean gnōrisē autēn ho anthrōpos, öti autē estin, anapauetai.*"
100. John Climacus *To the Shepherd* 5 (PG 88.1177a).
101. See Neilus the Ascetic *Letter to Rodomnio the Presbyter* 3.214 (PG 79.481a).
102. See John Chrysostom *To Stageirus on Sorrow* (PG 47.492).
103. See Macarius of Egypt [pseud.] *Homilies* 21.4 (PG 34.657c).
104. See Abba Zosimas *Thoughts* 4 (PG 78.1685b).
105. See John Chrysostom *Commentary on Hebrew* 24.3 (PG 63.171–172).
106. See Nicodemos the Hagiorite, *Exomologētarion*, 181–182.
107. See Dorotheos of Gaza *Discourses* 14.151 (SC 92.426). See also Isaac the Syrian, *Ta askētika*, hom. 81, 382.
108. See Abba Zosimas *Thoughts* 4 (PG 78.1688b).
109. See ibid. 3.1 (PG 78.1684c).
110. See Elder Païsios the Hagiorite, *Logoi*, vol. 2, 73.
111. Elder Païsios the Hagiorite, *Logoi*, vol. 5, 113–114.
112. Dorotheos of Gaza *Discourses* 5.66 (SC 92.260). See also John Cassian *Conferences* 2.16.10 (PL 49.1025a).
113. See Barsanuphius, *Texts*, vol. 3, no. 694, 312. Cf. Phil 2:7.
114. See Origen *On the Psalms* 4.5 (PG 12.1141d).
115. See Didymus the Blind, *Psalmen-Kommentar* (*Tura-Papyrus*), ed. Michael Gronewald (Bonn: Michael Gronewald, 1969), part 3 (Psalms 29–34), 222.12–14.
116. Jerome *Commentary on Ezekiel* 6.18.1–2 (PL 25.168d–169a). See also *Letter to Salvina* 79.9 (PL 22.731).
117. See Jerome *Commentary on Matthew* 1.5.28–9 (PL 26.39d).
118. See Jerome *Commentary on Ephesians* 3.6.9 (PL 26.543a–d).
119. See Evagrius *On the Eight Spirits of Wickedness* 4 (PG 79.1148d). See also ibid. 6 (PG 79.1152b).

120. See Origen *On First Principles* 3.2.2 (PG 11.306c).

121. Augustine *On the Trinity* 12.12.18 (PL 42.1008).

122. Mark the Ascetic *On Divine Baptism* 4 (PG 65.992b).

123. See Mark the Ascetic *On the Spiritual Law* 1.142 (PG 65.921d–924a).

124. See Mark the Ascetic *On Those Who Think They Are Made Righteous by Works* 2.179 (PG 65.957c).

125. See Origen *On the Psalms* 54.5 (PG 12.1465b).

126. Origen *On First Principles* 3.1.4 (PG 11.252c–253a).

127. See Philotheus of Sinai *Forty Texts on Watchfulness* 36 (PHIL 2.285).

128. Mark the Ascetic *On Those Who Think They Are Made Righteous by Works* 2.211 (PG 65.964c). Palmer, Sherrard, and Ware, *Philokalia*, vol. 1, 145.

129. Theodore Balsamon *Council of Neocaesarea* 4 (PG 137.1204d). See also PG 137.1205a. Cf. Agapios Monachos, ed., *Pēdalion*, 316; Ralli, ed., *Syntagma*, vol. 3, 75–77.

130. See Augustine *On the Sermon on the Mount* 1.12.34 (PL 34.1246). See also Pope Gregory the Great *Pastoral Rule* 3.29 (PL 77.109a).

131. See Maximus the Confessor *Centuries on Love* 2.84 (PG 90.980b).

132. See Mark the Ascetic *On Those Who Think They Are Made Righteous by Works* 2.211 (PG 65.964c). See also Hesychius the Presbyter *On Watchfulness and Holiness* 1.46 (PG 93.1496c) and 2.71 (PG 93.1536a).

133. John Climacus *Ladder* 15 (PG 88.896d). Holy Transfiguration Monastery, 115–116.

134. See Philotheus of Sinai *Texts on Watchfulness* 35 (PHIL 2.285).

135. John of Damascus [pseud.] *On Virtues and Vices* (PG 95.93a). Palmer, Sherrard, and Ware, *Philokalia*, vol. 2, 338.

136. See Maximus the Confessor *Other Chapters* 2.27 (PG 90.1456b). See also Ilias the Presbyter *Gnomic Anthology* 123 (PG 127.1172d).

137. John Climacus *Ladder* 15 (PG 88.896d). Holy Transfiguration Monastery, 116.

138. See John of Damascus [pseud.] *On Virtues and Vices* (PG 95.93b). Palmer, Sherrard, and Ware, *Philokalia*, vol. 2, 338 [translation slightly modified].

139. See Maximus the Confessor *Other Chapters* 2.27 (PG 90.1456b).

140. Pope Gregory the Great *Pastoral Rule* 3.29 (PL 77.109a).

141. See Mark the Ascetic *On Those Who Think They Are Made Righteous by Works* 2.211 (PG 65.964c).

142. See John of Damascus [pseud.] *On Virtues and Vices* (PG 95.93b). See also John Climacus *Ladder* 15 (PG 88.897a) and Philotheus of Sinai *Texts on Watchfulness* 35 (PHIL 2.285).

143. John Climacus *Ladder* 15 (PG 88.896d). Holy Transfiguration Monastery, 116. Cf. John of Damascus [pseud.] *On Virtues and Vices* (PG 95.93a) and Philotheus of Sinai *Texts on Watchfulness* 35 (PHIL 2.285).

144. See John of Damascus [pseud.] *On Virtues and Vices* (PG 95.93c). Cf. John Climacus *Ladder* 15 (PG 88.896d) and Philotheus of Sinai *Texts on Watchfulness* 35 (PHIL 2.285).

145. See Hesychius the Presbyter *On Watchfulness and Holiness* 1.46 (PG 93.1496c). See also Theodore of Edessa *Century of Spiritual Texts* 19 (PHIL 1.307) and John of Damascus [pseud.] *On Virtues and Vices* (PG 95.93c).

146. See Maximus the Confessor *Centuries on Love* 2.31 (*PG* 90.993c).

147. Pope Gregory the Great *Pastoral Rule* 3.29 (*PL* 77.109a).

148. See Nicodemos the Hagiorite, *Exomologētarion*, 49–50.

149. See Ilias the Presbyter *Gnomic Anthology* 128 (*PG* 127.1173b).

150. Tito Colliander, *The Way of the Ascetics* (Crestwood, NY: Saint Vladimir's Press, 1960), 50.

151. See Theodore Balsamon *Council of Neocaesarea* 4 (*PG* 137.1204d). Cf. Agapios Monachos, ed., *Pēdalion*, 316; Ralli and Potli, eds., *Syntagma*, vol. 3, 75–77.

152. See John Climacus *Ladder* 15 (*PG* 88.897b). See also Philotheus of Sinai *Forty Texts on Watchfulness* 35 (*PHIL* 2.285).

153. See Symeon the New Theologian *Catechetical Discourses* 3.8 (*SC* 96.300–302).

154. John of Damascus [pseud.] *On Virtues and Vices* (*PG* 95.93c). See also John Climacus *Ladder* 15 (*PG* 88.897b); Maximus the Confessor *Other Chapters* 2.27 (*PG* 90.1456b); and Hesychius the Presbyter *On Watchfulness and Holiness* 1.46 (*PG* 93.1496c).

155. John Cassian *Institutes* 6.8 (*PL* 49.284a). Cf. Greek summary in *On the Eight Thoughts of Wickedness* (*PHIL* 1.64).

156. See Kallistos Aggelikoudis *Texts on Prayer and Attention* (*HPE* 21a.237).

157. Pope Gregory the Great *Pastoral Rule* 3.29 (*PL* 77.109bc).

158. See Alford and Beck, *Integrative Power*, 12.

159. See ibid., 16.

160. See J. S. Beck, *Cognitive Therapy*, 95.

161. See Beck and Emery with Greenberg, *Anxiety Disorders and Phobias*, 9, 10.

162. See J. S. Beck, *Cognitive Therapy*, 172. This initial incredulity with respect to one's own opinions is a skill that requires some effort. Elder Païsios the Hagiorite advocated a similar approach when he advised people to tell themselves, "This thought passed through my mind, but I don't know if it is correct." *Logoi*, vol. 5, 70.

163. See J. S. Beck, *Cognitive Therapy*, 148, 172.

164. A. T. Beck, *Cognitive Therapy and Emotional Disorders*, 243.

165. See J. S. Beck, *Cognitive Therapy for Challenging Problems*, 272.

166. See Beck and Emery with Greenberg, *Anxiety Disorders and Phobias*, 168.

167. Ibid., 70.

168. See ibid., 72.

169. See ibid., 70–71.

170. See A. T. Beck, *Love is Never Enough*, 30, 33, 47.

171. See ibid., 157.

172. See ibid., 104–105.

173. See ibid. 18, 102, 105, 199.

174. See Beck et al., *Cognitive Therapy of Substance Abuse*, 166.

175. See ibid. 35.

176. See ibid. 36.

177. See ibid. 45–46.

178. See ibid. 32, 52.

179. See Lk 10:42.
180. Elder Païsios the Hagiorite, *Logoi*, vol. 1, 227–228.
181. Jn 21:6–11.

Chapter Six

1. For example, Michael Mahoney remarks, "Psychotherapists are, after all, akin to modern confessors and clerics." In his *Constructive Psychotherapy: Theory and Practice* (New York: The Guilford Press, 2006), 206.

2. See Hieromonk Spyridon Servou, *Euchologion to mega* [Great prayerbook] (Athens: Astër, 1992) 677. Cf. Nicodemos the Hagiorite, *Exomologētarion*, 54.

3. See Socrates Scholastikos *Ecclesiastical History* 5.19 (PG 67.613a–620a); Hermias Sozomen *Ecclesiastical History* 7.16 (PG 67.1460ab).

4. See Theodore Balsamon *Council of Laodicea* 2 (PG 137.1345b). Cf. Agapios Monachos, ed., *Pēdalion*, 343; Ralli and Potli, eds., *Syntagma*, vol. 2, 173–174.

5. See Augustine *Sermon on Matthew* 56.8.12 (PL 38.382); idem, *Sermon on Luke* 98.7.7 (PL 38.595); Theodoret of Cyrus *Letter to Rufus* 170 (PG 83.1477c).

6. See Augustine *Sermon on Matthew* 68.2.3 (PL 38.434).

7. See Nicodemos the Hagiorite, *Exomologētarion*, 54.

8. Basil of Caesarea *Letter to Amphilochius on the Canons* 2.217.84 (PG 32.808c–809a).

9. See John the Faster *Service and Rubrics for Confessants* (PG 88.1889a–1901d).

10. John Chrysostom *On the Priesthood* 2.4 (PG 48.635).

11. Theodore Balsamon *Council in Trullo* 102 (PG 137.868c). Cf. Agapios Monachos, ed., *Pēdalion*, 255; Ralli and Potli, eds., *Syntagma*, vol. 2, 549. Gregory of Nazianzus expresses a similar principle in *Oration* 2.30 (PG 35.437c).

12. See John Chrysostom *On the Priesthood* 2.4 (PG 48.635).

13. See Academy of Cognitive Therapy, *Candidate Handbook* (Philadelphia: Academy of Cognitive Therapy, 2005), 8.

14. See ibid., 3–4.

15. J. S. Beck, *Cognitive Therapy* 45. See also ibid., 8,25.

16. See Alford and Beck, *Integrative Power*, 12; Beck et al., *Cognitive Therapy of Substance Abuse*, 97.

17. See J. S. Beck, *Cognitive Therapy*, 45–60; idem, *Cognitive Therapy for Challenging Problems*, 154–175.

18. Christine Padesky notes, "Cognitive therapy has been taught using principles of collaboration, guided discovery, conceptualization, and structure," which is to say, using the principles that define a typical therapeutic session. See Christine Padesky, "Developing Cognitive Therapist Competency: Teaching and Supervision Models," in Salkovskis, ed., *Frontiers of Cognitive Therapy*, 271. See also ibid., 289.

19. Ignatius of Antioch *Epistle to the Ephesians* 7 (PG 5.649c–652a).

20. Ibid. 6 (PG 5.737a).

21. See Jn 17:23.

22. Augustine *Sermon on John* 138.5.5 (PL 38.765).

23. Justin Martyr *Dialogue with Tryphon* 34 (PG 6.548b).

24. Heb 4:12.

25. See Ambrose of Milan *On the Decease of his Brother Satyrus* 2.41 (PL 16.1384a).

26. John Chrysostom *On the Priesthood* 4.2.3 (PG 48.665).

27. Rufinus *Apology to Saint Jerome* 1.1 (PL 21.541a).

28. John Chrysostom *Commentary on Ephesians* 21 (PG 62.152).

29. John Climacus *To the Shepherd* 7 (PG 88.1181d). Holy Transfiguration Monastery, 235-236.

30. See Antiochus the Monk *To Eustathius on Abbots* 111 (PG 89.1780ab).

31. See Archimandrite Sophrony [Sakharov], *On Prayer*, trans. Rosemary Edmonds (Essex, UK: Stavropegic Monastery of St. John the Baptist, 1993), 90, 108; Archimandrite Zacharias [Zacharou], *The Enlargement of the Heart* (South Canaan, PA: Mount Thabor Publishing, 2006), 169, 174. Cf. Col 4:6.

32. Ignatius of Antioch *Letter to Polycarp* [Syriac version] 1 (PG 5.720b-d).

33. See Archimandrite Zacharias [Zacharou], *Enlargement of Heart*, 164, 167; Archimandrite Sophrony [Sakharov], *On Prayer*, 88.

34. Rom 12:15.

35. See Archimandrite Sophrony [Sakharov], *On Prayer*, 113.

36. Metropolitan John [Zizioulas], "Nosos kai therapeia stēn orthodoxē theologia," 76-79.

37. Larchet, *Mental Disorders*, 70.

38. Blessed Augustine refers to "*medicinae confessionis*" in both *On Lying* 35 (PL 40.511) and *On the Psalms* 86.22 (PL 36.1093). Similarly, Gregory of Nazianzus writes "*Mega kakias pharmakon kai homologia kai phygē tou ptaismatos.*" See *Orations* 16.17 (PG 35.957c).

39. See Gregory of Nazianzus *Orations* 39.17 (PG 36.356a); John Chrysostom *Commentary on Matthew* 6.5 (PG 57.69); John Climacus *Ladder* 5 (PG 88.764b).

40. Archimandrite Sophrony [Sakharov], *On Prayer*, 88.

41. Heb 8:1.

42. 1 Pet 1:25.

43. J. S. Beck, *Cognitive Therapy for Challenging Problems*, 17.

44. Academy of Cognitive Therapy, *Candidate Handbook*, Appendix D, Case Write-up Directions, 52-53.

45. See J. S. Beck, *Cognitive Therapy*, 138-139.

46. See J. S. Beck, *Cognitive Therapy for Challenging Problems*, 23-24.

47. P. C. Kendal and K. M. Benis, "Thought and Action in Psychotherapy: The Cognitive-behavioral Approaches," in M. Hersen, A. E. Kazdin, and A. S. Bellack, eds., *The Clinical Psychology Handbook* (New York: Pergamon Press, 1983), 566.

48. See J. S. Beck, *Cognitive Therapy*, 13, 18.

49. See Beck et al., *Cognitive Therapy of Substance Abuse*, 81-83.

50. See J. S. Beck, *Cognitive Therapy*, 26.

51. See Aaron Beck, Tony Tang, and Robert DeRubeis, "Cognitive Therapy," in Dobson, ed., *Handbook of Cognitive-Behavioral Therapies*, 351,353.

52.   See Jeffrey Young and Aaron Beck, "Cognitive Therapy Scale Rating," (Philadelphia: Academy of Cognitive Therapy, 1980), 12–13.

53.   See Beck et al., *Cognitive Therapy of Depression*, 92.

54.   See Beck and Emery with Greenberg, *Anxiety Disorders and Phobias*, 199–200.

55.   See ibid., 260. John Cassian provides an impressive list of such behaviors that include having a blank glance, fidgeting, coughing, and twiddling one's fingers. See *Institutes* 12.27 (*PL* 49.468c–469b).

56.   Bruce Liese and Robert Franz, "Treating Substance Use Disorders with Cognitive Therapy: Lessons Learned and Implications for the Future," in Salkovskis, ed., *Frontiers of Cognitive Therapy*, 475.

57.   See Ellis and Harper, *Guide to Rational Living*, 129–130,137; Ellis and Dryden, "Rational-Emotive Behavior Therapy," in Dobson, ed., *Handbook of Cognitive-Behavioral Therapies*, 296.

58.   John Chrysostom *Commentary on First Corinthians* 33.5 (*PG* 61.283). Saint Syncletica puts a medical twist on this adage: "Hate the sickness [*noson*], not the person who is sick [*nosounta*]." *Sayings of the Fathers* Σ.13 (*PG* 65.425c). See also Isaac the Syrian, *Ta askētika*, hom. 60, 244.

59.   John Chrysostom *On the Hieromartyr Phokas* 2 (*PG* 50.701).

60.   Maximus the Confessor *Questions and Answers* (CCSG 10.9.8). See also his *Centuries on Love* 2.82 (*PG* 90.1009d) where he defines evil as the mistaken use of ideas followed by the misuse of the things themselves. Similarly, Methodius notes, "For a man is evil on account of his actions. For he is said to be evil, because he is the doer of evil. Now what a person does, is not the person himself, but his activity, and it is from his actions that he receives the title of evil." *On Free-will* (*PG* 18.256c).

61.   *On Man's Perfection in Righteousness* 2.4 (*PL* 44.294). See also idem, *On the Nature of the Good against the Manicheans* 36 (*PL* 42.562).

62.   Maximus the Confessor *To Thalassius* 43 (*PG* 90.413b).

63.   See Maximus the Confessor *Commentary on the Divine Names* 4 (*PG* 4.240a, 4.253d).

64.   Maximus the Confessor *To Thalassius Introduction* (*PG* 90.253b).

65.   See Antiochus the Monk *To Eustathius* 49 (*PG* 89.1585b).

66.   Macarius of Egypt [pseud.] *Homilies* 18.8 (*PG* 34.640c).

67.   See Fr. John Romanidis, *Rōmaioi ē rōmioi pateres tēs ekklēsias* [Roman and romioi fathers of the church] (Thessaloniki, Greece: Pournara 1984), 27.

68.   See Nicodemos the Hagiorite, *Exomologētarion*, 9, 54.

69.   See Augustine *Tractates on John* 55.2 (*PL* 35.1809).

70.   See Cyprian of Carthage *Letter to Antonianus* 10.16 (*PL* 3.807b). See also John Chrysostom *On the Priesthood* 2.4 (*PG* 48.635).

71.   See Gregory the Great *Pastoral Rule* 3.24 (*PL* 77.95b).

72.   See Elder Païsios the Hagiorite, *Epistoles*, 198.

73.   See Augustine *Against the Epistle of Manicheus* 3.3 (*PL* 42.475).

74.   John Chrysostom *Commentary on Colossians* 11 (*PG* 62.377).

75.   See Abba Macarius *Sayings of the Fathers* M.39 (*PG* 65.281a).

76.   See Augustine *On Christian Doctrine* 4.13.29 (*PL* 34.102).

77. See Abba Poimen who writes, "To teach your neighbor is similar to reproving him." *Sayings of the Fathers* Π.157 (*PG* 65.360d).

78. See Elder Païsios the Hagiorite, *Logoi*, vol. 2, 76, 79. Isaac the Syrian offers the same advice. See *Ta askētika*, hom. 23, 95.

79. Elder Païsios the Hagiorite, *Epistoles*, 157. See also his *Logoi*, vol. 2, 77.

80. John Chrysostom *Commentary on First Corinthians* 44.3 (*PG* 61.377).

81. See Dorotheos of Gaza *Letter to Overseers* 2.184 (*SC* 92.498).

82. John Chrysostom *Commentary on Colossians* 11.2 (*PG* 62.376–377). Cf. Col 4:6.

83. Nicodemos the Hagiorite, *Exomologētarion*, 59.

84. See John Chrysostom *An Exhortation to Theodore after his Fall* 1.4 (*PG* 47.282).

85. See John Chrysostom *Commentary on Ephesians* 14.1 (*PG* 62.101).

86. John Chrysostom *Commentary on Matthew* 21.1 (*PG* 57.295).

87. See Tan, "Cognitive Behavior Therapy," 106.

88. See Beck et al., *Cognitive Therapy of Depression*, 53; Beck et al., *Cognitive Therapy of Substance Abuse*, 63, 65.

89. See Beck et al., *Cognitive Therapy of Substance Abuse*, 58; J. S. Beck, *Cognitive Therapy*, 37–38.

90. Beck et al., *Cognitive Therapy of Personality Disorders*, 110. For an excellent discussion on the normalization of psychoses, see David Kingdon and Douglas Turkington, *Cognitive Therapy of Schizophrenia* (New York: The Guilford Press, 2008), 84–85, 87–91.

91. Beck et al., *Cognitive Therapy of Personality Disorders*, 81.

92. See J. S. Beck, *Cognitive Therapy*, 27. David Burns notes that research reveals a direct correlation between perceived therapeutic empathy and clinical improvement. See D. Burns and A. Auerbach, "Therapeutic Empathy in Cognitive Therapy: Does it really make a difference?" in Salkovskis, ed., *Frontiers of Cognitive Therapy*, 144.

93. See Beck and Emery with Greenberg, *Anxiety Disorders and Phobias*, 174.

94. See J. S. Beck, *Cognitive Therapy*, 27.

95. Beck et al., *Cognitive Therapy of Depression*, 53; J. S. Beck, *Cognitive Therapy*, 58–59; Alford and Beck, *Integrative Power*, 107.

96. See Beck and Emery with Greenberg, *Anxiety Disorders and Phobias*, 175.

97. See J. S. Beck, *Cognitive Therapy*, 5, 41

98. See Beck et al., *Cognitive Therapy of Depression*, 84.

99. See J. S. Beck, *Cognitive Therapy*, 41; idem, *Cognitive Therapy for Challenging Problems*, 68.

100. See J. S. Beck, *Cognitive Therapy for Challenging Problems*, 67. See also R. J. DeRubeis and M. Feeley, "Determinants of Change in Cognitive Therapy for Depression," *Cognitive Therapy and Research* 14 (1990): 469–482.

101. J. S. Beck, *Cognitive Therapy for Challenging Problems*, 118.

102. Ibid., 125.

103. A. T. Beck, *Prisoners of Hate*, 235.

104. See J. S. Beck, *Cognitive Therapy*, 94. D. Burns and A. Auerbach, "Therapeutic Empathy in Cognitive Therapy," in Salkovskis, ed., *Frontiers of Cognitive Therapy*, 153.

105. See Beck et al., *Cognitive Therapy of Personality Disorders*, 205.

106. See A. T. Beck, *Cognitive Therapy and Emotional Disorders*, 221.

107. Beck et al., *Cognitive Therapy of Substance Abuse*, 74–78.

108. See J. S. Beck, *Cognitive Therapy for Challenging Problems*, 74–77; D. Burns and A. Auerbach, "Therapeutic Empathy in Cognitive Therapy," in Salkovskis, ed., *Frontiers of Cognitive Therapy*, 159.

109. See Clement of Alexandria *Stromateis* 7.7 (PG 9.468d).

110. John Chrysostom *Commentary on First Corinthians* 33.5 (PG 61.285).

111. See John Chrysostom *On the Priesthood* 2.3 (PG 48.634).

112. John Climacus *To the Shepherd* 7 (PG 88.1184b). Holy Transfiguration Monastery, 236.

113. See Eusebius of Caesarea *Ecclesiastical History* 1.4.7 (PG 20.77c) and Clement of Alexandria *Stromateis* 7.16 (PG 9.537b).

114. Gregory of Nyssa *Answer to Eunomius's Second Book* 12 (PG 45.925d).

115. John Chrysostom *Commentary on Romans* 15.31 (PG 60.512).

116. See Augustine *On the Psalms* 41.4 (PL 36.457).

117. Augustine *On the Sermon on the Mount* 1.1.1 (PL 34.1229–1230).

118. Basil of Caesarea *Letter on Perfection* 1.22.1 (PG 32.288b).

119. See Cyril of Jerusalem *Catechetical Discourses* 13.36 (PG 33.816b). See also John Chrysostom *Commentary on Colossians* 8.5 (PG 62.358).

120. See Athanasius the Great *Festal Letters* 3.5 (PG 26.1374d–1375a). See also Augustine *On the Psalms* 101.3 (PL 36.1296).

121. See John Chrysostom *Commentary on Ephesians* 1.3 (PG 62.14).

122. Augustine *Sermon on Luke* 113.2.2 (PL 38.649). See also his *Sermon on John* 131.1.1 (PL 38.729).

123. Rom 3:23.

124. Lanctantius *Divine Institutes* 6.24 (PL 6.723b).

125. Ambrose of Milan *On Repentance* 2.6.44 (PL 16.508c).

126. Leo the Great *Sermons* 44.1 (PL 54.301c). See also Lanctantius *Epitome of the Divine Institutes* 77 (PL 6.1081b).

127. See Leo the Great *Sermons* 44.4 (PL 54.304a).

128. John Chrysostom *Commentary on John* 5.4 (PG 59.59).

129. Augustine *Against Faustus the Manichaean* 26.3 (PL 42.480).

130. John Chrysostom *On the Statues* 8.2 (PG 49.99).

131. Ambrose of Milan *Letter to Theodosius* 1.51.3 (PL 16.1212).

132. The description of certain latinophone fathers involves a felicitous play on words that translates nicely into English. In Latin, the word *ac-cusare* implies movement toward accusation, whereas the word *ex-cusare* means movement away from accusation. See Augustine *On Continence* 13 (PL 40.357): "*Quibus instigat insuper peccatoram ad sua excusanda potius quam accusanda peccata.*" See also Tertullian *On Repentance* 9 (PL 1.1244b): "*Cum accusat, excusit.*"

133. See Augustine *On the Psalms* 91.6 (PL 36.1153).

134. See Tertullian *On Repentance* 9 (PL 1.1244a); See also John Climacus's description of the residents of the prison in *Ladder* 5 (PG 88.764d–776b).

135.   See Cyprian of Carthage *Letter to Moysen and Maximus* 26.7 (*PL* 4.304a); John Climacus *Ladder* 5.19 and 5.35 (*PG* 88.772a and 780b).

136.   St. John Chrysostom lists five paths to repentance: condemning our sins, forgiving our neighbor's sins, praying for forgiveness, giving alms, and being humble. *That Demons Do not Govern the World* 2.6 (*PG* 49.264).

137.   See Clement of Rome *First Epistle to the Corinthians* 56 (*PG* 1.321a).

138.   John Climacus *Ladder* 5.26 (*PG* 88.776d). Holy Transfiguration Monastery, 62.

139.   See John Chrysostom *Commentary on Ephesians* 18.13 (*PG* 62.122).

140.   See Ambrose of Milan *On Repentance* 1.15.81 (*PG* 16.490c).

141.   See Tertullian *On Repentance* 8 (*PL* 1.1243a).

142.   See ibid. (*PL* 1.1243a) and his *Against Marcion* 2.25 (*PL* 1.314c).

143.   See Cyril of Jerusalem *Catechetical Discourses* 4.18 (*PG* 33.480a).

144.   See Augustine *On the Psalms* 84.14 (*PL* 36.1079).

145.   See Augustine *On the First Epistle of John* 1.6 (*PL* 35.1982).

146.   Augustine *Tractates on John* 12.14 (*PL* 35.1492).

147.   See John Chrysostom *Commentary on Hebrews* 9.7 (*PG* 63.81a).

148.   Ambrose of Milan *On Repentance* 2.7.53 (*PL* 16.531b).

149.   See John Climacus *Ladder* 5 (*PG* 88.780b).

150.   See Augustine *On the Psalms* 94.4 (*PL* 36.1218) and 110. 2 (*PL* 36.1464).

151.   [Cyprian of Carthage?] *On the Glory of Martyrdom* 24 (*PL* 4.834c).

152.   See Phillip J. Leaf et al., "Factors Affecting the Utilization of Specialty and General Medical Mental Health Services," *Medical Care* 26, no. 1 (January 1988): 9.

153.   See Phillip J. Leaf et al., "Contact with Health Professionals for the Treatment of Psychiatric and Emotional Problems," *Medical Care* 23, no. 12 (December 1985): 1330, 1332, 1327–1328.

154.   See Michael First and Harold Pincus, eds., introduction to *Diagnostic Criteria from DSM-IV-TR* (Arlington, VA: American Psychiatric Association, 2000), vii–viii.

155.   See Ronald Kessler, James Reuter, and James R. Greenley, "Sex Differences in the Use of Psychiatric Outpatient Facilities," *Social Forces* 58, no. 2 (December 1979): 559, 565.

156.   Ibid., 558.

157.   See James Greenley, David Mechanic, and Paul Cleary, "Seeking Help for Psychological Problems: A Replication and Extension," *Medical Care* 25, no. 12 (December 1987): 1115.

158.   See Charles Kadushin, "Social Distance Between Client and Professional," *The American Journal of Sociology* 67, no. 5 (March 1962): 530.

159.   See Edna E. Raphael, "Community Structure and Acceptance of Psychiatric Aid," *The American Journal of Sociology* 69, no. 4 (January 1964): 346.

160.   See Greenley, Mechanic, and Cleary, "Seeking Help," 1227.

161.   See Kadushin, "Social Distance between Client and Professional," 531.

162.   See Kessler et al., "Sex Differences in the Use of Psychiatric Outpatient Facilities," 565.

163.   See Allan Horwitz, "Social Networks and Pathways to Psychiatric Treatment," *Social Forces* 56, no. 1 (September 1977): 100; Kadushin, "Social Distance between Client and Professional," 530.

164.   See James Greenley and David Mechanic, "Social Selection in Seeking Help for Psychological Problems," *Journal of Health and Social Behavior* 17, no. 3 (September 1976): 250; Leaf et al., "Contact with Health Professionals," 1333; Leaf et al., "Factors Affecting Utilization," 23.

165.   See Greenley and Mechanic, "Social Selection," 249; Greenley, Mechanic, and Cleary, "Seeking Help," 1113.

166.   See Leaf et al., "Factors Affecting Utilization," 23; Leaf et al., "Contact with Health Professionals," 1322, 1331.

167.   Horwitz, "Social Networks," 88, 99; See also Greenley, Mechanic, and Cleary, "Seeking Help," 1115, 1120.

168.   See Neal Krause, Christopher G. Ellison, and Keith M. Wulf, "Church-based Emotional Support, Negative Interaction, and Psychological Well-being: Findings from a National Sample of Presbyterians," *Journal for the Scientific Study of Religion* 37, no. 4 (December 1998): 725, 727, 736–737; Horwitz, "Social Networks," 102–103.

169.   See Nicholas Cummings and William Follette, "Psychiatric Services and Medical Utilization in a Prepaid Health Plan Setting: Part II," *Medical Care* 6, no. 1 (January/February 1968): 38.

170.   See Leaf et al., "Factors Affecting Utilization," 21.

171.   See Raphael, "Community Structure," 348.

172.   Leaf et al., "Contact with Health Professionals," 1331.

173.   See Jerome Myers and Leslie Schaffer, "Social Stratification and Psychiatric Practice: A Study of an Outpatient Clinic," *American Sociological Review* 19, no. 3 (June 1954): 310.

174.   See Greenley, Mechanic, and Cleary, "Seeking Help," 1227.

175.   See Greenley and Mechanic, "Social Selection," 261.

176.   See Deborah Haas-Wilson, Allen Cheadle, and Richard Scheffler, "Demand for Mental Health Services: An Episode of Treatment Approach," *Southern Economic Journal* 56, no. 1 (July 1989): 219.

177.   See Greenley, Mechanic, and Cleary, "Seeking Help," 1114.

178.   See Cummings and Follette, "Psychiatric Services," 31.

179.   See Butler et al., "The Empirical Status of Cognitive-Behavioral Therapy," 28.

180.   See Cummings and Follette, "Psychiatric Services," 38.

181.   See S. Shapiro et al., "Utilization of Health Services: Three Epidemiological Catchment Area Sites," *Archives of General Psychiatry* 41 (1984): 971.

182.   See David Bromley and Bruce Busching, "Understanding the Structure of Contractual and Covenantal Social Relations: Implications for the Sociology of Religion," *Sociological Analysis* 49, presidential issue (December 1988): S18.

183.   See Neilus the Ascetic *Ascetic Discourse* 26 (PG 79.753c).

184.   See Bromley and Busching, "Understanding Structure of Social Relations," S20–S21.

185.   Jer 31:13 (MT); 38:13 (LXX).

186.   See Mt 16:26.

Chapter Seven

1. The myth, recounted by Plutarch and others, is also used effectively as a literary device by church fathers such as St. Basil the Great. See the latter's *Letter to a Calligrapher* 3.334 (*PG* 32.1077b).

2. Mahoney, *Constructive Psychotherapy*, 73 (see chap. 6, n. 1).

3. Bandura, *Social Learning Theory*, 11–12 (see chap. 2, n. 77).

4. See J. S. Beck, *Cognitive Therapy*, 164.

5. See John Chrysostom *Commentary on Acts* 54.3 (*PG* 60.378).

6. See John Chrysostom *Commentary on Hebrews* 19.2 (*PG* 63.142).

7. See John Chrysostom *Commentary on Acts* 15.5 (*PG* 60.126).

8. See Elder Païsios the Hagiorite, *Logoi*, vol. 2, 297.

9. See ibid., 72, 282, 283.

10. See Arnobius *Against the Heathen* 2.8 (*PL* 5.823a).

11. See Hilary of Poitiers *On the Trinity* 3.2 (*PL* 10.76c).

12. See John Chrysostom *On the Statues* 1.5 (*PG* 49.23).

13. See Augustine *On the Harmony of the Evangelists* 2.56.98 (*PL* 34.1127). See also John Chrysostom *Commentary on Matthew* 1.7 (*PG* 57.22).

14. See Augustine *On Christian Doctrine* 4.23.52 (*PL* 34.115).

15. See Irenaeus of Lyons *Against all Heresy* 2.10.1 (*PG* 7.735b).

16. See Augustine *On the Harmony of the Evangelists* 13.43 (*PL* 34.1185).

17. See Abba Joseph *Sayings of the Fathers* I.8 (*PG* 65.229d).

18. See John Climacus *Ladder* 8 (*PG* 88.828c-836b), 14 (*PG* 88.864c-872a), and 15 (*PG* 88.8.880d-904c).

19. Phil 3:13–14 (italics mine).

20. John Chrysostom *Commentary on Philippians* 12.2 (*PG* 62.272).

21. See John Chrysostom *Commentary on Acts* 7.3 (*PG* 60.67).

22. See Justin Martyr *First Apology* 11 (*PG* 6.341b).

23. See Tertullian *On the Martyrs* 3 (*PL* 1.624c). In a homily of St. Isaac the Syrian extant only in Western and Eastern Syriac, he writes, "Even prison is pleasant for the man who dwells there with expectation." *Ascetical Homilies* hom. 24, 128.

24. Ambrose of Milan *On Repentance* 2.3.16 (*PL* 16.500c).

25. See Neilus the Ascetic [pseud.] *Encheiridion of Epictetus* 19 (*PG* 79.1292d).

26. See John Cassian *Conferences* 1.1.4 (*PL* 49.485b).

27. See ibid. 1.1.2 (*PL* 49.483b).

28. Ibid. 1.1.5 (*PL* 49.487c).

29. See John Chrysostom *Commentary on Second Corinthians* 5.3 (*PG* 61.431). See also *Shepherd of Hermes* 1.1 (*PG* 2.893).

30. See Gregory of Nyssa *On the Soul and the Resurrection* (*PG* 46.96c).

31. See Gregory of Nyssa *On Virginity* 11 (*PG* 46.368d).

32. See John Cassian *Conferences* 1.1.4 (*PL* 49.486a).

33. See Nicodemos the Hagiorite, *Aoratos polemos*, 41.

34. See Gregory of Nyssa *Great Catechism* 35 (PG 45.88b).

35. See Augustine *Tractates on John* 28.5 (PL 35.1624).

36. See Gregory of Nyssa *Against Eunomius* 6 (PG 45.652b).

37. See John Cassian *Conferences* 1.1.4 (PL 49.486a).

38. Augustine *On the First Epistle of John* 7.8 (PL 35.2033).

39. See John Chrysostom *Commentary on John* 4.1 (PG 59.45).

40. See Dorotheos of Gaza *Discourses* 14.154 (SC 92.432). See also John Chrysostom *Commentary on Hebrews* 1.2 (PG 63.16), *On the Statues* 4.7 (PG 49.68), and Basil of Caesarea *Letter to Chilona* 1.42.2 (PG 32.349d–352a).

41. See Gregory of Sinai *Other Chapters* 5 (PG 150.1301b).

42. See Nicodemos the Hagiorite, *Aoratos polemos*, 74, 139.

43. See Maximus the Confessor *Various Theological Texts* 3.51 (PG 90.1281c).

44. See Jn 1:45–46.

45. Archimandrite Zacharias [Zacharou], *Enlargement of Heart*, 155–156.

46. See Gregory of Nyssa *Answer to Eunomius's Second Book* 12 (PG 45.1100a).

47. See Clement of Alexandria *Stromateis* 6.17 (PG 9.388b): "*Hopou d'aneu theōrias tōn prōtōn aitiōn, tērēsei tōn homoiōn kat metabasei poiēsei tina hormēn kai systasin, empeiria prosagoreuetai.*"

48. See Arnobius *Against the Heathen* 2.18 (PL 5.837a).

49. See Augustine *On Marriage and Concupiscence* 1.21 (PL 44.426).

50. See Athenagoras the Philosopher *On the Resurrection of the Dead* 17 (PG 6.1008b).

51. Basil of Caesarea *Letter to Gregory* 1.38.5 (PG 32.336c).

52. See John Chrysostom *Commentary on Hebrews* 6.4 (PG 63.59).

53. John Cassian *Conferences* 3.23.21 (PL 49.1280a).

54. See ibid. 1.5.9 (PL 49.621a).

55. See John Chrysostom *Commentary on Philippians* 12.3 (PG 62.273).

56. Augustine *City of God* 16.32 (PL 41.510).

57. Neilus the Ascetic *To Eulogius* 24 (PG 79.1125b).

58. Augustine *On the Soul and Its Origin* 3.4.5 (PL 44.513). In a similar vein, St. Gregory Palamas notes how ridiculous it is when those bereft of experience contradict the experienced. *On Behalf of the Hesychasts* 1.2, vol. 1, 400.

59. See John Chrysostom *Commentary on Acts* 9.5 (PG 60.82); Augustine *Disputation Against Fortunatus* 2.22 (PL 42.225).

60. See John Chrysostom *Commentary on Acts* 10.5 (PG 60.94). See also his *On the Statues* 20.8 (PG 49.209).

61. See Elder Païsios the Hagiorite, *Logoi*, vol. 3, 48.

62. The experimental adoption of new spiritual practices can be seen in the ancient monastic republic of Mount Athos. For example, in one coenobitic monastery, everyone in the kitchen softly says the Jesus prayer at his own rate as he works; in another monastery, one monk is designated to say the Jesus prayer, while the others silently follow it as they fulfill their assigned tasks.

63. See A. T. Beck, *Cognitive Therapy and Emotional Disorders*, 95–96.

64. See Thomas D'Zurilla and Arthur Nezu, "Problem-solving Therapies," in Dobson, ed., *Handbook of Cognitive-Behavioral Therapies*, 225.

65. See D'Zurilla and Nezu, "Problem-solving Therapies," 215, 232; Mahoney, *Constructive Psychotherapy*, 74 (see chap. 6, n. 1); J. S. Beck, *Cognitive Therapy*, 194.

66. See Mahoney, *Constructive Psychotherapy*, 75.

67. See D'Zurilla and Nezu, "Problem-solving Therapies," 231–232.

68. See J. S. Beck, *Cognitive Therapy for Challenging Problems*, 128; Beck et al., *Cognitive Therapy of Substance Abuse*, 126.

69. J. S. Beck, *Cognitive Therapy for Challenging Problems*, 15; See also idem, *Cognitive Therapy*, 31–32.

70. See J. S. Beck, *Cognitive Therapy for Challenging Problems*, 135, 140–141.

71. See Bandura, *Social Learning Theory*, 162, 167.

72. See J. S. Beck, *Cognitive Therapy*, 86.

73. See A. T. Beck, *Cognitive Therapy and Emotional Disorders*, 227.

74. Beck et al., *Cognitive Therapy of Depression*, 118.

75. See Beck and Emery with Greenberg, *Anxiety Disorders and Phobias*, 264.

76. See Beck et al., *Cognitive Therapy of Depression*, 118; J. S. Beck, *Cognitive Therapy*, 154.

77. See Beck et al., *Cognitive Therapy of Substance Abuse*, 237–238.

78. See ibid., 149.

79. J. S. Beck, *Cognitive Therapy for Challenging Problems*, 23.

80. See Beck and Emery with Greenberg, *Anxiety Disorders and Phobias*, 268–269.

81. Ibid., 269.

82. See "*theoria, praxis*," *LSJ* 797, 1459 and *PGL* 648–649, 1127–1128.

83. See Maximus the Confessor *On Various Difficult Passages* (PG 91.1108b) and his *To Thalassius* 63 (PG 90.685c).

84. See Maximus the Confessor *To Thalassius* 54.6 (PG 90.528a).

85. See ibid. 37 (PG 90.385c).

86. See Clement of Alexandria *Paedagogus* 1.13 (PG 8.376a).

87. See Thalassius *On Love and Self-control* 3.65 (PG 91.1453c).

88. Dorotheos of Gaza *Discourses* 2.39 (SC 92.204).

89. John Climacus *Ladder* 25.58 (PG 88.1001a). Holy Transfiguration Monastery, 159.

90. See Neilus the Ascetic *Ascetic Discourse* 73 (PG 79.808ab); Dorotheos of Gaza *Discourses* 8.92 (SC 92.312); and Gregory of Nazianzus *Orations* 4.113 (PG 35.649c–652a).

91. See Ilias the Presbyter *Gnomic Anthology* 44 (PG 127.1156d).

92. Macarius of Egypt [pseud.] *Discourse on Love* 114 (PG 34.932d).

93. See Hesychius the Presbyter *On Watchfulness and Holiness* 2.63 (PG 93.1532d). See also Philotheus of Sinai *Texts on Watchfulness* 3 (PHIL 2.275).

94. See Dorotheos of Gaza *Letter* 5 (SC 92.510).

95. See John Climacus *Ladder* 4 (PG 88.709b).

96. Ambrose of Milan *On Duties of the Clergy* 1.21.90 (PL 16.55).

97.   See John of Damascus [pseud.] *On Virtues and Vices* (PG 95.85d). See also Abba Poimen *Sayings of the Fathers* Π.60 (PG 65.336c).

98.   See Gregory Palamas *To the Nun Xenia* (PG 150.1069d). See also John Climacus *Ladder* 15 (PG 88.888d).

99.   For example, see Ilias the Presbyter *Gnomic Anthology* 4 (PG 127.1129b); John of Damascus [pseud.] *On Virtues and Vices* (PG 95.85d–88a); Maximus the Confessor *Centuries on Love* 2.57 (PG 90.1033a); Nikitas Stithatos *Practical Chapters* 1.40 (PG 120.869c); Theodore of Edessa *Century of Spiritual Texts* 60 (PHIL 1.314); Peter of Damascus *Book One on the Seven Forms of Bodily Discipline* (PHIL 3.18). For the scriptural precedents on which these practices are based, see Neh 9:11; Jl 2:12; 1 Sm 15:11; Mt 17:21; Lk 6:12.

100.   John of Damascus [pseud.] *On Virtues and Vices* (PG 95.85d–88a). Palmer, Sherrard, and Ware, *Philokalia*, vol. 2, 334–335.

101.   See Thalassius *On Love and Self-control* 1.25 (PG 91.1429c).

102.   See Maximus the Confessor *Centuries on Love* 1.76 (PG 90.1005d) and Theodore of Edessa *Century of Spiritual Texts* 12 (PHIL 1.306).

103.   See Maximus the Confessor *Centuries on Love* 2.70 (PG 90.1005d–1008a); Nikitas Stithatos *Practical Chapters* 1.40 (PG 120.869c); 1.43 (PG 120.872a); and John Climacus *Ladder* 26 (PG 88.1028d–1029a).

104.   See Hesychius the Presbyter *On Watchfulness and Holiness* 2.10 (PG 93.1513d). See also ibid. 1.75 (PG 93.1504c).

105.   See Thalassius *On Love and Self-control* 3.35 (PG 91.1452b).

106.   See ibid. 3.14 (PG 91.1449b).

107.   See John Climacus *Ladder* 6 (PG 88.796b).

108.   See Peter of Damascus *Book One on the Third Stage of Contemplation* (PHIL 3.41–42). See also Theodore of Edessa *Century of Spiritual Texts* 34 (PHIL 1.309).

109.   See Peter of Damascus *Book One on How to Acquire True Faith* (PHIL 3.78).

110.   See Symeon the New Theologian *Practical Chapters* 1.26 (PG 120.615a).

111.   See Philotheus of Sinai *Texts on Watchfulness* 28 (PHIL 2.283).

112.   Thalassius *On Love and Self-control* 1.36 (PG 91.1432a). Palmer, Sherrard, and Ware, *Philokalia*, vol. 2, 309.

113.   See Ilias the Presbyter *Gnomic Anthology* 35 (PG 127.1156a).

114.   See Thalassius *On Love and Self-control* 3.11 (PG 91.1149a).

115.   See Amma Syncletica *Sayings of the Fathers* Σ.15 (PG 65.425d).

116.   See Abba Poimen *Sayings of the Fathers* Π.184 (PG 65.368a).

117.   See Diadochus of Photiki *On Spiritual Knowledge* 45 (SC 5bis.111).

118.   See Ilias the Presbyter *Gnomic Anthology* 57 (PG 127.1160b).

119.   See John Climacus *Ladder* 14 (PG 88.868b), 15 (PG 88.881c), and 20 (PG 88.910d).

120.   See Gregory of Sinai *On Stillness* 13 (PG 150.1325d).

121.   See John Climacus *Ladder* 26 (PG 88.1065b).

122.   See Nikitas Stithatos *Practical Chapters* 1.86 (PG 120.892b).

123.   See Gregory Palamas *To the Nun Xenia* (PG 150.1076d).

124. Dorotheos of Gaza *Discourses* 2.39 (SC 90.206). See also Abba Sisoe *Sayings of the Fathers* Σ.13 (PG 65.396b).

125. See Neilus the Ascetic *Discourse on Non-acquisitiveness* 25 (PG 79.1001c). See also John Cassian *Institutes* 2.14 (PL 49.105a).

126. See Evagrius *Rerum monachalium rationes* 8 (PG 40.1260d).

127. See John Climacus *Ladder* 14 (PG 88.868b).

128. Jerome *Letter to Rusticus the Monk* 4.125.15 (PL 22.1081).

129. See John Climacus *Ladder* 15 (PG 88.900c).

130. Ibid. 28 (PG 88.1133b). Holy Transfiguration Monastery, 215.

131. See ibid. 4 (PG 88.689a–d).

132. Augustine *Tractates on John* 58.4 (PL 35.1794).

133. See Gregory of Sinai *On Driving out the Thoughts* (PG 150.1332d). St. John Climacus gives similar advice for the same struggle. See *Ladder* 15 (PG 88.900d). St. Basil the Great, however, values such a stance only if the heart follows suit. See his *Commentary on the Prophet Isaiah* 1.35 (PG 30.188d).

134. See John Climacus *Ladder* 14 (PG 88.868a). Part of the preparation for the Beck diet plan involves a similar exercise of recording sensations throughout the day to learn the difference between desire for food, hunger, and craving. See Judith Beck, *The Beck Diet Solution Weight Loss Workbook* (Birmingham, AL: Oxmore House, 2007), 65.

135. See ibid. 4 (PG 88.701d).

136. Gregory of Nyssa *On Virginity* 23 (PG 46.405c).

137. See John Chrysostom *On the Statues* 13.4 (PG 49.141).

138. See Maximus the Confessor *Various Theological Texts* 5.59 (PG 90.1373a). See also his *On the Lord's Prayer* (PG 90.901b). See also Augustine *Letters* 11.4 (PL 33.76).

139. [Cyprian of Carthage?] *On Public Shows* 8 (PL 4.785d).

140. Bandura, *Social Learning Theory*, 188 (see chap. 2, n. 77).

141. See John Chrysostom *Commentary on Acts* 42.4 (PG 60.301). See also his *Commentary on Matthew* 2.6 (PG 57.30–31).

142. Dorotheos of Gaza *Discourses* 2.39 (SC 92.204–206). See also John Climacus *Ladder* 25.59 (PG 88.1001a).

143. See Lanctantius *Epitome of the Divine Institutes* 53 (PL 6.1075a). For a meta-analysis on the effects of media violence on children, see George Comstock and Haejung Paik, *Television and the American Child* (New York: Academic Press, 1991).

144. See *Paradise of the Fathers* 7.34 (SC 387.368). See also *Sayings of the Fathers* 11 (PG 65.89cd).

145. See John Chrysostom *Commentary on Acts* 29.3 (PG 60.217–218).

146. See Hesychius the Presbyter *On Watchfulness and Holiness* 1.33 (PG 93.1492c). Similar examples can be seen in the lives of the saints. For example, in order to quench fleshly lust, St. Benedict cast himself into briars, whereas St. Martianos stepped into a fire. See Pope Gregory the Great *Life of Saint Benedict* 2 (PL 66.131c) and *Life of Saint Martianos* (SYN 2.322). In passing, we note that these examples in spirit and in fact are unrelated to the psychologically questionable medieval Roman Catholic practice of self-flagellation as a form of penance.

147. See *Paradise of the Fathers* 5.26 (SC 387.262).

148. See Robert W. Lundin, *Theories and Systems of Psychology* (Lexington, MA: D. C. Heath & Company, 1985), 189.

149. See Beck et al., *Cognitive Therapy of Depression*, 119.

150. See A. T. Beck, *Cognitive Therapy and Emotional Disorders*, 325–326.

151. See ibid., 329.

152. Beck et al., *Cognitive Therapy of Depression*, 119.

153. See Beck et al., *Cognitive Therapy of Personality Disorders*, 86.

154. A. T. Beck, *Love is Never Enough*, 208.

155. See Beck et al., *Cognitive Therapy of Depression*, 140.

156. See A. T. Beck, *Love is Never Enough*, 212.

157. Beck et al., *Cognitive Therapy of Personality Disorders*, 366. For an instructive graph correlating psychopathology and behavioral versus cognitive interventions, see Arthur Freeman et al., *Clinical Applications of Cognitive Therapy* (New York: Kluwer Academic/Plenum Publishers, 2004) 59.

158. Bandura, *Social Learning Theory*, 78. See also ibid., 70–71.

159. Beck et al., *Cognitive Therapy of Personality Disorders*, 86.

160. See Beck et al., *Cognitive Therapy of Substance Abuse*, 147–149.

161. See Beck et al., *Cognitive Therapy of Depression*, 120, 129.

162. See ibid., 128.

163. Basil of Caesarea *Discourse on Asceticism* (PG 31.638d–649ab). See also Abba Nistheroos *Sayings of the Fathers* N.5 (PG 65.308c).

164. Hesychius the Presbyter *On Watchfulness and Holiness* 1.65 (PG 93.1501c).

165. Theophan the Recluse, *Put' ko spaseniju*, 152. *The Path to Salvation*, 172.

166. [St. Cyprian of Carthage?] makes a similar suggestion in his *On Public Shows* 9 (PL 4.816ab).

167. See Propst, *Psychotherapy in a Religious Framework*, 101–102 (see chap. 3, n. 5).

168. Bandura, *Social Learning Theory*, 212.

169. See J. S. Beck, *Cognitive Therapy for Challenging Problems*, 42.

170. Beck et al., *Cognitive Therapy of Substance Abuse*, 151.

171. See Beck et al., *Cognitive Therapy of Personality Disorders*, 359–360.

172. See Beck et al., *Cognitive Therapy of Depression*, 137.

173. See Theodore Balsamon *Council of Trullo* (PG 137.692c). Cf. Agapios Monachos, ed., *Pēdalion*, 219 and Ralli and Potli, eds., *Syntagma* vol. 3, 424–425.

174. Tertullian *On Public Shows* 10 (PL 1.643a).

175. Basil of Caesarea *On the Hexameron* 4.1 (PG 29b.80a).

176. [Cyprian of Carthage?] *On Public Shows* 6 (PL 4.784b).

177. John Chrysostom *Commentary on Acts* 4.5 (PG 60.301).

178. Augustine *On the Sermon on the Mount* 2.2.5 (PL 34.1271). See also John Chrysostom *Commentary on Matthew* 20.1 (PG 57.287–288).

179. See Jerome *Letter to Marcellus* 3.43.2 (PL 22.479). See also Augustine *On the Sermon on the Mount* 2.19.64 (PL 34.1298).

180. See John Chrysostom *Commentary on Matthew* 33.6 (PG 57.395).

181.   See Lauren Braswell and Phillip Kendall, "Cognitive-Behavioral Therapy with Youth," in Dobson, ed., *Handbook of Cognitive Behavioral Therapies*, 160.

182.   See Beck and Emery with Greenberg, *Anxiety Disorders and Phobias*, 248.

183.   See Beck et al., *Cognitive Therapy of Substance Abuse*, 152.

184.   See Beck and Emery with Greenberg, *Anxiety Disorders and Phobias*, 246–247.

185.   Beck et al., *Cognitive Therapy of Substance Abuse*, 150

186.   See Beck and Emery with Greenberg, *Anxiety Disorders and Phobias*, 281.

187.   (italics mine) Tertullian *On Flight during Persecution* 5 (PL 2.108b).

188.   Beck et al., *Cognitive Therapy of Substance Abuse*, 153.

189.   See Jean-Claude Larchet, *Thérapeutique des maladies spirituelles* [Treatment of spiritual sicknesses] (Paris: Les Editions de l'Ancre, 1991), 489. Cf. Mt 6:24; Gal 5:17.

190.   See John Chrysostom *Commentary on First Timothy* 6.3 (PG 62.534). Although the disturbed are not usually inclined to give alms, St. Diadochus suggests doing so to become calm. *On Spiritual Knowledge* 10 (SC 5bis.89).

191.   Alford and Beck, *Integrative Power*, 58–59.

192.   See Beck and Emery with Greenberg, *Anxiety Disorders and Phobias*, 269.

193.   John Chrysostom *Commentary on Second Thessalonians* 2.4 (PG 62.478).

194.   See Abba Agathon *Sayings of the Fathers* A.18 (PG 65.113c).

195.   See John Climacus *Ladder* 7 (PG 88.813b).

196.   See ibid. 6 (PG 88.796c).

197.   See Beck and Emery with Greenberg, *Anxiety Disorders and Phobias*, 274–275.

198.   Ibid., 278.

199.   See Beck et al., *Cognitive Therapy of Depression*, 132–134.

200.   See Beck and Emery with Greenberg, *Anxiety Disorders and Phobias*, 264–265.

201.   See ibid., 258, 283.

202.   Even the monastic life was not so much discovered by St. Anthony the Great as it was revealed to him by an angel whom he observed. See *Sayings of the Fathers* A.1 (PG 65.76b).

203.   For example, the advice of the desert fathers—"Go, sit in your cell and your cell will teach you all things"—can be understood according to psychological theory as "In order to solve the *problem* of ignorance about the monastic life, perform a *behavioral experiment* of going and sitting in your cell, and from this experiment you will attain the *goal* of learning about monasticism." The theory can be imposed on the text, but is not explicitly expressed by the text. See *Paradise of the Fathers* 2.1 (SC 387.134).

204.   See Hans Vaihinger, *Die Philosophie des Als Ob* [The philosophy of as if] (Leipzig: F. Meiner, 1922), 99; Marc N. Richelle, *B. F. Skinner: A Reappraisal* (East Sussex, UK: Psychology Press, 1999), 66; Gregory of Nyssa *Great Catechism* 35 (PG 45.88bc).

205.   Gregory of Nyssa *Great Catechism* 35 (PG 45.88bc).

206.   Jn 14:6.

Chapter Eight

1. This passage is attributed to various sources, including St. John Chrysostom (*PG* 63.941), St. Ephraim the Syrian (*Erga*, vol. 4, 176 and vol. 6, 42), and an anonymous elder (*Paradise of the Fathers* 2.35 [*SC* 387.144]).

2. Gn 8:11.

3. See Nm 13:13.

4. Mt 16:3.

5. Ex 3:8.

6. Tm 2:22.

7. The two most common English translations for the Greek term *theoria* are contemplation and divine vision. Some zealous Orthodox translators dislike the term *contemplation*, because of associations in the West with Ignatius of Loyola's imaginative and sensual *Exercitia Spiritualia*. Thus, they translate *theoria* as divine vision, emphasizing its experiential, supra-rational, and perceptual dimension. The fathers, however, do not use the term *theoria* solely in reference to vision [*orasē*]. In some texts, *theoria* refers to a quite rational mental recollection [*anamnēsē*], in which case the term *contemplation*, rather than the term *vision*, would be appropriate. A historical case for using the term *contemplation* could also be made by appealing to St. John Cassian, a father of unimpeachable Orthodoxy, who used the words *theoria* and *contemplatione* interchangeably: "*Videtis ergo principale bonum in theoria sola, id est, in contemplatione divina Dominum posuisse.*" See John Cassian *Conferences* 1.1.8 (*PL* 49.492a). Likewise, the standard Latin translation for the Greek philosophical dyad *praxis-theoria* was *actione-contemplatione*. See Augustine *City of God* 8.4 (*PL* 41.226) Since neither English translation adequately covers the full semantic range of the Greek term *theoria*, we have decided to leave it untranslated.

8. A. T. Beck, *Cognitive Therapy and Emotional Disorders*, 258.

9. Gregory of Sinai *Other Chapters* 5 (*PG* 150.1301b).

10. Gregory of Sinai *Chapters* 127 (*PG* 150.1292c).

11. Isaac the Syrian, *Ta askētika, Letter* 4, 374. See also Theognostus *On the Practice of the Virtues and Contemplation* 6 (*PHIL* 2.256) and Maximus the Confessor *Diverse Theological Chapters* 2.85 (*PG* 90.1252d).

12. Isaac the Syrian, *Ta askētika*, hom. 30, 129. See also ibid., hom. 69, 272.

13. Nicephorus the Monk *On Watchfulness and Guarding of the Heart* (*PG* 147.962a).

14. Theophan the Recluse, as quoted in *The Art of Prayer*, 182.

15. Nicephorus the Monk *On Watchfulness and Guarding of the Heart* (*PG* 147.961c).

16. Hesychius the Presbyter *On Watchfulness and Holiness* 1.6 (*PG* 93.1481d) and 1.7 (*PG* 93.1484b).

17. Ibid. 1.93 (*PG* 93.1508d) and 2.66 (*PG* 93.1533b).

18. [Symeon the New Theologian?] *Three Methods of Prayer* (*PG* 120.701bc).

19. Hesychius the Presbyter *On Watchfulness and Holiness* 2.18 (*PG* 93.1517b). For a reference to philosophy as the science of sciences, see John of Damascus *Philosophical Chapters* 3 (*PG* 94.533c).

20. Hesychius the Presbyter *On Watchfulness and Holiness* 1.50 (*PG* 93.1497b).

21. Philotheus of Sinai *Texts on Watchfulness* 3 (*PHIL* 2.275).

22. Maximus the Confessor *Texts on Theology* 2.79 (PG 90.1161d). Palmer, Sherrard, and Ware, *Philokalia*, vol. 2, 158.

23. [Symeon the New Theologian?] *Three Methods of Prayer* (PG 120.706b). Palmer, Sherrard, and Ware, *Philokalia*, vol. 4,

24. Hesychius the Presbyter *On Watchfulness and Holiness* 1.13–17 (PG 93.1485ac).

25. Gregory Palamas *Homilies* 12 (PG 151.153c).

26. Nikitas Stithatos *Practical Chapters* 1.8 (PG 120.853d–856a).

27. Hesychius the Presbyter *On Watchfulness and Holiness* 1.64 (PG 93.1501ab). See also Peter of Damascus *Book Two The Remembrance of Christ's Sufferings* (*PHIL* 3. 132).

28. Mark the Ascetic *Admonition to Nicholas* 5.2 (PG 65.1029d) and ibid. 6 (PG 65.1037b). See also Nicodemos the Hagiorite, *Aoratos polemos*, 42.

29. See Abba Philemon *Discourse* (*PHIL* 2.243).

30. Isaac the Syrian, *Ta askētika*, hom. 85, 347.

31. Ibid., hom. 23, 98. The Syriac adds "For many times has the power of theoria been aroused by reading the scriptures." *Ascetical Homilies*, hom. 4, 36.

32. See Mt 17:1–9; Acts 10:8–17; 2 Cor 12:12 respectively.

33. Theoliptos of Philadelphia *On Inner Work in Christ* (*PHIL* 4.7).

34. Maximus the Confessor *Texts on Theology* 1.43 (PG 90.1100a).

35. Isaac the Syrian, *Ascetical Homilies*, hom. 22, 113 [extant only in Syriac].

36. Isaac the Syrian, *Ta askētika*, hom. 39, 168. *Ascetical Homilies*, hom. 49, 239.

37. Ibid., hom. 38, 165.

38. See *Life of Saint Dionysius of Zakinthos* (SYN 12.489–490).

39. Gregory of Sinai *Chapters* 127 (PG 150.292a).

40. Maximus the Confessor *Texts on Theology* 1.70 (PG 90.1109a). Palmer, Sherrard, and Ware, *Philokalia*, vol. 2, 128.

41. Neilus the Ascetic *Ascetic Discourse* 26 (PG 79.753c).

42. Ilias the Presbyter *Gnomic Anthology* 33 (PG 127.1153d–1155a).

43. John Climacus *Ladder* 26 (PG 88.1029c).

44. The dogmatic of vespers in the grave tone. *Paraklētikē*, 299.

45. Abba Neilus *Sayings of the Fathers* N.3 (PG 65.306b).

46. Maximus the Confessor *Centuries on Love* 3.90 (PG 90.1044d).

47. John Cassian *Institutes* 5.10 (PL 49.225b).

48. Gregory Palamas, *Homilies* 51, Sophokleous Oikonomou, 116.

49. See ode nine for Tuesday matins of the fifth week of Great Lent. *Triōdion katanyktikon* [Lenten service-book of three compunctious odes] (Athens: Phōs-Xeen, 1989), 285.

50. For example, see ode five for Tuesday matins in tone one (*Paraklētikē*, 29), second kathisma for Tuesday matins in tone four (*Paraklētikē*, 170), aposticha for vespers in tone one (*Paraklētikē*, 24), and Sunday vespers aposticha in tone one (*Paraklētikē*, 19).

51. *Ōrologion to mega*, 616.

52. Nicodemos the Hagiorite, *Exomologētarion*, 44–45.

53. Barsanuphius, *Keimena diakritika kai hēsychastika* [Texts on discernment and stillness], vol. 2 (Kareas, Greece: Etoimasia, 1997), no. 304, 164.

54. Dorotheos of Gaza *Letter* 8.193 (SC 92.516). See also Phil 4:13.

55. Nicodemos the Hagiorite, *Exomologētarion*, 47.

56. Ephraim the Syrian, *Other Beatitudes*, 20, *Erga*, vol. 2, 272. For another version of the same advice, see also his *Discourse on Repentance and Judgment, Erga*, vol. 4, 236.

57. Peter of Damascus *Book One on Dispassion* (*PHIL* 3.64). Palmer, Sherrard, and Ware, *Philokalia*, vol. 3, 148–149.

58. Dorotheos of Gaza *Letter* 8.193 (SC 92.514).

59. Nicodemos the Hagiorite, *Aoratos polemos*, 103.

60. Hesychius the Presbyter *On Watchfulness and Holiness* 2.51 (PG 93.1528d).

61. Nicodemos the Hagiorite, *Aoratos polemos*, 103.

62. Hesychius the Presbyter *On Watchfulness and Holiness* 1.88 (PG 93.1508c).

63. Isaac the Syrian, *Ta askētika*, hom. 59, 242.

64. Ilias the Presbyter *Gnomic Anthology* 65 (PG 127.1161a). See also John Chrysostom *Commentary on Ephesians* 15.3 (PG 62.109).

65. Theodore of Edessa *Century of Spiritual Texts* 70 (*PHIL* 1.316–317).

66. Barsanuphius, *Keimena diakritika kai hēsychastika* [Texts on discernment and stillness], vol. 1 (Kareas, Greece: Etoimasia, 1996), no. 91, 216–218.

67. Isaac the Syrian, *Ta askētika*, hom. 34, 148–149.

68. John Climacus *Ladder* 26.193 (PG 88.1085c).

69. Hesychius the Presbyter *On Watchfulness and Holiness* 2.36 (PG 93.1521d). Palmer, Sherrard, and Ware, *Philokalia*, vol. 1, 186.

70. Mark the Ascetic *On Divine Baptism* 4 (PG 65.1016d).

71. Theoliptus of Philadelphia *On Inner Work in Christ* (*PHIL* 4.12). Palmer, Sherrard, and Ware, *Philokalia*, vol. 4, 186. See also John Cassian *Institutes* 6.37 (PL 49.198a).

72. Dorotheos of Gaza *Discourses* 1.25 (SC 92.184).

73. Athanasius the Great *Life of Saint Anthony* 55 (PG 26.924c).

74. Maximus the Confessor *Diverse Theological Chapters* 2.76 (PG 90.1248d–1249a).

75. See Abba Poimen *Sayings of the Fathers* Π.20 (PG 65.320a) and Π.21 (PG 65.328a). St. John Chrysostom also uses this analogy in *On the Saying to Avoid Fornication...* 1 (PG 51.209).

76. Nicodemos the Hagiorite, *Exomologētarion*, 48–49.

77. Elder Païsios the Hagiorite, *Epistoles*, 2, 120.

78. See Paul M. Salkovskis, "The Cognitive Approach to Anxiety: Threat Beliefs, Safety Seeking, Behavior, and the Special Case of Health Anxiety and Obsessions," in Salkovskis, ed., *Frontiers of Cognitive Therapy*, 71–72.

79. Elder Païsios the Hagiorite, *Logoi*, vol. 5, 63.

80. *Paradise of the Fathers* 18.38 (SC 498.88).

81. Abba Macarius *Sayings of the Fathers* M.3 (PG 65.264b) and (PG 34.241b). Other fathers also followed this practice. See Palladius *Lausaic History* 12 (PG 34.1034b).

82. Jerome *Letter to Monk Rusticus* 125.12 (PL 22.1079).

83. *Mikron euchologion* [Small prayerbook] (Athens: Apostolikë Diakonia, 1996), 84.

84. See Mt 4:1-11; Lk 4:2-13.

85. See Augustine *On the Psalms* 90.1.1 (*PL* 36.1149). See also John Chrysostom *Commentary on Matthew* 13.4 (*PG* 57.212); Antiochus the Monk *To Eustathius on the Thoughts* 81 (*PG* 89.677bc); and Nicodemos the Hagiorite, *Aoratos polemos*, 47.

86. John Cassian *Conferences* 1.7.8 (*PL* 49.678a). See also Jas 4:7.

87. Macarius of Egypt [pseud.] *On Freedom of the Intellect* 6 (*PG* 34.961d-964a).

88. Maximus the Confessor *Centuries on Love* 3.88 (*PG* 90.1044c).

89. See Antiochus the Monk *To Eustathius on the Thoughts* 81 (*PG* 89.1677bc); Augustine, *On the Psalms* 137.12 (*PL* 36.1773-1774); Jerome *Letter to Eustochius* 22.6 (*PL* 22.398); Ambrose *On Repentance* 2.11.105 (*PL* 16.523a-524a); John Cassian *Institutes* 6.13 (*PL* 49.234b-285a); Hesychius the Presbyter *On Watchfulness and Holiness* 2.56 (*PG* 93.1529d); and Dorotheos of Gaza *Discourses* 11.116 (*SC* 92.362).

90. See Gregory of Nyssa *Against Eunomius* 1 (*PG* 45.249cd) and Origen *Against Celsus* 7.22 (*PG* 11.1453b).

91. Eph 4:22.

92. Hesychius the Presbyter *On Watchfulness and Holiness* 2.36 (*PG* 93.1521d).

93. Abba Zosimas *Thoughts* 5 (*PG* 78.1688c).

94. Antiochus the Monk *To Eustathius on the Thoughts* 81 (*PG* 89.1677cd).

95. Hesychius the Presbyter *On Watchfulness and Holiness* 2.49 (*PG* 93.1528b).

96. Abba Sisoe *Sayings of the Fathers* Σ.22 (*PG* 65.400c).

97. Nicodemos the Hagiorite, *Exomologētarion*, 46-47.

98. Mark the Ascetic *On Divine Baptism* 4 (*PG* 65.1000d).

99. Neilus the Ascetic *Ascetic Discourse* 39 (*PG* 79.768cd). See also Augustine *On the Psalms* 48.6 (*PL* 36.548); John Cassian *Institutes* 4.37 (*PL* 49.198b); and Gregory of Nyssa *On Prayer* 4 (*PG* 44.1172bc).

100. Gregory Palamas *To the Nun Xenia* (*PG* 150.1068).

101. John Chrysostom *Commentary on Ephesians* 24.2 (*PG* 62.171).

102. Evagrius *On Various Bad Thoughts* 16 (*PG* 79.1217d-1220a).

103. Nicodemos the Hagiorite, *Aoratos polemos*, 46-49.

104. Ephraim the Syrian, *To Neophytus the Monk*, 40, *Erga*, vol. 2, 230-231.

105. Ephraim the Syrian, *To Eulogius*, 47, *Erga*, vol. 3, 263-264.

106. *Life of Saint Syncletica* (*SYN* 1.120).

107. Evagrius *On Various Bad Thoughts* 7 (*PG* 79.1208d).

108. Macarius of Egypt [pseud.] *On Freedom of the Intellect* 2 (*PG* 34.937a). Palmer, Sherrard, and Ware, *Philokalia*, vol. 3, 337. Cf. also Ez 33:11.

109. Maximus the Confessor *Centuries on Love* 4.48 (*PG* 90.1057d). Basil of Caesarea *On the First Psalm* 2 (*PG* 29b.212d).

110. Ephraim the Syrian, *To Egyptian Monks*, 35, *Erga*, vol. 3, 163. See also Ps 24:18 (LXX).

111. Jerome *Letter to Salvinas* 3.79.9 (*PL* 22.730-731).

112. See Evagrius, *Discourse of Evagrius on the Eight Bad Thoughts* (addit 14578 fol. 34^{b8}-77$^{a\alpha}$) in Wilhelm Frankenberg's *Evagrius Ponticus*, (Berlin: Weidmannsche Buchhandlung, 1912), 472-544.

113. Backus, *Hidden Rift with God*, 123 (see chap. 4, n. 11).

114. Elaine Leong Eng, "Faith and Psychology: Integration or Separation?" *Journal of Health and Religion* 37, no. 1 (Spring 1998): 46.

115. Propst, *Psychotherapy in a Religious Framework*, 105–107. Cf. Mt 26:75 and Jn 21:7.

116. Fr. Anthony Coniaris also lists biblical responses to psychologically maladaptive bad thoughts. See his *Confronting and Controlling Thoughts*, 94–95 (see intro., n. 26).

117. Maximus the Confessor *To Thalassius* 16 (PG 90.300d).

118. Evagrius *On the Various Bad Thoughts* 27 (PG 79.1232c-d).

119. Maximus the Confessor *Centuries on Love* 3.42 (PG 90.1029b). Palmer, Sherrard, and Ware, *Philokalia*, vol. 2, 89.

120. Ibid. 3.43 (PG 90.1029b) and Abba Joseph *Sayings of the Fathers* I.3 (PG 65.229ab).

121. Symeon the New Theologian *Catechetical Discourses* 25.9 (SC 113.66). See also Evagrius *On the Various Bad Thoughts* 8 (PG 79.1209c).

122. Theophan the Recluse, *Put' ko spaseniju*, 287.

123. Maximus the Confessor *Centuries on Love* 3.20 (PG 90.1021c).

124. Beck et al., *Cognitive Therapy of Depression*, 146.

125. J. S. Beck, *Cognitive Therapy*, 81.

126. Beck et al., *Cognitive Therapy of Depression*, 148.

127. See his *Book One A List of Passions* (PHIL 3.107–108).

128. J. S. Beck, *Cognitive Therapy*, 100–101.

129. Ibid., 83–84.

130. J. S. Beck, *Cognitive Therapy for Challenging Problems*, 213.

131. J. S. Beck, *Cognitive Therapy*, 100–102.

132. Augustine *City of God* 11.30 (PL 41.344). Cf. Ws 11:20.

133. Neilus the Ascetic *Those who Dwell in Cities Differ...* 24 (PG 79.1089b).

134. Nicodemos the Hagiorite, *Exomologētarion*, 182. St. John Chrysostom makes the same recommendation in his *Commentary on Hebrews* 31.5 (PG 63.216).

135. Weishaar, *Aaron T. Beck*, 112.

136. J. S. Beck, *Cognitive Therapy*, 107.

137. *Fusion of Psychiatry and Social Science*, 83 (see chap. 4, n. 38).

138. Ibid., 216.

139. A. T. Beck, *Cognitive Therapy and Emotional Disorders*, 243.

140. Beck and Emery with Greenberg, *Anxiety Disorders and Phobias*, 206.

141. A. T. Beck, *Love is Never Enough*, 62.

142. J. S. Beck, *Cognitive Therapy for Challenging Problems*, 237–239.

143. Burns, *Feeling Good*, 63.

144. Beck et al., *Cognitive Therapy of Depression*, 287.

145. J. S. Beck, *Cognitive Therapy*, 126.

146. Ibid., 135.

147. Burns, *Feeling Good*, 64.

148. Weishaar, *Aaron T. Beck*, 92.

149.   J. S. Beck, *Cognitive Therapy*, 214–215.

150.   Evagrius, *Discourse of Evagrius on the Eight Bad Thoughts* (addit 14578 fol. 34^{b8}–77^{aa}) in Frankenberg's *Evagrius Ponticus*, 423.

151.   McMinn and Campbell, *Integrative Psychotherapy*, 201.

152.   Freeman et al., *Clinical Applications*, 53.

153.   Bandura, *Social Learning Theory*, 106 (see chap. 2, n. 77).

154.   J. S. Beck, *Cognitive Therapy*, 213.

155.   Phil 4:7.

Chapter Nine

1.   See Col 3:9–10.

2.   See Mk 4:26–28.

3.   See 1 Cor 3:6.

4.   Mk 4:28.

5.   See Hilary of Poitiers *On the Trinity* 1.34 (*PL* 10.47b).

6.   See Ambrose of Milan *On the Duties of the Clergy* 1.10.32–34 (*PL* 16.33a–34a).

7.   See John Chrysostom *Commentary on Matthew* 5.1 (*PG* 57.55).

8.   See John Chrysostom *On the Statues* 3.7 (*PG* 49.58) and *Commentary on Acts* 29.4 (*PG* 60.226).

9.   See John Chrysostom *Commentary on Matthew* 11.8 (*PG* 57.201).

10.   See Barsanuphius, *Texts*, vol. 1, no. 79, 200; vol. 2, no. 237, 52; vol. 2, no. 380, 270.

11.   See Dorotheos of Gaza *Discourses* 1.20 (*SC* 92.176–178).

12.   See Athanasius the Great *Interpretation on the Psalms* 118.60 (*PG* 27.489d). St. Jerome interprets this psalm in *Breviarium in Psalmos* 118 (*PL* 26.1194a) as follows: "I prepared myself to confess and was not disturbed by tribulations sustained for Christ's sake." See also Ambrose of Milan *Exposition on Psalm 118* 36 (*PL* 15.1378a).

13.   See [John Chrysostom?] *Interpretation on the Psalms* 118.9 (*PG* 55.687). Cf. Theodoret of Cyrus *Interpretation on the Psalms* 118.60 (*PG* 80.1840d–1841a).

14.   See Cyril of Alexandria *Commentary on John* 9.1 (*PG* 74.157d–160a).

15.   See John Cassian *Conferences* 3.19.14 (*PL* 49.1143bc). See also Severianus of Gabala [John Chrysostom, pseud.] *Homily on the Blind Man* (*PG* 59.609); John Cassian *Conferences* 3.19.16 (*PL* 49.1146a); and Basil of Caesarea *Homily on the Irascible* 10.5 (*PG* 31.364c).

16.   See Nicodemos the Hagiorite, *Aoratos polemos*, 63.

17.   See Theophan the Recluse, *Put' ko spaseniju*, 115.

18.   See Neilus the Ascetic [pseud.] *Encheiridion of Epictetus* 35 (*PG* 79.1300b). Cf. Epictetus *Discourse of Arrian* 3.15 (*LCL* 131.100) and *Encheiridion* 29 (*LCL* 218.506).

19.   See Neilus the Ascetic [pseud.] *Encheiridion of Epictetus* 9 (*PG* 79.1289a). Cf. Epictetus *Encheiridion* 4 (*LCL* 218.486).

20. See Neilus the Ascetic [pseud.] *Encheiridion of Epictetus* 48 (PG 79.1304d). Cf. Epictetus *Encheiridion* 33 (LCL 218.131).

21. See Beck et al., *Cognitive Therapy of Depression*, 135.

22. See Beck and Emery with Greenberg, *Anxiety Disorders and Phobias*, 230.

23. Maximus the Confessor *Centuries on Love* 4.54 (PG 90.1060c). Palmer, Sherrard, and Ware, *Philokalia*, vol. 2, 106.

24. See Gregory Palamas *On Behalf of the Hesychasts* 2.1.42 *Syngramata*, vol. 1, 504.

25. See John Cassian *Conferences* 2.13.3 (PL 49.902b).

26. Phil 4:8.

27. See John Chrysostom *Commentary on Philippians* 14.2 (PG 62.284).

28. See Isaac the Syrian, *Ta askētika*, hom. 56, 227.

29. See ibid., 38, 166.

30. See Dorotheos of Gaza *Letter Four to the Cellarer* 189 (SC 92.506).

31. See Isaac the Syrian, *Ta askētika*, hom. 52, 212. See also John Climacus *Ladder* 1 (PG 88.636d-637a).

32. Theodoret of Cyrus *Ecclesiastical History* 4.19 (PG 82.1176a).

33. Cyprian of Carthage *Letter to Fortunatus* 13 (PL 4.676a).

34. See Barsanuphius, *Texts*, vol 1, no. 135, 286.

35. See Leo the Great *Sermons* 67.1 (PL 54.368bc).

36. See Dorotheos of Gaza *Discourses* 12.128-129 (SC 92.388).

37. See John Chrysostom *Commentary on Hebrews* 26.3 (PG 63.182).

38. See Gregory of Sinai *Chapters* 130 (PG 150.1293d).

39. See Peter of Damascus *Book One on the Eight Stages of Contemplation* (PHIL 3.32-33). St. Nicodemos the Hagiorite likewise provides a similar list of topics to be used when the mind grows weary from noetic prayer. See his *Aoratos polemos*, 105-107.

40. Theophan the Recluse's list emphasizes the absolute character of those subjects. In particular, he mentions "the reigning power of God, the paradigm of salvation, the four finalities: death, judgment, paradise and hell." See *Put' ko spaseniju*, 211.

41. See John Cassian *Conferences* 2.11.9 (PL 49.855b-857a).

42. See ibid. 3.24.6 (PL 49.1295ab).

43. See John Climacus *Ladder* 6 (PG 88.796c).

44. See Theophan the Recluse, *Put' ko spaseniju*, 115.

45. See Neilus the Ascetic [pseud.] *Encheiridion of Epictetus* 28 (PG 79.1296b) and Diadochus of Photiki *On Spiritual Knowledge* 81 (SC5bis.139).

46. See John Climacus *Ladder* 6 (PG 88.796cd).

47. Theophan the Recluse, *Put' ko spaseniju*, 213-14. Cf. also Heb 9:27.

48. See Frank Dattilio, Elizabeth Davis, and Robert Goisman, "Crisis with Medical Patients," in Frank Dattilio and Arthur Freeman, eds., *Cognitive-Behavioral Strategies in Crisis Intervention*, (New York: The Guilford Press, 2007), 231.

49. See Freeman et al., *Clinical Applications*, 67.

50. See Ignatius Brianchaninov, *The Arena, An Offering to Contemporary Monasticism* (Jordanville, NY: Holy Trinity Monastery, 1991) 1,4. See also ibid., 21-23.

51. Theophan the Recluse, in *The Art of Prayer*, 246.

52. See Abba Epiphanius of Cyprus *Sayings of the Fathers* E.9 (*PG* 65.165b).

53. See Dorotheos of Gaza *Letters* 7.192 (SC 92.512).

54. See Cyprian of Carthage *On Jealousy and Envy* 16 (*PL* 4.649a).

55. See Paulinus and Therasia *Letter to Augustine* 1.25 (*PL* 33.101).

56. See Maximus the Confessor *Letter to Constantine the Treasurer* 24 (*PG* 91.609d–612a).

57. See John Cassian *Conferences* 1.1.14 (*PL* 49.508a). See also Isaac the Syrian, *Ta askētika*, hom. 23, 95.

58. See John Climacus *Ladder* 27 (*PG* 88.1116cd). See also John of Damascus *Exact Exposition of the Orthodox Faith* 4.17 (*PG* 94.1176c).

59. See Athanasius the Great *Festal Letter* 11.7 (*PG* 26.1408a).

60. See John Cassian *Conferences* 2.14.13 (*PL* 49.979b–981b).

61. Neilus the Ascetic *Ascetic Discourse* 36 (*PG* 79.764d): *"Hai gar synecheis tōn kalōn paradeigmatōn mneiai para plēsias eikonas encharattousi tais mē pany sklērais kai apokrotois psychais."* The same holds true for evil remembrances or impure images as he notes in his *Letter to Prisko* 3.288 (*PG* 79.525d).

62. See Isaac the Syrian, *Ta askētika*, hom. 56, 227.

63. See Thalassius *On Love and Self-control* 3.37 (*PG* 91.1452b). See also Isaac the Syrian, *Ta askētika*, 1, 4 and John Chrysostom *Encomium to the Martyr Barlaam* 4 (*PG* 50.682).

64. See Neilus the Ascetic *Discourse on Non-acquisitiveness* 20 (*PG* 79.996c).

65. Isaac the Syrian, *Ta askētika*, hom. 14, 53. *The Ascetical Homilies*, hom. 13, 81.

66. See J. S. Beck, *Cognitive Therapy*, 250.

67. See John Cassian *Conferences* 2.14.13 (*PL* 49.979a). Abba Dorotheos likewise referred to zeal in secular studies ·as a goad to similar fervor with respect to virtue. See *Discourses* 10.105 (SC 92.338–340).

68. John Chrysostom *On the Statues* 1.1 (*PG* 49.18).

69. See Elder Païsios the Hagiorite, *Logoi*, vol. 2, 100.

70. See Theophan the Recluse, *Put' ko spaseniju*, 233.

71. See John Climacus *Ladder* 27 (*PG* 88.1116d).

72. See Ignatius Brianchaninov, *The Arena*, 22.

73. Nicodemos the Hagiorite, *Aoratos polemos*, 69–70.

74. Gn 3:8; 2:19.

75. In the standard alphabetical collection of *Sayings of the Fathers* (*PG* 65.71a–440d), *"eipe moi rhēma"* is used eleven times, whereas the variant *"eipe moi logon"* appears five times.

76. See Jn 15:5.

77. See Larchet, *Mental Disorders*, 59.

78. Basil of Caesarea *Letter of Consolation* 2.101.1 (*PG* 32.508a).

79. See Maximus the Confessor *Letter to John the Presbyter* 8 (*PG* 90.445b).

80. See John Chrysostom *Commentary on Ephesians* 19.2 (*PG* 62.129–130).

81. Isaac the Syrian, *Ta askētika*, hom. 48, 198. *The Ascetical Homilies*, hom. 61, 296.

82. Leo the Great *Sermons* 12.2 (*PL* 54.169c–170a).

83. John Chrysostom *Commentary on Second Corinthians* 1.6 (*PG* 61.390–391).

84. Isaac the Syrian, *Ta askētika*, hom. 73, 284. *The Ascetical Homilies*, hom. 48, 229.

85. See Abba Zosima *Thoughts* 3 (PG 78.1684cd). For an additional comparison between doctors and those who trouble us, see Dorotheos of Gaza *Letter* 2.187 (SC 92.504).

86. See Philotheus of Sinai *Forty Texts on Watchfulness* 40 (*PHIL* 2.286).

87. See Dorotheos of Gaza *Letters* 2.187 (SC 92.504).

88. See Mark the Ascetic *On Those Who Think They Are Made Righteous by Works* 193 (PG 65.960d).

89. Dorotheos of Gaza *Discourses* 6.75 (SC 92.278).

90. Ibid. 7.84 (SC 92.296).

91. See Abba Isaiah *On Commandments for Believers* 7 (*HPE* 12.29) and 5.2 (PG 40.1122b).

92. See Elder Païsios the Hagiorite, *Logoi*, vol. 3, 71.

93. See John Cassian *Conferences* 3.19.14 (*PL* 49.1143d–1144a). Cf. Ps. 119:60 (MT); 118:60 (LXX).

94. See Dorotheos of Gaza *Discourses* 8.90 (SC 92.308).

95. Nicodemos the Hagiorite, *Aoratos polemos*, 55–56.

96. Jerome, *Letter to Algasias* 4,121,1 (*PL* 22.1007). Palladius likewise cites this saying with approval in *Lausiac History* 21 (PG 34.1091). Galens attributes this saying to Hippocrates on numerous occasions. E.g. *To Erasistratos*, *Clavdii Galeni Opera Omnia*, vol. 11, 167.

97. See Nicodemos the Hagiorite, *Exomologētarion*, 20–22. Gregory Palamas mentions some of these reasons in *Homily* 22 (PG 151.289b). See also his *To the Nun Xenia* (PG 150.1052d–1053a).

98. See Nicodemos the Hagiorite, *Exomologētarion*, 186.

99. See ibid., 1,6, 37–38.

100. Neilus the Ascetic [pseud.] *Encheiridion of Epictetus* 33 (PG 79.1297d).

101. Basil of Caesarea *Letter to Nektarius* 1.5.2 (PG 32.240b). Tertullian makes use of a similar reminder about the human condition [*conditionis humanae*] in order to encourage the faithful to look at martyrdom differently. See his *On Martyrs* 6 (*PL* 1.626c).

102. See Basil of Caesarea *Letter to the Spouse of Nektarius* 1.6.2 (PG 32.244ac). Theodore the Studite provides similar arguments in *Letter to Staurakius a member of the Ceremonial Bodyguard* 1.18 (PG 99.964d–965a).

103. See Ambrose of Milan *On the Decease of his Brother Satyrus* 2.3 (*PL* 16.1315c–1316b).

104. See Theodore the Studite *Letter to Thomas, the Two-term Consul* 1.12 (PG 99.952b). See also Ps 142:7 (MT); 141:8 (LXX).

105. See Elder Païsios the Hagiorite, *Epistoles* 5, 225.

106. See Freeman et al., *Clinical Applications*, 117, 127; Kingdon and Turkington, *Cognitive Therapy of Schizophrenia*, 172.

107. John Chrysostom *On the Statues* 2.9 (PG 49.37).

108. See John Chrysostom *Commentary on John* 77.4 (PG 59.418).

109. Ibid. 45.4 (PG 59.255–256).

110. See Abba Kronio *Sayings of the Fathers* K.2 (PG 65.248bc).

111. See Neilus the Ascetic *Ascetic Discourse* 51 (PG 79.781d).

112. See Dorotheos of Gaza *Discourses* 12.125 (SC 92.382).

113.   See Abba Isaiah *On Commandments for the Believers* 44 (*HPE* 12.41).

114.   St. Maximus the Confessor's misattribution of this quotation to much earlier philosophers and rhetoricians such as Isocrates, Democratus, and Epictetus is understandable, given Libanius of Antioch's (AD 314–393) penchant for writing as though he lived during the pre-Christian era. See Maximus *Collection from Various Books* 28 (*PG* 91.880a). Cf. Libanius, *Fragmenta*, 88, 27, *Libanii Opera*, vol. 11, ed. Richard Forester (Hildesheim, Germany: Georg Olms Verlagsbuchhandlung, 1963), 665.

115.   See John Chrysostom *Commentary on Titus* 2.3 (*PG* 62.674).

116.   See John Climacus *Ladder* 26 (*PG* 88.1016bc).

117.   See Beck and Emery with Greenberg, *Anxiety Disorders and Phobias*, 217, 220.

118.   See J. S. Beck, *Cognitive Therapy*, 230–242.

119.   See Propst, *Psychotherapy in a Religious Framework*, 136–138 (see chap. 3, n. 6).

120.   See Elaine L. Eng, "Faith and Psychology: Integration or Separation?" *Journal of Health and Religion* 37, no. 1 (Spring 1998): 46; cf. Jn 15:1–5.

121.   Mt 5:13–14.

122.   Theophan the Recluse, *Put' ko spaseniju*, 121. *The Path of Salvation*, 143.

123.   See John D. Teasdale, "Clinically Relevant Theory: Integrating Clinical Insight with Cognitive Science," in Salkovskis, ed., *Frontiers of Cognitive Therapy*, 45.

124.   See John Chrysostom *Commentary on Second Corinthians* 5.3–4 (*PG* 61.432).

125.   See ibid. 3.5 (*PG* 61.411–413).

126.   See Theodore the Studite *Catechetical Discourse* 99 (*HPE* 18a.364).

127.   See Theophan the Recluse, *Put' ko spaseniju*, 121.

128.   See John Chrysostom *Commentary on Romans* 14.10–11 (*PG* 60.537–538).

129.   See John Chrysostom *Commentary on Acts* 7.4 (*PG* 60.69–70).

130.   Ibid. 31.3 (*PG* 60.232). St. John Climacus also compares angry reactions to physical vomiting. See his *Ladder* 8 (*PG* 88.829d).

131.   See John Chrysostom *Commentary on Acts* 50.3 (*PG* 60.348).

132.   See ibid. 31.3 (*PG* 60.232).

133.   See ibid. 50.3 (*PG* 60.349).

134.   See John Chrysostom *Against the Jews* 8.7 (*PG* 48.939).

135.   See Elder Païsios the Hagiorite, *Epistoles*, 2, 108.

136.   John Chrysostom *Commentary on Acts* 31.3 (*PG* 60.231). For a similar exhortation calling to mind Job, the poor Lazarus, the apostles, prophets, and righteous see his *On the Statues* 1.10 (*PG* 49.30).

137.   See *Life of Saint Syncletica* (*SYN* 1.129).

138.   See John Moschus *Spiritual Meadow* 208 (*PG* 87c.3100d).

139.   John Climacus *Ladder* 26 (*PG* 88.1065c). Holy Transfiguration Monastery, 184.

140.   See Theodore the Studite *Letter to Nikephorus the Hegoumenos* 1.4 (*PG* 99.921a).

141.   See Symeon the New Theologian *Practical Chapters* 1.47 (*PG* 120.621c).

142.   Ps 117:23 (LXX);118:23 (MT).

143.   See Freeman et al., *Clinical Applications*, 82.

144.   See Beck et al., *Cognitive Therapy of Personality Disorders*, 73.

145. Burns, *Feeling Good*, 234.

146. See Freeman et al., *Clinical Applications*, 84.

147. See Christine Padesky, "Schema Change Processes in Cognitive Therapy," *Clinical Psychology and Psychotherapy* 1, no. 5 (1994): 269.

148. See Beck et al., *Cognitive Therapy of Personality Disorders*, 61.

149. See Freeman et al., *Clinical Applications*, 84.

150. See Burns, *Feeling Good*, 241–249.

151. See J. S. Beck, *Cognitive Therapy*, 146.

152. See Burns, *Feeling Good*, 237.

153. See J. S. Beck, *Cognitive Therapy*, 148.

154. See Freeman et al., *Clinical Applications*, 86.

155. See Padesky, "Schema Change Processes in Cognitive Therapy," 269–270.

156. See Beck et al., *Cognitive Therapy of Substance Abuse*, 137.

157. See J. S. Beck, *Cognitive Therapy*, 160–161.

158. See ibid., 160.

159. Michael W. Kramer, *Managing Uncertainty in Organizational Communication* (Mahwah, NJ: Lawrence Erlbaum Associates, 2003), 89; Propst, *Psychotherapy in a Religious Framework*, 56.

160. See Wendy Doniger, *Britannica Encyclopedia of World Religions* (London: Encyclopedia Britannica, 2006), 220; Ewret Cousins, "The Humanity and the Passion of Christ," in Jill Raitt, Bernard McGinn, and John Meyendorff, eds., *Christian Spirituality: High Middle Ages*, vol. 2 (New York: Crossroads, 1987), 375.

161. Augustine *Tractates on John* 16.4 (PL 35.1468).

162. Idem *On the First Epistle of John* 9.3 (PL 35.2047).

163. Tertullian *Against Scorpiace the Gnostic* 11 (PL 2.145a).

164. Idem *Against Marcion* 4.22 (PL 2.413b).

165. Rom 12:2.

166. John Chrysostom *Commentary on Romans* 20.3 (PG 60.598).

167. See J. S. Beck, *Cognitive Therapy*, 156–158.

168. See Padesky, "Schema Change Processes in Cognitive Therapy," 270.

169. See Christine Padesky with Dennis Greenberger, *Clinician's Guide to Mind over Mood* (New York: The Guildford Press, 1995), 140–142.

170. See Padesky, "Schema Change Processes in Cognitive Therapy," 271–272.

171. See Padesky with Greenberger, *Clinician's Guide*, 144.

172. See Padesky, "Schema Change Processes in Cognitive Therapy," 272–273.

173. See 1 Tm 1:15.

174. Gn 18:27.

175. See Mircea Eliade, *The Sacred and the Profane* (Orlando, FL: Harcourt, 1959).

176. See Beck et al., *Cognitive Therapy of Personality Disorders*, 82.

177. See Padesky, "Schema Change Processes in Cognitive Therapy," 274.

178. See J. S. Beck, *Cognitive Therapy*, 186; Beck et al., *Cognitive Therapy of Personality Disorders*, 82.

179. See Propst, *Psychotherapy in a Religious Framework*, 111.

180. See Beck et al., *Cognitive Therapy of Personality Disorders*, 82.

181. See A. T. Beck, *Love is Never Enough*, 161, 248-250.

182. See Augustine *Retractions* 2.6 (PG 32.632).

183. For example, *Sayings of the Fathers*, Maximus the Confessor's *Collection from Various Books*, John of Damascus's *Sacred Parallels*, Paul Evergetinos's *Evergetinos*, and Chariton of Valamo's *Umnoe delanie o molitve Iisusovoy* [The mental art on the Jesus prayer].

184. See respectively, *Moja zhizn' vo Xriste* [My life in Christ] and *Dnevnik svjashennika* [Diary of a Russian priest].

185. See J. S. Beck, *Cognitive Therapy*, 177.

186. See Padesky, "Schema Change Processes in Cognitive Therapy," 277.

187. See ibid., 276 and J. S. Beck, *Cognitive Therapy*, 183-184.

188. Augustine *Confessions* 10.8.2 (PL 32.784).

189. See ibid. 10.13.20 (PL 32.787-788).

190. See Augustine *On the Trinity* 15.7.13 (PL 42.1066-1067).

191. Augustine *Confessions* 11.18.23 (PL 32.818).

192. See ibid. 10.8.12 (PL 32, 784).

193. See Augustine *On the Trinity* 11.8.15 (PL 42.996). Experimental cognitive psychology has likewise firmly established that the amount of information a person can process has clearly defined limits. See Teasdale, "Clinically Relevant Theory," in Salkovskis, ed., *Frontiers of Cognitive Therapy*, 38.

194. See Augustine *City of God* 7.3.1 (PL 41.196).

195. See Augustine *Confessions* 4.1.1 (PL 32.693).

196. See Augustine *On the Psalms* 70.2.2 (PL 36.892).

197. 1 Tm 6:12.

198. See Athanasius the Great *Life of Anthony* 10 (PG 26.860b).

199. See Elder Porphyrios, *Bios kai logoi*, 368-369.

200. See Padesky, "Schema Change Processes in Cognitive Therapy," 277; Dayton, *Trauma and Addiction*, 341-352 (see chap. 4, n. 153).

201. See J. S. Beck, *Cognitive Therapy*, 186.

202. See Beck et al., *Cognitive Therapy of Personality Disorders*, 312-313.

203. See J. S. Beck, *Cognitive Therapy*, 159-160.

204. See Backus, *Hidden Rift with God*, 153, 162 (see chap. 4, n. 11).

205. John Chrysostom *Commentary on Matthew* 44.5 (PG 57.408).

206. Cyril of Alexandria *Commentary on the Prophet Isaiah* 5.4 (PG 70.1296b).

207. Gregory of Nyssa *Commentary on the Song of Songs* 9 (PG 44.968c).

Chapter Ten

1. Clement of Alexandria *Exhortation to the Heathen* 1 (PG 8.60bc).

2. Lactantius [pseud.] *Phoenix* (PL 7.279).

3. Venantius Honorius On Pascha (PL 7.287).

4. For example, see John Chrysostom Homily on Elijah 6 (PG 51.343) and Encomium to the Great Martyr Drosida 3 (PG 50.687).

5. Stanley Rachman, foreword to P. Salkovskis, ed., Frontiers of Cognitive Therapy, xi.

6. In his article, "Beyond Belief: A Theory of Modes, Personality, and Psychopathology" (in P. Salkovskis, ed., Frontiers of Cognitive Therapy, 1–25), Beck proposes replacing the concept of mood with the concept of primal modes that are incrementally activated by experiences. John Teasedale's work on interactive cognitive substystems analysis promises other theoretical advances in the understanding of psychopathology. See his "Clinically Relevant Theory: Integrating Clinical Insight with Cognitive Science," 26–47 in the same volume.

7. M. E. Weishaar, Aaron T. Beck, 122.

8. See M. Mahoney, Constructive Psychotherapy, 109, 112, 114, 163, 212–213 (see chap. 6, n. 1).

9. David R. Hodge, "Spiritually Modified Cognitive Therapy: A Review of the Literature," National Association of Social Workers 51, no. 2 (2006): 164.

10. Padesky, Clinician's Guide, 50–51.

11. D. R. Hodge, "Spiritually Modified Cognitive Therapy," 165.

12. M. E. Weishaar, Aaron T. Beck, 79 citing David Clark.

13. Bromley and Busching, "Understanding the Structure of Social Relations," S23 (see chap. 6, n. 182).

14. Augustine City of God 2.21 (PL 41.66).

15. Hermias Sozomen Ecclesiastical History 3.16 (PG 67.1089ab).

16. Theodoret of Cyrus Ecclesiastical History 4.26 (PG 82.1189d).

17. John Chrysostom On the Statues 1.1 (PG 49.15–17).

18. Methodius of Olympus On the Free-will 1 (PG 18.241a).

✠ Bibliography ✠

1. Patristic Sources: Ancient and Contemporary

Agapios Monk, ed. *Hieron pēdalion*. Athens: Blastoy Barbarēngou, 1886.

Ambrose of Milan. *De excessu fatris sui Satyri*. Bk. 2. PL 16.1345–1412.

———. *De officiis ministrorum*. Bk. 1. PL 16.25–192.

———. *De poenitentia*. Bk. 1 and 2. PL 16.485–544.

———. *Epistolae*. Ep. 37, 51, and 70. PL 16.910–1341.

———. *In psalmi CXVIII expositionem*. PL 15.1257–1603.

Anastasius of Sinai. *Ek tou kat' eikona logos*. PG 89.1151–1180.

———. *Erōtēseis kai apokriseis*. PG 89.329–824.

Anonymous. *Apophthegmata tōn paterōn*. PG 65.71–440.

———. *Bios Maximou*. PG 90.67–110.

———. *Megas synaxaristēs tēs orthodoxou ekklēsias*. 12 vols. Athens: Ēlias Bakopoulos Monachos, 2001.

———. *Mēnaion tou apriliou*. Athens: Apostolikēs Diakonias tēs Hellados, 1977.

———. *Mēnaion tou ianouariou*. Athens: Apostolikēs Diakonias tēs Hellados, 1979.

———. *Mēnaion tou maiou*. Athens: Apostolikēs Diakonias tēs Hellados, 1977.

———. *Mēnaion tou septembriou*. Athens: Apostolikēs Diakonias tēs Hellados, 1959.

———. *Ōrologion to mega*. Athens: Phōs-xeen, 1992.

———. *Paradeisos tōn paterōn*. Bk. 2, 5, 7, and 18. SC 387 and 498 as *Les Apophtegmes des Pères*. 3 vols. Translated by Jean-Claude Guy. Paris: Les Éditions du Cerf, 1993–2005.

———. *Paraklitēkē ētoi oktōēxos hē megalē*. Athens: Apostolikēs Diakonias tēs Hellados, 1984.

———. *Poimēn tou Herma*. Bk. 1 and 3. PG 2.891–1010.

———. *Prōtē epistolē tou Barnaba*. SC 172 as *Épître de Barnabé*. Translated by Pierre Prigent. Paris: Les Éditions du Cerf, 1971.

———. *Triōdion katanyktikon*. Athens: Phōs-xeen, 1989.

Antiochus the Monk. *Logoi pros ton Eustathion*. Hom. 23, 49, 81, 111. PG 89.1421–1850.

Aristotle. *Nichomachean Ethics*. Edited by H. Rackhan. Vol. 73. LCL, 1962.

Arnobius. *Disputationes adversus gentes*. Bk. 2. PL 5.713–1200.

Athanasius the Great. *Bios kai politeia tou hosiou Antōniou*. PG 26.837–978.

———. *Epistoles heortastikes*. Ep. 3 and 11. PG 26.1310–1432.

———. *Epistolē pros ton Kastora peri tōn oktō tēs kakias logismōn*. PG 28.849–906.

———. *Exigēsis eis tous psalmous*. Pss. 44 and 118. PG 27.60–545.

Athanasius the Great. *Kata Areianōn*. Pt. 1. PG 26.1071–1084.

Athanasios the Great [pseud]. *Diagnōsis tou trimerous psychēs*. PG 28.1379–1408.

Athenagoras the Philosopher. *Peri anastaseōs tōn nekrōn*. PG 6.973–1024.

Augoustidis, Fr. Adamantios. *Hē anthrōpinē epithetikotēta*. New Smyrna, Greece: Akritas, 1999.

Augustine of Hippo. *Confessiones*. Bk. 4, 10, and 11. PL 32.657–868.

——. *Contra epistolam Manichaei*. PL 42.173–206.

——. *Contra Faustum Manichaem*. PL 42.207–518.

——. *De anima et ejus origine*. Bk. 3. PL 44.475–548.

——. *De civitate Dei*. Bk. 7 and 16. PL 41.13–804.

——. *De consensu evangelistarum*. Bk. 2 and 3. PL 34.1041–1228.

——. *De continentia*. PL 40.345–372.

——. *De doctrina christiana*. Bk. 2 and 4. PL 34.15–122.

——. *De mendacio*. PL 40.487–516.

——. *De natura boni contra Manicheos*. PL 42.577–602.

——. *De nuptiis et concupiscentia*. Bk. 1. PL 44.119–198.

——. *De origine animae hominis (Epistola 166)*. PL 33.471–1025.

——. *De peccatorum meritis et remissione ad Marcellinum*. Bk. 1. PL 44.119–198.

——. *De perfectione justitiae hominis*. PL 44.291–318.

——. *De sermone Domini in monte*. Bk. 1 and 2. PL 34.1229–1308.

——. *De Trinitate*. Bk. 11, 12, and 15. PL 42.819–1100.

——. *Enarrationes in psalmos*. Pss. 41, 48, 70, 84, 86, 90, 91, 94, 137, and 148. PL 36.67–1028 and PL 37.1033–1968.

——. *Enchiridion aud Larentium sive de fide*. PL 40.231–288.

——. *Epistolae*. Ep. 11. PL 33.61–121.

——. *In epistolam Joannis ad Parthos*. Hom. 1, 7, and 9. PL 35.1977–2062.

——. *In evangelium Joannis tractatus*. Hom. 12, 16, 28, 40, 55, 58, 77, and 90. PL 35.1379–1978.

——. *Retractionum*. Bk. 2. PG 32.583–659.

——. *Sermones ad populum*. Hom. 56, 68, 98, 113, 131, and 138. PL 38.23–995.

Barsanuphius, Abba. *Keimena diakritika kai hēsychastika*. 3 vols. Kareas, Greece: Etoimasia, 1996–1997.

Basil of Caesarea. *Eis tēn archēn tōn paroimiōn*. PG 31.385–424.

——. *Eis tēn hexaēmeron*. Hom. 4. PG 29b.77–94.

——. *Eis ton hebdomon psalmon*. PG 29b.227–250.

——. *Eis ton prōton psalmon*. PG 29b.209–228.

——. *Epistolai*. Ep. 5, 6, 22, 24, 38, 42, 101, 217, and 334. PG 32.67–1112.

——. *Hermēneia eis ton prophētēn Ēsaïan*. PG 30.117–668.

——. *Homilia kata orgizomenōn*. PG 31.353–372.

——. *Horoi kata platos*. PG 31.889–1052.

——. *Kat' epitomēn horōn*. PG 31.1051–1306.

——. *Logos peri askēseōs*. PG 31.625–648.

——. *Peri didachēs kai nouthesias*. Hom. 2. PG 32.1133–1146.

Basil of Caesarea. *Pros tous neous*. PG 31.563–590.

Chariton of Valamo. *The Art of Prayer: An Orthodox Anthology*. Translated by E. Kadloubovsky and E. M. Palmer. Edited by Timothy Ware. London: Faber & Faber, 1966.

Cicero. *De officiis*. Edited by W. Miller. Vol. 30. *LCL*, 1961.

Clement of Alexandria. *Logos protreptikos pros hellinas*. PG 8.49–246.

———. *Logos tis ho sōzomenos plousios*. PG 9.603–652.

———. *Paidagōgos*. Bk. 1. PG 8.247–684.

———. *Strōmateis*. Bk. 6 and 7. PG 9.207–558.

Clement of Rome. *Epistolē pros korinthious a′*. PG 1.201–328.

——— [pseud]. *Diatagai tōn apostolōn*. Bk. 2. PG 1.555–1156.

Colliander, Tito. *The Way of the Ascetics*. Crestwood, NY: Saint Vladimir's Press, 1960.

Coniaris, Fr. Anthony. *Confronting and Controlling Thoughts According to the Fathers of the Philokalia*. Minneapolis, MI: Light & Life, 2004.

Cyprian of Carthage. *Epistola ad Fortunatum de exhortatione martyrii*. PL 4.651–676.

———. *Epistolae*. Ep. 10 and 26. PL 3.709–856 and PL 4.191–483.

———. *Liber de lapsis*. PL 4.463–494.

——— [?]. *Liber de laude martyrii*. PL 4.787–804.

———. *Liber de opere et eleemosynis*. PL 4.601–622.

——— [?]. *Liber de spectaculis*. PL 4.779–788.

———. *Liber de zelo et livore*. PL 4.637–652.

Cyril of Alexandria. *Exēgēsis hypomnēmatikē eis ton prophētēn Ēsaïan*. Bk. 5. PG 70.9–1450.

———. *Hypomnēma eis to kata Iōannēn*. Bk. 4 and 9. PG 73.9–1056 and PG 74.9–756.

Cyril of Jerusalem. *Katēchēseis*. Disc. 4, 6, and 13. PG 33.331–1060.

Diadochus of Photiki. *Kephalaia gnōstika*. SC 5bis as *Œuvres spirituelles*. Translated by Édouard des Places. Paris: Les Éditions du Cerf, 1997.

Didymus the Blind. *Psalmen-Kommentar (Tura-Papyrus) Part 3 (Psalms 29–34)*. Edited by Michael Gronewald. Bonn: Michael Gronewald, 1969.

Dionysius the Areopagite [pseud.]. *Peri theiōn honomatōn*. PG 3.585–984.

Dorotheos of Gaza. *Didaskalia*. Disc. 1, 2, 5, 6, 8, 9, 10, 11, 12, 14, and 17. Ep. 1, 2, 4, 7, and 8. SC 92 as *Œuvres spirituelles*. Translated by L. Regnault and J. de Préville. Paris: Les Éditions du Cerf, 1963.

Ephraim the Syrian. *Erga*. 6 vols. Edited by Konstantinos Phrantzoles. Thessaloniki, Greece: To Perivoli tēs Panagias, 1989–1995.

Epictetus. *Arrianou tōn Epictētou Diatribōn*. Edited by W. Oldfather. Vol. 131. *LCL*, 1967.

———. *Encheiridion*. Edited by W. Oldfather. Vol. 218. *LCL*, 1967.

Eusebius of Caesarea. *Ekklēsiastikēs historias*. Bk. 1. PG 20.45–906.

Evagrius Ponticus. *Logos Evagriou peri oktō logismōn*. *Evagrius Ponticus*. Edited by Wilhelm Frankenberg Berlin: Weidmannsche Buchhandlung, 1912.

——— [Neilus the Ascetic, pseud]. *Peri diaphorōn ponērōn logismōn*. PG 79.1199–1234.

———. *Peri tōn oktō logismōn*. PG 40.1271–1273.

———[Neilus the Ascetic, pseud]. *Peri tōn oktō pneumatōn tēs ponērias*. PG 79.1145–1164.

———. *Praktikos*. PG 40.1219–1252.

Evagrius Ponticus. *Tōn kata monachōn pragmatōn ta aitia.* PG 40.1251–1264.

Galen. *Tinas dei ekkathairein. Claudii Galeni Opera Omnia.* Vol. 11. Hildesheim, Germany: Georg Olms Verlagsbuchhandlung, 1965.

Gregory of Nyssa. *Eis tēn proseuchēn.* Disc. 4. PG 44.1161–1178.

———. *Exēgēsis akribēs eis to asma tōn asmatōn.* Hom. 9. PG 44.755–1120.

———. *Logos katēchētikos ho megas.* PG 45.9–106.

———. *Peri kataskeuēs anthrōpou.* PG 44.123–256.

———. *Peri parthenias.* PG 46.317–416.

———. *Peri psychēs kai anastaseōs.* PG 46.11–160.

———. *Pros Eunomion antirrhētikos logos.* Bk. 1 and 6. PG 45.247–464, 709–738.

———. *Pros Eunomion deuteros logos.* Disc. 12. PG 45.909–1122.

Gregory of Sinai. *Hetera kephalaia.* PG 150.1299–1304.

———. *Kephalaia.* PG 150.1239–1300.

———. *Peri hēsychias.* PG 150.1313–1330.

———. *Peri planēs.* PG 150.1337–1346.

———. *Peri tou pōs dei diōkein tous logismous.* PG 150.1331–1334.

Gregory Palamas. *Kephalaia physika, theologika.* PG 150.1121–1226.

———. *Homiliai.* Hom. 12, 20, 21, and 22. PG 151.9–550.

———. *Homilia kb.* Hom. 51. Athens: Ekd. Sophokleos Oikonomou tou ex Oikonomōn, 1861.

———. *Pros Xenēn.* PG 150.1043–1088.

———. *Hyper hēsychazontōn.* Vol. 2. Edited by Panagiotis Christou. Thessaloniki, Greece: P. Christou, 1962.

Gregory the Great. *Epistola ad Theoctistam Patriciam.* PL 77.879–882.

———. *Moralia.* Bk. 31. PL 76.9–782.

———. *Regulae pastoralis.* Pt. 3. PL 77.9–148.

———. *Vita S. Benedicti.* PL 66.125–204.

Gregory of Nazianzus. *Epistolai.* Ep. 32 and 101. PG 37.21–386.

———. *Logoi.* Disc. 2, 4, 7, 16, 27, and 39. PG 35.387–1252 and PG 36.9–623.

Gregory the Wonderworker. *Metaphrasis eis ton ekklēsiastēn tou Solomōntos.* PG 10.987–1018.

Hermias Sozomen. *Ekklēsiastikē historia.* Bk. 3 and 7. PG 67.843–1630.

Hesychius the Presbyter. *Peri nēpseōs kai aretēs.* Cent. 1 and 2. PG 93.1479–1544.

Hilary of Poitiers. *De Trinitate.* Bk. 1 and 3. PL 10.25–472.

Hippolytus. *Refutatio omnium haeresium.* Patristische Texte und Studien. Vol. 25. Berlin: Walter de Gruyter, 1986.

Ignatius Brianchaninov. *The Arena, An Offering to Contemporary Monasticism.* Jordanville, NY: Holy Trinity Monastery, 1991.

Ignatius of Antioch. *Epistolē pros ephesious.* PG 5.643–662.

———. *Pros Polykarpon* [Syriac version]. PG 5.717–728.

Ilias the Presbyter. *Anthologion gnōmikon.* PG 127.1129–1148.

———. *Gnōstika.* PG 127.1147–1176.

Irenaeus of Lyons. *Elenchos kai anatropē tēs pseudonymou gnōseōs*. Bk. 2, 3, 4, and 5. PG 7.433–1222.

Isaac the Syrian. *The Ascetical Homilies of Saint Isaac the Syrian*. Hom. 22, 23, and 24 are extant only in the Syriac. Boston, MA: Holy Transfiguration Monastery, 1984.

———. *Ta eurhethenta askētika*. Hom. 1, 14, 18, 19, 23, 30, 34, 38, 39, 48, 52, 54, 55, 56, 59, 62, 65, 69, 72, 73, 75, 81, 83, and 85 (as numbered in the Greek edition). Edited by Nikēphoros Theotokis. Thessaloniki, Greece: Ekdoseis Basileiou Rēgopoulou, 1985.

Isaiah, Abba. *Fragmenta*. PG 40.211–1214.

———. *Peri entolōn pistōn*. HPE 12.

———. *Ta hiera parallēla*. PG 96.387–422.

Jerome. *Breviarium in Psalmos*. PL 26.821–1278.

———. *Commentariorum in Ephesianum*. Bk. 3. PL 26.439–554.

———. *Commentariorum in evangelium Matthaei*. Bk. 1. PL 26.15–218.

———. *Commentariorum in Ezechielem prophetam*. Bk. 6. PL 25.15–490.

———. *Contra Joannem Hierosolymitanum*. PL 23.371–414.

———. *Epistolae*. Ep. 22, 43, 79, 82, 107, 121, 125, 128, and 130. PL 22.325–1224.

John Cassian. *Collationes*. Disc. 1, 2, 5, 7, 10, 11, 13, 14, 17, 19, 23, and 24. PL 49.477–1328.

———. *De coenobiorum institutes*. Bk. 2, 4, 5, 6, and 9. PL 49.53–476.

———. *Peri tōn oktō tēs kakias logismōn*. PHIL 1.

John Chrysostom. *Eis ta kata ton Davīd kai ton Saoul*. PG 54.695–708.

———. *Eis to apostolikon rhēton dia de tas porneias hekastos tēn heavtou gynaika echetō*. PG 51.207–218.

———. *Eis ton Ēlian*. PG 51.337–348.

———. *Eis ton hagion hieromartyra Phōkan*. PG 50.699–706.

———. *Eis ton seismon kai eis ton plousion kai eis ton Lazaron*. PG 48.1027–1044.

———. *Eis tous andriantas*. Hom. 1, 2, 3, 4, 8, 13, and 20. PG 49.15–222.

———. *Engōmion eis tēn megalomartyra Drosida*. PG 50.683–694.

———. *Engōmion eis ton martyra Barlaam*. PG 50.675–682.

———. *Hermēneia eis tēn pros hebraious*. Hom. 1, 6, 9, 19, 24, 26, and 31. PG 63.9–236.

———. *Logoi kata ioudaiōn*. Disc. 8. PG 48.927–942.

———. *Logos parainetikos eis Theodōron ekpesonta*. Ep. 1. PG 47.277–308.

———. *Logos parainetikos pros Stageiron*. PG 47.423–494.

———. *Peri hierōsynēs*. Bk. 2 and 4. PG 48.623–692.

———. *Pros tous legontas hoti daimones ta anthrōpina dioikousi*. Hom. 2. PG 49.257–264.

———. *Pros tous ouk deon chrōmenous*. PG 51.311–320.

———. *Hypomnēma eis tas Praxeis*. Hom. 7, 9, 10, 15, 29, 31, 41, 42, 50, and 54. PG 60.13–384.

———. *Hypomnēma eis tēn a´ pros Korinthious*. Hom. 33, 38, and 43. PG 61.9–382.

———. *Hypomnēma eis tēn a´ pros Timotheon*. Hom. 6 and 9. PG 62.501–600.

———. *Hypomnēma eis tēn b´ pros Korinthious*. Hom. 1, 3, and 5. PG 61.381–610.

———. *Hypomnēma eis tēn b´ pros Thessalonikeis*. Hom. 1 and 2. PG 62.467–500.

———. *Hypomnēma eis tēn pros Galatas*. Hom. 1. PG 61.611–682.

———. *Hypomnēma eis tēn pros Ephesious*. Hom. 1, 12, 14, 15,18, 19, 20, 21, and 24. PG 62.9–176.

John Chrysostom. *Hypomnēma eis tēn pros Kolassaeis.* Hom. 8 and 11. PG 62.299-392.

———. *Hypomnēma eis tēn pros Philippēsious.* Hom. 12 and 14. PG 62.181-298.

———. *Hypomnēma eis tēn pros Rōmaious.* Hom. 14, 15, 20, and 27. PG 60.391-682.

———. *Hypomnēma eis tēn pros Titon.* Hom. 2. PG 62.663-700.

———. *Hypomnēma eis to kata Iōannēn.* Hom. 3, 4, 45, and 77. PG 59.23-482.

———. *Hypomnēma eis to kata Matthaion.* Hom. 2, 4, 5, 6, 11, 13, 20, 21, 33, 44, 59, and 81. PG 57.13-472 and PG 58.471-794.

John Chrysostom [pseud]. *Eis to rhēton to legon en poiai exousiai tauta poieis.* PG 56.411-428.

———. *Hermēneia eis tous psalmous.* PG 55.35-408.

———. *Peri hypomonēs kai peri synteleias tou aiōnos toutou.* PG 63.937-942.

John Climacus. *Klēmax.* Disc. 1, 4, 5, 6, 7, 8, 14, 15, 20, 25, 26, 28, and 29. PG 88.631-1164. Translated by Holy Transfiguration Monastery as *The Ladder of Divine Ascent.* Brookline, MA: Holy Transfiguration Monastery, 1979.

———. *Pros ton poimena.* PG 88.1165-1208.

John Moschus. *Pneumatikos leimōn.* PG 87c.2851-3112.

John of Damascus. *Ekdosis akribēs tēs orthodoxou pisteōs.* Bk. 2, 3, and 4. PG 94.789-1228.

———. *Kephalaia philosophika.* PG 94.529-674.

———. *Tōn oktō tēs ponērias pneumatōn.* PG 95. 79-85

John of Damascus [pseud]. *Peri aretōn kai kakōn.* PG 95.85-96.

John of Karpathos. *Pros tous en tēi Indiai monachous.* PHIL 1.

John the Faster. *Akolouthia kai taxis epi exomologoumenōn.* PG 88.1889-1908.

Justin Martyr. *Apologia prōtē.* PG 6.327-440.

———. *Pros Tryphōna ioudaion dialogos.* PG 6.471-800.

Kallistos Aggelikoudis. *Eklogē peri proseuchēs kai prosoxēs.* HPE 21a.

———. *Kephalaia peri proseuchēs.* HPE 21a.

Kallistos Kataphygiotis. *Peri tēs kata Theon henōseōs.* PG 147.835-942.

Kallistos Tilikoudis. *Peri hēsychastikēs tribēs.* PG 147.817-826.

Keselopoulos, Anestis. *Pathē kai aretes stē didaskalia tou hagiou Grēgoriou tou Palama.* Athens: Domos, 1982.

Lactantius. *Divinarum institutionum.* Bk. 6. PL 6.111-822.

———. *Epitome divinarum institutionum.* PL 6.1017-1094.

——— [pseud]. *Phoenix.* PL 7.277-243.

Larchet, Jean-Claude. *Mental Disorders and Spiritual Healing.* Translated by G. John Champoux and Rama P. Coomaraswamy. Hillsdale, NY: Sofia Perennis, 2005.

———. *Thérapeutique des maladies spirituelles.* Paris: Les Editions de l'Ancre, 1991.

Leo the Great. *Sermones.* Hom. 12, 44, and 67. PL 54.137-467.

Libanius. *Libanii Opera.* Vol. 11. Edited by Richard Forester. Hildenheim, Germany: Georg Olms Verlagsbuchhandlung, 1963.

Macarius of Egypt [pseud.]. *Logos peri agapēs.* PG 34.907-936.

———. *Logos peri eletherias noos.* PG 34.935-968.

———. *Logos peri proseuchēs.* PG 34.853-866.

Macarius of Egypt [pseud.]. *Homiliai pneumatikai.* Hom. 15, 18, 21, 22, and 27. PG 34.449-822.

Mark the Ascetic. *Peri nomou pneumatikou.* PG 65.905-930.

——. *Peri tou theiou baptismatos.* PG 65.985-1028.

——. *Peri tōn oiomenōn ex ergōn dikaiousthai.* PG 65.929-966.

——. *Pros Nikolaon nouthesiai.* PG 65.1027-1054.

Matsoukas, Nichos. *Dogmatikē kai symbolikē theologia.* 3 vols. Thessaloniki, Greece: Pournara, 1985-2005.

Maximus the Confessor. *Epistolai.* Ep. 2, 3, 5, 8, and 24. PG 91.363-650.

——. *Erōtapokriseis. Opera Maximi Confessoris Quaestiones et Dubia.* Vol. 10. CCSG, 1982.

——. *Hermēneia eis tēn proseuchēn tou pater hēmōn.* PG 90.871-910.

——. *Hetera kephalaia.* Cent. 1-4. PG 90.1401-1462.

——. *Kephalaia diaphora theologika.* Cent. 1, 2, 3, and 5. PG 90.1177-1392.

——. *Kephalaia theologika ētoi eklogai ek diaphorōn bibliōn.* PG 91.721-1018.

——. *Mystagōgia.* PG 91.657-718.

——. *Peri agapēs.* Cent. 1-4. PG 90.959-1080.

——. *Peri diaphorōn aporiōn.* PG 91.1031-1418.

——. *Peri theologias.* Cent. 1-2. PG 90.1083-1176.

——. *Pros Marinon.* PG 91.9-216.

——. *Pros Thalassion.* PG 90.243-786.

——. *Scholia eis to peri theiōn honomatōn.* PG 4.185-416.

——. *Syzētēsis tou agiou Maximou meta Pyrrhou.* PG 91.287-354.

Methodius. *Logos peri anastaseōs.* PG 18.265-330.

——. *Peri tou autexousiou.* PG 18.239-266.

Neilos the Ascetic. *Kephalaia.* PG 79.1249-1264.

——. *Epistolai.* Bk. 2: Ep. 65, 125, 282; Bk. 3: Ep. 214, 288, 293, 294. PG 79.81-582.

——. *Logos askētikos.* PG 79.719-810.

——. *Logos hoti diapherousin tōn en polesin ōkismenōn...* PG 79.1061-1094.

——. *Logos peri aktēmosynēs.* PG 79.967-1060.

——. *Logos pros ton monachon Eulogion.* PG 79.1093-1140.

——. *Peri proseuchēs.* PG 79.1165-1200.

——. *Peri tōn oktō tēs kakias logismōn.* PG 79.1435-1472.

Neilos the Ascetic [pseud]. *Encheiridion tou Epiktētou.* PG 79.1285-1316.

Nellas, Panagiotis. *Zōon theoumenon, prooptikes gia mia orthodoxē katanoēsē tou anthrōpou.* Athens: Armos, 1979.

Nicodemos the Hagiorite. *Aoratos polemos.* Athens: Phōs-xeen, 2002.

——. *Exomologētarion.* Athens: Agios Nicodemos, 1868.

Nicodemos the Hagiorite and Makarios of Corinth. *Philokalia tōn hierōn nēptikōn paterōn hēmōn.* 5 vols. Athens: Astēr, 1982. Translated by G. E. Palmer, Philip Sherrard, and Kallistos Ware as *The Philokalia.* 4 vols. London: Faber & Faber Press, 1979-1995.

Nikiphoros the Monk. *Peri nēpseōs kai phylakēs kardias.* PG 147.945-966.

Nikitas Stithatos. *Bios tou hagiou Symeōn, Orientalia Christiana.* Vol. 12, no. 45 (Rome: 1928).

Nikitas Stithatos. *Physikōn kephalaiōn.* PG 120.899–952.

——. *Praktikōn kephalaiōn.* PG 120.851–900.

Origen. *Kata Kelsou.* Bk. 3 and 7. PG 11.641–1632.

——. *Eis psalmous.* PG 12.1053–1686.

——. *Ek tou g tomou tōn eis tēn genesin.* PG 12.91–92.

——. *Epistolē pros ton Grēgorion ton thaumatourgon.* PG 11.87–92.

——. *Peri archōn.* Bk. 3. PG 11.115–414.

Païsios the Hagiorite. *Epistoles.* Souroti-Thessaloniki, Greece: Hieron Hēsychastērion Evangelistēs Iōannēs ho Theologos, 1994.

——. *Logoi.* 5 vols. Souroti-Thessaloniki, Greece: Hieron Hēsychastērion Evangelistēs Iōannēs ho Theologos, 1998–2006.

Palladius. *He pros lauson historia.* PG 34.995–1262.

Paulinus and Therasia. *Epistola venerabili Augustino.* PL 33.101–105.

Peter of Damascus. *Biblia* 1–2. PHIL 3.

Philimon, Abba. *Logos pany hōphelimos.* PHIL 2.

Philotheus of Sinai. *Nēptika kephalaia.* PHIL 2.

Photius. *Peri tou Hagiou Pneumatos mystagōgia.* PG 102.279–392.

Plato. *Cratylus.* Edited by H. Fowler. Vol. 167. LCL, 1977.

——. *Republic.* Edited by P. Shorey. Vols. 237 and 276, Bk. 4, 7, and 9. LCL, 1963.

——. *Meno.* Edited by W. Lamb. Vol. 165. LCL, 1990.

Polycarp. *Epistolē pros tous philippēsious.* PG 5.1005–1022.

Popovich, Fr. Justin. *Philosophie de la vérité: dogmatique de l'église orthodoxe.* 5 vols. Translated by Jean Louis Palierne. Paris: L'Age d'Homme, 1992–1997.

Porphyrios, Elder. *Bios kai logoi.* Chania, Greece: Hiera Monē Zōodoxou Pēgēs, 2003.

Ralli, G. and M. Potli, eds. *Syntagma tōn theiōn kai hierōn kanonōn.* Vol. 2, 3, and 4. Athens: G. Chartophylakos, 1852–1853.

Romanides, Fr. John. *Rōmaioi ē rōmēoi pateres tēs ekklēsias.* Vol. 1. Thessaloniki, Greece: Pournara, 1984.

Rufinus. *Apologiae in sanctum Hieronymum.* Bk. 1. PL 21.541–624.

Severianus of Gabala. *Homilia eis ton typhlon.* PG 59.509–610.

Socrates Scholasticus. *Ekklēsiastikē historia.* Bk. 5. PG 67.33–842.

Sophrony [Zakharov], Archimandrite. *On Prayer.* Translated by Rosemary Edmonds. Essex, UK: Stavropegic Monastery of the St. John the Baptist, 1996.

——. *We Shall See Him as He is.* Translated by Rosemary Edmonds. Essex, UK: Stavropegic Monastery of the St. John the Baptist, 1988.

Spiridons, Servou, ed. *Euchologion to mega.* Athens: «Astēr», 1992.

Symeon the New Theologian. *Biblos tōn ēthikōn logōn.* SC 129 as *Traités théologiques et éthiques.* Vol. 2. Translated by Jean Darrouzès. Paris: Les Éditions du Cerf, 1967.

——. *Katēchētikoi logoi.* Disc. 3, 4, 9, and 25. SC 96, 104, and 113 as *Catéchèses.* 3 vols. Translated by Joseph Paramelle. Paris: Les Éditions du Cerf, 1963–1965.

——. *Kephalaia praktika.* PG 120.603–688.

—— [?]. *Peri tōn triōn tropōn tēs proseuchēs.* PG 120.701–710.

Tertullian. *Ad martyras. PL* 1.619–628.

——. *Adversus gnosticos Scorpiace. PL* 2.121–154.

——. *Adversus Marcionem.* Bk. 2 and 4. *PL* 1.246–524

——. *De anima. PL* 2.641–752.

——. *De carne Christi. PL* 2.751–792.

——. *De fuga in persecutione. PL* 2.101–120.

——. *De poenitentia. PL* 1.1223–1248.

——. *De praescriptionibus adversus haereticos. PL* 2.9–74.

——. *De resurrectione carnis. PL* 2.791–886.

——. *De spectaculis. PL* 1.627–662.

Thalassius. *Peri agapēs kai enkrateias.* Cent. 1 and 3. *PG* 91.1427–1470.

Theodore Balsamon. *Canones tēs en Ankyrai synodou. PG* 137.1121–1196.

——. *Canones tēs en Gangrai synodou. PG* 137.1233–1274.

——. *Canones tēs en Karchēdoni synodou. PG* 138.9–456.

——. *Canones tēs en Kōnstantinoupolei en tōi troullōi synodou. PG* 137.501–874.

——. *Canones tēs en Laodikeiai synodou. PG* 137.1341–1422.

——. *Canones tēs en Neokaisareiai synodou. PG* 137.1195–1234.

Theodore the Great Ascetic. *Kephalaia. PHIL* 1.

Theodore the Studite. *Epistolai.* Bk. 1: Ep. 4, 12, and 18; and Bk. 2: Ep. 36. *PG* 99.903–1670.

——. *Katēchētikoi logoi.* Disc. 22, 99, and 100. *HPE* 18 and 18a.

Theodoret of Cyrus. *Ekklēsiastikē historia.* Bk. 4. *PG* 82.1172–1494.

——. *Epistolai.* Ep. 2 and 170. *PG* 83.1172–1494.

——. *Hermēneia eis tous psalmous.* Ps. 118. *PG* 80.857–1998.

Theognostus. *Peri praxeōs kai theōrias. PHIL* 2.

Theoliptus of Philadelphia. *Logos tēn en Christōi kryptēn ergasian diasaphōn. PHIL* 4.

Theophan the Recluse. *Put' ko spaseniju.* Moscow: Tipo-litografija I. Efimova, 1908. Translated by Fr. Seraphim Rose as *The Path to Salvation.* Platina, CA: Saint Herman of Alaska Brotherhood, 1996.

Venantius Fortunatus. *De pascha. PL* 7.285–288.

[Vlachos], Bishop Hierotheos. *Orthodoxē psychotherapeia kai paterikē therapeutikē agōgē.* Odessa, Greece: Hiera Monē Timiou Stavrou, 1986.

[Zacharou], Archimandrite Zacharia. *The Enlargement of the Heart.* South Canaan, PA: Mount Thabor Publishing, 2006.

[Zizioulas], Metropolitan John. *Orthodoxia kai synchronos kosmos.* Leukosia, Cyprus: Kentro Meletōn Kukkou, 2006.

Zosima, Abba. *Dialogismoi. PG* 78.1679–1702.

2. Psychology, Philosophy, Sociology, and Modern Religious Thought

Academy of Cognitive Therapy. *Candidate Handbook.* Philadelphia: Academy of Cognitive Therapy 2005.

Allport, Gordon W. *Becoming: Basic Considerations for a Psychology of Personality.* New Haven, NJ: Yale University Press, 1955.

Ayers, A. J. *Language, Truth and Logic.* New York: Dover Publications, 1952.

Backus, William. *The Hidden Rift with God.* Minneapolis, MI: Bethany House Publishers, 1990.

Bandura, Albert. *Social Learning Theory.* Upper Saddle River, NJ: Prentice Hall, 1977.

Beck, Aaron T. *Cognitive Therapy and the Emotional Disorders.* New York: Penguin Books, 1976.

——. Interview by Sidney Block. May 4, 2004. Philadelphia, PA. http://www.academyofct.org/ Library/ InfoManage/Guide.asp?FolderID=1169.

——. *Love is Never Enough.* New York: Harper & Row Publishers, 1988.

——. *Prisoners of Hate: The Cognitive Basis of Anger, Hostility, and Violence.* New York: Harper Collins Publishers, 1999.

Beck, Aaron T. and Brad A. Alford. *The Integrative Power of Cognitive Therapy.* New York: The Guilford Press, 1997.

Beck, Aaron T. and Gary Emery with Ruth Greenberg. *Anxiety Disorders and Phobias: A Cognitive Perspective.* New York: Basic Books, 1985.

Beck, Aaron T., Arthur Freeman, Denise D. Davis, and Associates. *Cognitive Therapy of Personality Disorders: Second Edition.* New York: The Guilford Press, 2004.

Beck, Aaron T., John Rush, Brian F. Shaw, and Gary Emery. *Cognitive Therapy of Depression.* New York: The Guilford Press, 1979.

Beck, Aaron T., Fred D. Wright, Cory F. Newman, and Bruce S. Liese. *Cognitive Therapy of Substance Abuse.* New York: The Guilford Press,1993.

Beck, James R. The Integration of Psychology and Theology: An Enterprise out of Balance. *Journal of Psychology and Christianity* 22, no.1 (2003): 20–29.

Beck, Judith S. *Cognitive Therapy for Challenging Problems: What to do when the Basics Don't Work.* New York: The Guilford Press, 2005.

——. *Cognitive Therapy: Basics and Beyond.* New York: The Guilford Press, 1995.

——. *The Beck Diet Solution Weight Loss Workbook.* Birmingham, AL: Oxmore House, 2007.

Becker, Ernest. *The Revolution in Psychiatry: The New Understanding of Man.* New York: The Free Press of Glencoe, 1964.

Bergin, Allen. Values and Religious Issues in Therapy and Mental Health. *American Psychologist,* 46 (1991): 394–403.

Bilgrave, Dyer P. and Robert H. Deluty. Religious Beliefs and Therapeutic Orientations of Clinical and Counseling Psychologists. *Journal for the Scientific Study of Religion,* 37, no. 2 (1998): 329–349.

Bobgan, Martin and Deidre Bobgan. *Psychoheresy: The Psychological Seduction of Christianity.* Santa Barbara, CA: East Gate Publishers, 1987.

Bromley, David G. and Bruce C. Busching. Understanding the Structure of Contractual and Covenantal Social Relations: Implications for the Sociology of Religion. *Sociological Analysis* 49 (1988): 15–32.

Burns, David. *Feeling Good: The New Mood Therapy.* New York: Signet Books, 1980.

Butler, Andrew, Jason Chapman, Evan Forman, and Aaron Beck. The Empirical Status of Cognitive-Behavioral Therapy: A Review of Meta-analyses. *Clinical Psychology Review* 26 (2006): 17–31.

Collins, Gary. *Christian Counseling.* Dallas, TX: Word Publishing, 1988.

Compte, Auguste. *Système de Politique Positive.* Vol. 2. Paris: Carilian Goeury et V. Dalmont, 1851.

Comstock, George and Haejung Paik. *Television and the American Child.* New York: Academic Press, 1991.

Copleston, Frederick. *A History of Philosophy.* Vol. 4, 6, 8, and 9. New York: Image Books, 1964.

Cummings, Nicholas A. and William T. Follette. Psychiatric Services and Medical Utilization in a Prepaid Health Plan Setting: Part 2. *Medical Care* 6, no. 1 (1968): 31–41.

Damascene [Christensen], Monk. *Not of This World: The Life and Teachings of Fr. Seraphim Rose.* Forestville, CA: Fr. Seraphim Rose Foundation.

Dattilio, Frank and Arthur Freeman. *Cognitive-Behavioral Strategies in Crisis Intervention.* New York: The Guilford Press, 2007.

Dayton, Tian. *Trauma and Addiction: Ending the Cycle of Pain Through Emotional Literacy.* Dearfield Beach, FL: Health Communications, 2000.

Descartes, René. *Rules for Direction of Mind. Great Books of the Western World.* Vol. 31. Edited by Robert Hutchins. Translated by Elizabeth Haldane and G. R. Ross. Chicago: Encyclopedia Britannica, 1952.

Dobson, Keith S., ed. *Handbook of Cognitive-Behavioral Therapies.* New York: The Guilford Press, 2001.

Doniger, Wendy. *Britannica Encyclopedia of World Religions.* London: Encyclopedia Britannica, 2006.

Dueck, Alvin C. and Kevin Reimer. Religious discourse in psychotherapy. *International Journal of Existential Psychology and Psychotherapy* 1, no. 1 (July 2004): 3–15.

Eliade, Mirchea. *The Sacred and the Profane.* Orlando, FL: Harcourt, 1959.

Ellis, Albert. *The Case against Religion: A Psychotherapist's View and the Case against Religiosity.* Austin, TX: American Atheist Press, 1980.

Ellis, Albert and Robert Harper. *A Guide to Rational Living.* Chatsworth, CA: Melvin Powers Wilshire Book Company, 1997.

Eng, Elaine. Faith and Psychology: Integration or Separation? *Journal of Health and Religion* 37, no.1 (1998): 45–47.

Entwistle, David. *Integrative Approaches to Psychology and Christianity: An Introduction to Worldview Issues, Philosophical Foundations, and Models of Integration.* Eugene, OR: Wipf & Stock Publishers, 2004.

First, Michael and Harold Pincus, eds. *Diagnostic Criteria from DSM-IV-TR.* Arlington, VA: American Psychiatric Association, 2000.

Fosdick, Harry Emerson. *On Being a Real Person.* New York: Harper & Brothers Publishers, 1943.

Freeman, Arthur, James Pretzer, Barbara Fleming, and Karen Simon. *Clinical Applications of Cognitive Therapy.* New York: Kluwer Academic/Plenum Publishers, 2004.

Freud, Sigmund. *Introductory Lectures on Psychoanalysis.* Translated by J. Strachey. New York: Penguin Books, 1982.

Goethe, Johann. *Theory of Colours.* Translated by Charles Eastlake. London: John Murray, 1840.

Greenley, James R. and David Mechanic. Social Selection in Seeking Help for Psychological Problems. *Journal of Health and Social Behavior* 17, no. 3 (1976): 249–262.

Greenley, James R., David Mechanic, Paul D. Cleary. Seeking Help for Psychological Problems: A Replication and Extension. *Medical Care* 25, no. 12 (1987): 1113-1128.

Deborah Haas-Wilson, Allen Cheadle, Richard Scheffler. Demand for Mental Health Services: An Episode of Treatment Approach. *Southern Economic Journal* 56, no. 1 (1989): 219-232.

Hersen, Michael, Alan Kazdin, and Alan Bellack. *The Clinical Psychology Handbook.* New York: Pergamon Press, 1983.

Hodge, David R. Spiritually Modified Cognitive Therapy: A Review of the Literature. *National Association of Social Workers* 51, no. 2 (2006): 162-166.

Horney, Karen. *Neurosis and Human Growth.* New York: W. W. Norton & Company, 1950.

Horwitz, Allan. Social Networks and Pathways to Psychiatric Treatment. *Social Forces* 56, no. 1 (1977): 86-105.

Hunter, Cornelius. *Science's Blind Spot: The Unseen Religion of Scientific Naturalism.* Grand Rapids, MI: Brazos Press, 2007.

James, William. *Some Problems of Philosophy.* New York: Longman's Green Company, 1911.

———. *The Varieties of Religious Experience.* New York: Penguin Books, 1982.

Johnson, W. Brad and Stevan Lars Nielsen. Rational-Emotive Assessment with Religious Clients. *Journal of Rational-Emotive and Cognitive-Behavior Therapy* 16, no. 2 (1998): 101-123.

Jones, Stanton L. and Richard E. Butman. *Modern Psychotherapies: A Comprehensive Christian Appraisal.* Downers Grove, IL: Intervarsity Press, 1991.

Kadushin, Charles. Social Distance Between Client and Professional. *The American Journal of Sociology* 67, no. 5 (1962): 517-531.

Kessler Ronald C., James A. Reuter, James R. Greenley. Sex Differences in the Use of Psychiatric Outpatient Facilities. *Social Forces* 58, no. 2 (1979): 557-571.

Kingdon, David and Douglas Turkington. *Cognitive Therapy of Schizophrenia.* New York: The Guilford Press, 2008.

Kramer, Michael W. *Managing Uncertainty in Organizational Communication.* Mahwah, NJ: Lawrence Erlbaum Associates, 2003.

Krause, Neal, Christopher G. Ellison, and Keith M. Wulf. Church-based Emotional Support, Negative Interaction, and Psychological Well-being: Findings from a National Sample of Presbyterians. *Journal for the Scientific Study of Religion* 37, no. 4 (1998): 725-741.

Lampe, G. H. W. *A Patristic Greek Lexicon.* Oxford: Clarendon Press, 1961.

Leaf, Philip J., Martha M. Livingston, Gary L. Tischler, Myrna M. Weissman, Charles E. Holzer, Jerome K. Myers. Contact with Health Professionals for the Treatment of Psychiatric and Emotional Problems. *Medical Care* 23, no. 12 (1985): 1322-1337.

Leaf, Philip J., Martha Livingston Bruce, Gary L. Tischler, Daniel H. Freeman, Jr., Myrna M. Weissman, Jerome K. Myers. Factors Affecting the Utilization of Specialty and General Medical Mental Health Services. *Medical Care* 26, no. 1 (1988): 9-26.

Lewis, C. S. *The Abolition of Man.* San Francisco, CA: Harper Press, 2001.

Liddell, Henry G. and Robert Scott. *Greek-English Lexicon.* Oxford: Clarendon Press, 1996.

Linzey, Gardner, Calvin S. Hall, and Richard F. Thompson. *Psychology.* New York: Worth, 1975.

Lundin, Robert W. *Theories and Systems of Psychology.* Lexington, MA: D.C. Heath & Company, 1985.

Mahoney, Michael J. *Constructive Psychotherapy: Theory and Practice.* New York: The Guilford Press, 2006.

Manzaridis, George. Aristotelikē ēthikē kai christianismos, reprint from Aristotelika. Thessaloniki, Greece: Panepistēmio Thessalonikēs 1980.

Matsouka, Nikos. Historia tēs philosophias me syntomē eisagōgē stē philosophia. Thessaloniki, Greece: Pournara, 2001.

McMinn, Mark R. and Clark D. Campbell. Integrative Psychotherapy: Toward A Comprehensive Christian Approach. Downers Grove, IL: Intervarsity Press, 2007.

McMinn, Mark R. and Timothy R. Phillips, eds. Care for the Soul: Exploring the Intersection of Psychology and Theology. Downers Grove, IL: Intervarsity Press, 2001.

Meichenbaum, Donald H. Changing Conceptions of Cognitive Behavior Modification: Retrospect and Prospect. Journal of Consulting and Clinical Psychology 61, no. 2 (1993): 202–204.

Miller, Joseph and Archbishop Chrysostomos of Etna. Science and Orthodox Christianity: Two Orthodox Psychologists Offer Their Views. Monographic Supplement Series Number 34. Etna, CA: Center for Traditionalist Orthodox Studies, 1998.

Morelli, Fr. George. Internet Continuing Education Course in Christian Spirituality and Therapy (n.d.), http://www.ocampr.org/CCC_course.asp.

Myers, Jerome and Leslie Schaffer. Social Stratification and Psychiatric Practice: A Study of an Outpatient Clinic. American Sociological Review 19, no. 3 (June 1954): 307–310.

Muse, Stephen, ed. Raising Lazarus: Integral Healing in Orthodox Christianity. Brookline, MA: Holy Cross Press, 2004.

Niebuhr, H. Richard. Christ and Culture. New York: Harper & Row, Publishers, 1951.

Overholser, J. Elements of the Socratic Method. Therapy 30 (1993): 67–85.

Padesky, Christine. Schema Change Processes in Cognitive Therapy. Clinical Psychology and Psychotherapy 1, no. 5 (1994): 267–278.

Padesky, Christine with Dennis Greenberger. Clincian's Guide to Mind over Mood. New York: The Guilford Press, 1995.

Peale, Norman Vincent. The Power of Positive Thinking. New York: Prentice-Hall, 1952.

Piaget, Jean. La representation du monde chez l'enfant. Paris: Presses Universitaires de France, 1926.

Polanyi, Michael. The Tacit Dimension. Glouchester, MA: Peter Smith, 1983.

Propst, L. Rebecca. Psychotherapy in a Religious Framework: Spirituality in the Emotional Healing Process. New York: Human Sciences Press, 1988.

Raitt, Jill, Bernard McGinn, and John Meyendorff, eds. Christian Spirituality: High Middle Ages. Vol. 2. New York: Crossroads, 1987.

Raphael, Edna E. Community Structure and Acceptance of Psychiatric Aid. The American Journal of Sociology 69, no. 4 (1964): 340–358.

Richelle, Mark N. B. F. Skinner: A Reappraisal. East Sussex, UK: Psychology Press, 1999.

Russell, Bertrand. A History of Western Philosophy. New York: Simon & Schuster, 1945.

Salkovskis, Paul, ed. Frontiers of Cognitive Therapy. New York: The Guilford Press, 1996.

Shapiro, S., E. Skinner, L. Kessler, et al. Utilization of Health Services: Three Epidemiological Catchment Area Sites. Archives of General Psychiatry 41 (1984): 984–992.

Sorabji, Richard. Emotion and Peace of Mind: From Stoic Agitation to Christian Temptation. Oxford: Oxford University Press, 2000.

Still, Arthur and Windy Dryden. Ellis and Epictetus: Dialogue vs. Method in Psychotherapy. *Journal of Rational-Emotive and Cognitive-Behavior Therapy* 21, no. 2 (2003): 37-55.

Sullivan, Harry Stack. *The Fusion of Psychiatry and Social Science.* New York: W. W. Norton & Company, 1964.

Tan, Siang-Yang. Cognitive Behavior Therapy: A Biblical Approach and Critique. *Journal of Psychology and Theology* 15, no. 2 (1987): 103-112.

Theokritoff, George and Elizabeth Theokritoff. Genesis and Creation: Towards a Debate: Review of Seraphim Rose, *Genesis, Creation and Early Man: The Orthodox Christian Vision. St. Vladimir's Theological Quarterly* 46, no. 2 (2002): 365-390.

Thermos, Fr. Vasileios. *Anthrōpos ston horizonta! Prosengizontas tē synantēsē orthodoxēs theologias kai epistēmōn psychismou.* Athens: Grēgorē, 2006.

Tillich, Paul. *The Courage to Be.* New Haven, NJ: Yale University Press, 1952.

Tjelveit, Alan. The Ethics of Value Conversion in Therapy: Appropriate and Inappropriate Therapist Influence on Client Values. *Clinical Psychology Review* 6 (1986): 515-537.

Vaihinger, Hans. *Die Philosophie des Als Ob.* Leipzig, Germany: F. Meiner, 1922.

Van Leeuwen, Mary Stewart. *The Person in Psychology: A Contemporary Christian Appraisal.* Grand Rapids, MI: William B. Eerdman's Publishing Company, 1985.

Vitz, Paul C. "Beyond Psychology." Lecture to an audience of priests. New Westminster, BC, September 29, 1995, http://catholiceducation.org/articles/civilization/cc0004.html.

Weishaar, Marjorie E. *Aaron T. Beck.* London: Sage Publications, 1993.

Wessler, R. L. Idiosyncratic Definitions and Unsupported Hypotheses: Rational Emotive Behavior Therapy as Pseudoscience. *Journal of Rational-Emotive and Cognitive-Behavior Therapy* 14 (1996): 41-61.

Woloschak, Gayle. *Beauty and Unity in Creation: The Evolution of Life.* Minneapolis, MI: Light & Life, 1996.

Woterstorff, Nicholas. *Reason within the Bounds of Religion.* Grand Rapids, MI: William B. Eerdmans Publishing Company, 1984.

Young, Jeffrey and Aaron Beck. *Cognitive Therapy Scale Rating.* Philadelphia: Academy of Cognitive Therapy, 1980.

✤ Index ✤

❖D❖

daily schedules, 188
daily thought record
    ascetic self-observation and, 258
daily training in virtues, 218–220. *See also*
    virtue
Darwin, Charles, 36
data logs, 243–244
De doctrina christiana, 9
demonic thoughts. *See* bad thoughts
dependent personality disorder, 88
depression
    automatic thoughts in, 150
    behavioral interventions for, 186–188
    cognitive distortions in, 78, 86–87
    cognitive rehearsal in, 220
    daily logs in treatment of, 243–244
    egocentricity in, 97
    existential questions and, 269
    metacognition and, 122
    problem-solving in, 177–179
    self-constricting schemata in, 71
Descartes, René, 33
developmental schemata, 69–70
Dewey, John, 40
diagnosticians, cognitive therapists as,
    150–152
diaries, 243–244
Diderot, 36
Didymus the Blind, 127
diet plans, 305
Dionysios of Zakinthos, Saint, 198
discerning openness
    in Orthodox pastoral theology, 19–20
    in patristic counsel and cognitive
        therapy, 251–253, 262
    Platonism and, 17
    priorities in, 49
The Discourses, 224
dishonesty, 211
disqualifying the positive, 85–88, 123
Divine Providence,
    assumed by Chrisitans, 45
    changes metacognition, 125
    human methods vs., 120
    preserves humanity, 28
    schema modification and, 223–226

undermined by evolutionary theory, 38
    visible to faith, 118
divine *theoria*, 198–199
Dorotheos of Gaza, Abba
    on ascetic practice, 183–184
    on bad thoughts, 201–202
    on children, 101
    on courage, 81
    The Discourses of, 224
    on higher logical will, 112
    on humble-mindedness, 127
    on meaning assignment, 52
    overgeneralization of, 90
dove as metaphor, 214–215
downward arrow technique, 236–237
DTR (dysfunctional thought record), 211–214
dysfunctional schema, 70–73
dysfunctional thought record (DTR), 211–214
    core belief worksheets and, 244
    downward arrow technique vs., 237
    sample of, 212

❖E❖

Eastern Orthodox Church, views of. *See*
    Orthodox pastoral theology
ecclesiastical sketch of spiritual fathers,
    142–144
educators, cognitive therapists as, 150–152
egocentricity
    in Beck's theory of cognitive distortions, 83–88
    as cognitive distortion, generally, 89–90
    cognitive therapy on, 90–91, 95–98
    conclusions about, 254–255
    philautia vs., 91–95
Egyptian paganism, 9
Elchaninov, Father Alexander, 244
Ellis, Albert
    on guilt, 44
    introduction to, 3
    on meaning assignment, 51
    on religion, 274
    on self-statements, 65
    on sin, 38–39